Classical and Contemporary Perspectives of Indian Philosophy of Religion

Classical and Contemporary Perspectives of Indian Philosophy of Religion

Edited by
Manoranjan Mallick

PRINTWORLD
Publishers of Indian Traditions

Cataloging in Publication Data — DK
[Courtesy: D.K. Agencies (P) Ltd. <docinfo@dkagencies.com>]

National Seminar on "Indian Philosophy of Religion" (2022 : Bhubaneswar, India)
Classical and contemporary perspectives of Indian philosophy of religion / edited by Manoranjan Mallick.
pages cm
"... National Seminar on "Indian Philosophy of Religion", held in the Department of Philosophy, Utkal University, Bhubaneswar, on 22-23 April 2022" – Acknowledgements.
Includes index.
ISBN 9788124612545

1. Philosophy, Indic – Congresses. 2. Hindu philosophy – Congresses. I. Mallick, Manoranjan, 1979- editor. II. Utkal University. Department of Philosophy, organizer. III. Title.

LCC B131.N38 2022 | DDC 181.4 23

ISBN: 978-81-246-1254-5
First published in 2025

Printed and published by:
D.K. Printworld (P) Ltd.
Regd. Office: *Vedaśrī*, F-395, Sudarshan Park
(Metro Station: ESI Hospital), New Delhi - 110015
Phones: (011) 4172 2626, 98713 94815
e-mail: indology@dkprintworld.com
Website: www.dkprintworld.com

Dedicated to
all my Teachers

Acknowledgements

THIS anthology is an outcome of the contributions and presentations made by eminent scholars in the National Seminar on "Indian Philosophy of Religion", held in the Department of Philosophy, Utkal University, Bhubaneswar, on 22-23 April 2022. On behalf of the Department, I am thankful to all the contributors for their insightful writings which encouraged us for venturing to publish this volume.

I am very thankful to the Indian Council of Philosophical Research (ICPR), New Delhi for the substantial grant for organizing the National Seminar. I am also extremely grateful to the World Bank–Odisha Higher Education Program for Excellence and Equity (WB–OHEPEE), Utkal University for a partial financial assistance to conduct the National Seminar and for providing the grant for printing this anthology.

I express my sincere thanks to Professor Sachchidananda Mishra, Member-Secretary, ICPR, New Delhi, who delivered the keynote address of the seminar. I am grateful to the Vice-Chancellor, Professor Sabita Acharya, Utkal University for providing her support, able guidance and unmatched leadership. I am profusely thankful to Professor Saroj Kumar Mohanty, Former Professor and Head, Department of Philosophy, Utkal University for chairing the valedictory session of the seminar and giving valuable remarks on the theme of the seminar.

I also extend a deep sense of gratitude to Professor S. Panneerselvam, Former Professor and Head of the Department of Philosophy, University of Madras, Professor Laxmikanta Padhi,

Department of Philosophy, University of North Bengal and Dr Saroj Kanta Kar, Formerly Programme Officer, ICPR, New Delhi, and my colleague at present for their inspiration, motivation and guidance at every step in bringing out the anthology to the light of the day.

I am indeed thankful to Professor Vikram Singh Sirola, my PhD supervisor at IIT Bombay for his constant and unconditional inspiration at every stage of my career. I express my indebtedness to my revered teacher, Dr Harischandra Sahoo, Professor of Philosophy, Bhima Bhoi Research Chair, KISS University for his everlasting encouragement and support, which I have been receiving from the beginning of my academic career.

Further, my colleagues in the Department of Philosophy, Utkal University, Dr Sudhakar Jally, Dr Nandini Mishra, Dr Pragyanparamita Mohapatra and Dr Kabita Das deserve my gratitude for their constant support throughout the seminar. I acknowledge the extensive support and help from the research scholars, students and staff of the Department of Philosophy, Utkal University for making the seminar a grand success.

I am extremely grateful to the former Chairpersons of the P.G. Council, Utkal University, Professor Basanta Kumar Mallick and Professor Durga Shankar Patnaik for their moral and physical support for organizing the seminar.

I am indebted to my family members for their support and silent contributions.

Last but not the least, I am thankful to Mr Susheel Mittal, Director of the D.K. Printworld (P) Ltd., New Delhi for accepting my proposal for publication of this anthology.

Manoranjan Mallick

Contents

Introduction

अनेकशास्त्रं बहु वेदितव्यम् अल्पश्च कालो बहवश्च विघ्नाः ।
यत्सारभूतं तदुपासितव्यं हंसो यथा क्षीरमिवाम्बु मध्यात् ॥

Anekaśāstraṁ bahu veditavyam alpaśca kālo bahavaśca vighnāḥ ।
Yatsārabhūtaṁ tadupāsitavyaṁ haṁso yathā kṣīramivāmbu madhyāt ॥

There are many Śāstras (bodies of knowledge/doctrines) and an abundance of knowledge. But we have limited time with a lot of obstacles. Therefore one should study the essence of the Śāstras, like a swan extracts milk from a mixture of milk and water.

Indian philosophy of religion critically examines the religious traditions and practices that originated in the Indian subcontinent. It appreciates Hinduism, Buddhism, Jainism and Sikhism, including their subsects and similar traditions while reviewing certain aspects therein. In Indian tradition, philosophy and religion are not poles apart. Instead, they are related in theory and also to some extent in practice. Every Indic religion has a certain philosophy in its background and most of them assure the ultimate destiny of man, the fulfilment of human life, by the accomplishment of *puruṣārthas* (*dharma*, *artha*, *kāma*, and *mokṣa*). There have been vibrant, argumentative religious traditions, lived experiences and foundational institutions in all Indic religions explaining life and ultimate human destiny. There is no closed compartment for religious views. One may encounter absolutely new viewpoints and methodologies to explore fundamental questions concerning the meaning of life, or the ultimate human destiny. One of the important elements of Indian philosophy of religion is that it investigates the nature of religion that underlines the essential human duties by upholding moral and spiritual values for life by transforming the material to spiritual, profane to sacred, and natural to supernatural. It also explains the inexplicable and attempts to access the inaccessible in the paths of reason, devotion and action in symbiosis. This serves as the foundation of religions in India. Indian philosophy of religion moves on with an objective to resolve the doubts in the ideal plane, which seem more fundamental than any other material needs. In this context, this anthology aims to bring together the different views in Indian philosophy of religion as reflected in the Vedas, the Upaniṣads, the Purāṇas, and the modern perspectives thereof.

Indian religious and philosophical traditions are holistic. This is due to the accomodability in the understanding of various viewpoints ranging from polytheism, monotheism, pantheism, monism, and so on. Where there is no conception of God, the same place is given to a universal and objective truth and power. The Indic religions are neither God-centric nor man-centric, but holistic. Religious or divine knowledge is given importance in life as a source of understanding the very purpose of life and its relationship with the whole universe. It is only in this understanding or knowledge wherein the purpose of life is also fulfilled along with others; there is no purpose of God to be fulfilled as He is the ultimate and a complete whole. This includes a moderate man-centricity within the holistic spiritual achievements. God is not there at the centre of religion and religious beliefs, unlike in the Medieval West. There has been a focus on the philosophical debate and discussion on theism in the philosophy of religion. Theism forms a significant conceptual component of religions, such as Judaism, Christianity, Hinduism and Islam. In all these, the philosophy of religion has a rich and diversified history in comparison to other branches of philosophy. While considering, global religious enterprises, mainly the historicity of religious ideas, can be demarcated into four historical periods: the ancient, medieval, modern, and the contemporary world. In all these periods, the philosophy of religion in India has incorporated a neutral rational inquiry into the nature of divinity and the elements of scholasticism may be seen to be vibrant and lively. The scholars of religion have continuously debated innovatively by employing new methodologies to explore some vital old questions.

In Indian traditions, religion emphasizes spirituality and morality instead of merely believing in God and engaging in formal religious rituals. Merely believing in God and following religious rituals may not serve the aspirations generally expected from religion. The aspirations are fulfilled by imbibing the moral values for spiritual accomplishment. Religion is a matter of practising spirituality and this again depends upon practising moral values. Thus, the goal of religion is fulfilled by practising moral values. Sometimes, morality is equated with religiosity. Mahatma Gandhi says: "as soon as we lose the moral basis, we cease to be religious. There is no such thing as religious overriding morality." It may be questionable as to whether such emphasis on morality would suffice to determine the sense of religion, but as a matter of fact, there is no religion without morality. Buddhism, Jainism, and even some Vedic and Upaniṣadic passages have shown the possibility of sublime ethics without believing in a personal God.

B.K. Matilal, in his writings on "Moral Dilemmas and Religious Dogmas" raises some significant questions such as:

Can a moral act be religious by the same token? Or, is an act morally good because it is religious, or has a religious approval? Or, is an act religious because it is morally performed? In other words, when does an act become moral or when does an act become religious? Can a truly religious man transcend his so-called religious dogmas and put moral concerns over narrowly religious ones? The answers to all these questions put morality at the centre of all religions. These questions are also vital in order to understand the meaning of religion in any society. As a result, religion is concerned with society and humanity at large. Religion promoting morality is believed to be necessary to individuals and society because it helps to establish harmony in society being based upon the moral norms and practices within the framework of religion. In this context, this anthology attempts to delve into the issues of religion and religious beliefs or faiths discussed by the different traditions of Indian philosophical systems in the context of the crisis of moral values in individual life and society. Religion provides its believers a meaning to life, and the morals to guard it, and thereby helps them to work constructively for shaping out a healthy society. In this way, religion gets extended beyond mere faiths or beliefs and rituals. It becomes a mode of practising morality, and thereby, it remains as the mainstay of society.

Further it can be viewed that the concern should be on the spirit of religion, rather than the rituals and practices in it. Usually, scholars of the philosophy of religion no longer think that mere "faith" as the vital element of religions. In some religious traditions, people express their faith in something as it is said in the scriptures, authorities or followed by traditions and that seems to be sometimes dogmatic. Others follow the religious dictums with rational and moral examinations, whether in performing rituals or following particular religious principles in their daily lives. This has led to an emergence of two distinct categories: (1) dogmatic faith, and (2) rational belief for the religious practices. For the second category, religious practices demonstrate a combination of (a) rational beliefs and convictions, and (b) primacy of morality and human values. The Indian religious sphere can be seen to have been maximized with the second category of rational beliefs and moral practices.

The main objective of religion is happiness, here and hereafter. The dictum is to live happily and have a final deliverance from a sorrowful life. According to the religious scriptures, the ultimate human aspiration is salvation which is differently described as deliverance, release, or liberation. Deliverance from suffering and bondage arises when a man is shrouded by wonder, fear, and mystery and there he conceives the sense of the sacred and the divine as redeemer and protector. This happens to be the foundation of most of the religions. If there were no dangers, no fears, no insecurities, man would have never thought of any divine protector. But since man seeks protection, he develops different ways of worship to get the help from the divine. The ways of worship somewhere started with the torments of Nature, horrific violence, bloodshed and awe, which somehow have been pacified by some peaceful practices, Vedic rituals, and romantic worship in religion. Thus, the originally inexplicable wonder is approached as the holy, the divine, the supernatural, to which man has different progressive approaches – rational, moral, spiritual and yogic which may be segmented under the paths of knowledge, devotion and action. This also becomes the part and parcel of the foundation of religion promising the final deliverance.

The spectacular growth and vibrancy of the contemporary philosophy of religion provide a wide range of exciting debates from which the following three categories are significant:

- Debates involving attacks on religious beliefs,
- Debates in favour of religious beliefs, and
- Internal evaluation of the coherence between beliefs in a particular religion.

In the first two categories, the debates go on between theists and non-theists. In the last category, the debates are primarily between religious believers who differ from the implications of their belief patterns and commitments. These debates are supposed to provide an ideal comprehension, not simply for the philosophers, but also for the students to explore the vital issues in philosophy of religion.

Our world, in many ways, is a religious world, where most of the people adhere to some or other forms of religious beliefs and practices. Some affirm the ultimate reality and the universe as one; some believe in many deities; while some others believe in personal deity. Some others again believe in no deity at all, and most importantly, many believe in reality as pure consciousness from which the world has come into being and into which everything will ultimately return. Thus, the differences are multifarious. However, there are also similarities as most of religions have their beliefs in the divine, carry on the ideas of sacred and profane, and follow the practices centered around a transcendental reality that is supposed to provide ultimate meaning and purpose to life. Such intricate and essential human necessities are rendered by Indian philosophy of religion that can sharply come up to shape out a strong foundation for a new civilization of coherence and compatibility between people belonging to different religious belief patterns.

As elaborated in the essay "Religion, Religiosity and Secularity" of Prafulla Kumar Mohapatra, one of the most problematic situations for humanity is *dharmāndhatā*. It often masquerades as *dharmīyatā*. Another problem is religious fundamentalism which goes with and sometimes in the guise of secularism. As a result, there is religious intolerance, violence and terrorism. These factors are brazen show against morality, which is the very foundation of religiosity in the context of any religion. On the other side, the fundamentalist religion fails to the scientific temperament and reason, and for this reason, it is scrutinized by the rationalists. The matter is so much muddled that the rationalists and moralists have to be the born foe of religion. The situation bewilders the common man. But is there nothing in religion that is rational and secular, and leads to a peaceful life instead of conflict? On this question, it may be seen in the discourse that the very basis of any religion is the unity of humanity and all that in the cosmos itself because, as religion says, all are the expressions of the divine or coming from the same divine source. It commands the moral order of unity and fraternity, leading to peace and harmony. Religious dictum says not to behave to the other in a way that is harmful to one's own self (*ātmānaṁ pratikūlāni pareṣāṁ mā samācaret*). All religions preach truth, non-violence and non-stealing (*satya*, *ahiṁsā* and *acaurya*). These are the indispensable principles of all religions. Primacy of the ethical is the mark of genuine religiosity and the same has to be regarded, not the religious fundamentalism.

Bijayananda Kar in his paper "Valuation on Mahimā Philosophy" attempts to depict the importance of human values, propagated by Bhīmā Bhoi. Mahimā Dharma is the most humanistic (Mānavavādī) among many sects and subsects in various religions. Its humanism has two aspects. First, it prays and appeals for the well-being of all, animate, inanimate, with the understanding that "all are the manifestations of the same divine". Mahimā Dharma is the foremost promoter of *ahiṁsā* on the emotional ground that *hiṁsā* involves unbearable pain and torture. Imagining and sympathizing the others and their pain on one's own self, one may abstain from *hiṁsā* for all. Second, humanism of Mahimā Dharma is reflected in treating all humans equally. It does not allow any discrepancy on caste, creed, men, women, etc. for practising Mahimā Dharma. Humanism goes with the rationalization. For this, it does not spread blind beliefs as other religions often do. It is a movement against elaborate and exploitative ritualism and belief systems comprising many gods and goddesses. Mahimā Dharma minimizes its rituals to simple adoration of the *guru* and the divine. At the centre of all these, there remains the concern of the human plight and the miserable conditions of all beings up to the insects, worms and plants. Bhīmā Bhoi devotionally weeps before the divine for redeeming the sorrow of all.

Ramesh Chandra Pradhan in his paper "Religion and Spirituality: Some Reflections on the Hindu View of Life" makes an attempt to study the relation between religion and spirituality in Hinduism. For him, the Hindu philosophy of religion accords spirituality the highest value in view of the fact that it aims at establishing the spiritual way of life in the world. The central philosophy of the Hindu religion is that the supreme Godhead is one, though it allows for the possibility of the plurality of forms of the Ultimate Reality. That is, according to Hinduism, though the Ultimate Reality is one, it can have various names such as *Brahman*, *Īśvara*, Viṣṇu and Śiva. Though there are many sects within Hinduism, all accept the reality of one supreme Godhead. The basic contention of Pradhan's argument is that Hinduism is not a doctrinal religion based on the teachings of one founder and one holy book. It is not dogmatic in its beliefs regarding the nature of spirituality. It opens up many ways of attaining spiritual freedom. Since spirituality is its essence it does not feel constrained by any rigid doctrine about how one can attain spiritual liberation. The realization of the Divine in the present life is the ultimate goal of Hinduism which aims at achieving the spiritual freedom of the human beings.

Ganesh Prasad Das in his essay "Conflict between Religion and Science Revisited" tries to debate the conflict between religion and science as an issue which has been discussed in different aspects and sought to be resolved in the contemporary climate of thinking. Religion and science seem to be opposed to one another with the rise of new knowledge during the period of Renaissance and Enlightenment. Knowledge in science and technology has, to some extent, appeared to jolt the belief in religious reality, but advanced knowledge in these fields shows that both are on the even path searching for deeper realities of life. For him, the search of both is spiritual at the core. It is not accurate to say that religion and science are complimentary to each other, because religion is a complete system of thinking without the support of science, whereas science cannot be a complete system of thinking without the support of religion. As the scientists admit, they work at a level above, not at the deep most level. Giving primacy to religion especially Hindu religion as it is originally known, but better called Sanātana Dharma, he concludes that it conceives the whole world as one abode, and life in this abode is one of love, coexistence, brotherhood, synergy and peace. Sanātana Dharma is India's contribution to the humanity at large for organizing the structure of man and of society of men.

In "A Creative Cultural Tradition of India in the Context of Religious Values" the author, S. Panneerselvam reflects upon Indian culture and its relation to traditions in the context of religious values. There are three parts in his paper. In the first part, he points out that the culture carries the values to the future generation and hence the values of it must be preserved. Individual as well as the social values constitute the culture. Culture is the guardian of the people. Culture endows people with their identity. The basic contentions of his arguments are:

1. The world of the great tradition in which the mythological past lies in the present, and
2. The modern world of science and technology by which we have seen a marvellous development because of which we are competing with the rest of the world.

He brings out the uniqueness of Indian culture and values by maintaining a balance between the past and present. The second part deals with the application of the notion of lifeworld in the context of Indian situation. Here, he claims that lifeworld of the Hindu religious tradition always allows interpretation and reinterpretation as lifeworld is always linguistically constituted. The Hindu tradition appreciates the role of language since language is viewed as a pointer to the knowledge of God. Panneerselvam further discusses how religious statements are based on faith from two different approaches, Western and Indian, in the third part of his paper. He tries to bring Wittgensteinian Fideism approach on this issue which holds that religious statements have their validity within their framework, they regulate one's life. In this sense, religious statements correspond not to any matter of fact, but rather, to a certain attitude to life. It also holds that how according to Wittgenstein, religion, belief, faith, conviction, etc. are reflected in the form of life.

Godabarisha Mishra in his paper "Dharma, Religion and Ethical Relativism: Altruistic Obligation and Motivated Ordination in Indian Philosophy of Religion" has dealt with various interpretations of *dharma* from the standpoint of the Indian traditions of philosophy. He has discussed how *dharma*, ethics and religion are interconnected in the Indian context. Among the many contextual connotations of the term *dharma*, Mishra has presumed ethics or morality to be the proximate meaning of the term because in most of the cases, it is used in association with performance of an action physical as well as psychological. Further, he holds that religion is the inspiration of morality since all religions uphold certain common moral values. Since there are some religions that defend certain values that are considered unethical by practitioners of other religions, we cannot derive an unequivocal connotation and speak about universal ethics as far as "religion" is concerned. But when we look at the term *dharma* as ethics, the matter seems to be different because it seems to have universal ethical implications and more than it, is also has metaethical and meta-religious dimensions. In the analysis of religion vis-à-vis *dharma*, we find that religions are manifold and are conditioned by space, time, personal contingencies and factors connected with their propagators and practitioners. *Dharma*, in its pristine sense, can be understood as one – as the ethical essence of all the religions having eternal value. Mishra has argued in favour of the universality of ethics and offered arguments to support the idea that though the principles associated with *dharma* are patently relative there are some ethos which have absolute implications.

Laxmikanta Padhi in his paper "Does Religion Create or Discover Meaning of Life?" aims to observe some pertinent questions regarding life. "Is life meaningful?" or "Is the meaning of life discovered or created in the context of religion?" He has contrasted "discovering the meaning of life" and "creating meaningful life". Padhi has discussed the clues from Russell to the existentialists and Schopenhauer, and tried to get a brief idea of how religion is concerned with the meaning of life. The meaningfulness of life is created rather than discovered, and a meaningful life must involve both subjective satisfaction and an objective moral and religious component. For him, all religions are not merely focused on a belief in a god, gods, or supernatural forces; they can provide a basis for moral thought and behaviour. Religion regulates all our duties as divine commands. Our understanding of who we are to become and our modes of being in the world are influenced by the aims and objectives by which we define ourselves and create meaning for our lives. To be fully human is to create meaning by establishing deep relationships, committing ourselves to the aims and objectives that give order and purpose, and placing our lives in the context of meaning-creating aims and objectives.

In the paper titled "Bhīmā Bhoi: The Revolutionary Poet-Philosopher", the author, Sarat Chandra Panigrahi explains the metaphysical and humanistic standpoints of Bhīmā Bhoi. From the perspective of metaphysics, Bhīmā Bhoi is a monist, as he regards reality is one, *śūnya* and indeterminate which is manifested in many. Going against ritualism, Bhīmā deplores the worship of other gods and goddesses. He vehemently criticizes ostentatious ritualism. It is because rituals militate against the realization of godhood. Ritualism, including worship and pilgrimage, leads to sectarianism and religious fundamentalism, and then blind faiths and exploitations. Bhīmā Bhoi's surging love for his fellowmen made him appear as a non-compromising crusader against social discrimination. For him, spiritualism admits no distinctions of caste, colour or creed. Mahimā Dharma gives hope to all that there is one caste. For him, love and compassion are the inevitable expressions of spiritual vision and serve as the cementing force to keep the diverse people together. The spirituality in the hands of Bhīmā Bhoi comes to embrace the whole within its ambit and it entails a form of humanism that transcends man while securing the interest of man to the highest possible extent. Bhīmā Bhoi aimed at the salvation of the humanity at large from the clutch of eternal suffering.

In "A Tightrope Walker: Appraising K. Satchidananda Murty on Religion and Morality", the author Vikram Singh Sirola has attempted to discuss K. Satchidananda Murty's views on religion and morality from Wittgenstein's perspective. The paper is not an attempt to make a comparison between these two thinkers, rather, the author has provided certain solutions to the complexities found in Murty's writings. The first complexity originates when Murty mentions a person who feels he has caught a glimpse of the realm which transcends the world. The second complexity, which is not clearly spelt out in Murty's writings, is that the religious dogmas do not blind a religious thinker and, with an awareness of this realm, realizes the lack of evidence and certainty in religious doctrines. But the questions arise: How would such belief guide him in comprehending human life and performing actions in practical life? Will his being religious suffice to lead a moral life in all spheres of his existence? In other words, how would he make sense of the religious rituals and creeds, and see them together in his experience of morality? In his attempt to answer these two complexities, Sirola has proposed a solution by revising Matilal's concluding remarks on "being religious" which is concerned with the popular view of religion and religious belief. The author's proposal is: religious attitude or temper or religiosity may get primacy over morality if it is identified with love, commitment, responsibility and sincerity towards life. It is like giving heart and emotions to cold-blooded Kantian morality. Morality and religiosity do not limit each other to just a system of propositions establishing a code of conduct for working in our lifeworld. It would be complete as an experience of value when weaved around the individual finding the right way of living.

Ranjan Kumar Panda in his paper "Vairāgya in the Realm of Awakening Consciousness" aims at articulating the philosophical significance of *vairāgya* in the realm of awakening consciousness. For him, *vairāgya* is a significant religious-ethical concept firmly grounded in the metaphysics of Indian philosophy. *Vairāgya* suggests *detachment* and *dispassionate association*. Contrary to that *rāga* exhibits a *pravṛtti* of passionate involvement which suggests indulgences with worldly affairs. The passionate attachment is celebrated in the realm of pleasure-centric condition of the materiality of life; its association with other psychological factors such as ego, greed and aversion are binding factors that cause suffering – *duḥkha*. In this context, the pertinent question here is: where does *vairāgya* fit in as a meaningful religious-ethical concept? Panda has argued that *vairāgya* as an intentional epistemic and normative attitude that helps the self and strengthen the *self-knowledge* developed through *vivekakhyāti*. Unless *vairāgya* is practised (*abhyāsa*), it is hard to attain self-knowledge and thereby, it causes further difficulty for the self to free from suffering.

In "Epistemic Foundation of Religions in India" Saroj Kanta Kar makes an attempt to depict the epistemic foundation of religions in India. Religions are epistemically based upon religious experiences and reason, which are personally experimented on and tested by reason. If verified as true, then upholding the same, the scriptures or teachers are accepted. This epistemic verification is exemplified in Buddhism, Jainism, Vedism, Śaivism, Śāktism, Tantra, Yoga, Nātha Sampradāya and even in Bhakti movements. Religions are based not upon baseless faiths, beliefs, blind beliefs or unquestionable authorities (as found in other religions). The paper claims that there is no ultimate faith-based system, though initial trust in teachers and scriptures is provisionally required to go with it in the preliminary stage. The inherent religious matters are experiential, rational and critical in the major religions in India. In these respects, religions in India are different from the Semitic religions and religions that are based solely on unverifiable faith and authorities in other parts of the world. While focusing on the epistemic foundation, this discourse also points out other major epistemic foundations of religions and how religions in India were viewed by Western scholars under the rubrics of Hinduism. In this context, this paper humbly attempts to depict the epistemic features of the major religions in India in both critical and descriptive modes.

In the paper titled "Can Religious Tradition Overcome the Crisis of Climate Change?", the author, Jhadeswar Ghosh investigates the role of religious tradition in dealing with the issues of environmental degradation in particular to climate change. For him, it is realized by the research of climatologists, geologists, oceanographers and other scientists that the Earth's climate is changing due to human activity. The crises of climate change occur in the wrong direction. Man tries to change or modify the environment according to his requirements and, so, the environment is being exploited to the fullest extent for the benefit of man. The basic contention of Ghosh's argument is, how we live our lives today will determine the fate of future generations, as well as other species. The mere analysis of climate science through the frame of technology is inadequate because all these human-made environmental issues cannot be resolved through technology. In this sense, he has pointed out that religion has a part to play significantly and influences our responses to the crisis of climate change. Religion is multifariously depicted as a symbolic system, a social institution, a relationship with the divine, or a moral code which could be applied to the issue of climate change. It also deals with an understanding of the human–environment relationship within the concept of nature, culture and religion which involve one another to resolve the crises of climate change.

In his paper, "The Universal Religion Swami Vivekananda and Bhīma Bhoi", Basant Kumar Dash has argued that Swami Vivekananda has proposed for universal religion, derived from the standpoint of practical Vedānta to resolve the conflicting claims of various religions. It is a synthetic approach to understand religion, which is nothing more than perceiving the fundamental unity that exists in all religions. It is neither a separate religion nor a religion to be accepted by all universally. It is rather an attitude to one's religion and also towards other religions. It is based on the Vedāntic truth of oneness. So, its key concept is in acceptance rather than tolerance. The difference that we find in different religions is only of outward appearance. But, in the core aspect, all religions believe in the realization of the reality. So, they are one in their essence. Dash has further established that Vivekananda's notion of universal religion is reflected in the writings of Bhīmā Bhoi, the great poet-philosopher and the exponent of Mahimā Dharma. For Dash, in the conceptual framework of Bhīmā Bhoi, the sacred is equated with the secular. He contends that the sacred core of all religions is one and the same, consisting of the set of cardinal values which help us to bind together. So, what is truly sacred is truly secular.

In the paper titled "Sociocultural Significance of Mahimā Dharma", Harischandra Sahoo illustrates the sociocultural importance of Mahimā Dharma which originated in late nineteenth century in western Odisha. In this paper, the author establishes that Mahimā Dharma was a protest against the prevailing evil practices in the society and degradation of moral values due to caste system, exploitation of the *rājās–zamīndārs–gauṇṭias* (the ruling class) over the poor people belonging to the lower strata of the society. The two main propagators of this cult are Bhīmā Bhoi and Biswanāth Bābā. But their approaches are different. Biswanāth Bābā advocated Mahimā Dharma as an unalloyed Advaita theory (Viśuddhādvaitavāda) and tried to establish it on par with other foundational religious scriptures of India like the Vedas and Upaniṣads. Bhīmā Bhoi, on the other hand, composed *bhajanas*, *cautīsās* and poems dedicated to his *guru* in local vernacular language to make significant changes in the society. He was raising protest against caste and class system that divided the society into narrow fragments. Bhīmā Bhoi was a champion of Spiritual Humanism. He anticipated socialism and a better social order, free from blind beliefs. Bhīma's attempt to see a changed world of tomorrow is praiseworthy which is the central concern of this paper.

Patitapaban Das's paper "Mahimā and Mahāyāna: Decoding the Concord" is an attempt to decipher the nature and form of religious syncretism happened in Odisha. Though the brand of Odishan religious syncretism encompasses myriad religious movements prevalent in Odisha, this paper excavates the nature of seemingly syncretism occurred in two important religious traditions in Odisha, viz. Mahimā cult and Mahāyāna tradition. Taking clues from the writings and literature of Sant Kabi Bhīmā Bhoi, it is argued that the poet-philosopher exhibits a stupendous syncretic tradition in Odisha, which has now been swelled into a powerful living religious practice.

In his paper "Interreligious Dialogue and Reflective Equilibrium", Gopal Sahu argues that interreligious conflicts and conflicts between religious and democratic values are inevitable in liberal constitutional democracies. Interreligious dialogue is used not only as a means for promoting understanding and peace across different religious traditions but also for resolving conflicts between religious with other values and principles. Further, the author argues that because of certain inherent practical and philosophical problems, the interreligious dialogue, though may not resolve conflicts and establish consensus in the logical sense, will help in realignment and resolution in liberal democratic societies. The author proposes the use of the philosophical tool "Reflective Equilibrium" to strengthen the environment for mutual understanding, communication and integration in matter pertaining to the peace, harmony and general well-being among the interreligious traditions and for alignment between religious values with democratic values.

Surya Kant Maharana in his paper "Revelation in Classical Indian Philosophy of Religion: A Śaṅkarite Approach" intends to endorse Śaṅkara to be one of the finest philosophers of religion who impartially and rationally attempted to point out the nature and acceptability of Śruti as revelation on rational and honest grounds. The paper argues that revelation is the final aim of religious endeavour which remains as the vision of the Ultimate Reality. A mere logical or scientific analysis of revelation is incapable of producing such vision precisely because logic has its own limits in capturing the Ultimate, Infinite Truth. If such truth is not uncovered in lived experience, then it turns out to be an untruth and nonrevelation.

Akoijam Thoibisana's paper "Ambedkar's Deconstruction of [the] *Bhagavadgītā*: A Philosophical Appraisal" seeks to explicate some of the most crucial questions raised by Ambedkar concerning the nature of the *Bhagavadgītā*. The paper illustrates and examines the dogmas of the *Bhagavadgītā* and explicates how it provided the much needed philosophical insight of the Hindu religion from the lens of Ambedkar's reading of the same. According to author, the crux of the paper is Ambedkar's deconstruction of the *Bhagavadgītā*. The paper is accordingly divided into three sections. The first is a brief outline of Ambedkar's definition of what is the *Bhagavadgītā*. The second gives an account of the *Bhagavadgītā* as a counter-revolutionary act of Brāhmanism. The third elucidates the deconstruction of the *Bhagavadgītā* and the trial of the philosophy of Hinduism.

In the paper titled "Religious Understanding and Global Peace", Sudhakar Jally attempts to explain that how our understanding of the true sense of religion can lead to global peace. The basic contention of the author's argument is that religion is incredibly human-centric. A human-centred world view announces the importance of individual liberty and autonomy. In the domain of religion, there are no scope for intolerance, sectarian attitude, and narrow approach and outlook. All religions are equivalent and comparable in nature. Proper understanding of religion is the urgent necessity of the present-day world by means of which peace and prosperity will be possible in the human society. Further, the author argues that religion, in every sphere, needs change and reformation which not only the individual's personal life but also his social life as well. Hence, change and reformation are necessary at all levels for the cause of sustenance of global peace, along with personal, social, regional and national interest, and obligation.

Alakananda Parida, in her paper "Jainism: Meeting of the Sacred and Secular", intends to hold a unique deliberation of secularism in the context of religion. The paper stresses on the ethical, metaphysical and epistemic aspects of Jainism that are sacred and secular at the same time. Non-violence, non-stealing, truthfulness, etc. are the paramount ethical norms of Jainism, which are simultaneously secular norms. Similarly, the Jainas hold that all selves are qualitatively similar in their pure form, with all goodness, and the defilements are adventitious to them. This undoubtedly establishes the equality of all. The Jaina epistemology is most secular as it bears no religious stigma. Thus, Jainism upholds the meeting of sacred and secular.

In the paper titled "J.N. Mohanty on the Structure of Religious World and Religious Experience" the authors, Manoj Kumar Panda and Pragyanparamita Mohapatra have discussed about J.N. Mohanty's view on the structure of religious world and religious experience. They have tried to show how a phenomenological approach can be found in Mohanty's understanding. Phenomenologists uphold that our understanding of the structure of reality is possible by understanding the structure of our experience. Another complementing way to understand the reality by phenomenologists is through describing the way in which the phenomena is given in experience which is called as first personal givenness of the phenomena. This first personal givenness is the key to understand our situatedness and the phenomena surrounding us including our lived experience. These two primary viewpoints can be seen in Mohanty's view. Mohanty tries to understand the structure of religious world by means of understanding religious experience and his explanation on the structure of religious world is supplemented by the explanation of our lived religious experience. For Mohanty, the religious experience is part of our lived experience and does not transcend the world where we live. Our ordinary daily experiences can also be the key to understand the religious world.

In the paper "Universal Religion: Indian Perspective" the author, K. Om Narayana Rao, attempts to explicate that how far the idea of Universal Religion is relevant in the Indian context. The author argues that the Vedas are *apauruṣeya*; this implies their Divine origination. But the scriptures of the historic religions due to their origin under different social, economic and political conditions have varying conceptions, ideals, principles, norms, etc. This variation in the belief-patterns, if when taken as differently true views from their respective standpoints, becomes acceptable to the individual religions, then there is a possibility of Universal Religion that has a sense of mutual understanding, respect and acceptance of each other's views for the general well-being of all. In this light, the idea of universal religion in the Indian context can be historically traced back to the Vedic period and this idea can be seen to pass through the teachings of Buddhism and Jainism, Aśoka's Dhamma, Bhakti and Sufi movements, Akbar's Dīn-ī-Ilāhī, Mahimā Dharma, and the thought and conception of Gandhiji and Swami Vivekananda.

Religious beliefs and practices of the tribal world reflect human perceptions from ancient time to present day. They are significant in every religion. The tribal religious rituals and belief systems have a room for spirits, who participate in their way of life. They occupy prominent positions in natural events and therefore worshipped. Describing the same, the paper titled "Tribal Religious Beliefs and Practices: A Philosophical Study on Koraput Region", Lakshman Patra attempts to study the cultural depth of tribes of Koraput district of Odisha. The author indicates that most of the worships have been done for the material gain of people, family, animals, plants and the whole cosmos. Additionally, the author also focuses upon tribal practices and religious beliefs concerning the blessings of God in life.

In his paper "The Concept of Premādvaita through the Lens of Swami Vivekananda", Dibyendu Mondal has discussed how the way of devotion (*bhakti mārga*) is a method to find the truth. Following Swami Vivekananda, the author has stated that the truth of Oneness or the nature of non-dual reality can be realized even by accepting its perceived diversities. The feeling of oneness through the world of names and forms we can identify as "Premādvaita." The author has discussed, following Swamiji, that even though the path of devotion begins its journey with duality, the highest feeling of devotion is always non-dual. His view in this regard is at the lower level of *bhakti* (*gauṇī bhakti*), the student starts her spiritual practices (*sādhanā*) in a number of methods, such as symbols (*pratīka*), idols (*pratimā*), worship (*pūjā*), words (*mantra*), etc. can purify the body and mind; through this process the student constantly aspires to reach herself to the next level of devotion. At the highest state of devotion student realizes the beautiful and inspiring truth that Love, the Lover, and the Beloved are one.

Keynote address

1

The Need of Various Philosophies of Religion

Sachchidanand Mishra

THIS is indeed a matter of great pleasure to share my thoughts in this seminar organized by the Department of Philosophy, Utkal University on the very pertinent topic "Indian Philosophy of Religion". I would like to begin highlighting the nature of philosophy of religion. The *Internet Encyclopaedia of Philosophy* defines the philosophy of religion:

> Philosophy of religion is the philosophical study of the meaning and nature of religion. It includes the analyses of religious concepts, beliefs, terms, arguments, and practices of religious adherents. – https://iep.utm.edu/religion/

At the same place the *Internet Encyclopaedia of Philosophy* also highlights:

> The scope of much of the work done in philosophy of religion has been limited to the various theistic religions. – Ibid.

The philosophy of religion explores the religious ideas from different perspectives. However, this was done taking into account specially the religious ideas related to Christianity. There are two reasons for this attitude: one, Christianity is a monotheistic religion; it believes in the God who created this world out of nothing and such an idea of God was well received; it had an appeal; second, India had been suppressed by the British for a long time, hence the Indian religions were not accepted as true religions, rather pseudo-religions.

Consult any text on the philosophy of religion, the main point of discussion is this one: whether or not there are reasons to believe in the religious ideas pertaining to the existence and nature of God, problem of evil and so on. Almost all the books on the philosophy of religion begin with the Judaic-Christian concept of God. What does it convey? It appears to me that the whole development of the philosophy of religion is centred upon this Christian idea of God. And here we find, as the core idea, arguments for and against the existence of God and theistic beliefs. Whether or not theism is tenable? And here comes the thought: suppose that one accepts the existence of God, what problems are they going to face? What questions will there be to settle and answer? When we accept God who is all-powerful, omnipotent, on one hand, and very kind, on the other, the very knotty problem, the problem of evil arises. The ground for this problem is this: one, if God is omnipotent, He is capable of doing whatever he wishes and very kind-hearted, why there is then suffering in this world? Why does not He make this world free from all this suffering and evil? He is either not all-powerful, omnipotent or not kind-hearted. The big part of the history of philosophy of religion is covered by the discussion on the problem of evil. The one point what this discussion establishes without any iota of doubt is that the philosophy of religion is mostly theocentric. God is there in the centre of religion, religious thoughts and, therefore, there are questions regarding arguments for and against the existence of God. In the semitic religions the same idea of God was conceived, that idea of God is very much accepted in Judaism, Christianity and Islam. These all are monotheistic religions. Taking this idea of religion, the philosophy of religion was started to be studied and the ideal of monotheistic religions was taken to be the paradigm of religion. The chief current of monotheistic religions is this: there are no gods, but GOD. There is negation of many gods but acceptance of God who is all-powerful, the creator of this universe, the father of humankind and the master of all whatever exists. This paves the path according to which only monotheistic religions are true religions and all others are false religions. Here starts the study of the philosophy of religion.

Western religions are necessarily theocentric, one cannot think of a religion without God. But the first question arises is: Is there any proof to establish conclusively the existence of God? In Western philosophical tradition, there is a common acceptance that this universe had a beginning. And if this world had a beginning, this must have originated from somewhere. And here comes the idea of Ultimate Mover, the First Mover. So, there is the beginning of time. And from that, before that there is only one, and from that everything originates. There are arguments for and against the existence of God. Even now, we are witnessing so many philosophical texts written to prove or negate the existence of God. Now, in twenty-first century, science is so evolved that it is proposing that everything can be explained without even taking into account the idea of God. Following the footsteps of Hume, Kant and some other philosophers have concluded that conclusively the existence of God cannot be proved. So, the existence of God is not a scientific fact.

Second, if we believe that God has created everything out of nothing or from himself, there are certainly some problems which are to be settled. if someone, who is the origin of this universe, the creator of this world is endowed with all the good qualities, why there is evil in this universe. Why is there so much suffering in this universe? Basically, these are issues related to the philosophy of religion.

When we turn to India the basic question begs the answer: Does India have the philosophy of religion? In Indian philosophical and religious traditions, we witness that there is no necessity of God. God is not at the centre of religious beliefs. And hopefully it is the Indian side where there are many religions which do not accept the existence of God. There is no contradiction in the acceptance of religion without God. And there are so many such religions. It is supported by the law of economy of thought. If God is not accepted, we can get rid of so many problems which are bound to originate while accepting the existence of God and believing in the monotheistic religions. Truly speaking, India does not have the philosophy of religion in the same way as it is developed in the Western philosophical tradition. We find epistemology, we find metaphysics, we also find ethics, but the philosophy of religion is something unique and particular to Western thought and this is not without reasons. The first reason is that India has no single dominating tradition of religion which can be classified as monotheistic and traditionally philosophy of religion is inseparable from monotheistic thoughts.

The philosophy of religion is actually philosophizing religious thoughts. We cannot philosophize all the religions in the same manner taking into account the same set of questions. There cannot be same set of rules in every game because all the games are developed on different pattern. In the same way, there is no possibility of same set of questions which are to be answered while philosophizing religious ideas of a particular religion. For example, Jainas do not believe in the existence of a creator God; therefore, for them the idea of God is not meaningful, it does not serve any purpose. What we consider as Hindu religion that is not in itself one religion as Christianity and Islam; rather it has different types of religions under one umbrella. There are Naiyāyikas who advocated for a religion which is one shade of Hinduism. For more than 1,000 years, the Nyāya philosophy was a strong trend of Indian philosophical tradition. We find intellectual debates far more than 1,000 years between Buddhist philosophers and Naiyāyikas, and here the Naiyāyikas are taking the challenge. They are producing the arguments to support the existence of God. Very interestingly, and this also comes with a surprise, that the problem of evil is not discussed in the Nyāya philosophical tradition although it is a kind of monotheistic philosophy and religion.

I am a student of Nyāya philosophy and I found that the problem of evil, notoriously famous in Western philosophical traditions, does not appear here because the Naiyāyikas conceive the idea of God which supported by reason. This is not the case that the religious beliefs are given and we start philosophizing in order to justify them. When Nyāya says that God is omnipotent, at the same time omnipotence of God was so defined that the problem of evil does not appear easily. In the Western philosophical traditions, one could find very easily such questions related to the idea of God's omnipotence that if God is omnipotent can he make a triangle square. Why such absurd questions? Because beliefs are coming first and later the philosophers and religious persons started philosophizing. When the idea of omnipotence conceived, it is conceived that God is free from all the rules. He is free to play as he likes. He is the rule maker, rule breaker and he can do whatever he is willing to do because he is so capable that he could create this universe out of nothing without taking any help of anything at all. So, if this is accepted, so many other problems arise. However, the Naiyāyikas also believe in the omnipotence of God, but their omnipotence of God is so well defined that such type of questions does not arise at all. For the Naiyāyikas, God cannot create this universe out of nothing. But this does not make God limited in the sense that how one could do anything? We all are doers and without having freedom we can neither be held responsible nor doer. We must be *svatantra*. In Sanskrit there is a *sūtra*, *svatantraḥ kartā;* only if one is *svatantra*, he is a doer. And when we study the philosophy of religion there is another very important concept to discuss, called the problem of free will. The point that whether we are having free will or not, this is also very debatable. And here this is also very well accepted that we all are free. Why we are free because in Nyāya tradition it is said that we all are free. Why because God has not created ourselves. God has created the universe but he has not created the souls. He is able to create this universe, this inert world out atoms. But he has no ability to create us. We all are in the same way beginningless creatures, beginningless beings as God. We are very much equal to God in the sense that as God is not created, we are also not created. We have no beginning, no origination. So, what I highlighted, it is called the origin of time. So, time has an origination according to the Western thoughts, as this world has an origination. But here we have a cyclic idea of this world. There is an origination and there is a dissolution. Every creation or origination is followed by a dissolution and every dissolution is followed by another creation or origination. So, if in this way those problems of the philosophy of religion are seen, they disappear.

Now take for example Advaita philosophy. Advaita philosophy propounds that there is only one reality *neha nānāsti kiñcana*[1]

---

[1] *manasaivānudraṣṭavyaṁ, neha nānāsti kiñcana* ।
mṛtyoḥ sa mṛtyumāpnoti ya iha nāneva paśyati ॥ – *BṛUp* 4.4.19

"Only by the mind is it to be perceived. In it there is no diversity. He goes from death to death, who sees in it, as it were, diversity." – S. Radhakrishnan (tr.), 1990, *The Principal Upanṣads*, p. 277, Delhi: Oxford University Press and *ekamevādvitīyaṁ*,[2] there is no plurality there, there is only one reality, free from all the duality. But here again such problems do not originate which originate in the Western philosophy of religion. Why? Because despite this belief that there is only one reality, *jīvas* are believed to be beginningless. There are six entities, six *tattvas*, which are beginningless. *Jīva* is beginningless; pure consciousness is beginningless; *Īśvara*/God is beginningless; difference of *jīvas* and God is beginningless; *ajñāna* is also beginningless; the connection of *ajñāna* with *jīvas* is also beginningless. Many a time we study and find such statements of some writers that there is no difference between the Western Judaic concept of God and the Advaitic concept of *Brahman*. But on scrutiny it is evident that there are so many distinctions, so many differences. Why? Because in Christianity it is believed that the world has a beginning; we all also have a beginning. All the creatures have a beginning. Actually, for this reason, these are called creatures. But in Advaita philosophy, although non-dualism is accepted but these *jīvas*, *ajñāna* and also *Īśvara*, consciousness, etc. these six entities are considered beginningless.

I would like to highlight some salient features which might appear in Jaina philosophy of religion and also in Buddhist philosophy of religion. In Buddhist philosophy, there are different shades. There are mainly three branches. Vaibhāṣika-Sautrāntika, is one branch as we can take them together. Another branch of Buddhist philosophy is known as Vijñānavāda and

---

2 *sadeva somyedamagra āsīdekamevādvitīyam taddhaika āhurasadevedamagra āsīdekamevādvitīyaṁ tasmādasataḥ sajjāyata* || – *ChāUp* 6.2.1

"In the beginning, my dear, this was Being alone, one only without a second. Some people say in the beginning this was non-being alone, one only; without a second. From that non-being, being was produced." – S. Radhakrishnan (tr.), 1990, *The Principal Upanṣads*, pp. 447-48, Delhi: Oxford University Press

fourth school of Buddhist philosophy known as Mādhyamika (Śūnyavāda). So, here also in Śūnyavāda, Vijñānavāda, Vaibhāṣika and Sautrāntika, the philosophy of religion has to differ. You cannot take them for granted for all of them in equal way. Again, in Jaina philosophy of religion, God is not accepted. So, there is no problem of evil because now the problem does not arise, the question does not arise. Why is there evil at all? Because we all the beings, we all the *jīvas* are responsible for all that is good in this world and whatever is bad in this world. Again, there is Mīmāṁsā philosophy. Mīmāṁsakas belong to the Āstika branch of Indian philosophy, which does not believe in the existence of a god, or more precisely in the existence of a creator God. So, here again these problems do not arise.

But it does not mean that there are no problems at all in the Indian philosophy of religion. The problems may come into forefront from different perspectives and from a different angle. This is a pity that we try to find out and settle the same old problems which are not there for the context and basic religious frameworks are different. Therefore, we are bound to get disappointed if we try to search the same problems here. But we must note that we have plenty of opportunities here to do philosophy creatively. We will have to be very careful as the whole realm of the philosophy of religion in the context of Indian philosophical traditions is completely or almost ignored. Because, in brief, many of places in the texts, this is hinted, and those arguments are very sound. But we have to think over these arguments, those issues and taking those points into the new world, into the new dimension. This is twenty-first century where new challenges are arising. Taking religion in the same way as it had been taken earlier is not a wise thing to follow.

Before we tread on the path to discover the Indian philosophy of religion, we will have to chalk it out in the context of Indian philosophical tradition what religious beliefs are important to discuss and philosophize. We have to differentiate which challenges we are going to discuss and which challenges we are going to leave. Because there are some points which are very much related to *karma-kāṇḍa*s (rituals). So, those ritual parts of the *karma-kāṇḍa*s need not be philosophized. But there are certain things which are very important and those issues require a thorough discussion taking various perspectives separately. We may take Sāṁkhya point of view, Yoga point of view, Jaina and Buddhist points of view, and not only one Vedāntic point of view, but separately each Vedāntic school one by one. Here again, we will have to be very careful as the challenges, the questions would arise in Advaita philosophy surely those would arise in Dvaita philosophy of Madhvācārya. So, usually in every school of Indian philosophy there is a scope of the philosophy of religion. We will have to understand the framework of that philosophy and then we have to think what idea of religion is conceivable there. I invite the scholars, researchers to work on these issues which might open new paradigms of Indian philosophical traditions. Surely, we cannot think of the philosophy of religion in the Indian context as it is available in the West.

2

Religion, Religiosity and Secularity

Prafulla Kumar Mohapatra

ANTONY Flew was a prominent figure in Western analytic philosophy. As a strong proponent of atheism and rationalism, he had numerous followers and admirers. While doing research in the University of Keele in England I had heard an interesting story – a true fact indeed – about him. During the last few days before completing his famous book *God and Philosophy* (1966), Flew was confined to his chamber in the Philosophy Department and was engaged in writing the book, when this happened for days together – about a week or so – Mrs Flew was very upset and on a Sunday she called him and said, "please come home for some time at least; the children have started missing you". "Okay, okay, there is a little bit left, I am coming after finishing the book." When he did not come home even after saying so two/three times, Mrs Flew gave him the ultimatum: "Look, Tony, if you are not coming home in the next quarter of the hour, I am going to send the children to Sunday school." That's it! Book writing stopped there unfinished, and Flew left his chamber at once and ran homewards. For he did not want that his children should join the rituals in the church without even knowing or understanding anything about it. He was passionately opposed to any form of superstitions and indoctrination.

This would be an encouraging instance for the rationalists of today. Belief in God would not be acceptable for them since it is not in keeping with scientific knowledge. They would also oppose religion and religiosity since religion and belief in God almost go together.

On a slightly different ground, another opposing line of thinking against religiosity may be secularity or secularism. The secularists do not support any particular religion or religious way of thinking. Not because the religious beliefs are unscientific or illogical; they do it because of their commitment to equality of all religions (*sarva dharma sama bhāva*). The basic principle of secularism is to treat all religions as equal and to provide equal right and opportunity to people of all religions to follow and practise their own respective religions.

Considered from this point of view, there should be a certain distinction between rationalism and secularism. The rationalists would strongly oppose religious beliefs, but the secularists would extend a liberal support for all religions though not fully supporting any particular religious point of view. This should be the case as a matter of principle and logic. But nowadays it is being observed that the proponents of these two points of view are showing an opposing attitude for religion and religious beliefs. It is being observed that in most cases, especially in the case of modern young folks and elite educationists, secularism is being displayed as a wise alternative to religiosity. Religiosity is being considered as an impediment to progress and development, and religion is being taken as a stumbling block on the way to social progress. Therefore, though in personal life the modern man has not fully forsaken religiosity in his subconscious, he prefers to pose himself expressly as a secularist. A very special reason for this is the fast growing blind obsession with religiosity (*dharmāndhatā*) and religious fundamentalism issuing therefrom. The type of aggressiveness and violence that is being taken resort to by the fundamentalists in the name of religion is not only creating indifference for religion and religiosity among the common folks, it is also being the cause of a strong abhorrence for this. To make this problem more acute, our country is witnessing the emergence of the so-called Hindutvavāda, which is nothing but a political pretense of religious fundamentalism – to say this would not be an overstatement. The Hindu nationalists are highjacking our religious past and misusing it for an ulterior political motive – for earning votes. And the few people who are wholeheartedly emulating this ideology in their life are inadvertently displaying *dharmāndhatā* (blind obsession with religion) in the name of *dharmīyatā* (religiosity by falling prey to misguiding ideas). Like the fundamentalists of other religions, these people are not shying away from taking resort to aggressiveness and violence in order to "protect"(?) the Hindu religion. Thus, as a matter of fact there is no religion or nationalism of the fundamentalist and terrorist. Fundamentalism and terrorism are such a mindset which reveals itself irrespective of religion and nationalism, and causes damage to religion in every case. Hidden behind this is a political evil motive or illogical superstition regarding religion. As a result of this, not only the rationalists but many of those who have taken secularism as their ideal are also found to be opposing religion and religiosity. It is only natural that in the name of religion, obsession with extreme religiosity or blind adherence to religion has been the root cause of the said reaction.

But largely because of this the common man finds himself in a state of confusion and does not know what to do. It has become a sensitive issue for him to give open expression to his natural propensity for being and acting as a moral and religious person. On the one hand, there are the staunch injunctions of religious fundamentalism and, on the other hand, there are daunting browbeating of rationalism and secular preferences. Between these challenging choices the poor common man feels utterly helpless. It was the prime objective of Flew's philosophy to express free and independent points of view on religion, morality and good conduct. But the common man is under a lot of constraints and fear in expressing this kind of view. Freeing himself from the blind precepts of fundamentalism, if he wants to be a liberal-minded soft-hearted Hindu (or Muslim or Christian), he will have to face opposition from the religious fundamentalists; on the other side, his soft-hearted religiosity might lose itself in blind obsession with religion, and both these sorts of religious beliefs being unscientific would face resistance from the secularists and rationalists respectively. Being indulged in this kind of dilemmatic confusion, he is neither able to openly oppose institutional religion nor is he able to present his own logical liberal view as proper religiosity. Such type of dilemma and consternation of a liberal, religious and well-intentioned common Indian has been aptly depicted by the eminent writer and columnist Gurcharan Das in his recently published book entitled *The Difficulty of Being Good: The Subtle Art of Dharma* (2009). Two instances given by Das in his discussion are noteworthy. Born in a liberal Hindu family which believed in the beliefs and ritual practices of all religions, and himself having a flair for original, progressive thinking, this scholar expressed interest in reading the *Mahābhārata*, but then some of his friends jokingly asked if he had decided to join the saffron family. This kind of a joke hurt his sentiments. For it would be unfortunate to become the butt of ridicule by secularists and rationalists if someone wanted to probe with an open mind into our ancient tradition as described in the *Mahābhārata*. Citing another similar example, he tells us about the confounded consternation of a woman nurtured in Western civilization. The lady was a sincere devotee and a habitual visitor to a Śiva Temple in Chennai; but in the prevailing circumstances she would prefer to visit the temple "secretly" for fear of the so-called secularists.

The import of Gurcharan's citing these examples was that while the Hindu fundamentalists were blindly following our tradition or were making misuse of it for political purposes, the modern educated and successful Indians have neither the time nor the interest in properly understanding this tradition in right earnest. Rather, in the convenient garb of secularism, these people are thinking it preferable not to take any serious note of it. Even these people are in a way being forced to openly underplay the religious disposition and the related moral proclivity consolidated in their subconscious.

However, logic and factual support are not enough for resolving all humanitarian problems. This has been the opinion even of several established scientists like Einstein and Fritzof Capra. They were looking for truth in Eastern wisdom and were searching for some philosophical justification of science in this. In his book *Out of My Later Years* (1950), Einstein has remarked that for realizing the Ultimate Truth about life and the universe spiritual illumination and the direction of the inner voice is a better means than logic and scientific facts. Expressing a similar view, Gandhi had said, "Great causes cannot be served by intellectual equipment alone; they call for spiritual efforts and soul force" (Tendulkar 1960: 6). More effectively than logic, science and rationality, spiritual efforts and soul force can solve all prominent problems. The rationalists see only the negative and dark side of religion. They condemn religious intolerance, violent crusade and aggressive nationality – all of which result from superstition and bad cultural mindset. The secularists condemn communal violence and hatred that are perpetrated in the name of religion. But how successful they have been in stopping or eliminating them? Rationalist thinking and secular logic are not the phenomena of today; they have been there for quite a long time. Together with them, extreme religious obsession, interreligious intolerance and communal rivalry have also been going on in parallel manner. For any effective solution of all this, the basic spirit of religion has to be unveiled from the veil of extreme religiosity and be properly analysed. From the theoretical point of view, if belief in God is an indispensable aspect of all religions, then this one God is worshipped in different names in different religions. All men are the children of God; so there should not be any scope for distinction for myself and others in any religion. Belief in God is bound to promote universal love and fraternity. Besides this, the universally accepted basis of religion is morality. A wide and indisputable definition of religion (*dharma*) is moral code of conduct. The basic principles of religion in the *Bhagavadgītā* are nothing but a set of ideal codes of conduct. Do unto others as you would be done by, *ātmānām pratikūlāni pareśām mā samācaret* (*Mahābhārata* 5.15.7) - these are the inviolable directives of all religions. *Satya, ahiṁsā* and *acaurya* (truth, non-violence and non-stealing) are the indispensable principles of all religions. Primacy of the ethical is the mark of genuine religiosity. That is why God is speculated as the source of morality and as *maryādā puruṣottama.* Without morality, God-belief is only an unnecessary revelation in imagination. Buddhism in Indian philosophy is a glaringly exemplary case. It has been rated as a major religion of the world, despite giving no importance to the belief in God and stressing on the moral code of conduct. Because of emphasis on the primacy of the ethical, the basic principles and objectives of all religions must be the same: the difference would lie in the superficial rituals and celebrations. If by overlooking the real objectives and basic principles of religion, more than necessary importance is given to these rituals, that is bound to generate religious intolerance and communal hatred. Obeying the moral codes is thus the leading trait of really religious life. Overlooking this, if we become obsessed with religious superstitions, the idea of religion gets distorted and thereby the society moves backwards instead of moving forward. Naturally and rightly, the rationalists raise their voice against such distortion of religion resulting from unscientific evil culture. And from this point of view, it is also largely justified that the secularists express distaste for religion. But no one would have any opposition or objection to following a religion that is based on morality and value, and free from any evil cultural distortion. A person believing in such value-based religion free from superstition should be respected as a truly religious person rather than being a butt of ridicule. If morality and value is the essence of religion, equality of all religions (*sarva dharma sama bhāva*) should be its inevitable consequence. Being well set on the equality of all religions, secularity would not promote the case of any particular religion. And for this reason, also it would not be against religion and religiosity. Because the basic objective of religion is to promote welfare of all and effect everybody's spiritual elevation. From this point of view, a truly religious person should be really secular. Besides having deep belief in his own religion, this person would be sympathetic and cooperative to all other religions. Because he would see his own reflection is others by virtue of his soul force resulting from morality. For this reason, despite being an avowed Hindu himself, Gandhiji remains an ideal for people of all religions like Christians and Muslims, in fact, for all the people of the entire world. All men are equals, all have equal fundamental rights and everyone is equally independent and free – for people believing in all this, secularism is an indispensable way of life. There can be no incompatibility between real religiosity, even firm belief in God and the secular way of life. Both the ways of life are well established on morality and human values. Beyond the boundary of logic and science a world rich with morality and values is everybody's desired preference, acceptable to every religion and every community. Moving out of the unnecessary rituals and superstitions, this beautiful world can be found in our tradition and religious legacy. Here God is the source of morality; man here is glowing with divine qualities. In a tradition where God is present in everybody's person, one does not have to look for extra-terrestrial divinity. Instead of looking for proofs in favour or against the existence of God, the best way is to live one's life with divine ideals and inspirations. For this reason it is against the spirit of morality to ignore the people who revel in the love of God and *brahmānubhava* on the basic support of morality. True, their way of thinking may not have scientific support; but it is also not logical to think that all that is not supported by science are useless and devoid of sense. Despite being unsupported by science, the spiritual way of thinking has been the desirable ideal for many prominent scientists. It is not rare in the history of ideas to find cases of people inspired with this kind of thinking who have given leadership in establishing humanism and universal fraternity. To respect the opinion of others and to be sensitive to other people's beliefs is true religiosity. It is also secularity in the true sense.

References

Das, Gurcharan, 2009, *The Difficulty of Being Good: The Subtle Art of Dharma*, New Delhi: Penguin India.

Einstein, Albert, 1950, *Out of My Later Years*, New York: Philosophical Library.

Flew, Antony, 1966, *God and Philosophy*, New York: Harcourt, Brace and World.

Tendulkar, D.G., 1960, Mahatma, vol. 4, 2nd edn, Ahmedabad: Navajivan Publishing House.

3

Valuation on Mahimā Philosophy

Bijayananda Kar

Mahimā philosophy is quintessentially based on Mahimā Dharma, a section of Hindu faith, basically originated from Odisha (erstwhile Orissa) and gradually got spread to nearby states, thus commanding all-India acceptance and recognition in modern timses. It was founded by Mahimā Goswāmī, variedly known as Mahimā Gosāīṅ, Mahimā Swāmī, Jogeśvara Mahāprabhu and Mahimā Prabhu. There is no recorded information about him. He lives in legends and oral narratives. According to some sources, he was known as *dhūli bābā* (a saint simmered in dust). His philosophy was monotheism. It rejected the prevalent caste system and discriminations of all sorts.

This philosophy got widespread recognition and acceptance due to its principal proponent Bhīmā Bhoi (1850-95). He was a nineteenth-century saint who lived just for forty-five years. A mystical poet, he developed his philosophical and religious acumen listening to *bhajana*s and holy scriptures. His significance is so profound that he was an epitome of human love and stood for the emporal welfare and well-being of humanity, especially of the poor, illiterate and the downtrodden. His dictum – *mo jībana pāche narake paḍithāu, jagata uddhāra heu* (let my temporal life be put into hell; nevertheless, let the temporal worldly being be redeemed) – got the attention of the literate and illiterate alike and made ripples in the social structure of Odisha. This redemption of temporal life is not necessarily limited to the human being alone, but to all beings. In other words, Mahimā Dharma Darśana advocates humanitarian and humanistic principles in a wider sense of all-inclusiveness and not bound to all-exclusiveness.

There persists a strong belief among a large section of people (both illiterate common man and the so-called intellectuals) that Mahimā Dharma, in a denominational sense, is within the framework of Hindu religion as a particular entity. As there are several denominations within the Hindu religion like Śaiva Dharma and Śākta Dharma in the classical sense and that of Śiraḍī Śāī Dharma, Śāī Dharma and even Santoṣī Mā Dharma in the modern sense, Mahimā Dharma is another influential sect within the Hindu religious framework and philosopy. In many other widely known *dharma*s, we are aware of the existence of different sects like Hīnayāna and Mahāyāna Buddhism, Chinese Buddhism, and Japanese Buddhism. There exists sectoral differences among the Christians such as Catholics, Orthodox and Protestants. Historical and legendary sources reveal that there were strong enmity and bloodshed among the Catholics and Protestants in the name of religion. Similarly, there are wide differences between the religious practices and faith of Turkish Muslims and Afghan Muslims.

Even now, though we come across varied cultural backgrounds and faiths among the Hindus, any change or reform is normally unwelcome, due to many reasons, mainly orthodoxy. This is common with all religions. There exists a total indifference to any reform or renaissance. For example, the movements against child marriage, *satī*, widow remarriage, and women education, among many. The entire orthodoxy stood against the teachings of many social reformers like Raja Rammohun Roy, Swami Dayananda Saraswati, and Jyotiba Phule, to name a few. Despite such opposition and resistance, there emerged many socio-religious reforms in Bengal, Maharashtra, Telangana, Andhra Pradesh, Assam, Utkal (Odisha), Kerala, and in many parts of the north-east. Mahimā Dharma was no exception. It also had to face a lot of resistance and opposition from the larger section of Hindu religion.

Mahimā Philosophy

Mahimā Dharma, as mentioned earlier, is centred round in its belief in a single God Alekha, who is *Parama Brahman*, a formless and omnipresent God just like *Brahman* of Vedānta. It condems idol worship and stands against the teachings of Vaiṣṇavism. Its main propagator was Bhīmā Bhoi, a Khoṇḍ, an initiate and an ardent disciple of Mahimā Swāmī, who devoted his entire life to preach Mahimā Dharma and collected and disseminated the Mahimā philosophy through *bhajanas*. It decries casteism in its strict sense and finds no meaning in class hierarchy of any sort. According to scholars, the original terms used in Mahimā philosophy were not in tandem with those in the traditional Hindu pantheon, thereby it assumes some similarity with crypto-Buddhism, Jainism, and Tantrism. Its rejection of the caste system, it is believed, played a pivotal role in the socio-religious empowerment of India. Charity, particularly giving food to the needy, is an inevitable part of its adherents' life.

However, it is far from controversies. Though it does not have any specific deity, some counter dhārmic people advocated a propaganda that Mahimā dhārmic propagators and Mahimāites visited Śrī Jagannātha Temple at Purī and even have accepted the authenticity of the said deity. Some years back, when I visited the Mahimā Āśrama, near Khaṇḍagiri Junction (that is on the eastern side towards Bhubaneswar Bahāī Temple), I met one brāhmaṇa, a semi-old man, inside the *āśrama*. The main centre of Mahimā cult in Bhubaneswar accepts any believer or non-believer (not anti-believer) of Mahimā.

Mānava Dharma

One salient feature of Mahimā Dharma, either overtly or covertly, is that it does not repudiate or object the formation and propagation of other believers who believe in one form of worship personally or even at Mahimā monastery (*maṭha* or *āśrama*). But, at the same time, it does not approve such developments in a public forum. It does not believe in creating widespread propaganda causing disturbance to the nearby residents and the passers-by shouting slogans, and using loudspeakers, loud music, orchestra, etc. It advocates serious hygienic and academic pursuits. While Mahimā Dharma, it seems, does not object some section of its adherents follow some prevailing procedures, it strictly forbids them from creating difficulty and disturbance in the public locality even by stealing flowers, property and so on. For them, such activities are illegal, immoral and to be repudiated at any cost.

Well, what do such moral codes imply symbolically? For them, both thought and action, privately or publicly, are of temporal significance in the worldly plane (*jagata uddhāra heu*). It does not refer either affirmatively or negatively to anything beyond temporal sphere. That is Mahimā Dharma or Mānava Dharma in earthly sphere. Here, *mānava* is not limited to men in the narrow sense of human individuals. It rather implies men at the larger sphere, meaning men inclusive of all living beings and natural phenomena. Here, *sarve bhavantu sukhinaḥ* refers to human welfare in the wider sense of human beings and nature without creating any mutual disturbance and one has to coexist peacefully. In this sense, there seems to be no absurdity in suggesting Mahimā Dharma as Mānava Dharma.

4

Religion and Spirituality

Some Reflections on the Hindu View of Life

Ramesh Chandra Pradhan

Introduction

RELIGION and spirituality are intimately connected in the Hindu philosophy of religion. Most of the Indian religions like Buddhism and Jainism accept the importance of spirituality for the reason that without the spiritual core, religion itself becomes an empty shell. The idea that religion is an abstract system of doctrines is foreign to the Hindu view of religion and therefore there is emphasis on the fact of spiritual experience within the Hindu view of life (Aurobindo 1959; Radhakrishnan 1959). The concern for the spiritual elevation of the human being is the essence of the Hindu religion. The idea of spiritual evolution of the human self is of paramount importance in the Hindu philosophy of religion.

In this paper I will seek to highlight the content of spiritual experience in Hinduism in order to demarcate the authentic elements from the inauthentic ones in describing Hinduism as a true religion. Hinduism provides the framework within which a true religion can be identified as a spiritual religion. Hinduism is a spiritual religion par excellence.

How to Be Truly Religious

What matters for a truly religious person is the religious experience that he has. The experience of the Divine Being or God is one of the key elements of religious experience. In the absence of such an experience one could lead a simply ritualistic life which has no sense of the Divine within it. Therefore, there can be no authentic religious life in the absence of the sense of the Divinity because to be religiously authentic is to have the experience of the Divine or the Supreme Reality (Radhakrishnan 1932, 1959, 1967).

Hinduism like any other religion worth the name makes the demand that a mere performance of rituals and mere chanting of names of God does not make a religious person. The deeper sense of religion is associated with the intense feeling for the Infinite Reality that is the object of religious experience. There is no way we can call a religion an authentic religion if it does make way for the intense feeling of the Supreme Reality (Radhakrishnan 1967: 102-04). Hinduism in this sense is an experiential religion being based on the genuine spiritual experience of the Divine (Aurobindo 1959).

Hinduism has been unnecessarily characterized as a primitive religion because it allowed the worship of idols as the latter is supposed to be a case of a primitive ritual of the commo mass. Idol worship has been criticized by many reformist movements within Hinduism like Arya Samaj. But the fact of the matter is that there is no conflict between idol worship and true spiritual experience as shown by the religious practices of Ramakrishna Paramahamsa who is supposed to have attained the highest spiritual experience through the worship of Mother Kālī (Vivekananda 1989). The religious practices of many religions of India involve some form of idol worship like the worship of the idols of the Buddha and Mahāvīra.

Whether a religion is authentic or true is not known from how its followers worship God, whether with the help of the external objects like idols or by inward experience of the Divine. What matters are how one reaches God or how one connects oneself with the Divine Being. Hinduism allows every form of worship. Its pluralism is its strength, its greatness. Every man according to his capacity and disposition can adopt any mode of worship, be it the worship of any idol or any object religiously sanctified. Hinduism makes no distinction between a worshipper of idols and a non-worshipper of idols, between a meditative saint and one who chants the names of God. All are true worshippers as long as they experience the Divine in the true sense.

Experiencing the Divine

Hinduism has divided itself into different branches or sects on the basis of mode of experiencing the Divine. Those who can experience God through meditations and philosophical reflections such as the Vedāntic thinkers are given the highest place in the Hindu religion not because they reject idol worship but because they have transcended the form of worshipping God in the idols. The meditative practices of Hinduism which are given the highest place (ibid.) are the representatives of the practices of *jñāna-yoga* which is held in highest esteem (*Gītā* II). However, they do not constitute the only way of connecting to God; there are the practices of *bhakti-yoga* which include many varieties of experiencing godhead such as through chanting the names of God or by offering material objects as a token of *bhakti* (devotion) (*Gītā* XII). The practices under *bhakti-yoga* are the easiest way of connecting oneself with God because of the availability of the devotional way of making oneself God-connected (Vivekananda 1989).

The different sects and cults such as Śaivism, Vaiṣṇavism and Śāktism, which come under the general framework of Hinduism, may differ in the form of the godhead the devotee wants to worship such as the forms of Śiva, Viṣṇu, Durgā, Kālī, Gaṇeśa or Sarasvatī and many others. They differ in the modes of worship but all worship the same Divine Being (Rajagopalachari 1964). Hinduism believes in the oneness of the Divine Reality though it admits the different forms of manifestation of the same Reality. There is no contradiction between the oneness of the Ultimate Reality and the different forms in which the supreme godhead can be found to be manifest. The *R̥gveda mantra*: *ekam sat viprā bahudhā vadanti* (God is one, but the wise men give it many names) is the founding principle of Hinduism. This catholic spirit of Hinduism is its hallmark and its great strength in accepting other religions which differ from it like Buddhism and Jainism.

The question whether the Hindu religious pluralism contradicts the basic principle of oneness of Reality can be easily answered by placing the plurality of sects and the multiplicity of gods and goddesses under the single banner of "One God, one Supreme Reality". It is very spirit of Hinduism to search for unity in diversity and to accept the many forms of the Supreme godhead. The principle of unity underlies the principle of plurality. That is what makes Hinduism free from any dogma and also free from any hatred towards any other form of religious worship. As it has often been said by Mahatma Gandhi (1962), all religions are true in the sense that they all lead to the same godhead and open up ways to experience the same Divine.

One Reality, Many Forms

Hindu religion is founded on the Upaniṣadic principle that there is ultimately only Reality which is called *Brahman* or *Ātman* (Śaṅkara 2001, 2002). The Upaniṣads unanimously declare that *Brahman* alone is the source of everything and that it is infinite and unlimited in character. The Supreme Reality is *sat-cit-ānanda* which explains the variety of things and beings in the world. *Brahman* in itself cannot be fully described in language as it is infinite in nature and cannot be given a definite shape in any manner. This affirmation of the Supreme Reality as *Brahman* has been central to the Vedāntic philosophy of the later ages as propounded by Śaṅkara, Rāmānuja, Madhva and other *ācāryas*. The ancient heritage of Vedānta has been the mainstay of Hinduism as both a religion and philosophy in India (Hiriyanna 1932; Radhakrishnan 1923; Rajagopalachari 1964).

The philosophy of the One Reality as *Brahman* has led to the religion of One God in the Hindu pantheon. Hinduism accepts the Supreme Reality as both the unmanifest and the manifest Reality in the universe. The unmanifest *Brahman* as the *Nirguṇa-Brahman* is the highest principle of Advaita Vedānta. This is philosophically the most acceptable principle but it may not serve the religious purpose, so Hinduism accepts the manifest *Brahman* (*Saguṇa-Brahman*) to help the religious worshippers. Even the dualist Vedāntins accept the *Saguṇa-Brahman* as the Ultimate Reality. The distinction between the unmanifest and manifest *Brahman*, that is, between *Nirguṇa-Brahman* and *Saguṇa-Brahman* does not make any difference to the metaphysics of One Reality which is the underlying principle that holds all the sects and cults together. Metaphysically, Hinduism stands for the oneness of the supreme godhead but practically it leaves scope for the plurality of the manifest forms of the Reality.

Hinduism as a whole accepts the philosophy of One-in-Many because for it God (*Brahman*) cannot be defined only as manifest or unmanifest (*saguṇa* or *nirguṇa*), because God can manifest Himself in many forms (*Gītā* XI). The *Bhagavadgītā* (X, XI) has explained why God can be seen or realized in many forms because there is no way we can deny the universal form (*viśvarūpa*) of the Supreme Reality, the Divine Being (Aurobindo

1996). The unfoldment of the supreme *puruṣa* (*puruṣottama*) in the various forms in the manifest universe is the greatest act of divine creation in space and time. The integral nature of the supreme godhead is the fundamental principle of the Hindu metaphysics (Aurobindo 1959) which has made it a unique religion and philosophy in the world.

Hinduism does not take the world as *māyā* (illusion) because the world itself is a form of *Brahman*. No school of Vedānta accepts the unreality of the world except in the metaphysical sense as in Advaita Vedānta (Radhakrishnan 1923). The idea that the world as *māyā* or *mithyā* does not mean that the world as empirically or practically unreal as has been made clear by Śaṅkara (1972), the founder of Māyāvāda. The Hindu religion accepts the reality of the world as the form of God so as to make room for the religious practices leading to liberation (*mukti*).

Spiritual Freedom as the Final End of Life (Puruṣārtha)

In the Hindu view of religious life, spiritual freedom or liberation is the highest ideal or value (Balasubramanian 1996). The Hindus accept the fourfold nature of the ends or values of life called *puruṣārtha*s such as *dharma*, *artha*, *kāma* and *mokṣa*. *Mokṣa* (liberation) is the highest end of life in view of the progressive realization of the liberation of the self through the fulfilment of other ends of life such as *dharma* (moral duties) and the fulfilment of the economic necessities (*artha*) and psychological needs (*kāma*). Such being the nature of the diverse values concerning life, one is led to believe that the Hindu view of life (Radhakrishnan 1959) makes room for not only the values concerning the life in the world but also the values concerning the life beyond the world. *Mokṣa* does not stand for a value to be realized after the cessation of life, but to be realized in life itself. The value of *mokṣa* is the value of spiritual freedom from suffering caused by the bondage to the world.

The Hindu ideal of *mokṣa* has been misunderstood because the idea of liberation or freedom has not properly been understood by the interpreters of Hinduism. It has been suggested, though wrongly, that Hindu religion is other-worldly and life-denying. Liberation has been suggested to be an escape from life and therefore ought to be treated as a value which denies life itself. But this interpretation is not only wrong but also misguided. *Mokṣa* means freedom from the sufferings and miseries of life which are due our attachment to the world. The human suffering is due to man's alienation from the Divine which is caused by the non-realization of the transitoriness of the human existence and the world that we live in (*saṁsāra*). The only way to happiness is the spiritual life that can ensure the end of the human misery (*duḥkha*) (Balasubramanian 1996: 81-82).

In this connection, it is to be noted that Hinduism does not demand a wholesale withdrawal from life in order to realize spiritual freedom. For, spiritual freedom can be attained here and now provided we attain the right knowledge about our self and its relation to *Brahman* (Supreme Self). The fact that our self has the divine Reality within it can make us rise above our limited existence in space and time. Our existence as the limited selves (*jīvas*) is condemned to the life of misery because of our being disconnected from the Ultimate Reality (*Brahman*). But there is a way out of this situation by the realization of spiritual freedom. Liberation is basically freedom from ignorance and the related state of existence in the world.

Spiritual freedom is neither a cessation of life nor a denial of the world. It is a reaffirmation of the spirit of man over the material life in the world. It is in that sense a form of transcendental freedom (Krishna 1989: 221-29) rather than a mere freedom in the socio-economic sense. It concerns the transcendental value of living the life of the spirit or the life divine (Aurobindo 1973). This new life of the spirit at once transcends the life in the world and also is a spiritual transformation of it by virtue of making life itself a worthy instrument of the expression of the divine spirit.

The Divine Life in the World

Hinduism is not only a spiritual religion but also a spiritualizing religion that transforms the life of the enworlded self or the self-in-the-world (Balasubramanian 1996). It raises the human self above its existence in the world and transforms it into the divine self. There is no way spiritual freedom (*mukti*) can be taken as an escape from the world. It is a way of transforming the world as envisaged by the Upaniṣadic thinkers by making life itself the instrument of the expression of the Highest Reality (*Brahman*). The systems of Yoga developed by the spiritual thinkers are meant to be the ways in which one can attain the divine life (Aurobindo 2000).

The idea of the divine life in the world is paramount in the Hindu philosophy of life and world. For the Hindu thinkers, what is most important is to make life itself a divine phenomenon in the sense that God can be realized in this life so that one can be a truly spiritual person (Aurobindo 1973). This ideal of a spiritual life in the world is the essence of much of Hindu thinking about how to make life worthy of divine knowledge and thus attain spiritual freedom here and now. The transcendental freedom of the human spirit is attainable here and now (*jīvanmukti*). Those who think that spiritual freedom is never attainable in this life are ignorant of the fact that all Hindu thinkers demand spiritual transformation of life itself while it is lived in the world.

Hinduism abolishes the man–divine divide by suggesting that man himself is a replica of the Divine because every man is an embodiment of the divine spirit (*Brahman*). The individual man as the microcosm is one with Divine as the macrocosm in the sense that what is in the individual self (microcosm) is also in the divine spirit (macrocosm). The Upaniṣadic *mantra*: "Thou art That" (*tattvamasi*) reverberates in the Hindu scriptures as one of the axiomatic principles of the Hindu philosophy of life (Balasubramanian 1996). The fact of the matter is that Hinduism does not see any merit in the man–God divide which has led to the idea of man's eternal alienation from the Divine. Hinduism celebrates human life itself as a divine creation in the sense that what is human is essentially divine. The flow of the divine bliss (*ānanda*) is eternally going on in the world, the latter itself being an expression of the divine bliss as the Upaniṣad declare (*Taittirīya Upaniṣad* III.vi.1).

The idea of man and the world being the unfoldment of *Brahman* has led many to think that Hinduism does not have any scope for the scientific notion of the world which is alien to man and to God. Thereby, they argue, Hinduism leaves no room for science of the physical world. The world being only a divine reality it is the home of spiritual life and not for any scientific or secular life. But this is a misconception because the world being metaphysically divine is empirically physical as the scientists believe it is. Science and religion do not conflict in Hinduism because of the fact that the physical world is itself divine in nature; the same reality can be both scientifically studied and also spiritually understood from God's point of view (Rajagopalachari 1964).

Science and Spirituality

In the Hindu view of the world, there can never be any conflict between science and spirituality because their viewpoints converge on the fact that the world, man and God stand closer in reality as the human spirit is a part of the world-spirit and what appears as the physical world is inherently a spiritual world. Man and the world are all of the same Reality because *Brahman* manifests itself in them. Science studies man and Nature in its own way which does not cancel the spiritual view of the universe. The scientific understanding of the universe is empirically testable and can be confirmed in sense experience. This, in no way denies that there can be a higher religious point of view for the understanding the same universe (Rajagopalachari 1964).

Hinduism from its very beginning in the Vedas has promoted science in all its aspects because it has made it clear that there is no object in the world which cannot be studied through the sense-experience. Hindu philosophy never downgraded the sense-experience in favour of the spiritual experience; in fact, for all practical purposes, it incorporated sense-experience itself within the transcendental experience of the world. The sciences within the Hindu civilization have occupied a highly respectable position along with religion because there is much scientific temper in the Hindu religion itself. The greatest scientists of ancient India were spiritual seekers as well just as the spiritual seers in the Upaniṣadic ages were scientists in their approach to the world (Ranade 1968).

The West has witnessed a conflict between science and religion because in that context, religion is opposed to science and the findings of the scientists. Science and religion oppose each other because their viewpoints are diametrically opposite of each other. The scriptural declarations about the world actually go against the scientific evidences regarding the nature of the physical world. In Hinduism, however, science itself is taken as an achievement of the human spirit which is art of man's total achievement in the understanding of the world. In that sense, science is no less a spiritual activity of man just as art, literature and philosophy are. Religion includes all forms of spiritual activity from the Hindu point of view. The divide between science and religion is bridged because of the convergence of both in the study of the world. For Hinduism, the so-called physical world is not physical in the materialist sense of the term. The physical world is a manifestation of the world-spirit owing to the fact that the physical itself merges into the non-physical from a transcendental point of view.

Science and spirituality go together because of the unitary nature of the universe and man. The cosmic unity of man and the universe is highlighted in the sciences and spiritual practices. Just as science takes the cosmos as a single unity from which everything else follows as a matter of natural necessity, so also religion studies the cosmos and man from God's point of view. Religion especially studies the human existence as part of the cosmic reality from which it derives the meaning of human life. The metaphysics of the world-unity is presupposed by both science and religion in the Hindu philosophy and religion.

Ethics and Society

Hinduism, like many other Indic religions, puts maximum emphasis on ethical life which ensures the prevalence of *dharma* (moral law) at all levels. It leaves no stone unturned to make life, polity and society subserve the impersonal law of morality as it has been emphasized in all discourses on *dharma* (Dharmaśāstra). In this sense, Hinduism is an ethical religion in that its ethics prevails upon all religious practices and all forms of worship of the Divine. Though ethics for the Hindus is not the final destination of life, it does not make ethics a mere instrument of achieving some on-moral ends. Ethics in the sense of accepting moral law(s) is indispensable to spiritual life as the moral law ensures progress towards spiritual life.

The Hindu ethics is part of the Hindu religion, indeed, an indispensable part. In fact, in obeying the moral law one begins one's spiritual life. The moral virtues which the Hindu ethics demands from the spiritual persons follow from their spiritual nature because virtues are of the nature of the divine qualities in man (*Gītā* XVI). The moral virtues like truthfulness, non-violence and self-control are the divine qualities (*daivī-sampat*) because they are part of the higher self of man which transcends the biological life of the human beings. In this sense, the moral good is not simply a psycho-biological good or a social good but a spiritual good in the sense of the good being ultimately divine. This ensures that there is a continuity between ethics and religion in Hinduism. In this sense, ethics and spirituality go together to make divine life possible. Ethics does not dissociate itself from religion as it is the case in the West.

The Hindu ethics is both an ethics of law (*dharma*) and an ethics of virtues. Both issue forth from the same holistic vision of life in which ethics and religion converge. *Dharma* and virtues are an integral part of the spiritual life because there is no way we can make spirituality free of ethical content. The moral content of the spiritual life emerges from the higher self of man that is freed from ignorance about its own divine nature. While ethics indicates the absolute demands of obedience to the moral law and the cultivation of the moral virtues, spirituality demands the integration of the whole personality in the service of the Divine. Thus, moral life and spiritual life become one in the integral life of the spiritual persons (Aurobindo 1973).

There is a misconception that since the Hindu religion is obsessed with spiritual life, its ethics becomes asocial thereby pushing aside the social issues to the backburner. However, it is the case that the Hindu ethics and spirituality are not asocial, though they do not derive their authenticity from the social conditions of man. The social conditions themselves are part of the moral framework of *dharma* as the highest value. The social structures are envisaged in terms of the moral law because the Hindus pursue their social goals in accordance with the moral values. *Dharma* rules the social sphere as much as the moral asd spiritual spheres because ethical life and the social life become integral to the spiritual life of man. Society is not an independent reality on its own. It is integral with the human reality. In that sense, we cannot take society as independent of the human beings. Therefore, man's social life must be part of his ethical and spiritual life.

The political and social rules or laws must fall within the domain of the moral law because the former is to be in conformity with the moral laws. The latter are universal and impersonal laws while the former is conventional and temporal. They change as the society changes and so they must accept the supremacy of the moral law. The socio-political framework, whatever it may be, is ultimately founded on the moral law or *dharma* according to the Hindu view of the polity (Aurobindo 1959). Thus, society itself is never opposed to the ultimate aim of spiritual freedom; in fact, it facilitates the spiritual freedom through a value-based social order. Man is as much dependent on the society for his spiritual evolution as the society derives its value-aspiration from the individual spiritual persons (Krishna 1965).

Hinduism as Sanātana Dharma

Hinduism has been called the Sanātana Dharma for the reason that it has been founded on the eternal principles which define the nature of social, moral and spiritual life of the human beings. It is also called *sanātana* (eternal) because it has no founder and therefore no beginning in time. Its origin can be traced to no historical or prehistorical time. It has been part of the human civilization guiding the human race from the time immemorial. Hinduism has evolved from the Vedic sources which are themselves impersonal (*apauruṣeya*) and timeless (*kālātīta*). Such being the case, it can easily be appreciated that the principles of the Hindu ethics and religion are taken as the eternal principles.

As discussed above, it can be said in favour of Hinduism that it is not a religion in the Western sense of the term, which has a founder and a holy book, like Christianity, Judaism and Islam. Hinduism has not only no founder but also it has no holy book like the Bible or Quran which codifies its central message. Hinduism has grown like a mighty tree during the course of the development of Indian civilization. It has developed different branches all carrying its central message regarding spiritual life. The Vedic civilization has been coterminus with the Hindu religion because of their antiquity. The following are the central principles of Hinduism:

1. It accepts all forms of worship of God with open arms. It hates none, excludes none from its civilizational boundary.
2. It accepts all religions, great or small, as ways of spiritual life, whether they accept God or not as the Ultimate Reality.
3. It, as a religion, is both transcendental and immanent in its approach to the ultimate reality. It accepts the supreme godhead as both transcendent to and immanent in the space–time world.
4. It stands for a civilization rather than a mere form or forms of worship. It is a way of life and a way of living ethically and spiritually.
5. It stands for the excellence of the human spirit and accepts all human beings as the "sons of immortality" (*amṛtasya putrāḥ*).

Concluding Remarks

In this essay, I have tried to throw light on some aspects of Hinduism which have been part of the foundational features of Hinduism as a religion. I have shown that the Hindu religion is a deeply ethical and spiritual religion because its basic aim is to spiritually transform human life. Its main goal is to establish divine life on earth so as to make the human race spiritually enlightened.

Hinduism has shown the way as to how the human beings can live in peace and harmony beyond all racial and religious barriers. In that sense, Hinduism is at once a philosophy and a religion constituting the foundation of the Indian civilization. It has been wrongly identified by the historians of religion as a primitive religion, though, in fact, it is the most philosophically and spiritually enlightening religion in the world. It is indeed a universal religion with a universal spiritual message for the whole mankind.

References

Aurobindo, Sri, 1959, *The Foundations of Indian Culture*, 1st Indian edn, Pondicherry: Sri Aurobindo Ashram.

———, 1973, *The Life Divine*, Pondicherry: Sri Aurobsindo Ashram.

———, 1996, *Essays on the Gita*, 9th edn, Pondicherry: Sri Aurobindo Ashram.

———, 2000, *The Synthesis of Yoga*, Pondicherry: Sri Aurobindo Ashram.

Balasubramanian, R., 1996, *The Primal Spirituality of the Vedas: Its Renewal and Renaissance*, New Delhi: PHISPC and ICPR.

Gandhi, M.K., 1962, *All Religions are True*, ed. Ananda T. Hingorani, Bombay: Pearl Publications.

Hiriyanna, M., 1932, *Outlines of Indian Philosophy*, London: George Allen and Unwin.

Krishna, Daya, 1965, *Considerations Towards a Theory of Social Change*, Bombay: Manaktalas.

———, 1989, *The Art of the Conceptual: Explorations in a Conceptual Maze over Three Decades*, New Delhi: Indian Council of Philosophical Research.

Radhakrishnan, S., 1923, *Indian Philosophy*, 2 vols, London: George Allen and Unwin.

———, 1932, *An Idealist View of Life*, London: George Allen and Unwin.

———, 1967, *Religion in a Changing Society*, London: George Allen and Unwin.

———, 1959, *Eastern Religions and Western Thought*, Oxford: Oxford University Press.

Rajagopalachari, C., 1964, *Hinduism: Doctrine and Way of Life*, Bombay: Bharatiya Vidya Bhavan.

Ranade, R.D., 1968, *A Constructive Survey of Upanishadic Philosophy*, Bombay: Bharatiya Vidya Bhavan.

Śaṅkara, 1972, *Brahmasūtrabhāṣya*, tr. Swami Gambhirananda, Calcutta: Advaita Ashrama.

———, 2001, *Eight Upanishads*, vol. II (with a commentary), tr. Swami Gambhirananda, Kolkata: Advaita Ashrama.

———, 2002, *Eight Upanishads*, vol. I (with a commentary), tr. Swami Gambhirananda, Kolkata: Advaita Ashrama.

Vivekananda, Swami, 1989, *The Complete Works of Swami Vivekananda*, subsidized edn, Calcutta: Advaita Ashrama.

5

Conflict between Religion and Science Revisited

Ganesh Prasad Das

Deep issues in philosophy, once born, never die. They might get outmoded in a particular climate of thinking, but they get transmuted and strike the mind of new-age thinkers and pose afresh in the contemporary idiom. The issues concerning rationalism and empiricism, the inner and the outer, scepticism and certainty, metaphysics and no metaphysics, private and public, matter and life, etc. appear again and again in every philosophical tradition as new variants. The various issues concerning religion are no exception despite many a thinker writing its death warrant.

My article titled "Religion as an Instrument of Social Change" was published by the P.G. Department of Philosophy, Utkal University three decades back in a volume entitled *Religion and Social Change* incorporating papers presented at a national seminar. There I attempted to show how religion can create a society of peace and amity, in which men live together with mutual love, support, trust and compassion for each other

(Mohapatra 1993). S.N. Dasgupta, the celebrated author of *A History of Indian Philosophy*) published *Religion and Rational Outlook* (1954), which is rarely mentioned in discussions of such kind. It may be remarked, in passing, that the publication of *A History of Indian Philosophy* is having its centenary celebration this year, 2022. Dasgupta is not only an outstanding scholar in Indian philosophy, but also in Western philosophy, science, religion and aesthetics. In the above-mentioned book, he critically and dispassionately seeks to find out the nature of religion, its relationship with man and society, and its rejection by the established truths of science. In this paper, I would like to discuss the problems set out in the previous paragraph closely following Dasgupta's standpoint as I find it to be so much enlightening and relevant.

The word "religion" comes from the Latin word *religare*, which means "binding together". The English word "religion" is regarded as equivalent in meaning to the Sanskrit word *dharma*, which is derived from the root *dhṛ* and means "to hold together". Although, in respect of their root meaning, *dharma* and "religion" appear to be univocal, in use they are not so. The words *dharma* and "religion" are not used exactly in the same sense; although, in certain contexts, mutual translation of the two words might be regarded as harmless. When Wittgenstein says in one of his remarks that he is not a religious man, but he cannot help seeing every problem from a religious point of view, the sense of the word "religion" in the first part of the statement and that of its variant "religious" in the second are not the same (Rhees 1981: 94). To be a religious man is to accept and adopt all beliefs and rituals of a given religious creed that constitute the exterior or the accompanying characteristics of a religion. To act religiously is to be committed to the spirit of religion, i.e. to the very purpose and motive of the given religion. In other words, this is concerning its interior or the essential features. Similarly, the word *dharma* has multiple senses like "righteousness", "merit", "duty", "rights", "law", "conduct", "virtue" and "right way of living". Moreover, in India, there are different religions in practice, such as Sanātana Dharma (of which "Hinduism" is a misnomer), Islam, Buddhism, Christianity, Jainism, Zoroastrianism and some minor religious sects. Some of these like Buddhism and Jainism are regarded as both missionary religions and systems of philosophy.

Religious sensibility is particularly human; ethical sensibility too is uniquely human. When we look at religions of primitive men as well as those of civilized men, we find certain commonalities among them. Apart from that, there are certain features which are found in some religions and not in others. So, it becomes difficult to pronounce judgements that would hold good for all religions.

The so-called Hindu religion is a category apart when compared with other religions. The term "Hinduism" is calibrated by European writers to refer to the beliefs and practices of the community of people inhabiting the valley of the River Sindhu (from Sindhu to Hindu and from Sindu to Sind to Inde to India). The use of the word "Hinduism" would have been well accepted, if it would not have created confusion by placing it at par with the Abrahamic religions like Judaism, Christianity and Islam and other historical religions.[1] Historical religions

[1] Some sources report that when Alexander the Great first invaded India around 325 BCE, he renamed the River Sindhu as "Indu". He dropped the first letter "S" from the word and coined a simpler word for the Greeks to pronounce. Gavin Flood states that the term "Hindu" first occurs as a Persian geographical term for the people who lived beyond the River Indus as per the sixth-century BCE inscription of Darius I. It is mentioned in *Maharsi Śrī Dayānanda Sarasvatī aur Unakā Kāma* (ed. Lala Lajpat Rai and published from Lahore in 1898), that the name "Hindu" is based on a derogatory meaning. It is stated in the introduction of the book, "... it is correct →

come into existence with the emergence of prophets and their prophecies made available in the form of scriptures. Such religions are, therefore, called prophetic religions. Hinduism is neither historical, nor prophetic; it does not have a single scripture composed by a single author and does not prescribe any rigorous code of conduct. It is a way of life permeating all its states and stations, but not a rigid and ossified one. It is rather liberal and flexible, ready to accommodate all sorts of genuine beliefs that get evolved in the human domain. Therefore, it has a better nomenclature "Sanātana Dharma".[2] This is otherwise called "Ārya Dharma" as a person adhering to it and practising it becomes more and more civilized, social, moral and liberal. This is also known as "Yukti Dharma" as its beliefs and practices stand to reason and are based on verified statements and is bereft of dogmatic assumptions.[3] Louis Fischer, the European biographer of Mahatma Gandhi (1946), once observed that Hinduism is a sponge religion:

> It includes features of Buddhism, Christianity and Paganism ... Hinduism absorbs all dogmas and destroys none.

← that this name [Hindu] has been given to the original Aryan race of the region by Muslim invaders to humiliate them. In Persian, the word means slave, and according to Islam, all those who did not embrace Islam were termed as slaves." Many archaeologists claim that during 1352 CE, the kings of the Vijayanagara Empire increasingly started emphasizing on the word "Hindu" with great pride and honour, and the most specific amongst all was King Bukkal who described himself as "Hindu Rāya Suratrāṇa". According to researcher Devdutt Pattanaik, Raja Rammohun Roy was the first person to use the word "Hinduism" in 1816 and Chandranath Basu came up with the idea of "Hindutva" in 1894.

2 *sadā nayati* (directs at all times) *iti sanātana*.

3 These two terms are due to Pt. Nilakantha Das. *Vide*, *Gita Prabesha* to *Understanding the Gita* (tr. from Odia into English by Kali Prasad Rath), Toronto, Canada, 2021.

By saying that Hinduism accepts all dogmas, Fischer means to say that the dogmas are absorbed duly rectified by reason in the pervasive framework of reason. He draws an important conclusion that there is no Hindu fundamentalism, about which much hue and cry is raised now and again. According to him, all the fundamentals of Hinduism are in a constant state of flux. It is not, therefore, easy to define the nature of Hinduism within the range of a few fundamentals and essentials. One might have some success if one defines it in terms of its highest ideals and the perfections of its moral culture.

Some well-read persons and some not-so-well-read persons alike are not clear about what Sanātana Dharma is. It might be that they suppose it to be another historical religion, comparatively newly propounded by someone like, say, Dīn-ī-Ilāhī, Bahāi or Swami Vivekananda's Universal Religion. They need a precise definition, nature and practice of that religion. We have already stated that India has given to the world a religion, which is applicable to and aims at the welfare of, all the people of the world. This conception of Sanātana Dharma is enshrined predominantly in the *Mahābhārata* (mentioned 157 times), the *Manusmr̥ti* (mentioned seven times), the *Garuḍa Purāṇa* (mentioned four times) and there are numerous other sources.

According to the *Amarakośa*, the synonyms of *sanātana* are *śāśvata*, *dhruva*, *nitya* and *sadā*. Translated into English, *śāśvataḥ* means "eternal", "ever-lasting" and "perennial"; *dhruvaḥ* means "constant" involving "consistency"; *nitya* means "invariability", "fixedness" and "temporarily eternal" and *sadā* means "permanent" in the sense of "continual". Here, we may particularize the universal concept Sanātana Dharma following *Mahābhārata* 3.281.34, thus:

adrohaḥ sarvabhūteṣu karmaṇā manasā girā ।
anugrahaś ca adānaṁ ca satāṁ dharmaḥ sanātanaḥ ।।

> The eternal duty of the good consists of not harming any creature by action, thought or speech, and of kindness and giving.

All of the values mentioned above – compassion, kindness and generosity – are qualities that are upheld by the good people. Any individual in society can acquire and cultivate them. While this list of values does not specify the people who uphold them (apart from those who are "good"), other instances of Sanātana Dharma include principles that should be upheld by a specific group of people. The specificity is based on the individual's personal or professional role in the society. According to *Garuḍa Purāṇa* 221.24:

> *satyaṁ damastapaḥ śaucaṁ santoṣaśca kṣamārjavam* ।
> *jñānaṁ śamo dayā dānam eṣa dharmaḥ sanātanaḥ* ॥
>
> Truthfulness, self-control, practice of austerities, purity, contentment, forbearance, simplicity, knowledge, compassion and charity – these are the eternal virtues.

Here, a list of universally accepted morals is provided, all of which constitute the fabric of Sanātana Dharma. These tend to build up a man of character – pious, dutiful, strong, self-reliant, upright, righteous, gentle and well-balanced characters which will give him the credence of a good man and a good citizen. The fundamental principles of religion that govern the general view of life and of life's obligations are alone sufficient for building such a character (Besant 1916).

As already explained above, religion plays a role in social cohesion. Some of the external features of religion that include rituals and even dogmas contribute to hold people together. Those are congregational forms of worship like Durgā Pūjā in West Bengal, Odisha and elsewhere, Gaṇapati Mahotsava in Maharashtra and there are many more examples; prayers like group *namāẓ* in Masjids or Suliā Yātrā of Ādivāsīs in Balangir district of Odisha, Śrī Kṛṣṇa Janmāṣṭamī celebration, Hemis festival of Buddhists, Mahāvīra Jayantī of Jainas, etc. in different parts of India. Thus, some religions seek to bind together people of a particular region or nationality, whereas the Bauddha Dharma seeks to bind not only the whole of humanity, but also the whole of living beings, and the Sanātana Dharma seeks to bind, uphold and sustain the whole of living beings and non-living beings as well, or better, it sustains all the *prajā*, i.e. all the created beings, to use a term of the *Bhagavadgītā*. It is said that King Aśoka, the Great, was a Buddhist and he was indoctrinated by saint Upagupta (claimed to belong to Odisha). Whether these are historical facts or not is questionable, but it is true that he did not show any preferential treatment to the Buddhists as distinguished from members of other religions. In his rock edicts, he prescribed gifts to brāhmaṇas and Buddhists alike, and allowed Jaina temples to be built near the Buddhists temples.

Religion and science appear to be opposed to one another with the rise of new knowledge during the period of Renaissance and Enlightenment. It was seen that many beliefs supported and propagated by Christianity were shown to be unfounded. For example, once upon a time, it was believed that the earth is the centre of the universe, and the Sun, the Moon and the stars encircle it. This belief officially belongs to the Egyptian astronomer Ptolemy. Italian astronomer Galileo, on the basis of observation through an instrument developed by him, doubted this belief and propagated that the earth is going round the Sun. He was considered as a sinner and confined in jail. He thought that if he remains in jail throughout his life, then he would not achieve what he wanted to do. So, he submitted to the king that Ptolemy's view was right and he was released from jail. But then he was convinced in his heart of hearts that the Christian view was incorrect. Later on, Copernicus proved the geocentric view to be unfounded and the heliocentric view to be scientifically grounded. Many similar beliefs in astronomy and physics supported by religion were set aside by science.

W.P. Alston in his book *Perceiving God* (1991) discusses about the alleged opposition between science and religion. It is alleged that the beliefs of Christian religion are contrary to facts established by science through the method of observation and experiment. Alston says that there is a methodological difference between the veracity of the beliefs of Christian religion and hypothesis/theories of science. It is undeniably true that Christian beliefs cannot be supported in the same way as scientific hypotheses and theories, but this does not mean that there is any conflict or incompatibility between the two. They are different in the same way as mathematics and empirical science are different. The results of pure mathematics cannot be established in the same way as the hypotheses and theories of empirical science and they are not incompatible as they deal with different subject matters, different problems and proceed in appropriately different ways.

Alston suggests that we should not ignore the various respects in which scientific developments come into conflict with Christian and other religious beliefs. He gives an example. Astrophysics first advocated a beginningless universe. After that it advocated the Big Bang theory. The Christian religion advocated that the universe was brought into existence by God some finite period of time ago. Science assumes materialism and causal determinism for its investigation. This does not hold good of God as God is no matter and He is not produced by anything. It is said to be *causa sui*. So, God does not form any part of the subject matter of science. Hence, there is no conflict between science and religion. No scientific hypotheses/theories that come into serious conflict with the Christian faith have reached even the lowest level of confirmation. Of course, the Freudian theory of religion contradicts the Christian faith, because it contradicts the claim that this faith was initiated by God's self realization. But Alston doubts that even the hardest Freudian would suppose that this theory is to be counted among the assured results of science (1991: 241).

Now, the point is that religion has been the source of intolerance, evil and superstitions that block the progress of the human mind and produce things that are inhuman, barbaric, cruel and vulgar. The development of science in its different branches: physics, chemistry, anthropology, sociology, psychology and along with science, philosophy too, struck at the roots of religion and weakened its hold on the human mind.

In the era of modern science that encourages cultivating scientific temper, nationalism springs up as a force of social integration. The development of science and technology contribute many things raising people's standard of living, promoting the means of production and opening up market opportunities for the products. Thus, economic generation and growth become the order of the day.

Nationalism is a secular idea and does not have anything to do with religion, holy scriptures, high priest, sacred congregation and rituals. It has a government installed by the people, a constitution for governance, a national flag and a national language to go with. Under the flag, people of the nation unite and live and die for their land. In case of war, with any adversary for any cause, they stand as one and fight for the unity of the nation. A nation seeks to be self-sufficient in every respect. But, there is a reverse kick. From the point of view of economic growth, there must be trade and commerce among nations, as otherwise, there cannot be progress and prosperity. For this, a developed nation would search for territories, where it can sell goods produced by it. There would be competition between nations for the same. Hence, clash between nations would be there and consequently, there would be loss of life and properties of people. So, nationalism as an integrative principle cannot contribute to amity between nations and bring about universal brotherhood of man.

Science and technology go a long way to foster comfort, pleasure and happiness of the people as already stated. In this way, there is improvement in the physical condition of living. But, unless the nature of people develops in respect of morality and spirituality in keeping with the physical development, that creates imbalance in personality. Personality is not merely or predominantly a psychological concept. By personality, Dasgupta means

> our entire complex structure, including our biological or animal tendencies. It includes within it our cravings, temperament, character, emotions, emotional outlook, will and conduct, in fact, the totality of our interrelated experiences and their potential tendencies. – 1954: 28

The spirit attempts to reveal itself in and through the entire personality in religious activity. One has to help it. Every man has an equal right to the development of each potentiality to the attainment of happiness and indeed everything that these two imply. Mere recognition of such right does not satisfy the religious spirit as demanded; fellowship and love are required. The motto of every religion must be "love all men as thyself". The religion that compels the ignorant to remain ignorant and the poor to be poor is not religion but a visitation.

Technology has made the world a global village, but the primitive sense of the village being a single family is absent in it. As explained above, they are caught through economic competition among nations creating envy, hate, betrayal and such other subhuman qualities. Aldous Huxley said once, "technological progress has merely provided us with more efficient means for going backwards". S.N. Dasgupta observes that the development of civilization and culture has but slightly ennobled our nature. As a result, the people are as much brutish now as they were tens of centuries before. The development of science has placed weapons of unimaginable destruction in the hands of a comparatively civilized chimpanzee or gorilla. All the nations of the world now shiver within as they apprehend a global war that might begin with pushing of buttons by empowered world leaders at the slightest pretext. The world at present sits on an active volcano, as it were. The present wars bred by power politics are far more destructive than the wars bred by religious conflicts between creeds and communities in the past (not talking about *dharma-yuddha*).

In the present-day society, there is the tendency of over-mechanization. There are now hospitals with robot nurses taking care of patients, surgeons doing surgery, restaurants with robot attendants, factories with robot workers and shopping malls with robots at the help desk. There is undue emphasis on the attainment of economic and political powers. These lead to dissolution of natural bonds – man is set against woman, employers against employee, even one family member against another because of allegiance to two different political parties. The pursuit of art, literature, philosophy and religion suffers by disillusionments. The mechanical idea of religion which is realizable in power or wealth tend to break the ideals naturally born in the heart of men. In the words of Dasgupta (1954: 20):

> The cry of the modern civilization denounces restfulness, quietness and contemplation and the inner resource of happiness and joy are denounced as ideal and dreamy fancy.

According to him, the fault of the present culture and civilization lies in the disproportionate of scientific knowledge and learning in its various departments and the comparative backwardness of spiritual control.

It is true to some extent that the advancement of science and the growth of knowledge weaken the roots of religion. It is also true that the extent within which the dogmas and rituals surrounding a traditional religion do not yield intended results are not corroborated by observed facts. The dogmatic suppositions and rituals, however, do not constitute the essential characteristics of religion. Thus, they do not conflict with the most universal, fundamental and essential spirit of religion. These are the things which give the ultimate value to the personality of a person espousing a religious way of life and rejuvenate him/her with greater optimism. This is superior humanism when compared with its Western counterpart.

There are some thinkers who consider that the very idea of religion is harmful to mankind. There are others who do not hold such a drastic view. They consider that certain central ideas of a given religion are harmful and that can be abjured by conversion to a different religion that despises those ideas. B.R. Ambedkar, for example, felt that certain ideas of Hinduism are pernicious to social democracy, which is the root of the cherished ideal of political democracy (Keer 1991: 415). The democratic principles, which constitute the fibres of social life are the trinity of liberty, equality and fraternity. Indian society, according to his perception, was based on castes, which were exclusive in their lives (ibid.: 490). But this tends to tear the very fabric of social existence and engenders associated life between the people who form the society and endangers natural rights and freedom. Hinduism, he alleges, stands for inequality and oppression and it deprives its adherents of honour, money, food and shelter.

This is not, however, a faithful account of Sanātana Dharma, although there might be deviations from the ideals at the factual level. If self-conscious and decision-making human animals turn out to be vile, the ideals cannot be condemned. The ideal enshrined in *Ṛgveda* I.89.1 is *ano bhadraḥ kratavo yantu viśvataḥ* (let noble thoughts come to us from every side). *Mahā Upaniṣad* 71 projects the ideal *vasudhaiva kuṭumbakam* (*Yajurveda* 32.86) (the whole world is a family). Dasgupta proposes that religion must be so interpreted that it transcends both nationalism and internationalism.

The spirit of nationalism and internationalism, which discards religion as a bond of unity, is itself not able to establish the bond of unity insofar as global peace and universal brotherhood are concerned. These are two precious human values. How could the human being imbibe these values? It is a big question. It has to be discovered whether there is some possible sources in our own nature, which may be able to transform us and set us in the path of enduring virtue. The seeking is that people should naturally be opposed to wars, so that the spirit of aggression may die down. When we search within ourselves, we find that the tendency towards being good and doing well is in our elements. The distinctive characteristic of the human individual is rationality, and being good and doing well are internally related to rationality. The *Taittirīya Upaniṣad* in the section Ānandavallī tells that man emerges out of *ānanda* (bliss), is sustained through *ānanda* and merges in *ānanda*. This Upaniṣad is an important text in Vedānta that is regarded as both philosophy and religion. It is philosophy in the sense that there is thinking about the man and the world he lives in, in total perspective – a perspective of 360° turn. It is regarded as religion in the sense that is a way of life. The universals like *satya*, *ahiṁsā*, *asteya* and *aparigraha*, are not the ideas for toying with, but for living life through. Thought, speech and action of a human being must be constructed and construed on the basis of these pervasive ideas. Hence, we must make a distinction between the essential and inessential attributes of a religion; as envisaged by Dasgupta. We have to discover the extent to which our growth of knowledge may be found incompatible with religion. And we have to discover the extent to which religion remains unaffected by our scientific and other kinds of knowledge. We have also to find out the extent to which religion is regarded as a fundamental fact of experience and as ennobling us through morality to beyond morality (Dasgupta 1954: 11).

The last point of Dasgupta is very important. The purpose of religion in its core aspect not only seeks to make people moral, but also to take them beyond morality. What is there beyond morality? Beyond morality, there is religious experience. To live morality is to live rationally. In different steps of life, where moral decisions are to be taken like "to do or not to do and how to do", one exercises reason to find out a way. Here, the moral person owns responsibility for his/her action, but he/she performs the action on behalf of a totality – might be his/her family, society, community, country, the world – and the result thereof never accrues to himself/herself exclusively, but to that totality. An individual person subserves the needs, objectives and aspirations of the totality. The actions of the moral agent are for each other's well-being without causing any pain or harm to anybody. This expansion and growth of the individual self is in and through intellectual understanding of the individual. The objective of reason is precisely this, that is, to take the agent beyond the confines of his/her small interests to the large interests and aspirations of the totality. Thus, the individual is free to act, but not absolutely so. His/her will is restricted, but not predetermined.

The *Bhagavadgītā* puts forward a number of concepts that show how universal interests are related with and goes beyond personal interests. The concepts are: *lokasaṁgraha, parasparaṁ bhāvayantaḥ, niṣkāma karma* and *sarva bhūta hite rataḥ*.[4] The term

---

[4] *karmaṇaiva hi sansiddhim āsthitā janakādayaḥ* ।
lokasaṅgraham evāpi sampaśyan kartum arhasi ॥ – III.20

→

lokasaṁgraha is formed by two words *loka* and *saṁgraha*. Here, *loka* means "mankind" and *saṁgraha* means "holding together". According to the *Bhagavadgītā*, *lokasaṁgraha* means

> holding together all people with a unitary principle of service aiming at the well-being of each and every human being of the society.

Although this term is interpreted in several definitions, its precise purport is "community welfare". For Radhakrishnan, *lokasaṁgraha* signifies "the unity of the world, the interconnectedness of society". The purport of *lokasaṁgraha* is spacious, it embraces both the unity of the world and the welfare of the world.

The *Bhagavadgītā* seeks to say emphatically that in the personal domain one must be a *niṣkāmakarmī*, not abstaining from action, but performing action without intention for personal thrift and gain. One can make it possible if only one thinks beyond oneself. In other words, one must put oneself in a wider domain of the whole of created beings or *prajā*, as *Bhagavadgītā* III.10 calls it. The agent must think him/herself positioned in the widest domain of the universe in which everything and being are interconnected. It needs to be clarified here that this whole is not just a totality of the particular individuals that are amenable to sense perception. But then, the whole is not anything apart from the particular individuals. So, this feeling of the whole being over and above particular individuals is cognized in and through the particular individuals. Reason of human beings

---

← *parasparaṁ bhāvayantaḥ śhreyaḥ param avāpsyatha* ॥ – III.11

naiṣkarmya-siddhiṁ paramāṁ ... ॥ – XVIII.49

and

sanniyamyendriya-grāmaṁ sarvatra sama-buddhayaḥ ।
te prāpnuvanti mām eva sarva-bhūta-hite ratāḥ ॥ – XII.4

takes him beyond reason in and through reason. In this sense, Dasgupta talks about the ennobling human beings to beyond morality through morality.

Man is a social being. He is also a religious being. There is as much the social instinct as the religious instinct in him. Religion is prominently a human instinct. Both the social and religious instincts have well-being as their end. The aim of the social instant is individual good and common good in tandem. On the other hand, the aim of the religious instinct is attainment of good here and hereafter. The social instinct is expressed in social rites and rituals like dress codes, manners, etiquettes like doing handshake, saying "hello" and putting off hat. The conception of the hereafter is transcendental and quite significant. It is not that it is devoid of sense and it is not that it does not have scientific support in any way. To dilate upon that would be an unnecessary digression here.

From the above discussion, it would be amply clear that the concepts of religion and morality are wedded together right from the beginning. The sense of oughtness or obligatoriness is there in moral discourse. It is also there in religious discourse. According to Harriet Martineau, morality implies obligation and obligation implies obedience to the command of some lawgiver (cited by Dasgupta 1954: 14). The law-giver voices from within our heart and this is known in ordinary parlance as *viveka*, i.e.the capacity to distinguish between good and evil. In this sense, religion is not archaic something associated with dogmatic suppositions, but it is spirituality supported by reason. In the ordinary go of life, the so-called Hindu religion is associated with *pratimā* (image), *pūjana* (worship), *prārthanā* (prayer), *praṇāmī* (obeisance), *prasāda* (offering), *parikramā* (going round for gaining a holistic view) and *pārāyaṇa* (self-reading of books dealing with philosophic ideas). These could be dispensed with without losing its core despite the fact that these are needed by men with immature minds.[5]

We speak of God as an objectively existing deity. We suppose Him to be the Creator, Organizer and Destroyer of the world. But we have never seen Him in our physical eyes, not heard His voice in our physical ear. We can only realize Him as we might perceive Him in our mind and heart as Spinoza and Rāmānuja would say. Personal gods – Jesus, Allāh, Kr̥ṣṇa, Viṣṇu, etc. as conceived by human beings – are bound to be anthropomorphic and like them social. Our God is Truthful, Just, Benevolent, Merciful and Loving. These are the attributes, which we wish all good men to cherish, of God.

We value freedom of our spirit above all. If God comes in conflict with the freedom of our spirit, then the theological God and social God would not be good. It would remain as powerful only. God to be good must be founded on the normal yearnings of

---

5 *Śukla Yajurveda* 32.3 says: *na tasya pratimā asti* (there is no image of Him); *Kena Upanisad* 1.4 says: ... *tadeva brahma tvaṁ viddhi nedaṁ yadidamupāsate* (you realize that alone as *Brahman*, nothing that you worship); Ādi Śaṅkarācārya speaks about *nirguṇa mānasa pūjā*: *ātmano brahmatā jñānam nirājanam iha ātmanaḥ*.

Tolstoy's *The Gospel in Brief* implanted a Christian faith in Wittgenstein. Before going on night-duty at the observation post, he wrote: "Perhaps the nearness of death will bring me the light of life. May God enlighten me! Through God I will become a man. God be with me. Amen." – S. Greenstreet, "Wittgenstein, Tolstoy and the Folly of Logical Positivism", *Philosophy Now* (https://philosophynow.org/issues/103/WittgensteinTolstoy_and_the_Folly_of_Logical_Positivism).

A prayer in the Indian tradition is: *prātaḥ smarāmi hr̥di saṁsphurad-ātma-tattvam sac-cit-sukham parama-haṁsa-gatim turīyam* (in the early morning I worship That, which is beyond the mind and the speech).

the heart, as Dasgupta puts it. So, God must be conceived not as a powerful being, but as a Loving Being. In this way, only God can be ours and we can be God's. There is no good anywhere except in human aspirations. It is in the ideal of man. In this sense, God is a creation of the human heart. In the words of Dasgupta:

> Born there, he suffuses the whole world with glory, interprets the whole world not only as the world of reason but as the world of purpose and the world of love. It is with this God in our heart that we can transform the mechanistic universe into a universe which tends for the good and perfection of humanity. – 1954: 18

Thus, it does not matter if a particular religion does not admit the objective existence of God. Any religion that admits the idol worship admits love as the good and admits the existence of God in essence. The Buddha and Mahāvīra did not admit the objective existence of God, but they were trying to inculcate love and non-violence in the hearts of men. So, they are labelled as religion for that matter; they are said to be humanistic religions. The truth is that all religions are humanistic from this point of view.

We grow to maturity by learning from our father, mother, teachers, guardians and senior persons in the process of our socialization. The English poet Herry Wadsworth Longfellow scribes:

> Lives of great men all remind us, we can make our lives sublime, and, departing, leave behind us, footprints on the sands of time. – A Psalm of Life, 1838

These footprints are for those, who come down the timeline, to follow us as we did our predecessors. We regard the society as the judge, who punishes us in non-legal ways for our violations, the society being the result of an unwritten contract among the indwellers. The society is an organic unity, where the being and becoming of one is bound up with the being and becoming of others as already pointed out. We learn from biology that the life of an individual cell is a function of the conglomerated cells. Every cell in the body can live in and through this function. When we say that the individuals are organically related with one another, we want to emphasize the fact that the being of an individual is a function of the complex being of the society. In this way, morality vanishes into religion and religion overflows morality in the perfection of the union of human and the Divine (Dasgupta 1975: 20). This is the idea of a poised, peaceful and spiritual society.

In an article "God and Morality", Rajendra Prasad (1975) says that morality is autonomous and its alleged theological basis is unwarranted. According to him, it is not obvious that there is a relation of logical dependence between the concept of morality and a concept of God, or a conceptual complex involving a concept of God or of something else related to God. One can constantly maintain that sometimes an action may be right although it is not approved by God or that it may not be right even if it is approved by God. It is to be considered whether an action is right because God approves of it, or God approves of it because it is right. It will be possible if being right and being approved of by God are logically connected. If the two are logically connected, then it would be self-contradictory to say of somebody that he or she leads a good moral life but does not believe that there is any God. Examples are there of cases in which those who do not believe in God have been admired for doing morally excellent work and those believing in God are accused of committing immoral deeds. A particular action is said to be moral because it is approved of, or commanded by God, according to the theologian. But, according to Prasad, there seems to be no special reason for search for ethical justification to end only with theological premise. There is another attempt to justify the entire system of morality in terms of some reference to God. This amounts to exhibiting the obligatoriness of leading a moral life. Prasad remarks that this would not mean justifying the entire system of morality, because it has to be in terms of the concept of obligation and this is the part of the same moral system.

Bertrand Russell (1925: 5-6) advocates that fear of nature gives rise to religions that are based on dogmas. There exists an antithesis between things that can be affected by our desires and things that cannot be so affected. The line of demarcation between the two is neither sharp nor immutable. With the advancement of science, more and more things are brought under human control. Nevertheless, there remain things definitely beyond human control. All the facts of our world that are dealt with by astronomy are in this list. It is only facts on or near the surface of the earth that we can, to some extent, control to suit our desires. And even on the surface of the earth our powers are not unlimited. Above all, we cannot prevent death, although we can often delay it. Religion is an attempt to overcome this antithesis. If the world is controlled by God, and God can be moved by prayer, then we acquire a share in omnipotence. Thus, belief in God serves to humanize the world of nature and to make men feel that physical forces are really their friends. In the like manner, the idea of immortality removes the fear of death. People who believe that when they die, they will inherit eternal bliss may be expected to view death without horror. It does, however, soothe men's fears somewhat even when it cannot fully drive them away.

We can corroborate Russell's view by citing a case found in the religious philosophy of Vaiṣṇavism of India. King Parīkṣita completely drove away his fear of death that he was cursed with after listening to the *Bhāgavata* from saint Śuka for a week. The great epic discusses a view of the world from its creation to decay with every problem of being and becoming in between in their doctrine of *puruṣārthas*, the ultimate pursuits of life of man. According to Russell, good life is one inspired by love and guided by knowledge. Sanātana Dharma ensures good life for everybody precisely in this way. The Vedas, the Upaniṣads, the *Bhāgavata* and the *Bhagavadgītā* have put up essentially the roadmap of such good life or life of bliss (*ānanda*).

References

Alston, W.P., 1991, *Perceiving God: The Epistemology of Religious Experience*, London: Cornell University Press.

Besant, Annine, 1916, *Sanatana Dharma: An Elementary Textbook of Hindu Religion and Ethies*, Benares: Central Hindu College.

Dasgupta, S.N., 1954, *Religion and the Rational Outlook*, Allahabad: Allahabad Law Journal Co.

Fischer, Louis, 1946, *The Great Challenge*, Delhi: Rajkamal Publications.

Keer, Dhananjaya, 1991, *Dr. Ambedkar: Life and Mission*, 2nd edn, repr., Bombay: Popular Prakashan.

Mohapatra, P.K. (ed.), 1993, *Religion and Social Change*, Cuttack: Akash Publications.

Prasad, Rajendra, 1975, "God and Morality", in *Indian Philosophy Today*, ed. N.K. Devaraj, pp. 186-200, Delhi: Macmillan.

Rhees, Rush (ed.), 1981, *Ludwig Wittgenstein, Personal Recollections*, Maryland, MD: Rowman & Littlefield Pub.

Russell, Bertrand, 1925, *What I Believe*, London: Kegan Paul.

6

A Creative Cultural Tradition of India in the Context of Religious Values

S. Panneerselvam

> Whereas nature has no history, culture as value-seeking is inherently historical as it is bound up with a social and symbolic tradition within which its dialectical and "developmental" process operated. – Pande 1985: 11

Culture: Its Relation to Tradition

INDIA being a great nation, consists of rich tradition of ethical values and cultural background, will always see the means and the end together. India is a country where there is a plurality of cultures. It always appreciates each culture whether it is small and big, sharing each culture its due. Culture adopts itself to the situation. It considers the changes that are taking place outside. It is slow but steady. Culture unites men into one cultural group. The development of many cultures is due to various causes like physical habitants and resources, which are outer and cause like range of possibilities inherent in various areas of activity, which are inner. All cultures are cultures because they have some essential elements in common. The culture carries the values to the future generation and hence the values of it must be preserved. Individual as well as the social values constitute the culture. Commenting on the individuality as well as the universality of human nature, G.C. Pande (1996: 153) says:

> The individuality of Indian culture must be so interpreted as not to militate against the universality of human nature and value-seeking. At the same time, the unity of Indian culture must be interpreted with sufficient catholicity to include numerous communities, regions, and epochs, which have historically entered into its making. This search for the cultural identity of India, individual but inspiring after universality, one but inclusive of differences, continuous but developing, arises from the awareness of India's historic traditions.

Culture is the guardian of the people. Culture endows people with their identity. Pande emphasizes that there are three approaches to culture, viz. the scientific, historical and metaphysical. The scientific approach, according to him, is essentially modern whereas the historical is both modern as well as traditional depending on one's approach to history. The metaphysical approach is basically traditional and it has two varieties. The first one is identified with orthodoxy, i.e. the values which we have inherited from our Vedic times, and the other is with the content of mystical revelation or intuitive experience of Vedic seers.

India lives in two or more conceptual worlds at the same time:

1. the world of the Great tradition in which the mythological past lies in the present, and
2. the modern world of science and technology by which we have seen a marvellous development as a result of which we are competing with the rest of the world.

This is the uniqueness of Indian culture and values, thus striking a balance between the past and present. We need to develop alternative world views, alternative metaphysics, as the basis for reflection on technology vis-à-vis society and civilization. The way towards understanding the metaphysical roots of technology, must lead through the creation of an alternative world view which will enable us to grasp sharply and clearly ramifications and consequences of present technology for a future human society. It is here Indian culture and philosophy can contribute to the Western cultures. It is because Indians have holistic understanding of life. It is not anthropocentric, but cosmocentric in nature. We must re-examine our intellectual heritage and tradition in the light of our present situation. Tradition is always hermeneutical and accommodates new interpretation and understanding. This reconstruction means the reconstructing the present categories of knowledge. Man's mode of being-in-the-world helps a person to evaluate the tradition. It is not possible for a person simply to follow the tradition, but he has the right to evaluate the tradition. The world of historicity will have an impact on the tradition and it accepts evaluation and reinterpretation. This does not mean that we are revolting against the tradition, but interpreting them in the context of present historicity. The cultural world, which one belongs to, allows a radical interpretation of the tradition. This sort of interpretation teaches a way of looking at the tradition afresh from a new perspective, which will suit for our present situation and this explains how a particular person is placed in the surrounding world or tradition though his physical world is supported by scientific and technological society. Every man is placed in a tradition or culture, which cannot be avoided.

We need alternative view of knowledge. For example, philosophers, futurists and others who are interested in the future of technology and thus with the future of culture would be benefited by a dialogue with the alternative world views of Indian culture in which alternative basis for knowledge and of life is admitted. The Western or the technological society is based to a great extent, on the qualitative instrumental values. It is true on the basis of these values, the social and political assessments are made. As long as the quantitative instrumental basis remains unchanged and channels its imperative via descriptive science, through industrial profit-efficiency-oriented technology, the order of things will remain the same.

The West is now in search of quality of life. It has understood the emptiness of the quantitative approach. The modes of life governed by quantity are simply not sufficient. Quality of life is hard to define, although its absence is readily apparent. We know what is within the structure of our experience of it. Quality of life adds to our stature as human beings. Quality of life cannot be understood without a purpose in life. The purpose in life cannot be secured unless we ascribe some meaning to the world or at least some meaning to the human life – beyond the immediate gratification of our sensual desires. This means that the quality of life requires a transcendental dimension of life. Traditional cultures and religions, by providing these transcendental dimensions can contribute to our experience of the quality of life.

The increasing awareness that Western culture may be breaking down has made us search for causes and examine facets of modern society which we have hitherto ignored, neglected and overlooked. In technology, there is a focal point, in which conceptual and ideological paths meet. To understand these converging paths is to understand the main configurations of the network within which our civilization operates. For example, notions like progress, nature, invention, rationality and efficiency have a link with culture. To put in simple terms, the philosophy of culture is the philosophy of religion, a philosophy of man in a civilization which has found itself at an impasse, which is threatened by excessive specialization, fragmentation and atomization, and which is becoming aware that it has chosen a mistaken idiom for its interaction with nature. All these problems to some extent are due to our wrong approach to science and technology.

Man's Being-in-the-World: Contextualizing the Lifeworld of Religion

This part of the paper deals with the application of the notion of lifeworld in the context of Indian situation. I would like to see the relevance of lifeworld of Habermas and analyses how far we go further to interpret and understand tradition in better a way in Indian philosophy of religion. My concern here is to see the way in which religion enters the lifeworld, into man's mode of being-in-the-world. Lifeworld is included in myths, beliefs in God, etc. and is always characterized by tradition and historicity. In other words, it can be said that tradition is the constitution of the lifeworld and language is the vehicle of tradition. It is language, which gives unity to tradition by considering of its historical dimension. Being situated in Indian tradition, I would like to show how culture and tradition allow new interpretation and understanding. I feel that both allow the participant to see the different dimensions of understanding. Habermasian distinction between system and lifeworld is useful here. The uncoupling of the system and lifeworld is essential so that one can know the importance of lifeworld. A system has structure and the lifeworld has hermeneutic interpretation. A system is always a rigid and fixed, and allows no changes, whereas lifeworld is flexible and allows changes and, hence, it is hermeneutical. It allows a discourse of understanding. Tradition is always hermeneutical and accommodates new interpretation and understanding. Here, it may be mentioned that though in Habermas we find the distinction between structure and lifeworld, and the tension involved between them, Indian scholars like S.S. Barlingay (1983: 165) have tried to overcome this tension by presenting the unified perspective of both. According to Barlingay, the structure and lifeworld are known as (i) cosmocentric, and (ii) anthropocentric standpoints respectively. One presupposes the other and hence there is no tension between them. The relation here is not between the social and natural but between two aspects of the social itself and hence there is no conflict, says Barlingay.

The lifeworld of my religious tradition always allows interpretation and reinterpretation since lifeworld is always linguistically constituted. The Hindu tradition appreciates the role of language and how language can be viewed as a pointer to the knowledge of God. Thinkers like Wilhelm Dilthey, Edmund Husserl, Martin Heidegger, Jürgen Habermas and others have shown the way to go from consciousness to language, from egoity to intersubjectivity, from fact to meaning and from system to lifeworld. The lifeworld is a shared one and it alone can explain how shared meanings are transmitted in religious traditions. Multiple expressions of human life are made possible by it. The stories, legends and myths need interpretation. They need constructive, interpretive activity of thinking to arrive at a coherent understanding in ordinary language of the lifeworld from which they sprang. What it means is that to interpret the stories, legends and myths in a new perspective, one must be in the present situation and context. The lifeworld allows for the evaluation of culture and tradition. Man's mode of being-in-the-world helps a person to evaluate the tradition. The lifeworld, which I belong to, allows a radical interpretation of the tradition. This sort of interpretation teaches a way of looking at the tradition afresh from a new perspective, which will suit for our present situation. Every man is placed in a tradition, which cannot be avoided. Tradition and historicity play a significant role in the understanding of the myths and symbols of a religion that is expressed by language. It is language, which carries the tradition from one to the other. In the lifeworld, it is language, which ultimately interprets things, and passes the message from one generation to the other. It is the hermeneutics of facticity, which interprets factual life afresh. The tradition, which I belong to, shapes my lifeworld and this is common to all traditions.

All the time, the myths, legends and stories connected with a particular religious tradition need interpretation and it is inevitable because the lifeworld demands it and, hence, there is a connection between a particular religious tradition and a particular lifeworld. For example, a hermeneutical understanding of the study of myths would suggest that it is used as a form of discourse. The role of myths in human experience and reality cannot be easily rejected because, to some extent, it shapes our lifeworld. Myths have relevance in the social context. They transcend time and first-order reference. They are always used as a form of symbolism and ordinary language. They suggest something invisible. Mircea Eliade (1961: 12) says:

> Images, symbols and myths are not irresponsible creations of the psyche; they fulfil a function, that of bringing to light the most hidden modalities of being.

Lifeworld is concerned with the phenomenology of religion. It is the sharing of religious lifeworld – shared lifeworld with others. There can be friction but not a collision. It can be explained in this way. Religion contains certain mythical modes of experience. The relation between them is so implicit that one cannot be isolated from the other. The myths are taken away from its religious content and the world tries to give a new meaning. The individuals and the collectives interact with each other; thus, there is a dialectical movement. It is the philosophy of participation. It is the transformation of meaning. In a philosophy of participation, criticisms are inevitable. Criticizability is the essence of free and rational creativity of "what is objective" and of "what is subjective" (Chattopadhyaya 1996: 12).

It should be remembered that there may be different approaches to the tradition but the inner meaning should not be lost. For example, a text like the *Bhagavadgītā* has different approaches. It is said that, according to Gandhi, the *Gītā* is a move in *dharma*, i.e. a move in religion and morality. But for Bankim, the *Gītā* is a move in history. In other words, Gandhi had never placed the *Gītā* in the history, but Bankim did. For Bankim, Kṛṣṇa was a historical person and the *Mahābhārata* was a real war. But Gandhi believed that this sort of understanding would deprive the *Gītā* of its status as a religious text of the Hindus (Chandra 2000: 29). The question, whether the text is a historical or a religious one, is not very important in this context. What is important is the truth conveyed by the text. Bankim tries to emphasize the fact that his historical interpretation would substantiate the truth, viz. the text has some purpose for which it is written. This means whether it is a historical or religious a text which has some sacredness in it, must be understood by the role it plays in the lifeworld situation. Similarly, the mythologies must be interpreted in the lifeworld situation. The stories mentioned in it need not be true, but the inner meaning, which is conveyed, must be understood to preserve the tradition.

The objectivity and intersubjectivity play an important role in the religious as well as cultural tradition of India. The Indian tradition believes in the conception of the lifeworld, which includes the objective, social and subjective worlds operate at the level of culture, society and personality. In my dialogue with others, I take the responsibility for rational persuasion by which I try to understand and interact with others. In other words, in my dialogue with others two things are taking place: (1) I persuade others, and (2) I am also persuaded by others. Therefore, while dialoguing with others, I make certain claims and they become not only my claims but are claims made for the sake of others. In the lifeworld, it is the communicative action which plays a significant role. Only in the context of lifeworld there is narrative presentation of events, which makes the self-understanding possible and acceptable. Here one can think of Sundara Rajan's (1986) (1) distantiating, and (2) participatory modes of thinking. In the former, the object is held at a distance, there is a dissociation of the self from the object and the bond between them is replaced by a spectational mode of understanding, whereas in the latter there is a fellowship with the other. There is an interior or indwelling understanding of the object. This is the uniqueness of Indian culture and philosophy. Understanding of culture is ever new and always creative, this must be done to preserve the culture to which we belong. This is possible by participatory understanding of the tradition and culture. D.P. Chattopadhyaya (1992: 364), says:

> When people understand meanings by participating in a lifeform, their participation can never be complete or total ensuring unanimity in their understanding of the concerned cluster of meanings. This is also supported by Margaret Chatterjee who says as follows:
>
> The participation-understanding of a live tradition may be partial; it may show differences from the participant's understanding of an earlier generation, but it would illustrate neither "distancing" nor fusion of horizons, but a continuity which would accommodate both change and encapsulation of the experience of earlier generations. – 1992: 337

Very rightly Schutz says that the intersubjective experience involves the bodily presence of the other. This implies that in intersubjectivity, there is always lifeworldly presence of the other. Husserl's approach to this is interesting:

> ... this world is there for me not only as a world of mere things, but also with the same immediacy as a world of objects with values, a world of goods, a practical world. ... All that which holds me for myself holds, as I know, for all other human beings whom I find present in my surrounding world ... the surrounding world and mine are objectively one and the same world of which we are all conscious. – 1983: 51-52

The lifeworld is the basic structure of understanding. It is by which the social, political and cultural gain their meaning. It is which relates the individual to the society and vice versa. Pande (1996: 156) says:

> The private and the public are united by culture. The universal culture of man is not constituted simply by science and humanism but even more deeply by spiritual wisdom without which man would not be a moral being and humanism will prove a mirage.

The uniqueness of Indian cultural tradition is that in it we find the synthesis of spirit and matter. Some Indian scholars trace the cultural roots of India in Vedic tradition as follows:

> The earliest preoccupation of India, as expressed in the Veda, was the exploration of the spirit in matter and of matter in spirit; the intermediate preoccupation was with the seeking and experiment in a thousand ways of the soul's outermost and innermost experience in a thousand ways of the soul's outermost and innermost experience marked by various conflicts and even exclusive affirmations and denials under an overarching tendency towards multi-sided development of the spiritual, ethical, intellectual, aesthetic, vital and physical parts of the being and some kind of synthesis. – Joshi 1996: 175

Hermeneutical Understanding of Religious Statements

In the Hindu tradition, belief or faith is a mode of valid knowledge, and not something different from it. Knowing from an authoritative source is, as a rule, attended with confidence. There cannot be any knowledge if doubt prevails in the mind of the cognizer. A doubt cognition cannot rank with knowledge. No information gained is a valid knowledge for the cognizer unless he is convinced of its truth. According to Vedanta, implicit belief or faith usage acceptance if, or the reliance on the words of the trustworthy, which needs no verification. Reason is implicit in faith. Religious statements are based on faith. What is the validity of these religious utterances? We can discuss this from two different approaches, Western and Indian. For example, Wittgenstein sees that there is ultimacy of intelligibility and justification in religious utterances. But to put religious beliefs into non-religious terms is inevitably to take away their meaning. Religious assertions correspond not to any matter of fact, but rather, roughly, to a certain attitude to life (Gudmunsen 1986: 103). For a believer, there is a Judgement Day and for a non-believer it is not so. Religious believers do not use a totally idiosyncratic language peculiar to them and them alone. Religious belief is, in some sense, a logically self-contained universe of discourse. The language they use is ordinary language given a particular application (Hudson 1975: 153). According to Wittgenstein, religious beliefs have logical distinctiveness. He says that we learn to speak in a religious way very early in life – "the word 'God' is amongst the earliest learnt" (1966: 59). Although this word is used "like a word representing a person", Wittgenstein says, "if the question arises as to the existence of a god or God it plays an entirely different role to that of the existence of any person or object I ever heard of" (ibid.). If someone wrote on a blackboard 2 + 21 = 13. I' would say: "This is no blunder" (ibid.: 62). Of course, the person who wrote this might be mad or making fun, but

> ... there might be cases where I look for an entirely different interpretation altogether. In order to see what the explanation is, I should have to see the sum, to see in what way it is done, what he makes follow from it, what are the different circumstances under which he does it, etc. – Ibid.

Here, Wittgenstein argues that the above arithmatic may be a right one under different circumstances. We need to watch how someone is operating with numbers before we can tell whether 2 + 21 = 13 is a blunder or not. When people say things about their religious beliefs, they have a different significance. It is different from an empirical or a historical fact. So, one cannot reject them as a blunder. Wittgenstein holds:

> Whether a thing is a blunder or not – it is a blunder in a particular system. Just as something is blunder in a particular game and not in another. – 1966: 59

Wittgenstein thinks of the religious language-game as a member of a logically interdependent family of language-games. While talking about a religious belief, he introduces the notion of "using a picture". The language used in religion is qualified ordinary language. We should declare, how we modify or alter our ordinary language when we make some religious statements. Wittgenstein says that if somebody says "God's eye sees everything" (ibid.: 71), the person uttering the sentence is using a picture. Unless we explain the peculiar way in which we use words to explain the religious statements, others cannot understand it. Wittgenstein views a religious tenet not as a factual hypothesis, but something which affects our thoughts and actions in a different way (Pears 1975: 174). Wittgenstein is of the opinion that religious belief regulates one's life. It is one "given form of life".

Religious statements are not to be taken as empirical or historical facts. A religious statement like "There will be a Last Judgement" expresses a certain attitude to life. If one does not have this attitude, there is not much one can say about the Last Judgement. Wittgenstein (1966: 58) says:

> Why shouldn't one form of life culminate in an utterance of belief in a Last Judgement? But I couldn't say either "Yes" or "No" to the statement that there will be such a thing. Nor "Perhaps" nor "I'm not sure". It is a statement which may not allow of any such answer. ... If an atheist says, "There won't be a Judgement Day", and another person says there will, do they mean the same? – Not clear what criterion of meaning the same is. They might describe the same things. You might say, this already shows that they mean the same.

In Indian philosophy, language is closely related to transcendence and religion. The importance of "religious language" is not known unless we recognize the inclination towards "religion" in primordial language. The distinction between "religious language" and "non-religious language" is a derivative one. All religious languages are in propositional form. It could be in the form of injunction and prohibition (*vidhi* and *niṣedha);* or in the form of informative texts. The nature of Vedic language is *apauruṣeya* which means transpersonal. Language in its highest participation in *Brahman* is *śruti.* Language has a structure which is ultimately dependent on, and given by, *Brahman*. Statements about *Brahman* are statements of religious language. We cannot interpret these statements in the same way as we interpret ordinary statements that are used in language. These religious statements have their validity within their framework, they regulate one's life. For a believer, the statement "There is a Last Judgement" has a validity because he believes it so, whereas for a non-believer it is not so. In each and every religion, we find such statements. For example, Buddhism says, "All *dharma*s are empty". Advaita says, "The world is illusory". Each system has its own built-in philosophy, which cannot be tested on the basis of other systems. There need not be any factual agreement between people who would make such statements and those who would not. It can be explained as follows: One may say that the world is illusory and another may deny it. How can we reconcile these two opposite views? We can reconcile them by saying that "for those who are enlightened, the world is illusory" and "for those who are not enlightened, the world is real". This means that religious assertions correspond not to any matter of fact, but rather, to a certain attitude to life. So, someone who asserts that "the world is illusory" is not making any factual assertion but expressing something like an attitude to life.

The view that religious languages have their own validity within their framework can be explained in the following way. The Veda consists of two parts. The earlier part known as *karma-kāṇḍa* deals with rituals and the later part known as *jñāna-kāṇḍa* deals with knowledge. For Śaṅkara, the ritual section has meaning and is important to those who are committed to a particular form of life. Similarly, the knowledge section is also meaningful and are useful to those who are committed to a different form of life. This means each religious form of life has validity within its framework. Each is authoritative in its own sphere. The subject matter (*viṣaya*) of the two parts of the Veda are different. For example, *dharma* constitutes the subject matter of the *karma-kāṇḍa,* which begins with, "Then, therefore, the desire to know *dharma*". The *jñāna-kāṇḍa* begins with, "Then, therefore, the desire to know *Brahman*" and here the subject matter is *Brahman* which is ever-existent. Similarly, with regard to the qualification of study (*adhikārin*) and the fruit (*phala*) which accrues to one who follows the teaching of each, both *karma-kāṇḍa* and *jñāna-kāṇḍa* differ. One who desires to perform sacrifice and other rites, and who longs for heaven (*svarga*), etc. is the person qualified to study the *karma-kāṇḍa.* As a result of the study of this part of the Veda, one attains the knowledge of what is to be done (*kartavyatā-jñāna*). One who is equipped with the fourfold means of eligibility (*sādhana-catuṣṭaya*) and one who has no desires excepting the desire for liberation is the person who is qualified for the study of the *jñāna-kāṇḍa.* The fruit which accrues to one who undertakes the study of the *jñāna-kāṇḍa* after fulfilling the condition of eligibility is *Brahman*-realization (*brahma-jñāna*) or liberation (*mukti*) which is eternal. Thus, in respect of subject matter, condition of eligibility and the nature of the end which is to be attained, the two disciplines, according to Advaita are different.[1] In other words, each part has its own framework. One cannot be applied to the other. Each part regulates one's life in its own way. Each one is a "given form of life".

The relation between language, thought and reality is emphasized in Indian philosophical tradition. Human thoughts are expressed by words. But religious statements have a special significance. Patañjali says that the expression of thought is the sole purpose that is served using words. All thoughts have to be expressed in language. The relation between language and thought is a fundamental problem in linguistics and philosophy. The relation between language and thought has been explained by Gadamer. He says all thinking about language is already once again drawn back into language. Another great Indian thinker T.R.V. Murti says:

> The problem of what we can know is closely bound up with the question of what we can say. It is only thought, as expressed in words that can be understood, communicated and criticized. Language is not an accidental, dispensable garb which could

---

1 R. Balasubramanian, 2001, "The Two Mimamsas", *The Voice of Sankara*, X(3-4): 235.

> be put on and put off. It grows with thought, with thought, or rather thoughts grows with it. – 1983: 358

So it is only through the medium of lauguage, an expression provides a route to the understanding of thought and reality. In the case of religious statements, we go beyond the empirical framework to know their significance and they cannot be interpreted in an ordinary way.

References

Balasubramanian, R. "The Two Mimamsas", *The Voice of Sankara*, X(3-4): 235.

Barlingay, S.S., 1983, *Beliefs, Reasons and Reflections*, Indian Philosophical Quarterly Publications University of Pune.

Chandra, Suresh, 2000, "Religion and History: Gandhi–Bankim Controversy on Bhagavad-Gita", *Studies in Humanities and Social Sciences*, VII(1).

Chatterjee, Margaret, 1992, "Towards a Hermeneutic of Centrality in Indian Art", in *Phenomenology and Indian Philosophy*, ed. D.P. Chattopadhyaya, Lester Embree and J.N. Mohanty, New Delhi: Indian Council of Philosophical Research.

Chattopadhyaya, D.P., 1992, "Reflections on Papers" in *Phenomenology and Indian Philosophy*, ed. D.P. Chattopadhyaya, Lester Embree and J.N. Mohanty, New Delhi: Indian Council of Philosophical Research.

———, 1996, "Itihasa, History and Historiography of Civilization", *Journal of Indian Council of Philosophical Research*, Special issue, pp. 67-106.

Eliade, Mircea, 1961, *Images and Symbols*, London: Haveill.

Gudmunsen, Chris, 1986, *Wittgenstein and Buddhism*, London: Macmillian.

Hudson, W. Donald, 1975, *Wittgenstein and Religious Belief*, London: Macmillian.

Husserl, Edmund 1983, *Ideas Towards a Pure Phenomenology and Phenomenological Philosophy*, tr. F. Kersten, The Hague: Martinus Nijhoff.

Joshi, Kireet, 1996, "Significance of the Veda in Indian Religion and Spirituality", in *Science, Philosophy and Culture*, part I, ed. D.P. Chattopadhyaya and Ravinder Kumar, New Delhi: PHISPC in association with ICPR.

Murti, T.R.V., 1983, "The Philosophy of Language in the Indian Context", in *Studies in Indian Thought*, ed. H.G. Coward, Delhi: Motilal Banarsidass.

Pande, G.C., 1985, *An Approach to Indian Culture and Civilization*, Varanasi: Banaras Hindu University.

———, 1996, "Culture and Cultures", in *Science, Philosophy and Culture*, part I, ed. D.P. Chattopadhyaya and Ravinder Kumar, New Delhi: PHISPC in association with ICPR.

Pears, David, 1975, *Wittgenstein*, London: Fontana/Collins.

Sundara Rajan, R., 1986, *Innovative Competence and Social Change*, Pune: Indian Philosophical Quarterly Publications, University of Pune.

Wittgenstein, 1966, *Lectures and Conversations on Aesthetics, Psychology and Religious Belief*, ed. Cyril Barrett, Oxford: Basil Blackwell.

7

Dharma, Religion and Ethical Relativism

Altruistic Obligation and Motivated Ordination in Indian Philosophy of Religion[1]

Godabarisha Mishra

THE performance of duty only prevents the evil that is sure to befall man who neglects it. On the other hand, its performance, because it is aimed at the eradication of evil tendencies, signifies the destruction of past evil or *durita-kṣaya* as it is termed. – Hiriyanna 1975: 206

Manu, or whoever it was who wrote the *Mānava-Dharma-Śāstra*, is supposed to have concluded his discourse (chapter 12, verses 105-12) by reasserting the rational basis of *dharma*, and indicating that in matters of dispute, a jury consisting of people from different strata of society should be called upon to adjudicate. He talked about three well-known *pramāṇas*, sources of knowledge – perception, inference and various *Śāstras* (testimony) – which must be appealed to for the "purification" of the *dharma* ethics. It was said that "an assembly of ten or at least three should deliberate and reach

---

1 Revised version of the paper presented at the ICPR National Seminar at Utkal University, Bhubaneswar during 22-23 April 2022.

> a decision, and the jury of ten should be constituted by three scholars versed in the three Vedas, one logician (*haituka*), one dialectician (*tarkin*), one semanticist, who also knows etymology (*nirukta*), one versed in the Dharmaśāstras, and three laymen, that is one celibate student, one householder and one retired person". This clearly was an evidence for the rational-democratic principle which an author at least implicitly accepted. – Matilal 2002: 78

Introduction

Though the term *dharma* is used with multifarious senses, the nearer meaning which approximates the idea and ideal of *dharma* is ethics or morality because in most of the cases it is used in association with performance of an action, physical as well as psychological. The universal implication of the term is associated with common ideas like speaking truth, non-stealing and valuing life of others which have universal undertones for promoting peace and harmony. In practice, many factors influence and constrain the course of ethical action, such as religion and regional customs. There are many instances when ethics becomes contextual and its pertinence can be understood only in the background of that age and place and with situational requirements. However, there are some religions who uphold certain values that are not considered ethical by practitioners of other religions. In a given religion also, a particular practice at times is condemned as unethical in favour of another practice. Thus, religion is not unequivocal in speaking about universal ethics. But when we look at the term *dharma* as ethics, the matter seems to be different because taking the original meaning of the term into consideration, i.e. "which holds", it seems to have universal ethical implications and more than that can have meta-ethical and meta-religious dimensions. In the metaethical dimension of the term *dharma*, we find that it is basic as well as regulatory and ethical. In the meta-religious aspects, it has broader application and collective appeal than the so-called religions. In the analysis of religion vis-à-vis *dharma*, we find that religions can be many and are conditioned by space, time, personal contingencies and factors connected with their propagators and practitioners. *Dharma*, in its pristine sense, can be understood as one – as the ethical essence of all the religions having eternal value. In Indian context, the natural and almost instinctive appreciation of ethical values arises from the distinct feature – the experiential character of righteousness, which can be termed as *dharma*. *Dharma* has been explained as metaphysical and factual in keeping with its understanding and applications. But in application, it becomes flexible to adapt itself to the real-world situations. This paper would attempt to deal with different facets of *dharma* associated with different source texts and show how there is something unnegotiable in its understanding and application.

Dharma, in a broader and simpler sense, contains a concern for the other which goes alongside denying as well as caring for personal interests. The so-called religions (including their Indian counterparts) at times are indifferent to others and lack adequate openness to include the interest of the other as one's own self. In accepting and practising a dhārmic mode of life, the Indian society has been trying to surcharge itself with modernity and kept itself flexible to adopt the modes of living which are felt to be beneficial and good. Neither the *śreyas* (absolute good) has been completely rejected nor is the *preyas* (temporal enjoyment) blindly accepted. Thus, the flexibility of the dhārmic principles has given adequate authority to its base, the ground on which the Dharmaśāstras have operated and negotiated their boundaries wherein the precepts and practices are intertwined harmoniously.

In taking a universal view of *dharma* (as well as religion), the individual has been trying to be liberative and liberal in his approach towards the other and in and through the seeming opposition in practice and inherent contradiction in thinking, a balanced world view has been emerging which has universal implications across religious traditions. Hence, we cannot explain ethical norms in terms of cultural relativity and there should be an ethical non-dualism (unity) to address the culture-specific ethics which are neutral to either being moral or immoral. This is addressed in the concept of five obligatory rites (*pañca-mahā-yajñas*) in Indian traditions of religion.

Dharma and Religion

The Sanskrit term *dharma*, in its finer sense, does not connote religion. But in the absence of any other term in English, there is some similarity with the term religion where we find an association with a supernatural being like God and also a text to support such a view. Sometimes the text becomes very important and helps us in working out the peripheries of *dharma* by giving a broad outline of what is meant by religion. Scholars, Indian as well as Western, accept certain conditions like as the basic features associated in the religion. Those are belief in supernatural beings, differentiating sacred and profane, ritual acts associated with objects, moral codes associated with divine feeling of mystery, a world view based on the basis of religious teachings and a social togetherness associated with the religion as the factors associated with religion (Matilal 2002: 176). This is not something which can be accepted in all the religions, since there are religions like Jainism or Buddhism which do not accept God, and there are tribal religions which have no moral codes associated with the divine.

Matilal discusses the psychological aspects of religion by associating the religion with characteristics like other-worldliness, the relation to the supernatural with love and devotion, efforts to manage and handle death both emotionally and intellectually, conservation of permanent values, a constant association with the ideals of ethics and morality, and nurturing a sense of inadequacy in coping with the difficulties of life (Matilal 2002: 178). Having explained what are the basics of the concept of religion, let us discuss the ideal of *dharma* which is a multidimensional problematic in Indian context and how it has been a significant point in our life of knowledge and action.

Dharma: A Multidimensional Problematic

The concept of *dharma* has been basically understood in two distinct ways in Indian tradition. First, it has been understood as an "order", a social order, that goes with the concept of *varṇa* or social stratification which meant a simple social structure (*varṇa-dharma*) in the early days of its conception. Second, it has been understood as a moral order, which owes its allegiance to the former since social order is not possible to be attained without the moral order. This is called as *sādhāraṇa dharma.* In the six systems of Indian philosophy, the topic has been taken up for extensive discussion and *dharma* has been explained in diverse ways as an action, as unseen (merit), quality and so on. After the advent of Abrahamic faiths in India, the word *dharma* developed new connotations of faith of a race and got a new association with a designation like "Hindu Dharma".[2] Thus, *dharma* which was used in the sense of social and moral order and which was meant for strict observation, steadily lost its hold with new connotations associated with its usages. Traditionally, the term *dharma* was understood in a rationalistic way than having metaphysical implications as is the case with religions. In this

[2] The word "Hindu" was of a peculiar origin. The Parsis, identified the inhabitants who lived on the banks of the river Sindhu in this name as distinguished from Christians, Muslims and others. In the course of time, the term "Hindu Dharma" was used to identify the faith of those inhabitants in the sense of "religion" like that of Christianity, Islam, etc.

sense, Hinduism would not be taken as a religion in the strict sense of the term as it may go against the very definition of the term "religion", which has to be founded on certain speculations as well as stipulations since the time of its origin. So, despite all self-contradicting features, the term "Hinduism" emerged as a fairly acceptable term referring to a religion-like concept if not strictly a religion.

Here, I would like to highlight how the term *dharma* has been dealt with differently in different Indian texts. Later, I would also try to explain that it is social workability that has been the criterion in its formulation and hence there is nothing wrong in identifying it with a cultural system which is no more geographically bound. I would also discuss the flexible nature of the texts, which can adapt to the needs of the changing times rather than being imposing eternal fixed laws. In the last part of this paper, I would show how there is some universal implications of this term which is more of an altruistic duty than acting for selfish gratification.

Dharma: Types and Scope

The real significance of *dharma* lies in the profound Vedic perception of man's existence as a rational being which harmonizes the different purposes of life to be realized here and hereafter. Hence, it was deemed necessary that people were committed to respect *dharma* and acted accordingly to conduct their personal and social affairs. In keeping with these dual requirements, the concept was basically divided into two types, viz. *sādhāraṇa dharma* (man's universal duties) and *varṇāśrama dharma* (specific or class duties). In the latter, the word *dharma* denotes a social or moral order which holds the society together. In the beginning, this was a simple social structure, which in due course of time became differentiated into four classes or castes. Initially, it was a social necessity that gave rise to this stratification. For example, a society must secure itself from external threat and maintain internal order which necessitated the class of warriors (kṣatriyas). Similar needs led to the formation of other classes. In order to avoid chaos in regulating these classes, the concept of *dharma* evolved. It must be noted here that the Vedic Indians who were nature worshippers over a period of time changed their way of worship and the rituals became predominant. It was during this period that the brāhmaṇa priests got superior positions in the sacrificial activities. The caste system lost its original character and the idea of *jāti* was substituted to *varṇa* system and later on it came to be identified with the very birth of a person. The concept of *svadharma* which later on was understood with relation to the job assigned to a particular caste was not intended in the initial days of its adoption. Thus, the *varṇāśrama-dharma*s were not determined by the birth of a person like the present-day caste system. In the *Bhagavadgītā*, Kṛṣṇa clearly states that the four *varṇa*s were made by him in accordance with the characteristics possessed and the actions performed.[3]

As regards the precise character of *dharma*, there are three views. For Mīmāṁsakas, *dharma* is an action. Through the intermediacy of *apūrva* (unseen potency) it yields its fruit. According to Naiyāyikas, *dharma* is a quality that is present in the self. For theistic schools, *dharma* is neither a quality nor an action. It is through meritorious deeds that one accumulates *dharma*. It is instrumental in getting the desired result which is either attainment of something good or avoidance of some evil. In the Vedas, it is used in the sense of religious ordinances (ṚV I.181.1; Kane 1968, I: 1). In the Upaniṣads, the word *dharma* is equated with the word *satya* (*BṛUp* I.14.14). In the *Chāndogyopaniṣad*, it is described in terms of three features, viz.

3. *cāturvarṇyam mayā sṛṣṭaṁ guṇakarma-vibhāgaśaḥ* |
– *Bhagavadgītā* IV.13

sacrifice, study and charity. Here *dharma* denotes the peculiar duties assigned to different *āśramas*.[4] P.V. Kane describes *dharma* as fivefold: *varṇa-dharma*, *āśrama dharma*, *varṇāśrama dharma*, *naimittika dharma* and *guṇa dharma*, like the duty of the king is to protect (Kane 1968, I: 1-10).

In the scheme of *puruṣārthas* (human values), *dharma* is viewed as having intrinsic value and as being related to *ṛta* and *ṛṇa*. The human values, *puruṣārthas*, are divided into four viz. *dharma* (righteousness), *artha* (security or wealth), *kāma* (pleasure) and *mokṣa* (liberation). While *artha* and *kāma* are taken as empirical and instrumental values, *mokṣa* is deemed as trans-empirical value, *dharma* (as ethics) plays an intermediary role in connecting the two. Hiriyanna is of the view that philosophy, in this sense of grading the values, is a criticism of values (1975: 16). In the *Bhagavadgītā*, we find that *dharma* is a regulating principle of *kāma*.[5] Thus, we may say that in the scheme of Indian conception of values, i.e. *puruṣārtha*, *dharma* is taken as a regulatory principle and therefore we have *dharma-artha* and *dharma-kāma*, the empirical values, as they ought to be rather than as they usually are. The ethical theories extended by different philosophical schools had liberation as their goal and in that direction, they formulated their ethical practices. To quote Radhakrishnan (1958: 80):

> Any ethical theory must be grounded on metaphysics, in a philosophic concept of the relation between the conduct and the Ultimate Reality. As we think the Ultimate Reality to be, so we behave; vision and action go together.

---

4 *trayo dharmaskandhā yajño' dhyayanaṁ dānamiti, ...*
– *Chāndogyopaniṣad* 2.23.1

5 *dharmāviruddho bhūteṣu kāmo 'smi bharatarṣabha* ||
– *Bhagavadgītā* VII.11

I am the source of pleasure, if not conflicting with righteousness.

The *Arthaśāstra* enumerates *dharma* as sixfold: *ahiṁsā*, *satya*, *śauca*, *anasūyā*, *anṛśaṁsya* and *kṣamā*. Jaimini defines *dharma* as the object of injunction.[6] In Vaiṣeśika school, *dharma* is defined as that from which results happiness, i.e. prosperity (*abhyudaya*) and liberation (*niḥśreyasa*).[7] In *Manusmṛti* 2.1, that which is practised by the learned, who lead a moral life freed from hatred and partiality, is called as *dharma*. In Āpastamba and such other Dharmasūtras, it is said that *dharma* is that activity which is praised by the wise. In *Gautama-Dharmasūtra* I.1.2, it is said: *vedo' khilam dharmamūlam* (the Vedas are the sources of *dharma*). The Buddhist conception of *dharma*, earliest of which is found in the fourth rock edict of Emperor Aśoka, lays emphasis on non-injury. However, in Buddhist philosophical literature, it is also used in the sense of an entity similar to that of early Advaita.

In Sanskrit, the term *dharma* is derived from the root *dhṛ* to hold, bear, support or to nourish. As has been already seen above, it is translated contextually. The word has been interpreted severally in English to mean "virtue", "righteousness" and religion conveying finer nuances of its import. The whole concept of *dharma* thus seems to be related to the Vedic ideal of *ṛta* (universal order) and *ṛṇa* (the debts one is supposed to repay) and seems to be the particularization at the human level of the ethical order prevailing in the universe.

Dharma in the Dharmaśāstras

The Dharmaśāstra literature exercised substantial influence on the Indian perception of an ideal man in a society from the Vedic period onwards. The Dharmasūtras form a part of Kalpasūtras, which are referred to as Smṛtis. The Kalpasūtras deal with the practical side of the Vedas which deal with rituals as well as

---

6 *codanālakṣaṇārtho dharmaḥ* । – *Pūrva-Mīmāṁsā-Sūtra* I.1.2

7 *athāto dharmaṁ vyākhyāsyāmaḥ* ।
yato'bhyudayaniḥśreyasasiddhiḥ sa dharmaḥ ॥ – *Vaiśeṣikasūtra*, 1.1.2

common morality. In the process of their systematization and social adoption, newer materials have been incorporated into three texts to suit the demands of different places and periods. One aspect of these Sūtras deals with the elaborate details of Vedic rituals and has very little relevance for the common man.[8] Another category of Sūtras deals with the domestic rites, such as rites relating to birth, marriage and death.[9] The third category relates to the conduct of the individual and his religious duties emphasizing social and personal ethics. These are termed as Dharmasūtras which have enormous significance to society as they serve as the guiding principles to decide right or wrong and merit or demerit (*pāpa* and *pūṇya*).[10] Different Dharmasūtras were composed separately for different Vedas. These Sūtras were codified later after consolidation and necessary adaptation. The texts have been interpreted in different ways in successive periods giving rise to enormous literature in this field. These works have been broadly authoritative because of availability of a wide range of options. The subject matter of these treatises deals with three aspects:

1. code of conduct (*ācāra*),
2. propitiation (*prāyaścitta*), and
3. jurisprudence (*vyavahāra*).

In later periods, we find the texts of Manu, Yājñavalkya, Parāśara, Nārada and others, who codified the necessary social features based on their observations. Dharmaśāstras represent a sanctified tradition and are accorded high respect next to

[8] Those are called Śrautasūtras which mainly discuss the norms of various *yāgas* and modes of their performance.

[9] These are Gr̥hyasūtras which contain the rituals to be performed by a householder.

[10] The Dharmasūtras and the Smr̥ti are otherwise known as Dharmaśāstras.

only Śruti.[11] For example, Dharmaśāstras classify actions in terms of obligatory (*nitya-karma*), optional (*kāmya*), prohibited (*pratiṣiddha*) and occasional (*naimittika*) deeds. The last type, i.e. occasional deeds, are similar to obligatory deeds since one ought to perform them on the specified occasion. The first and the last type of deeds may be referred to as categorical imperatives (Hiriyanna 1975: 190). The optional ones deal with desired ends, which are performed for personal well-being aiming at a goal in this world or hereafter. The seeker should purify himself in accordance with the stated rituals which make him eligible to perform such action (*kāmya karmas*). Hence, these are hypothetical imperatives, which involve moral disciplines in the right direction. Thus, the Dharmaśāstras contain the disciplines of life which modify the external behaviour as well as the inner disposition of man. *Dharma* as enunciated in the Dharmaśāstras is the comprehensive umbrella term denoting all moral laws, ethics, codes of conduct and religious acts. *Ṛta* is the logical concept underlying *dharma. Ṛṇa* represents the obligation of man to make his life conform to *dharma* and *ṛta* (Barlingey 1998: 81).

Dharma: Resonating the Universal

Many of the disciplines stated in the Dharmaśāstras are universal in nature. These texts have considered man as an individual as well as a social being. The two types of *dharmas* discussed above were put forth as the

1. universal duties *sādhāraṇa dharmas*, in which we come across ethical facets which even deal with the protection of animals and honouring the feelings of the immovable entities; and

---

11 Even during the period of Kālidāsa, the Śruti commanded a superior position than that of Smṛti. It is known from the verse *śruterivārthaṁ smṛtiranvagacchat* । – *Raghuvaṁśam* 2.2

2. duties of an individual person in accordance with his state of life, which are called as *varṇāśrama dharmas*. For the former, i.e. *sādhāraṇa dharmas*, Manu asserts that the observation of the tenets of his *Dharmaśāstra* alone is sufficient to lead a fulfilling and rewarding life. His definition of *dharma* goes thus:

> Contentment, forbearance, gentleness, respect for other's property, purity, self-control, knowledge, philosophical wisdom, veracity and patience are the ten facets of *dharma*.[12]

In his commentary on the *Yogasūtra*, Vyāsa defines *dharma* as universal goodwill.[13] Thus we see that the normative aspect of *dharma* has universal implication in the sense that it regards other's interests in the society without harming one's own interests. As Hiriyanna (1975: 193-94) puts it:

> Thus, when a person practises the virtue of contentment, his conduct is sure to result in some positive advantages to others. ... If the duties are negative and self-regarding, they generally point to rights of others as their correlatives.[14]

The ideals put forth here have undertones of universal ethics which promote self-discipline for an individual and his social well-being. Yājñavalkya says that *kāma* (desire) as such is not bad and need not be suppressed, but it needs to be properly regulated.[15] Its social implications are so strong that one may tend to feel that *dharma* focuses more on bettering the society as

---

[12] *dhṛtiḥ-kṣamā-damo steyaṁ saucamindriyanigrahaḥ* ।
dhīrvidyā-satyamakrodhaḥ daśakam-dharma-lakṣaṇam ॥
– *Manusmṛti* 6.92

[13] *sarvathā-sarvadā sarvabhūtānām anabhidruhaḥ* ।
– *Vyāsabhāṣya* on *Yogasūtra* 2.30

[14] *ātmanaḥ pratikūlāni pareṣām na samācaret* ।

[15] *samyak saṅkalpaḥ yaḥ kāmaḥ* । – *Yājñavalkyasmṛti* 1.7

a whole than the individual. In the *Mahābhārata*, we come across the same concept of *dharma* as being in the mind and one should do good for all.[16] Thus, *dharma* represents the moral order of the universe which is meant for providing a sustainable society. It implies an order which has an existence above the ordinary human requirements. Taylor (1979: 75) puts it:

> To fulfil the true impulse of nature in us is not just to meet the biological needs but also to satisfy higher aspiration. It is at the same time, a more fulfilment. From Rousseau on, the true voice of nature is at one and the same time both the impulse of biological needs and an aspiration to what is experienced as moral self-realization.

It is for this reason, in Indian context, duty is more important than rights. This may be the idea why in Dharmaśāstras there is so much emphasis on the community *dharma* which views the society as an organic unity where individual interests are subordinated to the interests of the society (Pappu 1986: 138). In the last part of this paper, I would discuss this aspect to show that human action must have certain obligation for the society in view and how it has been so profoundly pointed out in the Dharmaśāstras.

Dharma: Its Regulatory Precepts

Though there are many kinds of *dharma*, they all, in different ways, involve the notion of regulation, and are therefore basically rules of action. In some sense, the prescriptive ordering of anything is said to be *dharma* (Koller 1972: 131). The Śruti or the Vedas are the basic sources of *dharma*. The vast literature of Śruti is considered as sacred and *apauruṣeya*, of superhuman origin and it has an overriding authority over the other texts, like Smr̥tis and Sūtras which are *pauruṣeya* (human-origin). The Śruti contains two types of statements:

---

16 *cittamūlo bhavet dharmaḥ* । – *Mahābhārata* 13.211.220

1. *Vidhi* – injunctive statements, and
2. *Arthavāda* – statements containing praise, etc.

Āpastamba, an early Smṛti writer, is of the opinion that the source of Smṛti should be *vidhi-vākyas* (injunctive statements) (*ĀpDhśā* III.14.13). Jaimini, on the other hand, says that the whole Veda consisting of *vidhi* as well as *arthavāda* can be taken to be authoritative. In the Smṛti and their commentaries, a lot of effort has been made to show that the rules of Smṛti literature were based on Śruti. Kumārila Bhaṭṭa is of the view that Vedic authority for a Smṛti can be given either by quoting the actual words or if the text is lost, by giving its contention which would be equally valid like Śruti (Sastri 1929: 187-88).[17] Manu, one of the early authorities on the subject, quotes Śruti only once.[18] Though there is an underlying effort to align with Śruti, it is never satisfactorily done by the Smṛti writers as Vedas themselves have very little to convey as far the subject matter of Smṛti is concerned. The content (*viṣaya*), the *adhikārī* (eligible person) for both of these are different and the results (*phala*) one could obtain thereby are also different.[19] The modes of reference are different in different texts. In other words, the normative status of Śruti is never violated but at the same time, social thought and institutions were recognized in the Dharmaśāstra literature. Now for the texts which dealt with *dharma* in the later periods, the earlier Dharmaśāstras become authoritative. Like Vedas, this later literature was recognized till the beginning of last century.

17 *vedo hīdṛśa evāyaṁ puruṣairyaḥ prakāśyate* ।
sa paṭhadbhiḥ prakāśyeta smaradbhirveti tulyabhāk ॥
tataśca śrutimūlatvāt bādhyodāharaṇena tat ।
vikalpa eva hi nyeyyastulyakakṣa pramāṇataḥ ॥
– Subba Sastri 1929: 187-88

18 *yanme mātā pralulubhe vicarantyapativratā* ... ।
– *Manusmṛti* 9.20; refer Altekar 1952: 59

19 *athāpi nityānuvādamavidhi māhurācāryāḥ* ।
– *Āpastamba-Dharmasūtra* 2.14.13

Since it was mainly meant for giving sanction to a certain prevalent custom in the society, its contents went on changing and many things which were in vogue during the earlier days were prohibited in the later periods (Sastri 1898: 296).[20]

Prescriptions and Practices

Gautama, Manu and other earlier Smṛtikāras are of the opinion that the Vedas, Smṛti (memory) and *śīla* (conduct) of those who know the Vedas are the sources of *dharma*. So, an amalgamation of conventions and traditions as remembered by Vedic scholars (which was learnt by rote) constitutes the Smṛti and hence they became authoritative. In the Vedic period, the society definitely did not need a *dharmaśāstra* in the manner it was found later. After the Vedic period, during the period of rituals (around 600 BCE) a few of the Dharmaśāstras were conceived and composed. Āpastamba views that Smṛtis are based on *samaya* (tradition) and *ācāra* (convention).[21] Śaṅkara and following him Madhusūdana Sarasvatī regard the *Bhagavadgītā* as a Smṛti.[22] Hence, though Śruti is recognized to be eternally a valid source of knowledge, in due course of time, by the accommodation of social changes and practices, Smṛti too gained significant validity. In seventeenth century, Lakṣmaṇa Bhaṭṭa, the author of *Ācārasāra* says that a direct conflict with Śruti does not

20 In the Vedic literature, we find reference to inter-caste marriage, women's right for Vedic Institution, unmarried daughter's right to father's property and the like which were prohibited in the later ages.

21 *athāto samayācārakān dharmān vyākhyāsyāmaḥ* ।
– *Āpastamba-Dharmasūtra* 1.1.1

Commenting on this Haradatta says: *samayaḥ samayamūla ācāraḥ, teṣu bhavaḥ samayācārika evambhūtān dharmān, samayācārikān pauruṣeyi-vyavasthā* । – Refer Altekar 1952: 60

22 *smarati ca bhagavān vedavyāsaḥ gītāyāṁ bhagavadvacanam* ।
– Madhusūdana Sarasvatī in *Gūḍhārthadīpikā* 1

invalidate the injunctions of Smṛtis.[23] There are many instances where the prescriptive base has been violated and overruled in favour of a social practice. As the changes occur frequently, the necessity for codifying them too becomes necessary. For example, Smṛti texts authored by Devala and Gobhila were written to cater to the then fresh needs of the society as old Smṛtis became obsolete. After the Muslim conquest of India, many people were converted forcibly into Islam. Later on, there came a need for re-conversion. Śruti and earlier Smṛtis never faced such a situation. This gave rise to *Devalasmṛti* which codified the ways for re-conversion to one's own religion.[24] *Samaya* and *ācāra* also differed from place to place and from time to time. For example, eating fish and meat was enjoined in certain religious practices like *yāga*s and also permitted on certain occasions and in certain parts of the country.

Hence, the writers of the Smṛti texts kept themselves open to the needs of the time. Medhātithi, an earlier commentator on Manu, says that during his time new Smṛtis were composed for the future generation.[25] Choices were open as there were many Smṛtis available. The Purāṇas and Nibandhas interpreted the Smṛti dictums and were considered to be authoritative in the areas of *dharma*. For example, in the *Nāradasmṛti*, we find that widows have no right of inheritance. But Mitra Miśra, while commenting upon the text, observes that since the word *strī*

---

23 *pratyakṣaśrutivirodhe 'pi smṛtīnām aprāmāṇyaṁ nāstītyuktamacāryaiḥ* ।
– *Ācārasāra* of Lakṣmaṇa Bhaṭṭa, quoted in Altekar 1952: 15

24 *sindhutīre sukhāsīnaṁ devalaṁ munisattamam* ।
sametya munayaḥ sarve idam vacanamabrūvan ॥
bhagavan mlecchanītā hi kathaṁ śuddhimavapnuyuḥ ।
– *Devalasmṛti* 1.3 refer Altekar 1952: 19

25 *adyatve ca evamvidhairguṇair yuktaḥ īdṛśenaiva ca hetunā grantha-mupanibandhiyāt* । *sa uttaresām manvādivat prāmāṇyam bhavet* ।
– Medhātithi on *Manusmṛti* 2.6

is used and words like *patnī* or *bhāryā* are not used, Nārada is not opposed to the inheritance of a legally wedded wife but to a concubine.[26] Certain customs which were practised in earlier Smr̥tis were prohibited later like inter-caste marriage, levitate and such other practices. In legislating the means and end of liberation for all in the society, Smr̥tis have pointed out that by the study of Purāṇas, those who do not have access to Vedas may get the liberating knowledge. Mitra Miśra states that since *ātma-jñāna* is the means for salvation, even the śūdras can have it by the study of Purāṇas.[27]

The next source of practice as per *dharma* is one's contentment (*ātma-tuṣṭi*). Its scope is comparatively limited as one has to follow a standardized path if a particular practice is not found in the Śāstras. Nyāya, reason, has been recognized as a source and such a source has been testified by the authorities like Manu, Gautama, Nārada and Yājñavalkya. After the codification of the Dharmaśāstras, there was no scope for *sadācāra* (the path followed by the wise) to be treated as a different mode of deciding good or bad. But before the codification and after, at the time of a sheer necessity where the text is silent, this aspect has been invoked in the Smr̥ti texts. The *Baudhāyana-Dharmasūtra* says that certain practices are to be invoked from the Smr̥tis and thereafter the social customs are to be followed.[28] *Sadācāra* is relative in nature since what is good for a particular place may not be good for another. Hence in the *Mahābhārata*, we find that the respectable people alone determine the nature

---

26 *yadyapi nāradaḥ tatstrīṇām jīvanam dadyāt iti tadavaruddhā strīparaṁ patniśabda grahaṇāt* | - *Vīramitrodaya-Prakāśa*, Vyavahārakāṇḍa, Satpratibandha-adhyāya, refer Altekar 1952: 64

27 *veda anadhikarīṇām śudrāṇām kathamātmasākṣātkāra iti cet purāṇaśravaṇāditi brūmaḥ* | - *Vīramitrodaya-Paribhāṣā*, p. 36, refer ibid.: 62

28 *śeṣakriyāyām tu loko anuroddhavyaḥ* | - *Baudhāyana-Gr̥hyasūtra* 1.5.131

of *dharma*.[29] In the same epic, in the context of five Pāṇḍavas' marrying Draupadī we come across a dialogue between Drupada, her father and Yudhiṣṭhira, the eldest brother of the Pāṇḍavas. Drupada turns down the proposal of Yudhiṣṭhira to marry Draupadī to all five brothers since it was not *dharma*. For this, Yudhiṣṭhira pleads that *dharma* is too subtle and cannot be scrutinized by ordinary persons.[30] Marrying the daughter of the maternal uncle or that of one's own sister were accepted as the *deśadharma*s (practices pertaining to particular places).[31] Śaṅkara, defending the slaughter of animals in sacrifices argues that what is *dharma* in a particular place and on a particular occasion and with a purpose is *adharma* in other such contexts.[32] In the *Yājñavalkyasmṛti*, we come across the fact that the council of elders is an authoritative body to decide the *dharma*-related topics (Goodall 1996: 296).

To sum up, my attempt here is to remove the pervading doubt that the Hindu law is static and does not show any sign of change or participation in the social transformation. Such contention is wrong. In fact, in Hinduism, the practice is more venerated than the precepts. It has been a flexible tradition and that is the reason why in spite of various onslaughts, it has survived the test of time. As Vasudha Dalmia remarks:

---

29 *tarko 'pratiṣṭhaḥ śrutayo vibhinnāḥ*
naiko muniryasya matam pramāṇam ।
dharmasya tattvam nihitam guhāyam
mahājano yena gataḥ sa panthāḥ ॥ – *Mahābhārata* 12.373.117

30 *sūkṣmo dharmo mahārāja nāsya vidmo vayaṁ gatiḥ* । – Ibid. 3.195.21

31 *udūhyate dākṣiṇātyaiḥ mātulasya sutā dvijaiḥ*
madhyadeśe karmakarāḥ (steyaratāḥ) śilpinaśca gavāśinaḥ
matsyadāśca narāḥ sarve vyabhicāraratāstriyaḥ ।
–Refer Altekar 1952: 68. Also refer Sastri 1909: 69

32 *yasmin deśakālanimitte ca yo dharmo'nuṣṭhīyate sa eva deśakāla-nimittāntareṣu adharmo bhavati* । – Śaṅkara's *Brahmasūtra-Bhāṣya* 3.1.25

> Such a construction is based on "tradition" – an entity which is neither a permanent and unchanging heritage of the past, nor entirely fictitious, but constantly being selected and modified in response to social change and to visions of the future. The process however need not always be an entirely natural one. It is usually propelled and steered by individuals and by spokesmen of interested groups. These may be tempted to take advantage of the fact that the constant adjustment and rearrangement of the constituents of tradition renders them particularly amenable to manipulation.
>
> – Dalmia and von Stietencron 1995: 21

In the foregoing pages, I have given an account of the concept of *dharma* as found in the original texts, i.e. in the dharmaśāstric literature from post-Vedic period up to the modern age. To suit a multi-formed society like India, and in the absence of any religious text (in the strict sense of the term as understood in Christianity and Islam) the necessity of the Dharmaśāstras cannot be undermined. But as it is stated earlier, these are not religious texts but those which contain prescriptions for a regulated society. In and through the ages, the Hindu society has been trying to surcharge itself with the requirements of modernity and has kept itself flexible to adopt the modes of living which have been felt to be beneficial and good. Thus, the flexibility of the dictums has given adequate authority to its base, the ground on which the Dharmaśāstras have operated and negotiated their boundaries with the practices (correct behaviour) than that of prescriptions (Goodall 1996: xvii). The older the Smṛti is, the practices relating to social behaviour is much less and because of interpolations many times we find ambiguous and contradicting features in these texts.

To summarize the above discussion, it is pertinent to bring out the important points:

a. There is no basic dogma associated with *dharma* as far as

Dharmaśāstras are concerned. The idea is to have uniform practices to develop a sustainable society and uniform modification of such practices for accommodating the changing practices.

b. The texts were written to cater to the needs of different times and hence there are seeming variations in the precepts which again have formed the part of the Smr̥ti literature.

c. Because of the elasticity of Smr̥ti dictums, there is broad-based practice of so-called religiosity in India and people feel a sense of togetherness in spite of different practices based on different precepts.

d. We find Hinduism has an innate dynamism which gives enough scope for adopting the changing needs of modern society.

There have been several instances when changes have been incorporated because of the requirements of the inner dialectic within its broad spectrum. Questioning has been the hallmark of this tradition and there are a number of developments when we find fresh tenets overtaking the old as we noticed in case of Vedāntic thinking in the place of ritualism, Vaiṣṇava dualism as a revolt against Vedāntic non-dualism and the like. Due to such a constant interaction between different modes of thinking, a noticeable growth has been observed in the history of Hinduism keeping the future possibilities open for incorporation of pragmatic considerations.

Altruistic Obligations: Non-optional and Universal

So far, we have seen how the Dharmaśāstras have dealt with individual actions and practices for social harmony. Herein, I would like to discuss such actions and practices which have universal relevance and are non-optional. Ancient Indian texts assumed that for developing a human individual and a harmonious society, to nurture peace, harmony, progress and sustainable growth of the entire humanity, these precepts are to be practised by one and all. In the Dharmaśāstras as well as in other literature these are spoken of as *nitya-karma*s or *niyata-karma*s which are meant for the all-around development of the society that includes physical, emotional, intellectual and spiritual well-being. In the Upaniṣads, these are spoken of as five reverential services (*pañca-mahā-yajña*s) that are to be observed for upkeeping fivefold infrastructure and their indispensability for the survival of humanity. The first one is family infrastructure, that is the integrity of the family needs to be taken care of and human actions should be directed towards this aspect. This aspect which prescribes preservation of one's own family is called *pitṛ-yajña*, reverential service to family including forefathers. Whether ritualistic or non-ritualistic, family-care is one of the important aspects for human survival. The second one is reverential service to the societal infrastructure, social harmony, in which one has to develop respect for others for a together living and this is called as *manuṣya-yajña*. Man's action should be directed towards bringing together all types of people by taking care of each other irrespective of differences which are perceived and practised.

Then the next one is *bhūta-yajña* which is to take care of environmental infrastructure. Tradition divides environment into two types, sentient environment consisting of animals and plants and insentient consisting of inert matter. This environmental is performed in a ritualistic form which is called as *bhūta-yajña* that includes worship of animals like cow and plants like *tulasī*. This envisages the responsibility of humans to take care of the animals and plants. There are many prayers addressed to this aspect in Indian tradition and these are meant for making one aware of the symbiotic relation between man and the world around him. Any action in this direction, is a part of *bhūta-yajña*.

Reverential service to the *pañca-bhūtas*, which are looked upon as the representatives of God or manifestations of God, is known as *deva-yajña*. This relates to human responsibility for caring of the insentient nature consisting of five elements, like space, air, fire, water and earth. Each of these is important for our survival. In Indian tradition, they are taken as symbols of *Īśvara* (God).[33] Taking this as an obligatory action, we not only symbolically worship those deities, but also create an awareness and treat the elements with reverence. The implication of this *yajña* is that we knowingly do not pollute the environment.

The last of the reverential services is known as *brahma-yajña*, which means respecting the Vedas, which are the basic source-texts for understanding the world and its relationship with the man. Reverential service to the Vedas is nothing but preserving and promoting the knowledge tradition which is leading a life devoted to learning guided by Vedas. The preservation of teaching–learning tradition is called *brahma-yajña* which is performed in a ritualistic form also. The *yajña* is an attitude of reverence, developing an attitude of coexistence with nature. It is becoming the leader of nature, not with the desire for its exploitation, but to nurture it so that man learns to nurture himself. Thus, the five reverential actions (*pañca-mahā-yajñas*) are obligatory in nature. One may not practise this in a ritualistic way as has been spoken in the Vedas and Dharmaśāstras, but the spirit with which they are projected as obligatory in Indian tradition is important and needs to be emulated by all if we want a sustainable society to live in. This is the way to curtail disparity in the society and take care of others, create a pollution less society which is eco-friendly so that man leads a meaningful life.

---

33 In south India, there are five Śaiva-kṣetras symbolizing five elements (*bhūtas*) like Cidambaram – Ākāśa; Śrīkālahasti – Vāyu: Tiruvannakaval – Āp; Thiruvannamalai – Agni and Ekāmreśvara – Pr̥thvīliṅgas.

The Dharmaśāstra gives so much importance to these aspects of living that the non-performer of these actions is deemed to earn sin (*pratyavāya*) and the performer gets no merit out of the performance of these obligatory actions.

In short, Dharmaśāstra contains the message that in order to live, you have to let others live meaningfully and in whichever way it is possible, you need to be a part of this world-sustaining phenomenon.

Conclusion

In my tracing the concept of *dharma* from its original form in the traditional literature to its application in the contemporary situation, I have tried to show how Hindu society has been trying to be liberative and liberal in its approach towards the concept of *dharma*. This is one of the key concepts which is very basic to Indian ways of thinking. At the same time, it is very comprehensive as it has varied implications. In and through the seeming opposition in practice and inherent contradiction in thinking, a balanced world view has been emerging in the Hindu world of religion and spirituality which is universal in nature. The ability to adapt to any age and place, to any changing circumstances and customs had been the hallmark of Hinduism in all the times. One more thing to be appreciated is that before Dharmaśāstras, there was a society in Vedic and pre-Vedic days in which the well-founded customs have their say in regulating the individual and the society. Hence, the *dharma* is not only liberal in the sense that it has multiple options for the social behaviour but is also liberational (*mokṣa* centric) for the person to pursue the highest scheme of *puruṣārtha*, the *mokṣa*. Such a state of liberation can be realized only when man knows his role in the society and his relation with the ecosystem he lives in, which is systematically disturbed in the last few hundred years. It is pertinent to add that the panacea for world-sustenance lies in understanding our relationship with each component of the Universe and developing a sense of care and respect for all animate and inanimate beings which perhaps would be realized by humanity before it is too late.

References

Altekar, A.S., 1952, *Sources of Hindu Dharma in Its Socio-Religious Aspects*, Sain Das Foundation Lectures, Sholapur: Institute of Public Administration.

Barlingey, S.S., 1998, *A Modern Introduction to Indian Ethics*, New Delhi: Penman Publishers.

Dalmia Vasudha and Heinrich von Stietencron, 1995, *Representing Hinduism*, New Delhi: Sage Publications.

Goodall, Dominic, 1996, *Hindu Scriptures* (ed. with new tr.), Berkeley, CA: University of California Press.

Hiriyanna, M., 1975, *Indian Conception of Values*, Mysore: Kavyalaya Publishers.

Kane, P.V., 1968, *History of Dharmaśāstras*, vol. I, Poona: Bhandarkar Oriental Research Institute.

Koller, John M., 1972, "Dharma: An Expression of Universal Order", *Philosophy East and West*, 22(2): 131-44.

Matilal, B.K., 2002, *Ethics and Epics*, Oxford: Oxtord University Press.

Pappu, S.S. Rama Rao, 1986, "Hindu Dharma, Western Liberalism and Contemporary Indian Society", in *Search of Hinduism*, ed. Cromwell Crawford, New York: Unification Theological Seminary.

Radhakrishnan, S., 1958, *Eastern Religions and Western Thought*, London: Oxford University Press.

Sastri, Subba (ed.), 1929, *Mīmāṁsādarśana with Śābarabhāṣya and Tantravārtika*, vol. 1, Anandasrama Sanskrit Series no. 97, Pune.

Sastri, A. Mahadeva (ed.), 1898, *Āpastamba-Dharmasūtra*, Government Oriental Library Series no. 15, Mysore.

———, 1909, *Social Reform on Sastric Lines: With an Exposition of the Principles of Vedic Exegesis*, Mysore: Government Branch Press.

Taylor, Charles, 1979, *Hegel and Modern Society*, Cambridge: Cambridge University Press.

8

Does Religion Create or Discover Meaning of Life?

Laxmikanta Padhi

येषां न विद्या न तपो न दानं, ज्ञानं न शीलं न गुणो न धर्मः ।
ते मर्त्यलोके भुविभारभूता, मनुष्यरूपेण मृगाश्चरन्ति ॥ – *चाणक्य नीति* 10.7

yeṣāṁ na vidyā na tapo na dānaṁ, jñānaṁ na śīlaṁ na guṇo na dharmaḥ ।
te martyaloke bhuvibhārabhūtā, manuṣyarūpeṇa mr̥gāścaranti ॥
– *Cāṇakyanīti* 10.7

Those, who do not have learning, have no austerity, do not give to charity and have neither knowledge nor character, have no good qualities, no righteousness. They, on this Earth, are being burdens, in the form of people and are animals that simply graze.

I

In our day-to-day life, we generally spend most of our time worrying about our health, caring for our friends, arguing with our opponents, wondering at our children, shouting at the officials, thinking over our consumer bills, buying our cars, complaining about taxes, answering our mail, playing games, regretting mistakes, buying clothes, making love, eating, sleeping, working, laughing and crying. We also have the extraordinary capacity to take a break and ask: "What does it all come to?" What it means to be a human is to wonder about what it means to be human. The uniqueness of being human is to puzzle over the meaning of that uniqueness.

Questions about the meaning of life lead to further questions, like "why am I here?", "Is the existence of an afterlife the nature of *nirvāṇa*", "whether God exists?" and "whether there is a spiritual realm beyond the physical world?" Bertrand Russell states: "Unless you assume a god, the question of life's meaning is meaningless." For Russell, all the labours of the ages, all the devotion, all the inspiration, all the noonday brightness of human genius are destined to extinction in the vast depth of the solar system, and the whole temple of man's achievement must inevitably be buried beneath the debris of a universe in ruins. According to Kai Nielsen, when we ask, "what is the meaning of life?" or "what is the purpose of human existence?", we normally ask questions like "what should we seek?", "what ends, if any, are worthy of attainment?". This question is, in reality, a question concerning human conduct or behaviour. According to G.E. Moore, a man's life is of some meaning if and only if the intrinsic value of the Universe as a whole (including past, present and future) is more remarkable, owing to the existence of his actions and experiences. Meaning of life refers to human nature: whether my mind can exist independently of my body and whether my actions are within my control. It also refers to value questions, i.e. regarding our conduct towards others and what kind of social structure will best facilitate happiness.

Albert Camus felt that human life is absurd, meaningless and senseless. "What is the meaning of life?" is the most urgent of questions because "I see many people die because they judge that life is not worth living. I see others paradoxically getting killed for the ideas or illusions that gave them a reason for living." In absurdist philosophy, the absurdity of life arises out of the fundamental disharmony between the needs and aspirations of human beings and the apparent meaninglessness of the Universe. Camus' Sisyphus is condemned forever to the pointless pushing of that rock. Indeed, Camus asserts that "there is but one severe philosophical problem and that is suicide". He adds, "judging whether life is or is not worth living amounts to answering the fundamental question of philosophy".

Arthur Schopenhauer asked "what is the meaning of life?". Struggling with personal misery and a sense of loneliness and isolation, he tried to find some understanding of himself and the world around him that appeared to him senseless. He was alone, with not a single friend, and between one and none, there lies infinity. Thus, for Schopenhauer (1883: 386-87):

> We have not to rejoice but rather to mourn at the world's existence. Its non-existence would be preferable. It is something which at the bottom ought not to be.

So, life is like a ship on the sea, tossed by every wave and by every wind; a ship headed for no port and no harbour, with no rudder, no compass, no pilot; simply floating for a time, then lost in the waves (Edwards 1967). Nietzsche wanted to give an affirmative philosophy of life instead of Schopenhauer's pessimistic, life-denying philosophy. In *The Will to Power*, Nietzsche (1975) speaks of "the creative strength is to create meaning or value". The meaning of life is to be created, not discovered. The mistake lies in thinking that our meaning is present in "things-in-themselves". We create it. All meaning is the will to power. The aim of ethical theory is the realization of self.

Bradley might respond that the question should be asked along the lines of "what am I to do or be?" or "what is the ideal I seek to realize?". Willing and acting following an ideal is a moral end.[1] An unrealized self necessarily conditions the realization of an ideal self. In this regard, his ethics does not provide a metaphysical basis for relating the thought of the ideal with the reality of the actual. The existential approach can act as a therapy for solving psychological problems, too. This approach is based on the client's responsibility and freedom. The existential approach believes that people have the capacity for self-awareness and choice. An existentialist tries to help the client find meaning in discontent and suffering by choosing to think and act authentically. According to existentialists, creativity, love and authenticity may enable people to live meaningful lives despite discontent and suffering. For Jean-Paul Sartre (1966: 754):

> All existing things are born for no reason, continue through weakness and die by accident. It is meaningless that we are born; it is meaningless that we die.

Man, concludes Sartre, "is a useless passion. It all sounds like Ecclesiastes' Vanity of Vanities ... all is vanity". In William Shakespeare's *Macbeth*,[2] it is mentioned that Life "is a tale told by an idiot, full of sound and fury, signifying nothing". For Tolstoy (1904: 60):

> The more intelligent we are, the less do we understand the meaning of life and the more do we see a kind of bad joke in our suffering and death.

Thus, it appears that all other questions are insignificant and only the question "is life meaningful?" is most important.

---

1 https://philosophy.lander.edu/intro/articles/bradley_why.html

2 https://www.sparknotes.com/shakespeare/macbeth/quotes/page/5.

II

Let us make three observations on the question, "How is life meaningful?" and is the meaning of life discovered or created?

1. The first is the contrast between "discovering the meaning of life" and "creating a meaningful life". Many discussions are made on this contrast nowadays as our way of talking reflects an attitude. When we talk of discovering, looking for or searching for the meaning of life, it is generally suggested that there is some meaning "outside there" that is hidden. If we meticulously explore, we will uncover it. It is here that the meaning of life is compared with a beautiful piece of music that, if discovered, would fill one's days with harmony.

   Nevertheless, if we talk about creating a meaningful life, it may suggest that we are responsible for its coming into being. This is a crucial shift in our attitude. A meaningful life may be compared to composing a piece of music, a composing in which the harmony that emerges is a product of the creative activity of the self. What follows is based on the conviction that a meaningful life is much more likely to be the product of creation than discovery. This places the responsibility for meaning where it should be, i.e. on us. From childhood, we have been taught that all of our lives rarely do anything of value come quickly. What is of more excellent value than a meaningful life? It is not easily discovered. It is, with meticulousness, created; it is not found, it is made.

   Some additional clarifications need to be introduced here. Say, for example, in our own experience, we are aware that our capacity for experiencing meaning is significantly dependent upon our relationship with our father/mother/family. In their strong attitude, they give us the greatest gift that parents can give their daughter/son. They delight in our existence. We are redeemed from a shallow and hostile life only by the sacrificial love and graciousness that we have pointlessly received from our parents/family. Determination, in a fundamental sense, implies that meaning is created rather than discovered. Furthermore, it need not result in ignoring the *giftedness* dimension of our life, which we have received from our father/mother/family.

2. The second observation is that there is both a subjective and objective component to a meaningful life. If an individual's life is to be judged meaningful in the most total sense, that person must feel that his or her life is worthwhile. Even if we judge a person's life to be meaningful, there is something wrong if that person sincerely declares verbally or behaviourally (say, for example, suicide) that life is not worth living. Meaning must involve pursuing a mission that affords satisfaction to the pursuer. Without subjective satisfaction, meaning is incomplete.
3. Third, one may feel that one's life is meaningful. One may be enthusiastically involved in the pursuit of a goal, and in the end, he may pursue the destruction of a race of people. Thus, the word meaningful in the sense of a meaningful life should not be used so that an autocrat's life must be judged meaningful just because he may have judged it so. We say that a meaningful life in the most total sense must have an objective moral component. It must be morally constructive, as well as provide subjective satisfaction. Questions of the meaning of life are typically questions of how the pursuit of subjective satisfaction and morally and religiously worthy missions can be achieved.

Thus, the meaningfulness of life is created rather than discovered, and a meaningful life must involve both subjective satisfaction and an objective moral and religious component. However, there are several values and religious judgements about what constitutes a meaningful life. When we ask, "what is the meaning of life?" we ask, "what, if anything, is worthwhile?" or "how should we live?". Such questions also call for value and religious judgements. Let us make such judgements by defending three foundations of a meaningful life.

One point must be explained very clearly in this context. I am not suggesting that the above three factors exhaust the characteristics of a meaningful life, but these dimensions are particularly crucial in discussing a meaningful life. The discussion in this context, although schematic, is suggestive too. If we refer to Karl Jaspers, a German existentialist, then we may find that in his early life, he became conscious of loneliness. Life, he asserted, was structured in such a way that individuals seem to relate to one another superficially, "not inwardly from the historicity of their souls". However, nothing was "more destructive than loneliness, especially amid social intercourse that deceives itself in a multitude of [superficial] friendships". Loneliness is tragic precisely because "the individual cannot [even] become human by himself. Self-being is only real in communication with another self-being. If the never-completed movement of communication succeeds with but a single human being, everything is achieved. One may say that the basic theory of Jasper's philosophizing is that nothing is so crucial in creating a meaningful life as the quality of one's relationships.

A question may be raised: "Why is this so?" To respond, let us consider two more possibilities.

- The first involves the notion of communication, and it is through communication with others involving openness, risk and sacrifice that we most often discover who we are. By doing so, we become aware of our potentialities as those potentialities are discovered by another and reflected in us in a moment of depth communication. In such communication, we discover possibilities about ourselves that we had never thought of. We discover truths about which we might become that we had never imagined. Out of such relationships and communication, meaningful lives are created. Nevertheless, such communications and moments are relational moments.

- The second involves the notion of community, and it is in a community that we care for and are cared for. The value of caring is not to be analysed instrumentally but intrinsically. That means to care and to be cared for are inherently valuable. To care and to be cared for are the most satisfying of human experiences. To care and to have cared for meet the deepest of human needs, which makes caring relational. Thus, whether we are talking about depth communication or a caring community, we are talking about the value and power of honest and supportive relationships. Such kinds of relationships are the medium by which meaningful lives are created.

What we have mentioned is about relationships and communication. However, when we are experiencing a particularly pessimistic moment, most of us would acknowledge that it is essential that our life counts. This requires a commitment to achieve a goal or an objective that gives us a sense of doing something worthwhile and the process provides a focus for our energy that helps order in terms of importance a multitude of secondary interests and concerns. Appropriately, much of what we do is inconsequential. However, if all activities are superficial, then the experience of emptiness and the sense of being internally scattered or lacking unity of purpose may be overwhelming. Thus, we need to discuss establishing ends or goals in which life becomes meaningfully structured.

However, what kind of goals and objectives should one want to pursue? We are not escaping the issue to assert that this is precisely the decision one individual and he or she cannot make for another. Moreover, that this decision cannot be made by one for another is why meaning cannot be passed out. For example, how many students over the years have sat in my class and said something like: "I am not motivated. As I move through the day, nothing matters. I ask myself, what is the point?"

Moreover, as much as one might like, there is no way one can reach across the desk and hand out purpose. Ends and goals, as Seren Kierkegaard wants to argue repeatedly, are the kinds of things that have to be subjectively appropriated by the self in a moment of creative choice. Furthermore, it is precisely such a choice that serves as the foundation for meaning.

There may be a tragic dimension in choosing lifetime goals and objectives to make lifetime commitments, as goals, objectives and commitments are often mutually exclusive or incompatible. To choose one end is to reject another. To choose one profession is to turn our back on another. To serve one agency is to turn down another. To choose to invest our time and money in these goals and objectives is to refuse another. These choices are often painful, but they are essential to the creative process of establishing meaning-giving order in one's life. In *Beyond Virtue*, Alasdair MacIntyre (1989: 326-48) argues that meaning in a moral context cannot be adequately understood apart from the notion of the story: "I can only answer the question 'What am I to do?' ". MacIntyre claims: "if I can answer the prior question 'of what story or stories do I find myself a part?' ", what we mean to say is that there has emerged in contemporary philosophy, theology and even in management theory an appreciation for the "narrative structure or structures of human life" and the role of such structures in the creation of meaning.

III

Generally, it is believed that the definition of religion involves cultural beliefs, world views, texts, prophecies, revelations and morals that have spiritual meaning to members of a particular faith. It can encompass a range of practices, including sermons, rituals, prayer, meditation, holy places, symbols, trances and feasts. While this is the fundamental definition, there are many different understandings of religion. Not all religions are centred on a belief in a god, gods or supernatural forces. Religion can serve a wide range of purposes. Religion can be a source of comfort and guidance. It can provide a basis for moral belief and behaviour. It can also provide a sense of community and connection to tradition. Immanuel Kant[3] states, "religion is the recognition of all our duties as divine commands."

While discussing the meaning of life, we can find that religion is one way in which humans have found meaning and purpose in their lives. Nevertheless, is it the only way? Albert Einstein once said that "to know an answer to the question 'what is the meaning of human life?' " *means* to be religious. For Sigmund Freud, "the idea of life having a purpose stands and falls with the religious system".[4] According to Freud, belief in God, in *Civilization and Its Discontents* (1930: chap. 2), is based on an infantile response: the terrifying

> feeling of helplessness in childhood aroused the need for protection which the father provided, and the recognition that this helplessness lasts throughout life made it necessary to cling to the existence of a father, but this time a more powerful one.

---

3 Internet Encyclopedia of Philosophy: Immanuel Kant: Philosophy of Religion.

4 https://courses.washington.edu/freudlit/Civilization.Notes.html

Some philosophers have endorsed the view that God is somehow the source of the meaning of life and God's existence is necessary for life to have meaning. Say, for example, some claim "that God has a plan for the universe and that one's life is meaningful to the degree that one helps God realize this plan". Some have argued that our lives would be meaningless without an objective moral code and only God could provide such a code. Some claim that without God, our lives would be "contingent" and therefore meaningless. Still, others claim that our lives would have meaning only insofar as they were intentionally fashioned by a creator, thereby obtaining the meaning of the sort that an art object has. Of course, objections have been raised to these views, and there are secular accounts of the meaning of life. Nevertheless, the religion-based approach has been and still is prominent in the philosophical literature on the meaning of life.

What we can say is that if God exists, then all lives have meaning, and if any life has meaning, then God is not the source of this meaning, i.e. God-based approaches to the meaning of life are problematic. God's existence would guarantee that our lives have meaning and so the existence of God is a sufficient condition for life to have meaning. In classical theism, God is a perfect being and would not create beings that have a meaningless existence. It is generally agreed that lives can have different degrees of meaning. Say, for example, one person's life might be more meaningful than another's. So it can be claimed that if God is omniscient, omnipotent and omnibenevolent, then no individual human life is utterly devoid of meaning, even if a given life might have less meaning than another life. Freudian assertion, as mentioned in this section, was highly influential and can often be seen as informing the idea, cited by many contemporary atheists that God is merely a projection formed in response to our human insecurities. However, there are at least two difficulties with this way of dismissing the religious impulse.

a. First, though the miserable helplessness of the infant is an apt image of the fragility of the human plight, that fragility is not confined to infancy. Our vulnerability, and that of our loved ones, to death, disease and accident is an inescapable part of the human condition, and this being so, to be appropriately aware of it seems what an average rational human *ought* to be.

b. Second, talk of God as a projection does not, in the end, advance the debate between theists and atheists very much since it cannot settle the question of whether the impulse to project our desire outwards to an external source does or does not have an objective counterpart.

It is believed that a religious believer/theist maintains that since our true destiny lies in union with the creator, we will naturally feel insecure and restless until we find God. Many ancient writers have discussed this belief in theistic spirituality. The result of the debate over projection thus lies in an argument: the fact that humans feel a powerful need for God loves protection logically says nothing about whether that protection is a reality. For the sake of argument, let me assume that there is no such divine reality as put forward by an atheist for life's significance, for which the following questions may be made:

- Would human life be empty and pointless?
- If God is dead, is everything permitted, and if there is no God, would everything be meaningless?
- Is it more important to be free or autonomous than to have a grand meaning or purpose in life?
- Does religion create or discover a grand meaning or purpose to life, without allowing humans to be free or autonomous?

Regarding meaning of life, Indian philosophy/ethos offers *four* distinct goals of life (*puruṣārthas*), which one needs to embrace in varying degrees during different periods in life. P. Nagaraja Rao's *The Four Values in Indian Philosophy and Culture: A Study of the Puruṣārthas* (1970) defines it as a conscious pursuit of a *rational* being with some elevated goal that is commensurate with his rationality along with pursuing the path mindfully. The point is to seek a solution that best addresses a specific life circumstance or problem.

The more creative we are in adding substance to the list, the less likely Gilgamesh's problem of death will overcome us, Sisyphus's problem of futility, Boethius's problem of cosmic insignificance, the problem of suffering, or any other problem that undermines our sense of purpose or happiness. We cannot criticize the lunatic's meaningless life if our lives are meaningless. There is always a religious purpose for life. An atheist can lead a meaningful life. However, a lunatic's only hope for a meaningful life is to pursue happiness. Ethical egoists pursue their interests, but everyday life gets happiness in pursuing something more considerable, i.e. a religious as well as an ethical life. We cannot say that immoral acts are not necessarily irrational. People should see that our best shot at a meaningful and responsible life is achieved by pursuing a religious life. Here, "responsible" means being accountable for thought word and deed. To have a renge of duty is to fulfil the tasks with reliability, dependability and commitment to God.

IV

It is quite understandable that when people lose all sense of the meaning of life, then the philosopher is almost the last man they are inclined to consult. The traditional theologians know the answer, and the sufferer, who knows what, he will say, cannot use it. However, the philosopher stands very low, partly because he is inclined to enormous generalities, whereas this question is concrete and near. Because the attitude of rational inspection and analysis somehow cuts across that average vital momentum in which meaning lies. Philosophy is committed to the view that the universe has a meaning and that human life has a meaning, too. Suppose its answers are husk that is not due to the nature of reasoning but too bad reasoning. If thinking interrupts action for a moment, then the resumption of action can still use true thinking. Moreover, if the present age is suffering as no previous age has suffered from the disease of meaninglessness, we cannot say that it is due to the deficiency of action.

When philosophy is searching for reality and asserts that it cannot be found by sense or intellect but must be an object of animal faith, philosophy is celebrating its failure. Moreover, when, similarly, philosophy seeks meaning, then it says that it cannot be found in immediate experience or thought but must be an object of animal instinct as if it is an achievement. Thus, concerning Bergson, the whole point of reversion to simplicity and vitality is not a new version of ancient irrationalism but just the opposite of vitality and intelligence.

There are, of course, a variety of aims and objectives in terms of which we may define ourselves from different philosophers' views. The challenge is to choose the aims and objectives that place life in a meaningful context. The religious challenge is to choose the aims and objectives that place life in a genuinely ultimate context. Our way of being in the world will be determined by the aims and objectives we interpret. Our consciousness of the past, i.e. our understanding of roots. Our consciousness about the present, i.e. our understanding of who we are now, and our consciousness about the future, i.e. our understanding of who we are to become, all of these modes of being in the world are influenced by the aims and objectives in terms of which we define ourselves, in terms of which we create meaning for our lives. To be fully human is to create meaning by establishing deep relationships, by committing ourselves to the aims and objectives that give order and purpose, and by placing our lives in the context of meaning-creating aims and objectives.

Religion and decision making in complicated circumstances are not simply the province of philosophers or theists. Our choices reveal our values and meaning to the world. These values and meanings are either unreflective and superficial or reflective and deep. Philosophical thought should help us to make our values and choices deep and thoughtful. This makes it more likely that our choices will be the right ones. Finding an appropriate list of responsibilities or obligations may seem like a philosopher's game. However, the business of making appropriate decisions is not a game. One practical goal of our responsibility is that it may help us to make appropriate decisions in complicated circumstances, which make our lives meaningful. We need to think that we are not bound to solve all the problems in the world; our duty is only to avoid creating problems. We must not be responsible for evil to others; we must not harm others; if we harm, we must repair the damage. This is called the *Religion of Responsibility* and the answer to the question: *Does religion create or discover the meaning of life*? Let me end with a reference to the *Cāṇakyanīti*, chap. 5:

> वृथा वृष्टिः समुद्रेषु वृथा तृप्तस्य भोजनम् ।
> वृथा दानं समर्थस्य वृथा दीपो दिवापि च ॥
>
> *vr̥thā vr̥ṣṭiḥ samudreṣu vr̥thā tr̥ptasya bhojanam* ।
> *vr̥thā dānaṁ samarthasya vr̥thā dīpo divāpi ca* ॥
>
> Rain which falls upon the sea is useless/meaningless; so is food meaningless for one who is satiated; in vain is a gift for one who is wealthy; and a burning lamp during the daytime is useless/meaningless.

References

Bradley, F.H., 1876, *Ethical Studies*, Oxford: Oxford University Press, pp. 58-84 passim.

Brown, D., 1971, "Process Philosophy and the Question of Life's Meaning", *Religious Studies*, 7: 13-29.

Cottingham, J., 2003, *On the Meaning of Life*, London: Routledge.

Davies B. (ed.), 2000, *Philosophy of Religion*, part V, Oxford: Oxford University Press.

Dwivedi, O.P. (ed.), 1990, *The Essence of the Vedas*, Varanasi: Visva Bharati Research Institute.

Edwards P., 1967, "Life, Meaning and Value", *The Encyclopedia of Philosophy*, New York: Macmillan.

Freud, Sigmund, 1916, *Introductory Lectures on Psychoanalysis*, Lecture XVII.

———, 1930, *Civilization and Its Discontents*; included *Standard Edition of the Complete Psychological Works of Sigmund Freud*, XXI, ed. J. Strachey, London: Hogarth (repr. 1953).

Gordon, J., 1983, "Is the Existence of God Relevant to the Meaning of Life?", *The Modern Schoolman*, 60: 227-46.

Haber, J., 1997, "Contingency and the Meaning of Life", *Philosophical Writings*, 5: 32-44.

Jernes, H. (ed.), 1958, *Encyclopedia of Religion and Ethics*, vol. II, New York: Charles Scribner Sons.

Kahane, G., 2011, "Should We Want God to Exist?", *Philosophy and Phenomenological Research*, 82(3): 674-96.

Levine, M., 1987, "What Does Death Have to Do with the Meaning of Life?", *Religious Studies*, 23: 457-65.

Mawson, T., 2012, "On Determining How Important It Is Whether or Not There Is a God", *European Journal for Philosophy of Religion*, 4: 95-105.

Metz, T., 2013, *Meaning in Life*, Oxford: Oxford University Press.

MacIntyre, Alasdair, 1989, After Virtue: A Study in Moral Theory, Review by R. Jay Wallace, History and Theory, 28(3): 326-48.

Nagaraja Rao, P., 1970, The Four Values in Indian Philosophy and Culture: A Study of the Purusarthas, Mysore: University of Mysore.

Nietzsche, Friedrich, 1975, *The Will to Power*, tr. W. Kaufmann and R.J. Hollingdale, New York: Random House.

Nozick, R., 1981, *Philosophical Explanations*, Cambridge, MA: Harvard University Press.

Padhi, L.K., 2020, "What Makes a Human Being Valuable?", *Jnanadeepa: Pune Journal of Religious Studies*, 24(2): 28-41.

Rowe, W., 1979, "The Problem of Evil and Some Varieties of Atheism", *American Philosophical Quarterly*, 16(4): 335-41.

Sartre, J.-P., 1996, Being and Nothingness, tr. Hazel Barnes, New York: Washington Square Press.

Schopenhauer, A., 1883, *The World as Will and Idea*, vol. III, tr. R.B. Haldane, London: Routledge & Kegan Paul.

Sehon, S., 2010, "The Problem of Evil: Skeptical Theism Leads to Moral Paralysis", *International Journal for Philosophy of Religion*, 67: 67-80.

Tolstoy, L., 1904, *My Confession and Critique of Dogmatic Theology*, tr. L. Wiener, New York: Colonial Press.

9

Bhīmā Bhoi

The Revolutionary Poet-Philosopher

Sarat Chandra Panigrahi

THE land of Odisha has been the meeting ground of almost all the chief currents of religious movements in India. The major religions of the world like Buddhism, Jainism, Christianity and Islam have been respected and accommodated in the mainstream of Indian culture. The culture of Odisha is represented by Jagannātha culture. The Jagannātha culture incorporates it all the ideologies and traditions of different sects, philosophers and preachers. The Jagannātha culture is universal in the appeal which is clearly evident from its acceptance by the different religious sects like the Bauddhas, Jainas, Śaivas, Śāktas, Gāṇapatyas, Vaiṣṇavas and Vedāntins which appear to be contradictory. All the different religious sects visited Lord Jagannātha to impose their own ideologies in Jagannātha culture but returned with culmination of their ideology in the Lord.

Different religious sects identified their deity as Jagannātha. Jainas treat his as Jina, Buddhists as Bauddha, Gāṇapatyas as Gaṇeśa, Śāktas as Bhairava, Śaivas as Rudra, Gauḍīya Vaiṣṇavas as Kr̥ṣṇa, Utkalīya Vaiṣṇavas as Buddha-Jagannātha. The *dharma* culture of Bengal also expresses similar view as stated in *Dharma Pūjā Bidhāna* as follows:

> In the ninth incarnation, God (Hari) was born as Jagannātha who was none but Lord Buddha and he settled in his residence at the Bea-coast where he has relieved the whole world by distributing to all the *prasāda* irrespective of caste and greed.
>
> – Quoted in Dasgupta 1995: 287

Every new form of *dharma* originates according to the contemporary situation of social and spiritual background. Mahimā Dharma also appeared as a reaction to social mindset and following the worthless ideas leading to a life of imperfection infested with social evils. Bhīmā Bhoi was not a system builder in philosophy propounding mere abstract theories but he was committed to translate theories into practice. According to him, *dharma* is self-complete when there is harmony between our psychic attitude and the stark reality which is practical and existential without any oddity we can say that he is an existential thinker. He was opposed to the Brāhmanism as he could find that there was a gap between true religion and religious behaviour. He tried to accuse rational awakening in human beings. So that, they can progress in proper direction. Though Bhīmā Bhoi is said to be a reformer but his approach is radical and revolutionary. He did not want to compromise with the prevalent social–religious system but he did not ignore the basic philosophical elements found in Upaniṣads, the *Gītā*, Advaita Vedānta, Buddhism, etc. C.R. Das (1982: 157) explains the role of Bhīmā Bhoi for social upliftment as follows:

> Mahimā Dharma was the last protest of saints against the established Hindu religion. It was not a Buddhist movement, neither had it to do with the Vaiṣṇava way of worship. It was an effort to give to those who stood at the lowest is a status

> infested society, a real sense of human dignity and sought to raise them up as equals and devotions.

Bhīmā Bhoi appeared at a time when religion was infected with sectarianism and dogmatism. His mission was to enlighten spirituality in the inert man. He opened the door of spiritual *sādhanā* for all irrespective of caste and creed.

Bhīmā Bhoi was not just a poet – showing his literary acumen. First of all he is a devotee and all his philosophical elucidating are outpouring of his spiritual experience. His writings are very lyrical, simple and in vernacular language that appeals to the common man. The writings of Bhīmā Bhoi are taken as the bible of Mahimā Dharma. His literary works are not meant for the followers of the Mahimā cult but a message for all to overcome the degeneration of values of the society.

The first exponent of Mahimā Dharma is the celebrated poet-metaphysician Bhīmā Bhoi. He is a poet of eminence, a humanist of high order, an abstruse metaphysician subscribing significantly to the Advaita view of Vedānta. Mādhyamika Śūnyavāda of Buddhism. Scholars are of the opinion that Pañcasakhā literature has laid a solid foundation of Mahimā Dharma, particularly the thoughts of Bhīmā Bhoi. Pañcasakhā is name assigned to a group of five saint-poets who assimilated and propagated the synthetic view of the previous religious trends flourished in Odisha and were exponents of Utkalīya Vaiṣṇava Dharma based on the metaphysics of the Jagannātha cult, in spite of the tremendous influence of Gauḍīya Vaiṣṇava Dharma propagated by Śrī Caitanya.

Bhīmā Bhoi is a creative genius par excellence. The philosophic-poetic expression of a rare and real insight into a superb vision and world view, Bhīmā Bhoi emerges as a towering torch bearer, an epoch-making eye-opener with solemn rededication to service of man turning man to divine, reaccentuating in lofty and lovely terms the age-old human values coupled with captivating originality and extraordinary sagacity. He is uncommon, a man among the multitude.

Like a lotus flower emerging from the muddy soil, Bhīmā Bhoi flourished against all adversities of life and ultimately became the pathfinder of the unique cult. A bird's-eye view on the life-profile of the towering personality seems to be quite relevant. It is difficult to give an exhaustive and proper account of the life-history of Bhīmā Bhoi due to the fact that his biography has not been recorded systematically and non-controversially. However, it has been generally accepted that he was born of a poor parentage and also in a tiny dark corner of western Odisha which was, so to say, cut off from the mainstream of Odisha culture. It is clear from his writing that he belonged to the aboriginal family known as Kandha and his father was Janardan, mother's name being Gurubari of the village Jatasingha. To his misfortune he lost his father at an early age and the poor mother had no option but to bring up the child with a great difficulty. At the early age of twelve Bhīma earned his livelihood by being engaged in grazing of cows of others. There has been a great deal of controversies regarding the blindness of poet. Some scholars uphold the view that he was born-blind while others reject this standpoint. It is not worthwhile to discuss about this as it will be sheer waste of time but our focus should be on the elucidation of his thought-provoking views.

The then village culture of Odisha was fostered in the *Bhāgavata tuṅgīs*. In fact, the *Bhāgavata* of the saint-poet Jagannāth Dāsa was read and discussed by the villagers every evening in the *tuṅgī*s in a serene atmosphere and it was a great source of inspiration for Bhīmā Bhoi. As a śūdra, he was not allowed to enter into the *tuṅgī* but by sitting outside he would listen to the discussion with deep concentration. It was, so to say, the training ground for the development of his literary acumen and metaphysical insight.

Bhīmā Bhoi's poetic genius and philosophic uniqueness owe their origin not to his own creativity alone but by the grace of the omnipotent Lord known as Mahimā Swāmī. The Mahimā Swāmī is the Ultimate Reality, the founder and preacher of the cult. It was the rare fortune of Bhīmā Bhoi to have a glimpse of the Lord at the early phase of his life when amidst the dreary gloom of darkness he was in search of light. The glow of the divine light was showered on him as a token of divine grace. Mahimā Swāmī blessed him to write *bhajanas* and *jananas* for the propagation of basic tenets of Mahimā Dharma. It is said that Bhīma used to compose four prayer songs (*bhajanas*) in one *rāga* at a time. He would first give out the refrain line of each of these four to the four scribes and then sing each of the *bhajanas*. From his *Bhajanamālā*, it is clear that they were composed in groups of four. In one *bhajana*, he says:

> In one *rāga* I composed four songs, I am the helpless Bhīma, but my *guru* is all-powerful, under his fearless banner, I have taken shelter and drink the nectar from his feet. With his grace I see the inner and outer reality with the eyes of knowledge.
>
> – Mohapatra 1996: 2

Bhīmā Bhoi advocates metaphysics of *śūnyatā* along with the social ideal of classless society. Another distinct feature of Bhīmā Bhoi's writings is their human appeal. It would be clear from his *Stuti Cintāmaṇi* that Bhīmā Bhoi aimed at the salvation of the humanity at large from the clutch of eternal suffering. The most appealing thought which brought Bhīmā Bhoi the national recognition are expressed in the words:

> *prāniṅka ārata dukha aparamita dekhu dekhu kevā sahu* ।
> *mo jībana pāche narke padithāu, jagata uddhāra heu* ॥
>
> – Bhīmā Bhoi, *Stuti Cintamaṇi*, p. 27

Metaphysically Bhīmā Bhoi was a monist, reality is one, *śūnya* and indeterminate which has manifested in many. He is of the nature of void having no form or contour – *rūpa rekhā nāhiṅ, he śūnya dehī.* Though every manifestation is divine, it is not to be equated with any of his finite expressions. The concept of immanence and transcendence is lucidly brought out in *Stuti Cintāmaṇi.*

This makes him vocal against the idol worship and religious institutions thriving on it. An idol is inert and lifeless. Man being essentially infinite, his cravings are infinite. A lifeless idol can hardly be a saviour of man. It is the height of ignorance to make worldly offerings to the idols with the hope of redemption.

> *acetare sinā janaprānimāne karuchanti deva pujā* ।
> *pādepadi rakṣākara boluchanti debu kṣiripurī gajā* ॥
> – Bhīmā Bhoi, *Stuti Cintāmaṇi*, p. 95

The ignorant are prepared to have loving fellowship with the inert, while the living God is ignored. He deplores how people prefer to worship rather than the one who has invested life in them.

> *jehu gadhi achi āpaṇā piṇḍa prāṇa*
> *tāku samarpaṇa nāhīṅ* ।
> *dāru pratimā mūrtiku boluchanti*
> *prāṇaku bañchā tuhi* ॥ – Ibid.

He was painfully aware and vehemently critical of ostentatious ritualism. Observances of rites and rituals mitilate against the realization of godhood. Ritualism witnesses the birth of sectarianism and religious fundamentalism. People mistake the superficiality of religious observances as the essence of religion. This, according to Bhīmā Bhoi, is the mockery of religion because religious conviction and participation have no meaning if it does not help one to share the weal and woe of one's fellow men. People waste their precious life in mechanical rites and rituals forgetting that it is only through love of the inner self – that immortality can be achieved.

japa tapa sandhyā homa yajña teji
dhari niraveda pāṭha ।
ātmabhagatire mṛtya saṁsāre
maṇili mu ekamāta ॥ – Bhīmā Bhoi, *Stuti Cintāmaṇi*, p. 33

He does not find any rationale behind the practice of pilgrimage. Since God exists in every particular and every place, everything is scared and every place is holy. Forgetting this the ignorant undertakes long pilgrimage with the hope of salvation. Since everyone is potentially God, one need not go outside, but has to turn the mind within and serve the creation which is manifestation of God.

na jāṇi chāridigare pheruacha
tīrthabrata bolikari ।
jāhīṅre loḍiba tāhīṅ achanti brahmā
bujhiba jebe bicāri ॥ – Ibid., p. 92

Bhīmā Bhoi's surging love for his fellowmen made him appear as a non-compromising crusader against social discrimination. Hinduism in its decadent form was instrument in dividing people on caste line. The sense of innate superiority and innate inferiority led to inhuman exploitation by the higher class. The distinction of caste is man-made. He wanted to bring home the spirit of unity by fostering the Vedāntic ideals.

Spiritualism admits of no distinctions of caste, colour, creed. Love and compassion are the inevitable expressions of spiritual vision and serve as the cementing force to keep the apparently diverse people together. He denied any distinction on the basis of caste; even he denied distinction between male and female.

chataisa kāla je bāuna pātaka je acha stiri puruṣa ।
ucā nīcā vāraṇa na kari nāma re saraṇa pasa ॥
– Bhīmā Bhoi, *Stuti Cintāmaṇi*, p. 92

Bhīmā Bhoi was the champion of equality. He argued that we should not make any distinction on the basis of caste and attributing privileges to a particular man. Mahimā Dharma gives hope to all that there is just one caste. He pointed out:

> When all become outcastes, Mahimā Swāmī appeared as the Lord to turn devotees to one caste. – Bhīmā Bhoi, *Bhajanamālā* 14

According to Bhīmā Bhoi, all human beings are equal; this is the harmonizing force in the vision of unity as Lord pervades in every human being. So, he tells all to be compassionate to others.

> *alekhapura bhavana nāhīṅ tāhīṅ baḍā sāna* ।
> *samānare dayā dr̥ṣṭi sarva jīvare* ॥
> – Bhīmā Bhoi, *Stuti Cintāmaṇi*, p.10

He further substantiates his view in the following verse:

> *Be they wicked as saintly,*
> *Servant or master*
> *Insect or bird,*
> *I see equally in all beings*
> *Neither less nor more than the other.* – Ibid., p. 27

So, he tells again and again never to discriminate between brāhmaṇa and cāṇḍāla, and never to bother about *jāti* and *gotra.*

> *kī abā brāhmaṇa kī abā cāṇḍāla anya na karibā citte* ।
> *jāti gotra hīṅ na pacāriba kichi hāni lābha tāva jete* ॥
> – Ibid., p. 85

Bhīmā Bhoi appears as an ardent fighter for the cause of women who were under subjugation and were prevented from the practice of spiritual *sādhanā*. He provided dignity to women and said that they should be given equal opportunity for complete unfoldment of their personality. His argument in favour of this is stated as follows:

> As the two (men and women) emerge from the same reality, both these *varṇas* are identical, as water and wind do not make any discrimination in the course of their flow, the level that a man can go can also be reached by a woman.
>
> – Bhīmā Bhoi, *Brahma Nirūpaṇa Gītā* XI

His view on equality is based on the metaphysics that *alekha puruṣa* pervades in every being equally irrespective of any distinction of caste and gender.

> *sadā sampūrṇare samāna*
> *tāhār nāhīṅ pāpa puṇya* ।
> *jāti ajāti tāra nāhīṅ*
> *purichi sarva ghaṭe sehi* ॥ – Bhīmā Bhoi, *Śrutiniṣedhagītā* I

The Vendāntic vision of unity made him think beyond the human species and embrance the non-humans in the sweep. He prays the *alekha* not only to save the human species but also the animals, birds, insects who are none other than the kindred selves and the lord himself.

> ... *rakṣya karā swāmī naraloka*
> ... *kīṭapataṅga jalapoka*
> ... *saraṇa sambhāli rakṣa e jantu jībaka*
> – Bhīmā Bhoi, *Bhajanamālā*, p. 17

Every manifestation is the living expression of God. The spirituality in the hands of Bhīmā Bhoi comes to embrace the whole within its ambit and it entails a form of humanism which transcends man while securing the interest of man to the highest possible extent. He never wished to lift man to the level of God though he prayed for the salvation of one and all. Salvation for him means removal of ignorance and discovery of the innate divinity present in him. This meant a life of perfection. What he envisioned for his fellow men was the society of men and women who not only share and care for one another but also imbued with the love for the rest of the creation. In him there is tension between spiritual optimism and stark realism. When the realist in him makes him lament that people with eyes are no better than blind and people with intellect are directionless – therefore he only wishes that his *summum bonum* of life is to be truly human.

cakṣyu thai kaṇā buddhi thāi baṇā
bātula heleni samaste he ।
je hebā manuṣya jāniba abasya
bujhāi kahuchi jete he ॥
– Bhīmā Bhoi, *Stuti Cintāmaṇi*, p. 66

A man cannot to be a human only by possessing a human structure. The human values in Bhīmā Bhoi does not mean the values pertaining to the well-being of human species but the values which disclose the real sublimity of human awareness. It is the values which bears the characteristic stamp of human rationality. It enables man to see the diversity as the multiple expression of the one. That is why he prays the lord to cause rational awakening in one and all so that there is efflorescence of universal love.

ekoisipura cauda bhuvana jeunthāre jehuchanti ।
sabu ghaṭe prabhu hetu cetā dia uṭhu alekha bhagati ॥
– Ibid., p. 40

In the conceptual framework of Bhīmā Bhoi, the scared is equated with secular. He contends that the scared core of all religions is one and the same consisting of the set of cardinal values which helps us to bind together. So the truly sacred is truly secular. A sacred need not involve reference to the transcendental and the secular need not be defined in terms of the profane. As the same spark of divinity throbs, there is no room for privilege or status quo. It is open for all irrespective of caste and creed.

sadguru dharma ehi, kāhāku manā nāhīṅ
eka janakara nuhanti ṭhākura
achi saburi bhāga ।
koṭha loka hebā antara nohibā
jeuṅ mane bhajuthibe āga ॥
– Bhīmā Bhoi, *Stuti Cintāmaṇi*, p. 62

Thus, he shows how spirituality in the practical domain takes the form of socialism. If humanism takes human beings as the highest reality and human interest as of focal concern, then it is bound to degenerate into individualism. Hence, humanism in order to be truly socialistic has to base itself in a mode of holistic living where every other is treated as the expression of one's own self. So Bhīmā Bhoi is a spiritualist whose humanism does not plead for the exclusive cause of human species but pleads for the welfare of all – *sarvabhūta hite ratāḥ.*

References

Bhīmā Bhoi, *Stuti Cintamani.*

———, *Bhajanamala.*

———, *Brahmanirupanagita.*

———, *Srutinisedhagita.*

Das, C.R., 1982, *A Glimpse into Odia Literature*, Bhubaneswar: Orissa Sahitya Akademi.

Dasgupta, S.B., 1995, *Obscure Religion Cults as Background of Bengali Literature*, Calcutta: Firma KLM.

Mohapatra, Sitakanta, 1996, "Saint-poet-Bhima Bhoi and Assessment", in *Santha Kabi Bhima Bhoi*, Bhubaneswar: All Orissa Adivasi Cultural Association.

10

A Tightrope Walker*

Appraising K. Satchidananda Murty on Religion and Morality

Vikram Singh Sirola

Introduction

THIS paper is a modest attempt to revisit K. Satchidananda Murty's writings in light of some insights I have gathered from Ludwig Wittgenstein on religion, religiosity, religious person and morality. Though the perspective I settle with in looking at religion and morality is Wittgensteinian, but I have intentionally avoided making a frequent direct comparison between the two. Also, such comparisons would not serve any serious philosophical purpose. Instead, the attempt is to draw insights from their writings and develop the ideas further using the strands on the theme from both the thinkers. The motivation to talk them together arises from the fact that there

* I wish to thank Professor S. Paneerselvam for initiating me to write on the works of K. Satchidananda Murty and present it in a conference at the University of Madras. After that, I presented this paper at Utkal University and IIT Kanpur.

is a noticeable similitude in their thoughts on the mentioned subjects. I begin with citing from the two works, *Culture and Value* and *The Realm of Between*:

Ludwig Wittgenstein in *Culture and Value* makes an intriguing remark on a religious person:

> An honest religious thinker is like a tightrope walker. He almost looks as though he were walking on nothing but air. His support is the slenderest imaginable. And yet it is really possible to walk on it. – 1977: 73

In a similar vein, K. Satchidananda Murty begins the Preface of his book, *The Realm of Between*, by quoting *Bṛhadāraṇyaka Upaniṣad* IV.3.9:

> तस्मिन्सन्ध्ये स्थाने तिष्ठन्नेते उभे स्थाने पश्यतीदं च परलोकस्थानं च ।
>
> *tasminsandhye sthāne tiṣṭhannete ubhe sthāne paśyatīdaṁ ca paralokasthānaṁ ca* ।
>
> Standing in this "intermediate condition", says the *Bṛhadāraṇyaka Upaniṣad*, "one sees both those conditions, namely being in this world and being in the other world". By putting himself in such a situation, it adds, man sees both evils and joys: *pāpmana ānandamś ca paśyati.* – 1973: ix

Murty highlights the significance of this "intermediate condition" a person finds her/himself in by citing further thoughts from Buddhist thinkers to Alexander Pope; and from George Santayana, Blaise Pascal and Friedrich Nietzsche to Rumi (Murty 1973: ix-xi). This intermediate position may be equated with what Wittgenstein refers to as "a tightrope walk" where a man is walking on a support which is almost nothing. He is aware of both immanence and transcendence, where a human may possibly enter into a relationship with the divine. It may be just a dream and myth, but he can become aware of himself as living such a relationship. This realm of between for Murty is *sandhyā sthāna*, the intermediate condition in which man realizes what he is and becomes aware of what he ought to be and can be (ibid.: xi-xii).

To appreciate and explicate Murty's standpoint on God, religion and morality, we have to assess whether religious faith could be conceived as a hypothesis; based on some evidence or grounded in a proto-religious attitude. Moreover, how important it is to ask, is there God before settling with the idea of truth, values and meaning of life? Like many other philosophers, psychoanalysts, anthropologists and scientists, Murty holds that religiosity or religious attitude cannot or need not be limited to theism. To adopt an ethical attitude, one is not required to have belief in God's existence. In fact, belief in religious metaphysics is not essentially a basis of one's religiosity. Ordinary standards of epistemic support may not be applicable in case of religious doctrines. That does not make them unreasonable. Though it is extremely difficult to define such a religious attitude, the complexity of the idea needs to be articulated in philosophy.

Religion as "Righteous Living": Two Complexities

I will briefly discuss Murty's perspective on religion, God and morality drawn primarily from two of his works, *The Realm of Between* (1973) and *Hinduism and Its Development* (2007). Though these works mainly contain his erudite reading of various philosophers in Western and Eastern traditions on the theme, my focus will entirely be on his thoughts appearing in these books in the form of short comments on various viewpoints of the philosophers he chose to discuss.

Emphasizing the practical relevance of religion, Murty defines religion as "righteous living" and "the practice of *dharma*" (Murty 2007: 41). Conformity to *dharma*, the inner law of one's own being and adherence to it constitutes the practice of religion. In the same book, he further writes:

> A true religious man does not alienate himself from anything that is of interest to humanity. ... Religion shows men how to live, a richer and fuller life. ... If it cannot be of any practical use, then who owns a religion. If religion is merely to alienate us from the suffering world, if it is merely to make us lose our sanity by dipping us into depths of unintelligibility masquerading under profundity of spiritual truth, if it is merely to ignore the tremendous assets of science and revel in the hallucinations of fancied heaven and angelic hosts, if it is merely to construct systems of reflection without any reference to the primary and empirical facts of the world and life, if it merely to make us adopt superstitious silliness and orthodox foolishness and if it is merely to cry halt in the name of God to every novel innovation and every new step in the ladder of human progress then, I am afraid, no sane man can be religious. If that is religion, the sooner we shake ourselves from its shackles the better. – Murty 2007: 42

Murty has been very open and candid in his elucidation of religion and morality. In *Realm of Between* he writes:

> Every society and civilization has a religion or religions; but there are religions which have no place for God or soul or both. Buddhism and some of the major religious traditions of China and Japan deny both God and soul. Jainism and some of the great Hindu systems – e.g. Mīmāṁsā and Sāṁkhya – deny God. Some Vedic and Upaniṣadic passages deny the soul's immortality. Till a late stage Judaism did not posit the immortal soul and another life. – 1973: 179

Murty points out:

> Even in the Hellenic philosophical tradition, the immortality of the soul was not a popular object of belief. Nevertheless, all these religions and belief systems arose within the societies and shaped their civilizational growth. The spiritual and material achievements of these societies, and the standards

> of the ethical life they produced, were not inferior to those of others. Drawing from *Ivan Karamazov*, he maintains that there can be virtue even if there is no immortality and even if there is no God, all things are not (un)lawful. – Ibid.

He is appreciative of these traditions, which have demonstrated the possibility of sublime ethics without a belief in the religious portrayal of a God or the immortality of the soul.

Further, he underlines contrasting exemplars where God and immortality may be accepted as central to the belief system and yet may utterly fail to fulfil the standards of morality. His examples from history and epics are (ibid.: 181): some of the Czars who accepted God and immortality but were known more as despotic rulers than some of the communist rulers; and some of the benevolent Buddhist and Jaina kings; Christian Machiavelli and the orthodox brāhmaṇa Kauṭilya were far below the moral level of the political theories of Confucius. He asks, was Medieval Europe more ethical than modern Europe? In what way is the contemporary Chinese civilization of Mao inferior to the contemporary civilizations of Catholic Latin America or the Muslim Middle East? He goes on to pick malevolent characters of Rāvaṇa and Duryodhana to establish the point that despite accepting Vedic authority, following a prescribed pattern of life, and believing in God, the other world, rebirth and the immortality of the soul, they were not virtuous. Therefore, Murty submits that atheism and denial of immortality need not necessarily lead to immorality and despotism. In a similar vein, he says, even acceptance of God and immortality of the soul, as in religions like Christianity, Islam or Hinduism, does not necessarily result in morality, democracy, justice and liberty (ibid.: 182).

I agree with most of what Murty broadly purports on religion and morality. Only that his writings, particularly in *The Realm of Between*, leaves you more curious about the philosophical treatment one may offer in developing those assertions further in some detail. As one of the reviewers of his book also conveys his dissatisfaction of

> not being helped by the book to choose one out of the many views so eruditely presented by. Cold impartiality in some places leaves you only with the goal and no clear direction or path. – De Marneffe 1978

When it is felt that Murty leaves the reader wanting for more deliberations on the mentioned issues, it gives away space for exploration in his propositions. I offer to highlight twofold complexities in his exposition of religion and morality. It is more pertinent to the reference to the idea of *sandhyā sthāna* (the realm of between). The first complexity originates when Murty mentions a person who feels he/she has caught a glimpse of the realm which transcends the world. Even if one had a glimpse of the realm, the vision remains short-lived. As he aptly quotes from *Phaedo*:

> Cicero makes one of his debaters confess that when he was reading Plato's book on the soul (*Phaedo*) he found himself assenting to what Plato said, but as soon as he put aside the book and reflected in his own mind upon the immortality of souls, all his previous assent (*adsensio*) melted away. – 1973: xii

Murty calls it a human predicament where a man, after having a glimpse of the realm, hangs in between, drifts in the ocean, having set sail for another shore without really "knowing" there is one and he can reach it (ibid.: xii). The glimpse of the realm also indicates that religious belief originating from such experience or glimpse may not be tenable and reasonable, but, as Wittgenstein says, "it need not be unreasonable either" (1966: 58). How may a rational person remain religious (believer in God) without deceiving himself? If possible at all, it is no less than a tightrope walk. To such a rational thinker, Murty recommends having faith. And faith alone embraces believing where we cannot prove; one has to act as if He existed by making him the inner spring of our action (Murty 1973: xiv). He quotes the *Gītā*, to sum up, "Man is made up of faith, as is his faith, just so is he". There is an answer Murty offers, but he remains elusive in addressing the complexity of the thought.

The second complexity, which is not clearly spelt out in Murty's writings, is that the religious dogmas do not blind a religious thinker and, with an awareness of this realm, realizes the lack of evidence and certainty in religious doctrines. How would such belief guide her/him in comprehending human life and performing actions in practical life? Will his being religious suffice to lead a moral life in all spheres of his existence? In other words, how would he make sense of the religious rituals and creeds and see them together in his experience of morality?

The First Complexity

The first complexity mentioned above originates from the idea of the "realm of between", where a true religious person finds herself/himself, confronting the problem of reconciling between "taking religious faith as not unreasonable" and "finding God's existence not relevant or necessary for such faith". One more straightforward way to reconcile both is to suggest expressivist construal of religious beliefs and creedal statements.

That is to say, religious experience and faith do not necessarily involve any metaphysical beliefs. Therefore, creedal statements may represent some figurative expressions of an attitude towards life. Accordingly, ritualistic practices become a part of an expression of such attitude. When people speak of God and the immortality of the soul, that has to be appreciated in that context of expressing an attitude rather than a metaphysical assertion.

This is a comprehensive elucidation of Murty's account of religion. However, the problem with such a conception of religion is much more intricate. Can a demythologized account of popular religion bereft of its metaphysical stimulants really substitute a religious faith people identify with? It would be a misleading description of ordinary believers' religious views. As William James writes in *Varieties of Religious Experiences*:

> It is precisely as being SOLEMN experiences that I wish to interest you in religious experiences. So I propose – arbitrarily again, if you please – to narrow our definition once more by saying that the word "divine", as employed therein, shall mean for us not merely the primal and enveloping and real, for that meaning if taken without restriction might prove too broad. The divine shall mean for us only such a primal reality as the individual feels impelled to respond to solemnly and gravely, and neither by a curse nor a jest. – 2002: 25

James suggests that the focus must be on personal religious experience rather than communal because, in this case, the personal is more fundamental than the communal or shared societal experiences. He holds that most religious movements or sects have commenced out of the intense experiences of a few people in the culture.

Einstein, talking of true religiousness, also expresses a similar sentiment about religion.

> The most beautiful emotion we can experience is the mystical. To know that what is impenetrable to us really exists, manifesting itself as the highest wisdom and the most radiant beauty, which our dull faculties can comprehend only in their most primitive forms – this knowledge, this feeling, is at the centre of true religiousness. In this sense, and in this sense only, I belong to the ranks of devoutly religious men.
>
> – Philipp 1947: 217-18

Religious faith may be appreciated from both intellectual and emotional–practical perspectives. That is, cosmological beliefs on the one side and rituals and practices on the other. One's approach to religion is more about its appeal to us personally. We see this clearly in Wittgenstein, who remains very sympathetic towards the Christian faith when he said:

> I could not possibly bring myself to believe all the things that they believe. – Malcom 1958: 60

> I cannot call [Jesus] *Lord*; because that says absolutely nothing to me. ... I cannot utter the word "Lord" meaningfully. *Because I do not believe* that he will come to judge me.
> – Wittgenstein 1977: 38

Wittgenstein attempts to describe religious belief as one which he personally finds intelligible, intellectually acceptable and morally desirable. It almost suggests that, in some sense, each of us must have our own "personal" religion. That does not mean we must put forth some empirical evidence to prove its reasonableness over others. Religious beliefs cannot rationally be based on any empirical evidence. In one of his lectures, Wittgenstein developed an interesting thought experiment:

> We come to an island and we find beliefs there, and certain beliefs we are inclined to call religious. The islanders may, for example, believe that there is an immensely powerful being that can punish them or reward them, and that they worship. But now suppose they take us to the peak of a mountain where indeed we see that powerful being: somebody who sometimes strikes people dead and sometimes cures people's illnesses by a touch of the hand. Then we will no longer call their attitude towards that being a religious belief; it has turned out to be a simple piece of knowledge of a superior person islanders submit to. – 1966: 58-60

Religious attitude as a way of experiencing the world becomes the pivot of faith. It is not a consequence of theoretical constructions drawn out of unique religious metaphysics. A radical singularity of religious beliefs gets rejected here.

Bob Plant presents a list of such acts and behaviour which are linkages between the common natural form of human behaviour and religious beliefs: Acts of pity in a both ordinary or religious sense, confession of love or guilt or of sins, devotion towards the loved ones or towards religious symbols and practices, conscience, trust – governs any human relation including the religious faith, notion of fate or predestination, expressions of basic human vulnerabilities and needs and prayer, and finally, certain eschatological beliefs can also be seen as corresponding to a natural aspiration for fairness and justice (Plant 2004: 455).

Showing these linkages between religious beliefs and the natural form of human behaviour should not be mistaken as an attempt to undermine the inherent complexity of religious beliefs and practices. However, it intends only to deny their radical singularity and pure theoretical constructions. The point which I would like to stress upon here is that religious beliefs are to be conceived as founded on human nature. Its roots lie in humanity's natural responsiveness to the world. It is quite a Wittgensteinian insight (Clack 1999: 129). We must look at the links between apparently incommensurable types of human activities. Even if one is not completely immersed in any religious world picture, it cannot detest her/him from not having a sympathetic attitude towards religious practices. So it is more of a reconciliation rather than severance between these seemingly conflicting inclinations by marking out those recurrent patterns of behaviour which manifest themselves in the life of humankind. Religious concepts make sense in terms of sin, guilt and responsibility towards others. These are the behaviours we share as human beings.

Genuine religious utterances do not describe a supernatural realm but direct us towards one's earthly life (Wittgenstein 1966: 32, 53). One would find the faith of Tolstoy's "illiterate peasant" more meaningful than the theology of "learned believers" who found themselves on the doctrinal and theological tradition and institutionalized ritual practices, which, as Tolstoy says, "destroys the thing it should be advancing" (1987: 63, 72, 74). This characterization of the religious man can be understood only in relation to the sense of responsibility one feels towards others. As in *The Brothers Karamazov*, Dostoyevsky writes:

> Every one of us is responsible for everyone else in every way, and I most of all. ... I don't know how to explain it to you, but I feel it so strongly that it hurts ....
>
> – 1967: 339

The sense of responsibility towards the other includes a more profound experience of guilt in not being able to live up to it.

Second Complexity

The second level of complexity in Murty's work is founded on the central question, how by being religious one ensures leading a moral life? How to see religious creeds and rituals together in one's experience of morality? B.K. Matilal shares a similar concern in one of his essays in *Ethics and Epics* and asks very pivotal questions concerning religion and morality: Can a moral act be religious by the same token? Or, is an act morally good because it is religious, i.e. has it got religious approval? To put it straight, is it that gods love what is morally right? Or, is a thing morally right because gods love it? He calls it a dilemma between the "religious-because-moral" theory and the "moral-because-religious" theory. For him, a moral dilemma is a species of action-guided dilemmas where more than one action is possible in a situation that is both "absolutely and unconditionally obligatory" (Matilal 2002: 3-4).

I will refer to one of Matilal's exemplars of a dilemma from the *Bhagavadgītā* to clarify the argument. The dilemma is the one where Arjuna, in the *Mahābhārata* warfield, is perplexed whether he should fight the bloody battle and kill his revered grandfather, teacher, uncle, brothers, etc. or, should he not? It is

> morally obligatory for him as a man – as a human being and a member of the family and a society – to feel revulsion about a bloody battle that would lead to the senseless killing of his own venerable relatives:

However, he also has an identity of a warrior – a kṣatriya royal prince whose *dharma* is to fight wars when challenged and to recover the lost sovereignty. So, shall he kill or shall he not? Could Arjuna be condemned for showing his perplexity and being snared with such moral concerns and dilemmas? Matilal responds by saying,

> No. For, this only typifies the moral dilemma of an agent. Arjuna, by showing this side of his mind, turn out to be more of a human not a gigantic killing machine. He had to get on the battlefield and kill, which was inevitable. Nevertheless, to weep for those he was killing is genuinely humane and religious. His dilemma was genuine. – 2002: 6-8

Another thought-provoking example from Matilal's *Ethics and Epics* is very relevant here (ibid.: 9). It is about Kṛṣṇa telling a story to Arjuna in a different context, that of a sage, Kauśika, who had always vowed to tell the truth. A group of gangsters chasing an innocent man came to ask him which way he had fled. Should he break his vow and tell a lie and save the man's life, or should he not? Kauśika, being a very righteous sage, told the truth, and the man was chased and killed. Kṛṣṇa remarks that after Kauśika died, he could not reach his *sidhanocita dhāma*. It gets explained by recognizing what found precedence for Sage

Kauśika – the selfish religious dogma of truth-telling or the selfless morality in saving a life of an innocent, even at the cost of violating the vow.

Matilal comments:

> Truth-telling may be morally admirable and hence, indeed, a religious virtue, but not under all conditions; one of the certain marks of morally superior (and in my scheme, "religiously" superior) action is its non-self-regarding character. – 2002: 9

This is in consonance with the moral and religious insights which Kr̥ṣṇa shared in his instructions to Arjuna. As Matilal points out, the issue's complexity, however, still needs to be settled. He cites the exchanges between Bankimchandra and Rabindranath Tagore, which takes the deliberations a step further. Tagore, filled with purist religious vigour, vehemently objects to Bankimchandra's depiction of Kr̥ṣṇa in his *Kr̥ṣṇa-caritra*. He says:

> Falsehood can never be true under any circumstances – even if respected Bankimbabu or Śrīkr̥ṣṇa himself says it can be.

Tagore's absolutist proposal is for adhering to truth-telling. He suggests a radical way out of the impasse where Kauśika should have told the truth and said, "Yes, I know, but I will not tell you. He could have saved the innocent man's life by renouncing his own". Here truth-telling is a moral absolute comparable with the religious absolute. In this proposal, a moral principle of truth-telling has been turned into a moral dogma.

Conclusion

The clear insight from these two examples is the possibility that both truth (adherence to religious principles) and humanity (acting in accordance with moral guidance) can win over blind adherence to certain principles or dogmas. Matilal concludes:

> This probably approximates the "ideal" resolution of the dilemma, by which I mean the poetic resolution of the dilemma. A truly religious man can transcend his so-called religious dogma and put moral concerns over narrowly religious ones. – Ibid.: 13

It is evident that what Matilal refers to as religious concern is just the popular view of religion and religious belief. However, if we go by the conception of religion subscribed above, we may suggest some revisions in his concluding remarks. My proposal is as follows: religious attitude or temper or religiosity may get primacy over morality if it is identified with love, commitment, responsibility and sincerity towards life, and not with Tagore's purist religious fervour. It is like giving heart and emotions to cold-blooded Kantian morality. Desiccated morality may not always be viable in complex human relations and situations. Tagore suggests: "Saving the life of the innocent men by giving his own is not just being morally upright." Matilal also agrees that justice (morality) reaches its noblest height when, in meting out punishment to a wrongdoer, the punisher sheds tears, being as much hurt as the one punished. He reverberates Dostoyevsky's "sense of responsibility for everyone else in every way".

Morality enlivened with religiosity would become an individual elucidation of life conduct. None limits itself to just a system of propositions establishing a code of conduct for working in our lifeworld. It would be complete as an experience of value when weaved around the individual finding the right way of living. Probably, this is what K.S. Murty meant when he says:

> When the sacred is not separated from the profane, all action become ritual. When the sacred is experienced as a person, all action becomes worship. – Matilal 2002: 83

References

Clack, B.R., 1999, *An Introduction to Wittgenstein's Philosophy of Religion*, Edinburgh: Edinburgh University Press.

De Marneffe, J., 1978, "Book Review of *The Realm of Between*", *Indian Philosophical Quarterly*, 5(3): 531-33.

Dostoyevsky, F., 1967, *The Brothers Karamazov 1*, tr. D. Magarshack, London: Penguin.

James, W., 2002, *Varieties of Religious Experience: A Study in Human Nature*, London: Routledge.

Malcolm, Norman, 1958, *Ludwig Wittgenstein: A Memoir* (with a biographical sketch of Wittgenstein by G.H. von Wright), London: Oxford University Press.

Matilal, B.K., 2002, *The Collected Essays of Bimal Krishna Matilal: Ethics and Epics*, ed. Jonardon Ganeri, New Delhi: Oxford University Press.

Murty, K. Satchidananda, 1973, *The Realm of Between*, Simla: Indian Institute of Advanced Study.

———, 2007, *Hinduism and Its Development*, New Delhi: D.K. Printworld.

Philipp, Frank, 1947, *Einstein, His Life and Times*, New York: Alfred Knopf.

Plant, B., 2004, "The Wretchedness of Belief", *Journal of Religious Ethics*, 32(3): 449-76.

Tolstoy, L., 1987, *A Confession and Other Religious Writings*, tr. J. Kentish, London: Penguin.

Wittgenstein, L., 1966, *Lectures and Conversations on Aesthetics, Psychology and Religious Belief*, ed. C. Barrett, Oxford: Blackwell.

———, 1977, *Culture and Value*, ed. G.H. von Wright, tr. P. Winch, Oxford: Blackwell.

11

Vairāgya in the Realm of Awakening Consciousness

Ranjan Kumar Panda

Introduction

Let me begin while drawing your attention to one of the exemplary moments[1] in the *Bhagavadgītā* when the war between the Kauravas and the Pāṇḍavas was about to start, and Arjuna, the greatest warrior in this epic poem, expressed his withdrawal by stating that "I shall not fight". This declaration of Arjuna shows a spark of *vairāgya* (detachment) as he was saddened by the consequence of the war and compassion for his enemies. Arjuna, during this conversation, further mentioned to Kṛṣṇa that "I see my people" and it would be sinful to be engaged in killing his *svajana*s – grandfather, teacher, uncles, brothers, sons and nephew. Kṛṣṇa might have been surprised to see this dejected attitude of Arjuna as he addressed the enemies as his people. How can Duryodhana be no more his enemy! Moreover, the statement "I shall not fight", for the sake of argument, is an

[1] This moment is like a *sandhi muhūrta* or *sandhyā kāla*, which is neither day nor night.

expression of *vairāgya* because it exhibits the loss of self-interest and despair. Arjuna had lost the self-interest in winning the war and, in despair, he had "grasped the inner meaning of war" (Gurcharan Das 2009: 92). While narrating the inner meaning of war, Das mentions:

> Once war begins, it inevitably escalates, without limit. ... Great tragedy is inescapable in war. ... Arjuna's conscience tells him that it is wrong to kill. – Ibid.: 94

To illustrate the statement that "I shall not fight" is the expression of conscience which certainly shows that it is not merely a statement of despair. Rather, Arjuna gives the impression that he understands the consequence of the war and the devastating consequence that results in the killing of his people – *my people* (*māmakaḥ*). Hence, the despondent Arjuna decided to give up arms. How does one understand this despondency of Arjuna? We investigate it from the perspective of the Indian philosophy of religion and discuss two strands of interpretations, viz. the ethical and the metaphysical.

The interpretation based solely on an ethical concern shows that Arjuna examines the consequences of the war on certain normative considerations. Hence, he judges that participating in the war will lead to devastation and ultimately will bring sorrow and pain, annihilating his well-being of life. He mentions that it will not be a place worthy of living after winning such a war. This is not a case of enlightened selfishness. Therefore, it is not merely psychological. Had it been so, he would have responded with pride.

On the contrary, he expressed his *unhappiness* stating that it would be a sin to slay his people – *māmakāḥ* or *svajanas*. Hence, Arjuna's attitude is ethical rather than merely psychological. It represents a case of social affection that maintains a deep community relationship. Causing death to his people is a sin from the religious and ethical point of view. Arjuna's conscience does not allow this sin to happen. Hence, this ethical attitude of Arjuna in the statement "I shall not fight" discloses a kind of awakening consciousness. Where he is awakened to understand something meaningful that he had possibly failed to do before coming to the warfield. Therefore, in this regard, the sense of *viṣāda* (despair) is a disclosure of awakening consciousness as Arjuna understands the deeper consequence of having a war.

However, does this awakening consciousness make an individual *fully* awaken? To illustrate this question, the second interpretation might be strategically helpful, to begin with. The second interpretation is based on a metaphysical explanation and is not entirely divorced from the ethical one. As a religious text, the verses of the *Bhagavadgītā* do not merely advocate the ethics or normative principle of Hindu religion, rather these verses are grounded on the metaphysics of Hindu philosophy. The metaphysical interpretation shows the telos of life and death in a larger normative framework of *puruṣārthas*. The realization of the purpose of life in that normative framework demands the self be awakened. In brief, the awakening self must act like a *sthitaprajña* who maintains equanimity and a steady mind. In the realm of awakening consciousness, a *sthithaprajña* transcends the realm of unhappiness and happiness. Thus, the normative and ontological identity of a *sthitaprajña* is melted down, forming self-knowledge of being in a state of awakening consciousness.

In this paper, I intend to delve into these two above-stated interpretations concerning the notion of suffering (*duḥkha*). Arjuna's despondency is an instance of a *sufferer* who is caught in the crisis of understanding and misunderstanding the other – the world. A restless despondent person fails to decide what is right and what is wrong. The despondency reflects a state of being caught in the complex nexus of the world of attachments where the mind is generally indulged in the world. Being world-minded, one remains confined to worldly pleasures and gratification of one's needs and desires which become a reason for unhappiness and suffering. A sufferer (*duḥkhī*) goes through a *complex feeling* of pain or agony where he or she neither fails to detach/disengage exclusively nor succeeds in attaching/engaging successfully with the world. This is a *paradox* of human existence. In this regard, one could raise the question that which one of these interpretations would take us away from the paradoxical life situation. Thus, for further analysis, let us discuss the first interpretation that addresses the question of suffering from a normative or ethical point of view. This viewpoint is mainly put forward by B.K. Matilal while critiquing the metaphysical interpretation of the Indian philosophy of religion maintained by S. Radhakrishnan. In the following section, these two viewpoints are concisely discussed. Furthermore, in the subsequent section, the nature of *svabhāva* will be brought to this discourse concerning the notion of world-mindedness or attachment (*rāga*) as an intentional condition of suffering. We conclude with the reiteration that the notion of detachment (*vairāgya*) helps us comprehend the significant difference between being in a normative and metaphysically awakening consciousness.

The Duḥkha-Thesis: A Normative Perspective

According to Matilal, the *duḥkha*-thesis represents suffering as a commonly addressed concept by almost all religions. Suffering is part of our everyday life. Life becomes a burden when there are sorrows and distress. One starts believing that there is no end to suffering; rather, one's consciousness sinks into a realm of thought that *sarvam duḥkham* (Matilal 2004: 14). Life seems meaningless when one suddenly encounters wars, calamities, diseases, poverty, and the loss of parents and friends. The current humanitarian crisis in Ukraine is an example. There is a lack of peace and the absence of desirable living conditions. All of a sudden, life seems to become burdensome, undesirable and empty. While describing the nature of suffering, Matilal underlines that it is subjective and relative as it varies from person to person. Hence, the philosophical study of suffering is not about any particular fact, rather, it is about the concept of suffering.

Narrating the significance of suffering, Matilal (2004: 22) writes:

> *Duḥkha* can be seen as man's sense of alienation from his essence or "own being" (*svabhāva*) or ultimate nature. A deep feeling of purposefulness and absurdity of life (T. Nagel) is then derived, in this theory, from this sense of estrangement, and the goal then would be *nirvāṇa*, cessation of estrangement. And the pain thesis in this way obtains a factual character. Nevertheless, the argument here is against such claims as undermining the totality of its evaluative character.

The *svabhāva* is fundamental to living as it forms reactive attitudes. Attitudes per se are not always normatively filtered, rather, we need normative criteria to evaluate the content of intended action. The evaluative character could effectively develop a character by appropriately perfecting the reactive attitudes that ultimately culminate in providing a sense of identity. Sometimes, the nature of suffering might cause alienation where the person is estranged from one's behaviour. Alienation entails the loss of self. In such a situation, life seems absurd as one feels the absence of meaning in one's existence and identity. The evaluative character brings back the sense of being; it has the power of putting life into order. Hence, for Matilal, *nirvāṇa* is not merely a natural outcome of undergoing suffering. Rather, it presupposes a normative outlook of examining oneself.

Matilal reiterates the Socratic slogan that an unexamined

life is not worth living to emphasize the primacy of the ethical in the philosophical discourse of religion. Morality is an integral part of religion. It is either higher than religion or the core of all religions (Matilal 2004: 29-30). The necessity of ethics is recognized for maintaining religious harmony and the survival of religions. Moreover, the ethical attitude flags the spirit analysing pain with a negative value. At the outset, we have cited the example of Arjuna's attitude of despair. For Matilal, Arjuna is a *mumukṣu* who exhibits an aspiration for realizing higher values in life. Arjuna's despondency does not remain throughout as his dialogues with Kr̥ṣṇa proceed. He understands the very purpose of life. As a *mumukṣu*, he undertakes the *nivr̥tti* – the path of renunciation and, thereby, considers duty more important than seeking the acquisition of the kingdom and its material wealth. So, Arjuna's consideration was not materialistic when he gave up his arms. Over and above, he considered killing to be immoral and ready to sacrifice almost everything.

Thus, Matilal's ethical interpretation of understanding religious action highlights that *duḥkha* is

> ... underlying the undesirability or non-finality of worldly life for a person who strives to discover a higher, better, greater and transcendent truth beyond all this. – Ibid.: 11

Suffering does create hindrance in the path of *nivr̥tti*, as a result, it is undesirable. But it cannot stop a *mumukṣu* completely in his/her endeavour to realize the higher values of life. The normative religious attitude becomes the source of transcending the given and embracing the higher realm of awakening the spiritual.

Grounding Normative Religious Attitude Beyond Ethics

The realm of the spiritual provides a metaphysical ground for normative religious attitudes. A religious person is not only an ethical person but also a spiritual person. The ethical and the spiritual are essential for living a religious life. As discussed in the previous section, Matilal emphasizes that ethics is an integral part of religion. On the other hand, Radhakrishnan maintains that spirituality is the core of a religion. According to him, the spiritual is the ideal that represents the divinity in humanity (Radhakrishnan 1940: 35). The presence of the divine connects to everything and helps comprehend the wholeness of life (ibid.: 38). Human beings as spiritual beings have higher purposes, that is, they must aim to establish "harmony and order among different parts of nature and must strive for an integral life" (ibid.: 37). The spirit is the underlying principle of the material, the vital and the intellectual. Therefore, the spiritual stands as a metaphysical principle in Radhakrishnan's philosophy of religion.

By integrating nature and all other beings in nature based on spirituality, Radhakrishnan tries to highlight the basic and unceasing quest for knowing the truth. Religion is nothing but a search for truth (ibid.: 346).[2] He writes:

> Religion begins for us with an awareness that our life is not ourselves alone. There is another greater life unfolding and sustaining us. Religion is man's search for this greater self will not accept any creeds as final or any laws as perfect. – Ibid.: 61

The religious life is not solitary; in the pursuits of religious life, we pray and meditate, but these religious activities make us perfect in knowing our being – the true nature of the self. Being religiously wise must exhibit perfection in our normative attitude of everyday engagement and further strengthen the deeper relationship that one upholds with the other.

---

[2] "Religion, or search for truth, is a necessity" (p. 3). The aim of religion and the aim of search for truth are treated equally as part of the cosmic process of human existence.

The religious, spiritual life is neither isolated nor a dogmatic life, rather, it is a life that aims to achieve perfection in understanding the highest knowledge concerning the self – *self-knowledge*. While claiming that there is no limit to perfection in living an ethical and religious life, the wise in that sense remains to awaken and, thereby, he further claims:

> The genuineness of one's awakening is directly proportionate to one's apprehension of truth. Wisdom liberates while ignorance binds, and the inner change is essential for perfection. – Radhakrishnan 1940: 95

The quest for perfection lies in being awakened to higher consciousness. The human psyche is generally world-minded and obsessively engaged in cultivating selfish interests that it often fails to distinguish between what is intellectual living and what is a spiritually awakening life. The quest for genuine understanding of the purpose of life/meaning of life awakens us from the selfish-egoistic attitude.

Self-knowledge is necessary to articulate action that changes the attitude by participating in the ethical process. States Radhakrishnan:

> Any ethical theory must be grounded in metaphysics, in a philosophical conception of the relationship between human conduct and Ultimate Reality. As we think the Ultimate Reality to be, so we behave. Vision and action go together. If we believe in absurdities, we shall commit atrocities. A self-sufficient humanism has its metaphysical presuppositions.
> – Ibid.: 80

Ethics is not merely exhausted by explaining moral conduct, rather its metaphysical aspect deals with the logical possibility of *self-evaluation*.[3] There are other metaphysical presuppositions,

---

3 "Self-evaluation – I value myself. An unconditional minimal self-evaluation admits of no degrees. ... This is the beginning of moral →

for instance, the existence of God as the Supreme Being. However, the notion of self-evaluation is an important ethical attitude that relates to the Ultimate Reality or Truth. The relation further shows the integration of how the value is conceptualized and undertaken in action.

From Viṣāda (Despair) to Vairāgya (Detachment): An Understanding of Awakening Consciousness

Valuing is an important act that relates one self-consciously to values. The despondent Arjuna decided thoughtfully not to kill his people and commit sin; he was certainly conscious of the devastating consequence of the war and the miseries that would follow. By stating that "I shall not fight", he exhibits a state of awakening consciousness, as I had mentioned earlier. In the awakening consciousness, one actively relates to the values and makes a self-evaluation of own actions. The self-evaluation reflects the reason for not undertaking a fight that somehow meets the divine reason. In the normative framework, violence that remains morally insignificant is ever well condemned. Arjuna is an example here, but there may be many such Arjuna(s) who have encountered this kind of despondent situation in their respective lives. And, like Arjuna, many also try hard to seek the right response so that their despondencies are rightly resolved.

Moreover, my point of contention here is not how to resolve the moral dilemma that we encounter in everyday life. Rather, to focus on the state of *awakening consciousness* that evokes a sense of *self-evaluation* and also detachment. The awakening consciousness is thus a source for constant evaluation of the intent of the action. An awakening mind seeks to know how to perform the right action. One must know or have a good sense (self-knowledge) about one's "*svabhāva* – the inclination to act

---

← wisdom. This wisdom is embodied in the religious conviction that all men are equally valuable in the eyes of God." – Gandhi 1976: 57

in a certain way" (Das 2009: 94). *Karma* is an outcome of that inclination that forms the intention. When Arjuna is intending not to fight and kill his people, there is something morally significant. Being moral is charged with self-evaluation, but Arjuna could not overcome his state of despondency because of his commitment to the other Pāṇḍavas. Thus, he appeals to Kṛṣṇa, his wise friend, to resolve this conflict and save him from his despondency.

While analysing the dialogue between Arjuna and Kṛṣṇa, on this particular point, Gurcharan Das mentions that there are two arguments, one from the viewpoint of morality based on *dharma*, and another from the viewpoint of metaphysics based on *ātman/jīva/śarīra* dichotomy. *Dharma*, particularly concerning *varṇāśrama* or his kṣatriya *dharma*, signifies his social duty as a warrior – he must protect. But when it comes to *svadharma*, the duty of the conscience, Arjuna had this conflict as his conscience voices that it is wrong to kill. These two normative outlooks had no convincing answer for Arjuna. On the other hand, the metaphysical outlook explicates the presupposition of birth and death – *punarjanma* related to the notion of life. All living beings are a combination of the eternal *ātman* and the impermanent *śarīra/jīva*. *Ātman* never dies. It is eternal, whereas the *śarīra* is transient and perishes with death.

Moreover, as the dialogue proceeds, these reasons did not impact Arjuna. Das (2009: 84) writes:

> Arjuna, however, is a man and appears to be impervious to metaphysics. So, the divine charioteer Kṛṣṇa resorts next to a *truly novel* (italics to emphasize) moral argument based on action. When an individual acts for the sake of his work rather than for his reward from it, Kṛṣṇa says the individual is likely to do the right thing. This moral insight is famously called *niṣkāma karma*. *Niṣ* means "without" in Sanskrit, *kāma* means desire; *phala* is fruit, *karma* is action – literally, "disinterested

> action" or action without thinking of its fruit. Kṛṣṇa expresses it famously in *Bhagavadgītā*'s verse II.47: Be intent on the action, not on the fruits of action.

What makes *niṣkāma karma* a *truly novel* moral thesis? Does the thesis of *niṣkāma karma* have no metaphysical ground? These questions are important because they are not included in the ordinary account of normativity viewed from the perspective of *svadharma* and *varṇāśrama dharma.*

While explaining *niṣkāma karma*, Keya Maitra (2018: 87) writes:

> Here Kṛṣṇa seems to be giving us a far more nuanced sense of the mechanics than what is often offered in Western deontological ethics given its focus on reason. Part of the reason for the robustness of Kṛṣṇa's response might originate in the synthetic or organic nature of Hindu philosophy where, unlike the Western tradition, the clear conceptualization between metaphysics, ethics and epistemology or between mind and body does not happen.

The mechanics of action, that Kṛṣṇa, develops is without attachment. That is to say, there must be a complete absence of ego (*ahaṁkāra*). The body, the mind, the intellect and the senses are engaged in performing the action that purifies the self. So that the self performs the action with complete detachment (*vairāgya*) for the fruit of the action. In this regard, *niṣkāma karma* maintains a different way of articulating action. Further, the intricacy of conceptualizing the metaphysical, ethical and epistemic is problematic because one is embedded in the other, particularly when we try to understand the ethics of action concerning *niṣkāma karma.*

The nuances of this problem concerning ethics of action here demand preparation rather than the result. Preparation unfolds the involvement of normative and epistemic processes in articulating the right action. The *svabhāva* ought to be rightly transformed to act without any kind of selfish motive. In this regard, the cultivation of the spirit of *vairāgya* is to be cultivated and practised to perform *niṣkāma karma.* A *vairāgī* could renounce the result of action – making an epistemic-logical separation between *karma* and *karmaphala. Vairāgya* is an expression of detachment that gradually and steadily develops along with the continuous practice of virtues like truthfulness, temperance, courage and compassion. A *vairāgī* gains control over one's mundane desire (*kāma*) and greed of life, and acts non-egoistically and fearlessly as if as a *kartā* – the intent of the action is above the intention of making any gain or loss. The intent of action thus discloses the will of *sthitaprajña.*

The renunciation is not just a psychological effort but epistemic – as it is linked up with discriminative knowledge – *vivekakhyāti.* Right knowledge unfolds the will to perform an action that aims at realizing peace, happiness and contentment. In this realm of awakening consciousness, a person is not easily affected by either failures/sorrows or success. At this stage of life, the consciousness transcends the psychological conditions and starts enveloping the *virtue of* equanimity[4] and the will of *sthitaprajña.* In brief, a *sthitaprajña* becomes a *guṇātīta,* and we know that *guṇa*s form the basic *svabhāva.* As *guṇa*s such as *sattva, rajas* and *tamas* are conceptualized metaphysically, not only in the Sāṁkhya–Yoga but also in the *Bhagavadgītā* where the person is characterized by the predominance of one of the *guṇa*s. The right transformation of *guṇa*s transforms the personality. For example, Prince Gautama, after he got enlightenment, was known as the Buddha. It is not merely an attitudinal change, but

4 According to Keya Maitra, the virtue of equanimity is one of the best virtues discussed in the *Bhagavadgītā.* See verses V.18-20. It has ethical, cognitive and social dimensions. But she doubts whether it can also be viewed with metaphysical necessity.

rather a change in one's identity. What is important here is the *virtue of equanimity* that endorses "the realization of sameness of every being" (*Gītā* V.24-29).

By maintaining the virtue of equanimity, a person demonstrates the ethical and cognitive dimensions of life that enable the internal transformation of the self, which also discloses its social dimension. While viewing the conceptual function of these dimensions, Maitra asserts that such an exercise makes a case for eternal freedom, but she still shows her reservations stating that these dimensions are to be viewed as a matter of metaphysical necessity.

Vairāgya and the Metaphysics of Religion

From the above discussion, Das and Maitra are apprehensive about relating metaphysics to religion or the semantic of religious experiences. In their interpretations, the Indian philosophy of religion can be well discussed within a normative framework of ethics (*dharma*). This goes well with Matilal's strong thesis regarding the four noble truths of Buddhism that "Noble truth is a truth of ethics and religion, rather than metaphysics" (2004: 23). This reservation of Matilal is based on the presupposition that says: *yuktisiddham vāco grāhyam*, as he translates, "No unexamined religion is worth practising or worth studying" (ibid.: 11). This slogan goes along with the spirit of Socrates' dictum that "The unexamined life is not worth living". This concern shows that everything in the religion must be grounded in logic and rationality that has the power to determine religious values. This reminds the positivistic spirit in which logic is treated as the foundation of understanding reality or everything must be logical or otherwise nonsensical. This is hard to accept as this interpretation is dismissive of the core religious truth, such as *mokṣa* (liberation) and the existence of God.

Similarly, the relationship between ethics and religion is necessary as it provides a functional account of religion that emphasizes the necessity of maintaining religious harmony. Such an account of religion will remain incomplete. To understand the *truly novel* aspect of *niṣkāma karma* and the metaphysical necessity of the virtue of *sthitaprajña* (equanimity) as pointed out by Das and Maitra, respectively, we need to explicate the metaphysical ground of the ethical that is not sometimes accessible to the realm of the logical. To resurrect the metaphysical ground for ethical religion or religious ethics, concerning the above discussion, we need to revisit Ramchandra Gandhi's concept of *self-evaluative* consciousness. That is, human beings are "unconditionally and logically self-valuing creatures" (Gandhi 1976: 58). This attitude is unique and has the power to unfold the metaphysical ground of religious experience and truth.

Vairāgya shows detachment which is an outcome of the self-evaluation. One is awakened to a realm of self-consciousness, which reveals that "all human beings are valuable and deserve minimal care". Arjuna not only cared for his *svajana*s but also expressed his despair because he was committed to fighting against injustice. To overcome the dilemma, despair, difficulties, mental agony, *duḥkha* (suffering) and death, in our *communicative* framework, we pray to God. As Ramchandra Gandhi asserts that "We are under a moral obligation to invoke God in the face of all these difficulties, and not merely in the face of death" (1976: 65). God is invoked in our prayer, we seek to address God and seek the care and presence of God. Here, there is no logical legitimacy; that is why it is so. For a religious person, God is the Ultimate Reality and the engagement is devotional, as there is no legitimate reason why one should invoke God. Hence, it is not a matter of logical necessity. But one who is praying and seeking the care of God without any philosophical inhibition is a true seeker. He or she gets into a solitary engagement while invoking God. This mode of engagement, for Ramchandra Gandhi, is a case of *non-cognitive transcendence* (ibid.: 99). The significance of this transcending moment lies in the spontaneous shift in consciousness while being engaged in spiritual activities. Transcendence is generally construed as *reflective transcendence* (Putnam 2004: 96) as one deliberately or rationally goes beyond the given experiences. In non-cognitive transcendence, the seeker is deeply motivated in his or her quest without any emphasis on making the goal an intellectual pursuit. Spiritual engagement such as prayer or being devotedly seeking care by invoking the presence of God are not intellectual pursuits, rather, they are spiritual pursuits which widen the availability of religious ideas.

Prayers are addressed to the divine. Similarly, in meditation, one constantly contemplates seeking the presence of the divine. Prayer and meditation as spiritual activities cultivated with the spirit of *vairāgya*. The form of detachment is disengaging oneself from one's greed, lust, ego, pride and anger. *Vairāgya* results from the cultivation of virtues such as temperance, truthfulness, kindness, courage and compassion. Cultivation is a mode of practice (*abhyāsa*) – *sādhanā* in which one cognizes the spiritual values of reality. One is rather awakened to engage with the other spiritually and disengages with their mundane self-interest. Thus, the *vairāgya* is not merely an awakening state of self-consciousness (*cetanā*) *self-knowledge. Vairāgya* helps in sustaining *self-knowledge.* It is a higher state of consciousness in which one is awakened to spiritual existence. Hence, God as the divine transcendent being is only available in the awakening consciousness.

The metaphysics of religion is grounded on the intentionality of evaluative self-consciousness which signifies the act of valuing. Mostly evaluation is a concept used in forming an ethical judgement in everyday life. I would discuss the metaphysics of religion later in the follow-up paragraph. Let us reflect on the formation of ethical judgement as it too has a metaphysical dimension. Evaluative intentionality shows that a person *ought* to evaluate the moral content that defines something reasonable or unreasonable. This very distinction suggests reason as a metaphysical faculty involved in the evaluation. One's pursuit of ethical life depends on this as one has to judge what is reasonable and what is not (Putnam 2004: 71). Putnam, who wishes to write an obituary on the ontology of the ethical, tries to convey that not everything is reducible to descriptive facts. Rather, certain descriptions are also construed from the *moral point of view* and valuing is not a descriptive fact (ibid.: 72). Therefore, the need here is to reflect fully on the cognitive activities where we often agree or disagree with something.

For ethical judgement, reflective thinking is necessary for the evaluation. But when the ethical questions become the species of practical questions, according to Putnam,

> we find that valuing involves a complex mixture of philosophical beliefs, religious beliefs, and factual beliefs as well. – 2004: 75

Valuing is something important that transcends what is being valued and what is not. To say that there is something about valuing the ethical is not nullified, rather it brings again the metaphysics of reason to the discourse showing how these different beliefs converge in forming practical reason for making a judgement. The primacy of the ethical in juxtaposition to metaphysics as argued by Emanuel Levinas only rejects metaphysics which is either inflationary or deflationary in nature. Levinas does not negate the existence of God as a universal religious metaphysical notion. Rather, according to him, the ethics of compassion is irreducible and it ought to be universal. In this regard, a person is necessarily obliged to help the other as he/she has infinite responsibility towards the other. Putnam does not disagree with Levinas, rather, it could be suggested in brief that Levinas who gives primacy to ethics in his philosophy does not rule out its integration with religion. In all human cultures, there is an emphasis on alleviating human suffering regardless of gender, race and caste. This conception is deeply rooted in the great religious traditions such as Judaism, Hinduism, Buddhism and Islam of the world (ibid.: 23). In this connection, we must engage in philosophizing the wide availability of religious ideas.

If valuing is a transcending feature of consciousness, then we need to know its metaphysical dimension. While illustrating what metaphysics can do concerning transcendent, R.C. Pradhan (2011: 318) writes:

> What makes the transcendent reality the pivotal axis of the human existence is its appeal to the higher values that are embedded in human consciousness. The transcendent acts as the source of values which leads man to a higher state of existence. This has been the central concern of all greater thinkers meditated upon human conditions.

Human conditions can be improved with a higher aspiration and performance of virtuous action. Compassion is a virtue. One must be committed to being compassionate to others. This kind of commitment unfolds how values direct us to a higher state of consciousness or become a motivating source of performance of virtuous action. While being compassionate one unconditionally relates to the other and helps the other to get rid of suffering. This is an awakening moment for any individual when one transcends world-mindedness and intends to realize the significance of values in life. Hence, the intentionality of valuing ultimately succeeds in transcending and transforming an ordinary individual into a moral person. The ordinary individual possesses mundane feelings and inclinations, such as *rāga* (attachment), *dveṣa* (hostility), *ahaṁkāra* (ego) and *lobha* (greed) which express the *pravr̥tti* of the person. On the contrary, *vairāgya* in the mode of dispassionate engagement animates *śraddhā* (affection and love), *karuṇā* (compassion), *nirbhaya* (fearlessness), *satya* (truthfulness), etc. which strengthen *self-knowledge* that unfolds the path towards *nivr̥tti*. Self-knowledge is a higher state of consciousness – the awakening consciousness that acts as a means of freeing oneself from the clutches of suffering. While dwelling in this state, the person acts freely and thoughtfully without any inhibition, rather for harmony, peace and happiness.

However, metaphysics provides a unifying principle that comprehends life as a whole. It does not compartmentalize life in the logical, ethical and religious framework only. Radhakrishnan (1940: 82) says:

> If ethical thought is profound, it will give a cosmic motive to morality. Moral consciousness must include a conviction in the reality of the ideals. If the latter is religion, then ethical humanism is acted as religion. When man realizes his essential unity with the whole of being, he expresses this unity in his life. Mysticism and ethics, other-worldliness and worldly work go together.

Here, the ethical is not dismissed, rather, the ethical process in which one acts in examining oneself presupposes self-consciousness and is integrated with a religious and logical perspective in which one grows in developing a holistic view of life.

I will conclude by saying that self-consciousness is an awakening consciousness. It is indeed a great challenge to remain in the realm of awakening consciousness. The articulation of the virtue of equanimity (*sthitaprajña*) is formed while one lives in the spirit of awakening consciousness that signifies unity in life.

> The genuineness of one's awakening is directly proportionate to one's apprehension of truth. Wisdom liberates while ignorance binds, and the inner change is essential for perfection.
>
> – Radhakrishnan 1940: 95

Arjuna, in the *Bhagavadgītā*, while being engaged in the divine dialogue with Kṛṣṇa, did aspire for realizing this perfection.

References

Das, G., 2009, *The Difficulty of Being Good,* New Delhi: Penguin/Allen Lane.

Gandhi, Ramchandra, 1976, "Theism, Non-theism, and Morality", in *The Availability of Religious Ideas,* Library of Philosophy and Religion, London: Palgrave Macmillan.

Maitra, Keya, 2018, *Philosophy of the Bhagavad Gita: A Contemporary Introduction*, London: Bloomsbury Academic.

Matilal, B.K., 2004, *Logical and Ethical Issues: An Essay on Indian Philosophy of Religion,* New Delhi: Chronicle Books.

Pradhan, R.C., 2011, *Metaphysics vs Metaphysics: An Essay in Transcendent Metaphysics*, Delhi: Academic Excellence.

Putnam, H., 2004, *Ethics Without Ontology*, Cambridge, MA: Harvard University Press.

Radhakrishnan, S., 1940, *Eastern Religion and Western Thought,* New Delhi: Oxford University Press.

12

Epistemic Foundation of Religions in India

Saroj Kanta Kar

Introduction

By "epistemic foundation of religion"[1] it is meant to discuss the knowledge-base of religion, its instruments and validity. The basis of any religion, at its inception, may be divine or mystic experience or speculation. It then goes through scriptural form and is disseminated to the followers, who accept the master based on reverence as the authority and the unverifiable matters in the religion are accepted based on faith. This is one of the

Acknowledgements: I am indebted to all my teachers for the knowledge and approach I received from them and used here. I am also thankful to Dr Manoranjan Mallick, convenor of the seminar, who invited me for this paper and waited patiently for its completion of this final script.

1 Where "epistemic" means concerning to knowledge itself and epistemological means concerning to the study or theory of knowledge; epistemic foundation of religion may mean relating to the foundational knowledge as well as knowing in religions or relating to the knowledge-base of the religion.

broader pictures of the knowledge-base of most religions, where only masters have genuine experience and followers have faith in the authority and that for the divine. Sometimes, the followers have some intuitive experiences, but they are hardly accepted on par with that of the masters. The authority and faith are taken as the epistemic basis of those religions. Any discourse on the epistemic foundation is close-ended. This is one of the weaknesses, which is always guarded by the authorities in many religions. The protection is sometimes aided by political high-handedness. In contrast to this, religions in India enjoy an ever-open-ended discourse upon the knowledge-base of religions. They always stand on scrutiny, prone to be contested and tested. The Buddha advised "accept my words by examination only". Not for reverence (*parīkṣamāṇa gr̥hya mad vācaḥ, na tu gauravāya*).[2] How to examine? By experience only. This is the answer of all systems in India. Vedānta says the same by pointing to direct experience (*pratyakṣāvabodha/aparokṣānubhūti*). Yoga, in its broader sense, is the path for everyone to relish the nectar by oneself. Extraordinary experience is a test for the Ultimate Truth for the followers, as it is similar for the masters. Everyone, and not only the masters, can return to or be with their divine essence. Speculation, which is the imaginative reasoning, a creative function of reason is somehow helpful. Scriptural authority, which does not mean to the visible book only, or as a carrier for the followers, but as the eternal knowledge compendium, is the place of origin of divine knowledge (*śāstra-yonitvāt*), and the divine himself is the source. The authority has

---

[2] The Buddha said: "Oh *bhikṣus* and wise men, just as a goldsmith would test his gold by burning, cutting and rubbing it, so you must examine my words and accept them, but not merely out of reverence for me." – Śāntarakṣita's *Tattvasaṁgraha* v. 3587, also in *Jñānasāra-samuccaya* in Narada Thera 1988: 285, also in the *Ghanavyuhasūtra/Gaṇḍavyūhasūtra*.

to be verified by experience in every individual's and follower's consciousness or in one's being. On this backdrop, this discourse attempts to discuss the experience as the strongest epistemic foundation, where *śruti*, not as a disseminator, but as the source of knowledge based upon the experience, is regarded as the representation of the experience and that for transformation of the individuals. In this sense, *śruti* is the compendium of the experience (*anubhava*) along with convincing reasonings and narrations. Blind persuasion of authority, as commonly believed and was also socially evidenced in medieval India are hardly the case in the face of incapability of individuals to experience by themselves. At the end of all, the truth that is experienced is eternal on which all religions in India rest on.

Status of Religions for Epistemic Inquiry

By religions in India, it is generally understood that the existing religions and their origins that happened in the Indian subcontinent (Bhārata) was once extended from the present Myanmar to Afghanistan. Religions in India may broadly be understood "to get along with God or Reality/Truth", which is the eternal source of all. This simplest umbrellaed comprehension of religion in the Indian context may hopefully be adequate (to work within this discourse). Religion in India is based upon certain basic truth and values which are eternal (*śāśvata*) and timeless (*sanātana*). In this sense, the basic religion in India is recognized as Sanātana Dharma. It is more *sanātanika*[3] than the sectarian Eurocentric, post-Eurocentric and Islamic approaches as well as depiction of religions in India.[4] "Getting

---

3 By *sanātanika* it is meant that the truth/value which is already there in and as any form.

4 The Arabs and Islamists did not have any free understanding and from the point of view of their narrow mindset, their Semitic religious brutalities and hate psychology, they did not have →

along with reality" by the basic truth and values also confirms the etymological meaning of religion.[5] In pre-Islamic Bhārata,

← sufficient humane ability to understand the religions in India. The pre-Eurocentric approach has its two branches. One is established from Christian missionary interest, by the establishment of three chairs in Oxford University, where Monier Monier-Williams, Max Müller and Winternitz were given the tasks to respectively working on compiling the dictionary, translating important ancient oriental literature related to philosophy and religion, and investigating the history of literature (which we are going along with other philologist and historians research). Among their contributions, very wisely they established the Aryan Invasion Theory according to the Christian and Colonialist agenda of showing the inferiority of the ruled countries. There were other Indologists, who with their preconception and structures of Semitic regions, coined Hindu religion based on some similar practices and common pantheon and divided the religious community as Hindu, Buddhist, Jaina, Sikh, undermining the one undercurrent among all of them. The divide and rule agenda of the English people were in its way. The leftist approach is too mundane and materialistic, which was never capable to understand religions in India, and Damodar Das Kosambi's work only expressed the leftist narrowness and mandate in understanding religions in India. Today also anybody will see the books published by Progressive Publishers in Old Russia, one may find the leftist mandate inserted very openly on almost every page. The Nehruvian intellectuals furnished some intermixture of anti-leftist, socialist and democratic approaches, and find themselves comfortable in the Eurocentric depictions, which may be labelled here as the post-Eurocentric approach. This started a "let us go" approach without any dignity and adopted an opportunist mask of secularism, ultimately depicting the culture and religions in India to be rotten by themselves. Against all these, scholars like S. Radhakrishnan, his followers and students, Ganganath Jha, P.V. Kane and other Sanskritists and Oriental scholars attempted for some authentic establishment of religions of India, which we may say *sanātanika.*

5 "Religion" from Latin *re* (back) + *ligare* (bind together). Religion binds back together with the divine source.

all *sampradāyas* excluding no one, started by different *gurus* and their successor, and subsects therein, treat *dharma* in the same manner and, therefore, they are one from the point of view of Sanātana Dharma. This was helpful to see the unity of religions at least by conceptions and all religions including the tribal religions bore the unity among themselves, until the foreigners employed their divide and rule policy, and depict the *sampradāyas* as different from each other on their points of differences, with undermining their points of similarity or unity.

While initiating any epistemic inquiry, it is important to see which religions are based upon sound epistemic basis. Semitic religions, which have had political upper hand, often failed to common sense, reason and scientific inquiry. For this reason, they saved themselves in the safe custody of faith. Of course, subjective, mystical and experiential factors visible in the teachers and in some ardent followers, kept on those religion safe for truth. However, they lack sound open-ended philosophy and, therefore, fails to uncompromising rational inquiry. Love for wisdom was disentangled from theology, except the scholastic attempt where reasons were given in asserting the matters of faith. Science, which went by reason and experiments, and was communicable and testable for proof or disproof, was not allowed to take up matters of religion, which went on only by faith. Any alternative and progress were hindered in the name as well as fear of blasphemy. This is the fate and factors in Christianity, Islam and some minor religions in West and other parts of world, where civilizations were not so developed to test the faiths. Similar paths were also developed in India. In reaction to this, a new movement, similar to Theosophical Society, Brahmo Samaj, Arya Samaj, etc. were developed in India to rationalize the matters of divine and to establish it on the pedestal of experiences and truth. This was the situation in

India before as well, when prominent Indian religions kept up the demands of philosophy and science for the truth, which is also visible now prominently in Upaniṣadic themes, Buddhism and systems that adopt some or other forms of Yogic method for divine experiences. In this backdrop, it is important to say that the early Western scholars could not find the contents of faith, reason, and experiences exclusive to each other in the Sanātana Dharma. that is to say, the matters of philosophy, science and religion are not exclusively and distinctively established in religions in India as it was in the West at that time. They could not also track down the notions of monism, monotheism or pantheism, or polytheism in their exclusivity, as they categorized in Western religions. Therefore, they mistook religions in India as an amalgamation, and stated it with their initial confusions or with agenda, though some handful of Western thinkers have already paid their tribute to Western philosophy and religions by that time (Barua 2017). The misconceptions went on to such an extent that thinkers sometimes ascribed that India "does not have any philosophy, but only religion" (Stewart 2016). In opposition to the ascriptions of Western thinkers, some of the contemporary Indian thinkers have proceeded to establish the contents of religion and philosophy separately. Prominently, S. Radhakrishnan, S.N. Dasgupta and their followers took up the agenda to write on the philosophy in the terms of Western thinkers, so that it can be understood to them. They tried to keep the critical and rational assumptions and arguments, and similarly the ethical parts separated from practices, stories, anecdotes, etc., so that the Westerners could recognize the philosophical contents as they are habituated in their own systems. However, there are many aspects in Indian philosophical contentions that could not be established within the conceptual framework of the then prominent Western thinkers. This awoke the second line of authors among whom some, like D.P. Chattopadhyaya (senior), tried to quarantine some aspects of Indian philosophy and revive some other reason-confirmed aspects, keeping religious connections or references at bay. He denounced the spiritual and religious contents to some extent (Chattopadhyaya 1976), whereas some others like S.C. Chatterjee and T.R.V. Murti attempted to strike a balance between philosophical and religious assumptions on some of their writings. Some oriental scholars, who experimented the religious practices to some extent, tried to keep and rationalize the mystic and transrational aspects with special attention. The astonishing fact that came to the fore was that religions in India were established upon certain sound philosophical foundations, and not on faiths or somebody's preaching as in the Semitic religions. Religion is the translation of philosophy in the form of practical living. This was the reason for Westerners to confuse philosophy with religion and their inability to differentiate them. It was astounding for them, the ordinary way of living, the entire life some people, and the society, were accorded by the principles of philosophy and towards divine longing in India. It was based upon an understanding as well as assumption that "all is divine or is created by the divine, who/which is the beginning and end of all". This made a religious life in India from time immemorial.

Foundations of Religion

Among the two most important foundations of religion, one is metaphysics combined with soteriology and the other is epistemology. Metaphysics provided the basis as well as the core of the religions in the forms or conceptions of truth/ reality. It describes the nature of reality in itself and its manifestation or modification or creation in the forms of the universe and everything in the universe. The reality is viewed in its substantive as well as in its active or regulative aspects.

The Veda says about *satyam* and *ṛtam*, which respectively stand for the substantive and regulative/active aspects of the reality. Some philosophers in ancient India highlighted on the substantive aspects like in the Vedic systems, whereas, some others, such as the Buddhists, focused upon the regulative aspects (which later on understood as "process philosophy" by the Westerners).[6] There are hard issues on the way of completely comprehending and explaining these two modes of metaphysics because of limited human capacity. For this situation, the issues are somehow fixed in some manners to comprehend the reality as it is. For this reason, Indian religious systems rely on some extraordinary power to realize or comprehend the reality or at least to comprehend its uncomprehensibility.

Comprehension is taken care of by the branch of knowledge called epistemology, the other foundation of metaphysics and religions. It opens access to the truth, and as per the access, the validity and extent of the religion are determined. As fine is epistemic exerts, so great and authentic is the comprehension, and so is the reality realized. In many respects, it is appropriate in the sense that we picture the reality as per our inquiry. The method is important for matters of investigation. For this reason, an appropriate epistemology and its validity always remain a matter of concern.

Upon these two foundations of religion, metaphysics and epistemology, as mentioned above, there develops an intermediary superstructure of morals. Morality is like a flow of smoke, water, fire or energy. It is in the sense that, it is something, but the determination of it in most of the times remains dynamic like water, smoke, fire and energy. This

6 Process philosophy as it is understood for keeping the process, not substance, in the centre of philosophy, perhaps dates back to Heraclitus, and last elaborated by A.N. Whitehead.

nature of morality, of course, baffles the human mind and, for this reason, debates about the nature of morality touch the sky. Morality develops upon the dynamic aspects of reality which is also the source expressed as causality, transformation, creation – all outside and inside the man (i.e. his propensities). Epistemology helps to know some aspect of metaphysics and when accepting them, man decides for himself what should be done, and from this inquiry he develops the sense of morality. Morality becomes another foundation of the religions in India.

When established upon some specific aspects of metaphysics, morality turns into intense spirituality. It is in this sense that the reality, viewed as the spirit, is somehow different and somehow similar in different systems as an individual or universal or both or specific ones. Recognition of the spiritual is the contribution of metaphysics. This understating makes up knowledge, which further exerts man to choose and do for betterment. It prompts the effort, which again converts into action, and many actions with certain motives make up life. The successive causal chain of *jñāna-icchā-yatna-kṛti* makes up life, of course, if motives are running through the causal chain. From this point of view, metaphysics of spirit remains at the initial stage of *jñāna*, then ultimately the *kṛti* (action) will always be invested in getting along with the spirit, if there are no faults (*vyabhicāras*). This way of life becomes spiritual in the effort of living in accordance with the awareness of the spirit, the truth/reality, and tending towards it. Knowing the reality and then living by it makes a spiritual living. This spiritual living is one of the core aspects of the religions. Hence, spirituality is another foundation of religion. Often, when the objective and universal spiritual essence of any or all religions are referred to, spirituality is preferably used as a synonym for religions. In this sense, religions in India are better expressed as spirituality.

Epistemic Foundation of Religions in India

Among all the foundations as mentioned above, the epistemic foundation is crucial. It is in this sense that knowledge is the door to reality/truth. Knowledge indeed is one of the components of the reality/truth for which the power of knowing is already bestowed in the person and its manifestation is the inherent property of the truth. So, reality/truth is primary. This being so, knowing the reality/truth, i.e. epistemology, is also primary from the point of view of the knower, just in the similar way as metaphysics is primary from the point of view of the known. Similarly, morality and spirituality, which are also most important than epistemology in the sense that they can make the person perfect, who even does not have any knowledge of epistemology. Still, for the matters of knowledge, epistemology is before all, since it sharpens its instruments and process data and thereby becoming door to other branches of knowledge and practice. Thus, there is the importance of epistemology in religion or epistemic foundation of religions. The religion becomes great and perfect where its epistemic foundation is perfect.

Epistemic Status of Śruti and Anubhūti with Perspectives

Epistemic foundation can be viewed from subjective and objective perspectives. From the subjective point of view, for any person, the medium or the disseminator (in the form of preceptor or scripture) is the first foundation of any spiritual or religious knowledge. For this reason, scripture is considered as the origin of divine knowledge (*śāstra-yonitvāt*) – *Brahmasūtra* 1.1.3. The first exposure of the person happens to her/his parents and teachers, who are revered as the *gurus*. Some thinkers, through their writings, speeches, preaching and actions, also become the disseminators of knowledge. Such persons, who are qualified with great virtues, knowledge and powers, are also called *āpta puruṣas* (authoritative persons). All of them are understood as the first source of religious knowledge from the subjective point of view, simply because they serve as the first door to knowledge. All these authorities, viz. *śāstras*, *āpta puruṣas* and *gurus* as well as other disseminators, are regarded as indirect sources of knowledge from the subjective point of view.

It may be questioned, "what is the source of knowledge for the disseminators at all?" That is to say, "wherefrom the *Śāstras*, *āpta pūruṣas* and *gurus* get the knowledge?". The answer is, all religious (and similarly all) knowledge is either discovered or created or both, and somehow modified by creativity by certain or superhuman or human being at any point in time.

a. For those, who accept the discovery, religious knowledge is eternal (*śāśvata/sanātana*) and itself is part and parcel of the reality or godhead. Human beings are only its discoverer and carrier by their experience and efforts, and then become disseminator by their teaching, preaching or writings, which is recognized as *śruti*. A human being is the local locus of religious knowledge, whereas the source is the divine itself.

b. Those who accept the creation/invention of religious knowledge, considers superhuman or human being as both the first source as well as the locus of religious knowledge. In this case, the human being, and therein through his experience, intuition or understating, his being or his consciousness becomes the first fountain of knowledge. In this sense, consciousness in its certain level is the first *gomukha* of religious knowledge. Anybody can go to that level of consciousness or mind to discover or invent or create religious knowledge as happened to in the past. In this context, the knowledge itself, or the divine or the consciousness or the person or his experience is the first source of religious knowledge. This is the objective point of view of the epistemic foundation of religion.

Thus, it is clear that from an objective point of view, the divine or its reflection in subjective consciousness or conscious experience is the first foundation of religious knowledge, whereas from the subjective point of view, *śruti* (scripture) or any representative of authority, is the first foundation of religious knowledge. However, where *śruti* refers to the revealed knowledge and that knowledge is accomplished by extraordinary experience, the experience is the same as *śruti*, in the sense that *ṛṣi*s as *āpta puruṣa*s experienced the *śruti*. Thus, the consciousness of the experiencer or the divine is the ultimate source of knowledge. This is the objective viewpoint. Herein the subjective differences between expressions of the truth by different persons are natural due to time, place, the level of experience, the experiencer, mode of disseminations and the audiences. Thus, as *śruti* is nothing but a compilation of the *anubhūti*s (experiences) of truth/reality, as stated above, they are only different forms of the same content (the experience is rationalized).

Status of Śruti and Śāstra as Epistemic Foundations of Religions in India

Apart from *śruti*, *śāstra*, i.e. *smṛtiśāstraḥ* or *dharmaśāstraḥ*, is also considered as the scriptural epistemic foundation of religious knowledge. While *śruti* is just listening to the reality as it is revealed to the experienced person, expressing the same and remembering without anything added, modified or lost, *śāstra* is the conceptualization, creation and compilation of the knowledge of reality, where the roles of mind, subjectivity and intentionality contribute to or modify the truth as to be practically adopted. In such amalgamation and interference, mind sometimes is able to keep the *śruti* as it is, and sometimes differs from some aspects of *śruti* and sometimes augments or distorts the truth in it. *Śāstra* or *smṛti* keeps the practical point of view as to be suitable in guiding the fellows, and in this sense, is somehow pragmatic and contextual in being relevant to a specific time, space and for the definite people. Whereas, *śruti* springs forth universal and eternal knowledge as it is. *Śruti* is objective and descriptive. *Smṛti* is subjective and mostly prescriptive in religion. In this sense, as religion is concerned to some people and for certain time and space, it is more governed by *smṛtiśāstra* than *śruti*. As *Śāstra*s predominated over *śruti* in matters of religion, it takes on the interpretation, which takes on the form of hermeneutical mode of exposition or a type of activity, akin to scholasticism,[7] due to certain agenda. If scholasticism comes into force in interpretation, reason could never remain free and impartial than serving the agenda of the interpreter. This has given rise to different tumultuous effects in the religious sphere in India as the following.

Interpretation of Vedic *mantra*s started in a hermeneutic way. The Veda declared that all beings, higher and lower, depend on each other and by *yajña* man could fulfil the relationship with the others. Then the scholastic attempts in the Indian religions were started in Brāhmanic systems by rationalizing their agenda with quoting and favourably interpreting the *śruti* and *smṛti*. They allowed predominance of *karma-kāṇḍa* and thereby fulfilment of desires of living and non-living entities. Initially, the *karma-kāṇḍa* was supposed to give rise to mystic power, called *dharma*, which were examined by the fruitful ways as in the Purāṇas: for example, *yajña*, *dāna* and *tapasyā* have their fruits/results as described in the *Rāmāyaṇa* and *Mahābhārata*. Imitation to that the brāhmaṇas of the later period

---

7 Scholasticism is a medieval approach to use different methods of arguments to establish something. The people use this approach to advance arguments even to establish anything they want.

were claiming the similar power of *yajña* and all rituals, but unlike the descriptions in Purāṇas, most of the *yajña*s and *karma-kāṇda*s were visibly futile. For this reason, the interpretations were made describing the results as unseen (*adṛṣṭa*). Most of the benefits are explained for the dead and afterlife spiritual as well as material gains, which could not be verified in all cases. While all promises for spiritual benefits for the common people were described to be met in afterlife, the brāhmaṇas used to have their material benefits in this life. The brāhmaṇas as performing *purohita*s were lacking any Yogic or spiritual power as the *ṛṣi*s in ancient period possessed, as described. Along with this, some of the Vedic lines were conveniently interpreted to build on a rigid caste system and its byproduct, the untouchability, was inconveniencing ordinary life. When it becomes too much with keeping unquestionable faith in the scriptures, intended interpretations, neglecting the authentic religious experiences, the religious exploitation touched the sky. In opposition to this interpretation and practice, arose Jainism and Buddhism under *śramaṇa*s, which disqualified the authority of such interpretations and their supporting scriptures. This was one of the main reasons, for which the brāhmaṇa interpretations and their *karma-kāṇḍa* of the Vedic system were criticized by both the *śramaṇa sampradāya*s. They discard the Vedic belief structures and against them emphasize upon free reason and self-realization or experience. However, as time goes by, Buddhism and Jainism of Śramaṇism also gradually slipped into the same track of unquestionable scriptural prescriptions and rigid rituals, as Brāhmanism once did. Buddhism also developed Tantra forms of practices putting the social codes into much confusion. A dark period loomed over the religious firmament of India, allowing confusion, blind worships and unsocial practices to a large extent in different parts. Then came different *guru*s to steer clear the matters of religion based upon reason and experiences, which gradually gave rise to new *sampradāyas* and religions. Once again, some restorations were attempted on the strength of reason and experience, where *śruti* and *śāstra* were taken cautiously or remained as distant references.

In modern times, *śruti* and *smṛti* are looked upon with great reverence where it expresses the truth and lead to great heights of human destiny without any blind follow up. It is never acceptable, where it denounces human values and speaks satanic or prescribes rituals. This is due to the self-awareness, right discrimination and utility of the *śruti* and *smṛti*. Providing solace to the ordinary people, who were deprived of *śruti* and *smṛti*, the literary compositions of the Bhakti movements, by poets and *santa*s, were regarded highly. The *Grantha Sāheb* of Sikhs is the glowing example of representing the teacher. As the *Gītā*, so also the *Dhammapada*, were taken with adoration, but not as unquestionable authority as the Koran and the Bible were taken in other religions. The uncontestable status of the scriptural authority lost its constricting power, but preserves its guiding status where it satisfies reason and experience. No one is forced to take up the scriptures in a definite prescriptive way, but it is helpful to her/him or to large extent. Scriptures are liberating windows than binding shackles now in the Indian religions, which by allowing reverential critiques, make themselves refined and usable from time to time. They preserve their epistemic value, when lost too much of authoritarianism.

Reason in Religions in India

Reason (*buddhi*) in forms of rationality and its activity in argumentation have both positive and negative epistemic roles in religions in India. Spiritual thinkers always find the reason as somehow helpful and somehow hindering spiritual progress. As a major mental function, reason is directly concerned with the four of five propensities (*vṛttis*) like *pramāṇa, viparyaya, vikalpa* and *smṛti*, according to the *Yogasūtra*.[8] These *vṛttis* are responsible for worldly life. When these are conquered by systematic Yogic ways, reason will stop its normal working by transforming into intuition and then to pure awareness. It is because as *vṛttitva* is lost gradually, it becomes pure consciousness, as one ascends to the higher level of consciousness. The person gets established in his original state; Yoga describes it as *samādhi*. In Buddhism, this state is a perfect awakening (*sambuddha*). Reason in this way is the key for achieving higher levels of consciousness, as described in the theory of *cakra* in Tantra or in the context of successive higher levels of mind as described in the journey from "mind" to "super-mind" by Sri Aurobindo. At certain higher levels, the mind becomes free from the propensities and becomes universal and extended in time and space. The mind ceases to be ordinary, and in that state, reality can be revealed. Thus, the reason is the fundamental mental faculty to initiate and help in primary stages, but in some sense inhibits and, in some other contexts, accelerates the final goal in spiritual realization, which is fundamental in Indian religions.

Reason is most important in religious life for its two primary functions. One is a conceptual as well as a logical function, and the other is a normative or a moral discriminatory function. The first one may be recognized as *mati*,[9] employed with the conceptuality. The second may be recognized as *viveka* (moral conscience), an action-oriented discriminatory function of reason. *Mati* functions for factual truth, factual rights and wrongs, whereas *viveka* functions in the context of moral justifications as well as discrimination of right and wrong. The reason is the rational play of mind with positive and negative

---

8 *vṛttayaḥ pañcatayyaḥ kliṣṭākliṣṭāḥ* । - 1.5
pramāṇa-viparyaya-vikalpa-nidrā-smṛtayaḥ । - 1.6

9 The use of *mati* in this article is taken from the Jaina use of the word, where all mental knowledge is covered.

attitude, or with or without intentions. The reason as *mati* helps in the phenomenal and metaphysical issues to discover as well as establish the truth/reality and matters of fact. In the case of religion, when it is abandoned or sacrificed for the sake of faiths, religion goes astray and adopts blind beliefs and faiths. When it is adopted in its proper purview, it leads to the truth as in the Upaniṣadic teachings. It is the rational analysis in the *Śvetāśvatara Upaniṣad*, that convinces one *sarvaṁ khalvidaṁ brahma*, by analysis of pervasion of salt in water. Argumentation, questions and explanations, which are due to reason, are the ways of deliberation starting from the times of Upaniṣads till the age of Purāṇas. All genuine great *guru*s encouraged the arguments and questions as in the Upaniṣadic story of Indra–Virocana and Haṁsa–Sanatkumāra, and some true *santa*s and *guru*s appreciate the questions and arguments, whereas only some of the medieval and modern *guru*s discourage the trend of questions and arguments to hide their insufficiency.

It is true that for the highest truth, reason becomes insufficient and as *vṛtti* is to be abandoned. Ordinary functions of reason or mind is said not to be applied there (*naiṣā tarkeṇa matirāpaneya*), because the reality is beyond its purview (*atarkyaṁ*). Except for the highest level of truth, reason as *mati* is said to be the main instrument in religious matters. It makes the religions cultured and progressive. This golden path of rationality when was abandoned or is shrouded by the dusts of any ism or agenda, the dark age of religions started in India. Argumentative Indians gradually became imitative-authoritative Indians in religious affairs. This made faith-based religious life with a wrong quoting of the adage that God is achievable by faith and is far away to reach by reason (*viśvāse milai hari tarke vahu dūre*). From another point of view, from the modern negative perspectives, people also use reason to denounce religion. The modern scholars, who had only the exposures of Christianity, made reason a dreaded alternative to religion, so much so that, when science developed, it represented reason, and options were given to choose either reason or religion, depicting them mutually explicit or as antagonistic alternatives. However, this was not the state of Indian religions in Upaniṣadic ages and, many times much after that, when free reason for conviction was appreciated. This was because, reason was one of the epistemic bases of religions in India.

The reason as *viveka* in the specific sense of moral conscience is much more important for religions. It may be questioned "how has moral conscience any epistemic value?". True, it may not have any direct epistemic value, but it certifies the truth knowledge and makes important conjunction in epistemic matters. For example, just after his awakening, the Buddha could visualize his accomplishments and the state of multitudes of mortals. Then he felt *anukampā* for the hapless state of the others and resolved to distribute the nectar of knowledge to all. Here, his visualization or realization of truth is an epistemic factor. This promotes the heartfelt function of *anukampā* for others. This promotion certifies the height and completeness or perfection of his awakening. If one is perfect in knowledge, moral perfection will also be its automatic outcome. This perfection is insight and it is lacking in most of the modern-day's professors, who boast for knowledge. It is lacking in people for which animal sacrifices and damages to nature and environment happen as an everyday phenomenon. Knowledge and emotion may not be logically connected, but very much causally connected. This causal connection and play of moral conscience are at the root of religions in India. Vivekananda's Neo-Vedānta, Rammohun Roy's Brahmo Samaj, Keshua Chandra Sen's Prarthana Samaj and most of the *santa paramparā* carry this moral insight, making religions in India humanist and progressive.

Role of Emotion as an Aid to Epistemic Foundations in Indian Religions

Emotion has tremendous contribution to epistemic affairs of religions in India, nay the world. To say that emotion has epistemic contribution may attract criticism. But it is unlikely true in the sense that wrong and excess uncontrolled emotion adversely affects the right view. Conversely, right and controlled emotions augment the right view. Further, as per Kant, sensibility is the first processing window of stuff of knowledge, which is further processed by the categories of mind. The processing sometimes is affected by emotions. The sensibilities are also affected by emotions. All animals sense mostly by feelings, and emotions apart from sense faculties. All human beings recognize their mothers, first by sensibilities and feelings, and then by emotions. Favourable emotion leads to better understanding and greater realizations. Blind emotion is indeed hazardous, but emotion with awareness and actions contributes to most of the accomplishments. Particularly, for the religious matters, feelings and emotions are expressed in many forms, which is deliberated by Abhinavagupta as a means to realize the divine. For him and some followers of Tantra, some types of feelings and emotions are the sure ways of *siddhis*. *Bhakti*, in its nine forms, is essential to realize the divine.[10] The *Yogavāsiṣṭha*, *Nārada Bhaktisūtra* and *Śrīmad Bhāgavatam* establish *bhakti* as the essential way to realize the divine as well as the knowledge of the divine. Some knowledge of God is indeed essential which kickstart *bhakti*, but the intensity of *bhakti* then leads to realization, which is the completion of knowledge. Śrī Caitanya Mahāprabhu might be a learned person, Mīrabāī was not so learned, but *bhakti* of both

---

10 Nine forms of *bhakti:*

śravaṇaṁ kīrtanaṁ viṣṇoḥ smaraṇaṁ pādasevanam ।
arcanaṁ vandanaṁ dāsyaṁ sakhyam ātmanivedanam ॥
– *The Śrīmad Bhāgavata Mahāpurāṇa* VII.5.23

of them lead to their God-realization by self-sacrifices. Hence, divine emotion with knowledge is highest epistemic basis of religions in India.

Concluding Remarks

The aforesaid discussion describes some important aspects of epistemic foundation of religions in India. Among them, the *śruti* gives objective knowledge of truth, whereas *smṛti* provides the subjective prescriptions upon the objective knowledge. Blind follow up of them or outright rejection of them is never appreciated. Interpretation in hermeneutic way is appreciated, but that in scholastic manners remained obliterated by time. *Śruti* as scripture is one of the representative modes of experienced truth, and in certain cases, particularly when the Vedic *ṛṣi*s listened or saw the Vedic *mantra*s or realized the truth/reality, all of them are actually some sorts of experiences. Therefore, *śruti* is the same as the truth and experiences of the truth. In this sense *śruti* and truth is the same and one experiences the same in an empirically *samavāya* relation. Hence, experience, as ordinary, Yogic and *bhakti*, is the fundamental epistemic foundation of religions in India. Reason and emotion have their both advancing and adverse roles for the religions. Perfect attenuation of emotion and conscience-guided reason lead to befitting religious life, thus making them another foundation. Morality is the test as well as a mark of religious perfection, as it testifies the spiritual heights, for example, *catur brahmavihāra*s and *ṣaṭ-pāramitās*[11] in Buddhism, forbearance (*sahanaśīlatā*) and pardon (*kṣamā*) of Vasiṣṭha.

Post-Script: The next write-up in this sequel will elaborate the stuffs of epistemic foundations in descriptive way of all major religions.

---

11 *catur brahmaviharas,* such as *maitrī/mettā, karuṇā, muditā, upekṣā/upekkhā* and *sat paramitās,* such as *dāna, sīla, kṣānti, vīrya, dhyāna, prajñā.*

References

Barua, Arati (ed.), 2017, *Schopenhauer on Self, World and Morality: Vedantic and Non-Vedantic Perspectives*, Springer; 1st edn.

Chattopadhyaya, Debiprasad, 1976, *What Is Living and What Is Dead in Indian Philosophy*, New Delhi: People's Publishing House.

Narada Thera, 1988, *The Buddha and His Teachings*, 4th edn, Kuala Lumpur: Buddhist Missionary Society.

Stewart, Jon, 2016, "Hegel's Criticism of Hinduism", *Hegel Bulletin*, 37(2): 281-304.

13

Can Religious Tradition Overcome the Crisis of Climate Change?

Jhadeswar Ghosh

The Crisis of Climate Change and Religious Tradition

CLIMATE change is the major environmental problem of our time.[1] A most effective and fast characteristic of climate change is its potential to basically affect every corner of the planet. The increasing frequency and intensity of extreme weather events (including heatwaves, droughts, bush fires, tropical and extratropical cyclones, tornadoes, hailstorms, floods and storm surges) and the historically unprecedented economic losses have intensified the ongoing international debate about the possible adverse impact of climate change on global weather patterns. The position is clear, if we imagine someone living in 1923 or 1823 predicting what life would be like today. Climate refers to the "average" weather occurring within a given geographic location over a long period of time. More specifically, climate

---

[1] I have done some research on a related topic of climate change and disaster management: philosophical approaches. Please see Ghosh 2017, 2020.

refers to all the elements that cause changes in the atmosphere, such as solar radiation, humidity, cloud cover, and wind and ocean currents. Weather implies the conditions of temperature, humidity, precipitation, atmospheric pressure and wind on a day-to-day basis. By the research of climatologists, geologists, oceanographers and other scientists, it is realized that the earth's climate is changing due to human activity. The climate change issue is, at its heart, an ethical problem. Burning fossil fuels, releasing methane into the atmosphere and destroying the rainforest threaten us with an unprecedented fast global warming. This climate change will alter the living conditions for the entire planet and lead to what Bill McKibben (1989) calls the "end of nature". Here McKibben shows us in a convincing way that the world is out of control. By the end of nature, he says that it is not the end of the world. This is a certain set of human ideas about the world. But the death of those ideas begins with concrete changes in the reality around us – changes that scientists can measure and enumerate. More and more frequently, those changes will clash with our perceptions, until, finally, our sense of nature as eternal and separate is washed away, and we will see all too clearly what we have done. That is, an earth in which *everything* bears the stamp of human acts, because *everything* is affected by the human altered climate. Global warming will cause unforeseen damage to agriculture, wild lands and animals; and the rise of the oceans from melting polar ice caps will submerge coastlines and threaten the lives of island people. We are running towards dangerous climate change so rapidly. To study the ethics of climate change, we need to understand how climate change will affect people around the world, now and in the future. Many groups have actively involved with global climate agencies and civil society organizations on anthropogenic climate change. We rely on the Intergovernmental Panel on Climate Change (IPCC), an international agency that was set up to report the scientific understanding on climate-related issues in periodic reports. While there is an agreement that climate change is occurring and that it is caused by humans, it is extremely difficult to predict the impact of carbon emissions on people living 100 or 200 years in the future. As an intergovernmental body jointly established in 1988 by the World Meteorological Organization (WMO) and the United Nations Environment Programme (UNEP), the IPCC has provided policymakers with the most authoritative and objective scientific and technical assessments in this field. Beginning in 1990, this series of IPCC Assessment Reports, Special Reports, Technical Papers, Methodology Reports and other products have become standard works of reference. In the 1980s scientists noticed that the earth's climate was changing. The IPCC quickly gained credibility by offering cautious conclusions concerning climate change that were grounded in rigorous scientific studies.[2] It is clear that the global environmental tragedy is most centrally an ethical failure, and one that implicates our institutions, our moral and political theories, and ultimately ourselves, considered as moral agents.

Travelling from environmental crisis in general to climate change in particular, there is much to show about how religious beliefs, institutions and practices around the world pursue the idea of climate change. The recent climate change is predominantly caused by human activities from an apprehension of the research of science and technology. Merely seeing climate science, or discussing it from the standpoint of technology, is obviously inadequate. All these human-made environmental issues cannot be resolved through technology. To accomplish

---

[2] Weart (2003) rightly pointed out the views of climate scientists that the world was warming at a rate without precedent during at least the last ten millennia, and that warming was caused by the increase of greenhouse gases from human action.

a sustainable society, we need the differentiated skills of many people. Thus, we can claim that religion has a part to play and can influence our responses to climate change. Among social institutions, religions are often assumed to be one of the most significant approaches for values, motivations, morals and world views. Religion is multifariously depicted as a symbolic system, a social institution, a relationship with the divine or a moral code. Religion is often exhibited as determinative of values, it also admits world views, institutions, integrative practices and meaning-making procedures. Religion has ongoing implications at individual, national and global levels, and dealing ethical roles and determining the normative responses to the problem of climate crisis. Religious traditions also have an effect in the public arena outside their impact on individual followers' views and activities. Religions have the potential to provide connectivity and be able to engage a broad audience, many of whom accept and respect their moral authority and leadership. Each of these characteristics could be applied to the issue of climate change. Nowadays, the world's most religious traditions have developed more and more concerned with environmental and climate crisis matters and an extensive research literature is formulating on religion and nature.[3] There is much to present about how religious beliefs, institutions and practices throughout the world engage with the idea of the crisis of climate change and its consequence, thereby extending rich research programmes with which religious scholars can help to develop a healthy environment. The religious tradition and its moral philosophy prioritize working on a swift resolution to the theory–action gap, viz. the gap between adopted moral values

[3] In the twentieth century, the environmental problems increased rapidly, it can be visualized by the religious assigning environmental responsible behaviour. In this connection see the exposition of Chapple 2011.

and the actions that reflect such values. We must, therefore, consider the effects of our collective inactiveness on this major global challenge and take action to avoid having further damage.

Among the religious traditions, Buddhism has a hope for an environmental ethic, because it develops an interest for the other animals and nature as well as human beings. In Buddhist religious literature, we find many texts that address moral issues for the development of a calmer, more incorporated and compassionate personality. The guide for this process of transformation has been the *Dhamma*. If we look at Indian and Tibetan literature, Buddhist ethics seems to be *śīla* (moral discipline), something that is the subject of monastic Vinaya codes, Abhidhamma scholastic, *bodhisattva* literature, Jātaka tales and narrative Avadāna literature, some Mādhyamika treatises, even Tāntric texts and so on. Humanity is often described as presented with the crisis of climate change, which suggests a large trouble from which we find a quick resolution, lest we die. The teaching of the Buddha and its philosophy was a way of life which emerged in India in the sixth century BCE (over a gulf of more than 2,500 years). While the development of the field of "climate ethics" is a relatively recent phenomenon, and there were no such specific studies in the time of the Buddha, we see today. But the relationship between humans and the natural world was given a rigorous analysis in the Buddhist tradition.[4]

Religious World View and the Status of Nature

Human beings have lived on the earth for hundreds of thousands of years with their natural environment. The climate of earth was natural, it means that it is not affected by the activities of early human beings. In the last 200 years, however, this natural co-

[4] For a full discussion of the contemporary environmental crisis and Buddhist perspectives for environmental education, see De Silva 1998.

existence has rapidly changed due to the widespread application of science and technology. New agricultural techniques have greatly increased the productivity of the land and enabled the population to rise rapidly. The Industrial Revolution greatly increased the living standards in many countries, but at the same time it has polluted the earth to an unprecedented degree. This pollution is changing the face of the earth and its climate at an unforeseeable rate. Thus, to keep a clean, healthy, safe, secure, beautiful environment and want to hand it over to our children, grandchildren and great grandchildren, it is most essential to realize the value of the environment and understand the healthy balance of the ecosystem.

Human beings have a relationship with nature, it is very close and intimate, which involves food, living space, recreation, spiritual connectedness, climatic conditions, clean air, water, etc. Thus, they feel nature was God's creation and ultimately God's property, not our own. God is creator, nature is creation, they are logically and ontologically different. Divinity is part of nature, just as nature is part of divinity. Nature is both creative and created, and the logico-ontological difference between creator and creation plays out along a continuum of self-organizing forces on the one end and receptive matter on the other. The rightful place of humans is within nature and the right thing to do is to live in harmony with the natural environment. Nature, after all, is sacred and thus deserving of respect and care. Climate change will alter the relationship between man and nature everywhere on the planet. There is a great deal of talk about nature and its endeavour to protect nature in the age of the crisis of climate change. In 1992, the United Nations Conference on Environment and Development (UNCED) was convened in Rio de Janeiro, Brazil. A significant outcome was the development of the "Rio Declaration on Environment and Development", the first principle of which is:

> Human beings are at the centre of concerns for sustainable development. They are entitled to a healthy and productive life in harmony with nature.

The declaration emphasizes the importance of environmental sustainability to human well-being, as well as the obligation to consider the welfare of future generations.

The philosophical traditions like pre-Socratic philosophers are called "Investigators of Nature". The generic propensity of pre-Socratic philosophy is that it searches to find a principle of the derivation of nature. The pre-Socratic philosophers disapproved of classical mythological statements for the processes they assured around them in promoting rational thinking. They came out to involve questions like where did everything come from, and why is there such variety, and how can nature be described scientifically? They tried to see the universal principles to explain the whole of nature. Nature is an arranged physical system regulated by law. It is invariably rearranging, changing and renewing itself in a fitted mode. Natural element is the basic element according to the pre-Socratic philosophers. Thales is the first one who claimed the question regarding the interpretation of nature. He evoked that the fundamental reality which is ever changing but still renewing itself is "water". This is the ground of all things. All comes from water and all returns to water. Anaximander was known as the younger contemporary of Thales. He too had the idea that all that exists is corporeal. It is not any definite substance such as earth, air, fire or water. It is the compound of all contrary elements. It is neutral in the cosmic strife which exists between the elements, i.e. earth, air, fire and water. All things originate from it and return to it. But he did not approve of any "one" or the other element as the basis of the world. From this thinking he came to the conclusion:

> Prior to all perceptible bodies there must be an indefinite

> something with none of the incompatible qualities implied by perceptibility.[5]

Anaximenes is the last thinker belonging to the Milesian school. He suggests that the fundamental, boundless and self-changing substance in nature is air. All things are constituted from air through the operation of activity (water, earth and stone) and concentration (fire).

> This (theory) was condensation and rarefaction, the former of which he associated with cold and the latter with heat. Air as it rarely becomes fire; condensed, it turns first to wind, then to cloud, water, earth, and stones.[6]

The earth itself was formed through condensation, together with air. Air is the principle of life. Life is a warm breath. The fact of the air surrounding the whole world and of the breath being the condition of life seem to have led him to this hypothesis. The whole cosmos is integrated by the air that surrounds it. Pythagoras is the most famous name in the history of philosophy before Socrates and Plato. According to Pythagoras, not only the animate beings in our sense but also the cosmos itself is a living creature. He was the first one to use *cosmos* meaning "order". It is an order of unity where man is a part. He says that all things are numbers. All things are made of numbers, points, lines and surfaces. These numbers give the measure of each thing. Numbers can account for the wide range of different natures of different things. The order and harmony of the universe is explainable in terms of numbers. Numbers constitute the essences of things. Number is the key to nature.

With Plato's world, which is known as Plato's cosmological concept, the idea of a philosophical as well as a scientific

5 I have followed the exposition of Guthrie 1978: 305.

6 For a complete explanation, see Guthrie 1962: 89; Stace 1960; Burnet 1924.

cosmology comes into being. Here, in Plato's dialogue *Timaeus*, a powerful craftsman creates the world according to a perfect model, viz. the "cosmos" of the Platonic ideas. Like a perfect living being, the cosmos turns out to be an animated rational being, as a visible God in the form of a perfect sphere. Its soul, the "world soul", has an astronomical nature: it is formed by the mathematical order of the trajectories of the planets. At the same time the planets function as "tools of time"; time, arising with the heavens, is an image of eternity. The planets are visible and created gods,[7] the earth is the most venerable Goddess in the heavens. Man in the cosmos, which consists of purely Godlike entities and is itself a living God, is compared with a plant, which roots "not in the earth but in the heavens"; he connects the earth with the heavens related to him. Later on, in Christian thought, i.e. in Christian Platonism, the world of Platonic ideas to which the craftsman refers as a perfect model, becomes the realm of thoughts of God creating the world. Unlike a *Plato world*, which, apart from the mythical language in which it is presented, is governed by mathematical (geometrical) and astronomical laws, Aristotle's world is a world of natural things that consist of matter and form and have within themselves a source of motion. Motions caused by such a "natural" source are "teleological" motions, i.e. they make a thing into what, according to its own nature, it really is, or they lead it, in the form of a "natural" local motion, to its "natural" place.

Immanuel Kant's approach to aesthetics introduces a more nuanced position regarding the proper human attitude towards the natural world.[8] He thinks that aesthetic consciousness is a

---

[7] Regarding the concepts of "visible and invisible Gods", at the end of *Timaeus*, Plato asserts that the living cosmos is a visible, perceptible God, see Francis Macdonald, 1937, Cornford, *Plato's Cosmology: The Timaeus of Plato*, London: K. Paul, Trench, Trubner.

[8] The aesthetic consciousness is an awareness of the intelligibility →

felt awareness of the intelligibility and significance of natural forms, a kind of awareness closed to reason and science. Kant gives us reason to think on the issue of climate crisis and nature that aesthetic experiences and pure aesthetic judgements put us in touch with nature. He also gives us reason to believe that it is important to think about how to relate aesthetic experiences of natural beauty to the aims of conservation and to reflect about the moral dimension of nature. Kant possesses a philosophical anthropology which places him in a "rational" tradition of philosophy, dating from Plato and Aristotle and characterized by a normative concern with the most appropriate mode of life for human beings. Kant urges us to refrain from wanton cruelty against animals not because we are bound by any direct duties to them, but because we have duties towards other rational beings. Martin Heidegger addressed the issue of what he called "the devastation of the earth" and hence to have been involved with nature in the sense, roughly, of the natural environment. He argues that the modern metaphysical and scientific interpretation concerning the nature of the real as determinate material quantity not only grounds the practice of scientific research but also regulates even ordinary experience and perception of the world.[9] And this interpretation of the nature of being as a manifold of objective facts subject to quantitative representation sets the stage for a more technological kind of thinking. He asserts that in the modern age, the "earth itself can show itself only as the object of assault (Heidegger 1988b: 100). Nature is represented as nothing but raw material available for human use and consumption, and this representation holds "complete dominion over all phenomena that distinguish the age" (ibid. 1988c: 115). In *Being and Time*, Heidegger describes

← and significance of natural forms, for an elaborate discussion, see Kant 1991: 238-43.

[9] For this discussion see Heidegger 1988: 26-27; 1988a: 268-69.

the world or nature so construed as something "present-at-hand" and argues that it is parasitic on a quite different mode of understanding the world, as something "ready-to-hand" or "equipmental" (1980: 97). In *Being and Time*, Heidegger remarked that there are two conceptions of nature, a "primordial" and a "privative" one. Nature as a totality of readymade "equipment" and nature as a "world-stuff" set over against separated human cognition. He also comes up with a third conception such as "the nature which stirs and strives", which assails and enthrals us" (ibid.: 70). In later writings such as *An Introduction to Metaphysics and Contributions to Philosophy*, Heidegger remarked that this "primordial" conception is identified with the pre-Socratic Greek notion of *physis*. In experiencing nature as *physis*, the Greeks encounter as a "process of arising", as a "self-blossoming emergence" or "upsurging presencing" for us of the natural world.[10]

Christianity has a long historical tradition of reflection on nature and human relationship and responsibility. The ecological problems are often set down these days to the Judeo-Christian tradition and Christian attitudes to nature are often held to uphold these problems. According to Lynn White's widely republished essay "The Historial Roots of Our Ecology", these roots lie in the Judeo-Christian belief that man, being made in God's image, is set apart from nature, and that the entire physical creation was brought into being for human benefit and rule. As will be seen, White explains the change of the human role vis-à-vis nature introduced by Christianity. Passmore is not agreeing with White's view that the Old Testament must be interpreted as exploitative, though he holds that it does not proscribe despotic attitudes and that its laws requiring various forms of consideration for animals are either responses to heathen rituals

10 For the concept of experiencing nature as *physis*, refer Heidegger 1959: 14-15.

or motivated by concern for property. He admits that belief in human dominion can be taken not as despotic but as implying that humanity, as the steward or bailiff of God's creation, has responsibilities for its care. Lewis W. Moncrief (1970) points out that environmental stress is not peculiar to Christian cultures and holds that even if religious beliefs have contributed to the problems, their influence will have been indirect, and is no better evidence than the ties between Christianity and capitalism. Moncrief predominately rules out White's thesis as it refers to the medieval period, and Coleman, despite an understanding with White, grants much of Moncrief's case here and also on the need to distinguish a numerosity of factors leading to the despoliation of nature. Moncrief refuses White's thesis as it concerns the medieval period and also on the need to recognize a multiplicity of factors contributing to the despoliation of nature.

Degradation of Natural Climate and the Participation of Religion

Religions were acknowledged by scientists in the early 1990s as having an important role to protect the crisis of climate change. They recognized the importance of religion as key repositories of deep civilizational values and indispensable motivators in moral transformation around consumption, energy use and environmental protection. The environmental crisis requires radical changes not only in public policy, but in individual behaviour. It makes clear that religious learning, example and leadership are strongly able to determine personal conduct and loyalty. We realize that what is esteemed to be sacred is more likely to be dealt with attention and regard. Our terrestrial home should be considered. Accomplishments to protect and love the environment need to be infused with a vision of the religious. In the document "World Scientists' Warning to Humanity", by the Union of Concerned Scientists in 1992 and signed by over 2,000 scientists, including more than 200 Nobel Laureates. The document suggests that the planet is facing a severe environmental crisis and will require the assistance of spiritual commitment to protect the planet. It tells: A new ethic is required – a new attitude towards discharging our responsibilities for caring for ourselves and for the earth. We must be aware that our Earth has limited capacity. We must realize its vulnerability. We must no longer admit it to be destroyed.

A three-year international conference series took place at Harvard Divinity School's Center for the Study of World Religions from 1996 to 1998. The Harvard conferences were also designed to foster interdisciplinary conversations that drew on the synergy of historians, theologians, ethicists and scientists as well as on the work of grassroot environmentalists. The goal was to examine the varied ways in which human–earth relations have been conceived in the world's religions and to provide a broad survey that would help to ground a new field of study in religion and ecology. The intention was to avoid simplistic ecofriendly or apologetic readings of scriptures written in vastly different times and circumstances. The scholars were engaged in critically retrieving aspects of the religious traditions for re-examination and re-evaluation in the contemporary context. This has been part of the dynamic unfolding of religions historically as they have struggled to balance orthodoxy with the urgencies of adapting to new circumstances or cultures. Religious traditions have never been monolithic, but rather have embraced a broad range of interpretive positions ranging from Orthodox to Reform. Discerning appropriate change and the abiding value of tradition has been an important part of the life of religious teachers for centuries. Jewish *rabbīs*, Christian theologians and Islamic *imāms* in the West, and Hindu *paṇḍits*, Buddhist monks and Confucian scholars in Asia have all been involved with interpretation of their respective traditions over time. The Harvard project drew on that ongoing process of discernment so as to move towards a constructive phase. In the constructive phase the scholars of the various religions could point towards actual or potential sources of ecological awareness and action from within the particular traditions.

As the field of religion and climatology emerges within academia and beyond, it is clear that religions offer both promise and problems for ameliorating environmental issues. Religions have sustained human aspirations and energies for centuries, but they have also contributed to intolerance, violence and fundamentalist views of various kinds. The world's religions may thus be seen as necessary but not sufficient for climate change solutions. Religions have their problematic and dogmatic tendencies and have been late in coming to recognize the scale and scope of the global climate change crisis. The academic study of religion and ecology is drawing on other disciplines and thinkers to develop theoretical, historical, ethical, cultural and engaged dimensions. Among many thinkers, some of the theoretical and historical foundations have been laid by key philosophers. These include Clarence Glacken, who developed a study of nature in Western culture, and Arne Naess, who drew on Baruch Spinoza and south Asian thought to elaborate a theory of deep ecology emphasizing the primacy of the natural world over human prerogatives. Other philosophers and ethicists such as Baird Callicott and Holmes Rolston have helped to develop the field of environmental ethics. The cultural dimensions are influenced by the work of anthropologists such as Julian Steward, who coined the term *cultural ecology* to describe the relations between the environment, and the economic and technological aspects of society.

Religion as Cultural Resource

We feel our world is in crisis. The most pressing problems facing humanity today is climate change as a result of which it destroys all the hard-won gains of civilization. The enormous success of science and technology has generated terrible results: a destructive technology, a consumer society devoid of community, social "progress" that has destroyed both cultures and ecosystems. The anthropogenic climate change is caused by specific human practices related to specific attitudes and ideologies, and since it will more or less directly affect human societies and cultures, the humanities need to further engage in spiritual sciences. There is a strong need for more systematic and comparative interdisciplinary, interreligious and intercultural research on the role of religion and culture in a more general sense in global climate change. Nature, culture and religion involve one another. We generally understand nature as the planetary biosphere and culture as the human sphere. Religion, more or less, can be specified as a sum of spiritual beliefs. Nature is separate from culture, but culture determines nature just as nature determines culture. Religion differs from culture, but religion changes culture just as culture changes religion. The interaction of these areas is complex but not unintelligible. Their mutual agreement leads to how they alter each other. Thus, religion occupied a central space within culture. Belief systems occupy a crucial cultural place by means of the power of their ideas. Religious ideas impact cultural identity, both historically and collectively. Religions can be considered as cultural practices under which people live and develop their lives.[11] The past of religions is intimately associated with cultures from which the inward plurality of religions also came out. It is clear that the

11 For discussion of religions and cultural practices, consult Reder 2012.

sources of religion have always been integrated in particular sociocultural settings.

Religions always introspect the strengths and weaknesses of several cultures, even though they claim universal world views and ethical imperatives that indeed may transcend any particular culture and enable them to drive internal reforms.[12] The common characteristic of all religions is that they establish a comprehensive practice that enables discussion and reflection on a transcendent dimension of reality. But the way they realize this practice depends on the different cultural backgrounds involved. Therefore, from Schleiermacher's approaches is that, religion and culture are always interconnected. Thus, Nicholas of Cusa expressed this idea in the fifteenth century that the authority – God – is interpreted in different cultural ways.[13] The plurality of religions emerged from their interconnection with various cultural systems.[14] The concept of religions may be interpreted as a comprehensive cultural practice, which expresses a transcendent dimension of reality that cannot be objectified.[15] Religions express this transcendence in differentiated rites and semantic forms by which a comprehensive world view is founded. The different social forms of religions emerge from their irreducible relations to cultural backgrounds.[16]

---

12 Regarding discussion of the relationship between religion and culture, see Casanova 2010.

13 For a more detailed discussion on the concept of religion and culture, refer to Cusa 2002 and Bulhof 2002.

14 For this discussion, see Reder 2009.

15 Religions may be interpreted as a broad cultural practice in many instances; culture and religion are not so different, with cultural patterns becoming "religionized" and religious ideas turning part of the culture. For this discussion, see Derrida and Vattimo 1998.

16 The interreligious and intercultural dialogue about world views could help to strengthen religious activities concerning climate →

The interreligious and intercultural dialogue is necessary to strengthen religious activities concerning climate protection. The aim of such dialogues is to facilitate an exchange between different world views concerning the impacts of climate change. Interreligious dialogue is most successful when people share everyday life in the form of such cultural practices.

Buddhist Approaches to the Crisis of Climate

Climate change – and its most life-threatening consequence like the rapid overheating of the planet – is mainly a task and a challenge for ethics. It is very clear that the crisis of climate change and global warming of today was not existent during the Buddha's time or even 1,000 years after his death. Hence, he or his followers did not think over these problems. The Buddhists never had any doubt about a direct link between human actions and climate change. These are the modern problems born out of scientific developments, industrialization, deforestation, etc. which were unknown to the people in 600 BCE. However, it does not mean that we should not attempt the solution of the crisis of climate change from Buddhist orientations. An analysis of the climate change ethics and Buddhism includes a study of all human beings in terms of their physical, social, psychological and spiritual involvement. All the significant events of the Buddha's life were associated with nature like his birth, enlightenment, missionary activity and death.[17] The philosophy and ethical teachings of early Buddhism as advocated by the Buddha, and practised especially by the early monks who were his followers, are a kind of accommodate with nature emerging from their

← protection and the fight against poverty. For an elaborate discussion, see Müller and Reder 2009.

[17] Buddhist life and ethical conduct are nourished by universal compassion for all living beings. For this discussion, I closely follow the exposition of Jha 2006-07: 1059-60.

lifestyles and the practice of meditation. The advice to go to the forest, to the roots of trees and empty places is recovered time and again in the discussions of the Buddha. The open, empty and tranquil woods, groves, meadows and the foothills provided the ideal environment for those who went in search of spiritual solace. They initially lived in natural surroundings, under trees; forest dwellings came to be built as a residence for monks. Regarding the plants, trees and the natural environment, what is emphasized is a gentle human–nature orientation. The ethical principle involved for the monks is to keep away from activities that would unintentionally injure living creatures. The human domination of nature in a contemporary context may be seen as disorientation and disconnection of humans in relation to both society and nature. For Buddhists, all eco-systems with their inhabitants and organisms mean religion (*dhamma*). As a matter of fact, Buddhism propagates kindness and compassion towards all creatures of this universe – men, animals, birds, plants and even the earth itself. It tells us to live in harmony with nature. Hence, this philosophy has very often been referred to as ecological religion or religious ecology. The survival of human beings on earth depends on the availability of a clean environment. Nature can be protected only when there is a good understanding of the climate. For this, the general public have to become aware of the underlying issues associated with maintaining a clean environment and protecting nature.

Buddhism may be stated in terms of morality and its teachings. Its Four Noble Truth and the Noble Eightfold Path constitute its most fundamental elements, which are correlated with the crisis of climate in our planet. The core teachings of Gautama are summarized as the Four Noble Truths:

1. there is suffering (*duḥkha*);
2. there is a cause of suffering, viz. all forms of craving and attachment;

3. there is the cessation of suffering (*nibbāna*, which means literally "extinction"); and
4. there is a path to the cessation of suffering, known as the Buddha's "Eightfold Path" (Mitchell 2002: 34; Emmanuel 2013: 228).

The truth of suffering is described in the following words: birth (*jāti*), decay (*jarā*), disease (*vyādhi*), death (*maraṇa*), sorrow (*soka*), lamentation (*parideva*), pain (*dukkha*), grief (*domanassa*) and despair (*upāyāsa*) are referred to as suffering. The Four Noble Truths, often marked as the Buddha's verbalization of his enlightenment experience, provide the basis for developing an approach to climate ethics. The first and second Noble Truths promote particularly productive reflections applicable to ecological ethics. The first Noble Truth states that conventional lifestyles inevitably result in suffering; the second Noble Truth states that suffering stems from desire rooted in ignorance. The modern world is confronted with the unprecedented crisis caused by ecological imbalance. Humanity is advancing towards the twenty-first century with an unprecedented growth of industrialization and technological progress in all spheres. Large-scale industrial units had to be set up to satisfy the unlimited wants of the people. The raw materials to feed these industries have to be extracted from nature in large quantities which are non-renewable.

The basic orientation for the ethics of Buddhism is embedded in the Noble Eightfold Path. The ultimate spiritual goal of Buddhism is *nibbāna* and the path to the attainment of this goal is the Noble Eightfold Path. The path to *nibbāna* is described in terms of the following eight components: right view (*sammā diṭṭhi*), right resolve (*sammā sankappa*), right speech (*sammā vācā*), right action (*sammā kammanta*), right livelihood (*sammā ājiva*), right effort (*sammā vāyāma*), right mindfulness (*sammā sati*) and right concentration (*sammā samādhi*). This eightfold noble path presents in a compact way a methodology to all those who make a commitment to practise the teachings of the Buddha. The Buddha's important doctrine is dependent origination which describes the origin of suffering. In this manner, the concept of dependent origination provides a basis for developing a viable human–nature orientation. The dreadful growth in greenhouse gas and pollution stage which has resulted in dangerous environmental and ecological damage is the largest concern today. The survival of human beings on earth depends on the availability of a clean environment. Nature can be protected only when there is a good understanding of the ecology. Buddhist philosophy exerts the talk in certain contexts of physical objects like chairs and tables or trees and mountains, and animals and humans in terms of solidity (*paṭhavi*), liquidity (*āpo*), heat (*tejo*) and mobility (*vāyo*). But fundamentally, the Buddha sees the world as a network of many-sided, reciprocal causal patterns which interact. All processes within the universe are subject to change. The explanation *paṭicca samuppana dhamma* refers to phenomena dependently originated. The object and the subject in experience have no independent existence. This notion of dependent co-arising presents a deeper philosophical basis for understanding the causal patterns that bear on the climate change crisis. The Buddhist philosophy presented that suffering does not just happen. All creatures on the earth can suffer or experience *dukkha*. Part of our current environmental perplexity is that the earth is "suffering" and cannot improve the natural life support systems at a rate that can keep up with current rates of depletion and destruction. A fundamental concept in climate change science is that of the interconnectedness of everything in nature.

Ecological Holism and Spiritualism

Climate change is holistic, multifaceted and integrative. "Climate" is nothing specific or concrete. Solving the crisis of climate change with a holistic approach is inevitable. Wholes are more than sums of parts because they are *the way* parts work together within a sum. A whole is to a sum what a dynamic outcome is to a static aggregate. A move towards considering wholes rather than individuals can be shown to be advantageous. It involves social, cultural, moral and spiritual approaches to resolve the crisis. The climate is changing in the wrong direction. Change is inevitable. It is a difficult task, when we are confronted by two choices, between life and death, then we need to take a stand, we must change, though it is difficult. We understand the crisis in our relationship with nature; it could have potentially catastrophic results for the sustainability of civilization and even the habitability of the planet. New interdisciplinary and multidisciplinary collaborations have arisen between scientists and policymakers to examine the extremely challenging issues raised by global change but these are not sufficient to control the crisis of climate. We choose life, we change our way of life, despite the odds. Human and climate are of equal importance. Humans need a healthy climate and the climate needs humans, not to destroy but to take care. In this case, we need to develop an ethical relationship, just like an ethical relationship between human and human. We need to treat the climate as we treat human beings. We have a moral duty to do or to protect the environment like other human beings. Thus, the new relationship between human and climate is no longer between subject and object but it is a subject to subject because of equal importance. The philosophy of Martin Buber, interpersonal relationship, *I-Thou/You*, must be applied in which one is treated as an independent subject, not an object to be misrepresented.[18]

Humans need to build a harmony with the environment because damaging the environment can cause harm to the humans. Destroying the environment is destroying harmony. The idea of Baruch Spinoza may support the argument. He equated God and nature. He disagrees that God alone is perfect and the natural order is less than perfect. Spinoza equates reality with perfection. Since it is true that nothing in nature could be otherwise than it is, and all things in nature are a part of God and follow necessarily from his nature, God would not be complete without the whole natural order. Spinoza equated God (infinite substance) with nature, which is consistent with Einstein's belief in an impersonal deity. Spinoza's conception of God reveals the orderly harmony of what exists, not in a god who concerns himself with the fates and actions of human beings (Russell 1967 and also Jaspers 1966). Dwelling on this idea means humans need to see themselves as a part of a bigger whole, they are part of a bigger reality which is God and that God reveals himself in the harmony of nature. Building a harmonious relationship with others with nature is the same as building a relationship with spirituality. Destroying nature means we are destroying God and in return we are punished through climate change disaster. Arne Naess believes that an ecological holism can be substantiated in Spinoza's metaphysics, where "the whole" constitutes the totality of finite beings, equivalent to Spinoza's phrase *Deus sive Natura* (God or Nature). An ecological

---

18 An *I-Thou* acquaintanceship creates one wholly human by building up our integrity and comprehends a world of personal relationship. Buber considered it by coming together between *I* and *Thou* as the most significant view of human occurrence as it is the relationship that we become fully human. For this discussion, see Friedman, 2018 and Brody 2018.

holism is, as we have seen, a particular moral position which considers the interests of wholes (whether ecosystems or the whole earth) above, or more important than, the interests of individuals. Anyone familiar with Spinoza's work will know that such a moral position – whether of wholes or of individuals – is alien to Spinoza's thought, for any holistic philosophy assigned to Spinoza would have to be amoral or without prescription. Although Spinoza does not openly categorize his system as holistic, Naess believes that Spinoza's philosophy is founded upon a metaphysical holism which sees the "whole" as real. It is this metaphysical picture which Naess uses to substantiate the claim that the whole earth should be morally considered, since all beings are interconnected and part of the same "self". In this context, Leopold's conception of ecological holism plays an important role to controlling the day by day degradation of climate conditions. He articulates that our traditional ethical discussion only considers the relationship between the individual and the society but there is no ethics that deals with man's relation to land, animals and plants. There can be an ethical relationship between humans and land only if we can see, feel, understand and love it. Land ethics implies three values, i.e. integrity, stability and beauty (Leopold 1949: 224-25). These three values should be preserved in each and every ecosystem. This forms a foundation for the spiritual aspect for the protection of "wholes" such as species and habitats of our planet.

Conclusion

A great deal has been discussed about the crisis of climate change and the role of religious traditions. Climate change is already taking place and it cannot be avoided. The biggest threats we face are climate change in the planet earth on which life depends. It is often said that climate change is a matter of individual moral responsibility, due to the modern technology, industrialization as well as consumerism which are responsible for a changing global climate. As a result of this, the earth's temperature is increasing. Human activities have added greenhouse gases to the atmosphere: CO_2, mainly from deforestation and fossil fuel combustion, methane and nitrous oxides from agriculture and waste, and fluorinated gases from industrial processes. The basic reasons for our failure on these factors are not lack of economic resources, but simply our lack of ethical concern and seriousness. It shows an irrational lack of concern for our future. We must, therefore, consider the effects of our collective inactiveness on this major global challenge and take action to avoid having further damage of our planet.

Religion is practised, not just believed; it consists of a number of characteristics – such as cosmology, values, social organization and lived experience symbolically interpreted – that vary among and within religious traditions; religion arrives at from individual disciples through aggregations, groups, institutional bodies, and transhistorical and transnational traditions. These are aspects of religions that must be taken into account in order to understand religious engagement with anthropogenic climate c+hange. The world's religions may thus be considered as inevitable but not enough for the climate change crisis, because religions have their problematic and dogmatic attitudes. Thus, we are thinking about the academic study of religion and environment. This can draw other fields and intellectuals to develop theoretical, historical, ethical, cultural and engaged dimensions for the climate crisis. We should rethink their approaches, methodology and the basic ideas about the nature of nature, human nature, and the proper relationship between humans and the nature from the philosophical point of view. Buddhism has great hope for the climate crisis, because it teaches the ethics for animals, nature as well as our fellow humans. Buddhist approach is a unique framework from its metaphysical and epistemological outlook regarding the human situation and the cosmos. Buddhism provides critical tools for evaluating the state of human–nature relationship and for envisaging this relationship in its ideal form. Thus, a new form of religious approach is necessary to build up our responsibilities for ourselves and for the healthy climate and ecological balance of the earth. A new way of thinking is required – a new orientation towards carrying out our obligations for loving ourselves and for Mother Earth. We must understand its vulnerability. We must no longer admit it to be destroyed.

References

Brody, Samuel H., 2018, *Martin Buber's Theopolitics*, Bloomington, IA: Indiana University Press.

Bulhof, I.N. (ed.), 2000, *Flight of the Gods: Philosophical Perspectives on Negative Theology*, New York: Fordham University Press.

Burnet, John, 1924, *Greek Philosophy*, part I, New York: Macmillan.

Casanova, K., 2010, "Religion in Modernity as Global Challenge", in *Religion und die Umstrittene Moderne*, ed. M. Reder and M. Rugel, pp. 1-16, Stuttgart: Kohlhammer.

Chapple, Christopher Key, 2011, "Religion and Environment", *Annual Review of Environment and Resources*, 36: 441-63.

Cusa, Nicholas of, 2002, *Vom Frieden zwischen den Religionen*, Frankfurt am Main: Insel.

De Silva, Padmasiri, 1998, *Environmental Philosophy and Ethics in Buddhism*, New York: Palgrave Macmillan.

Derrida, Jacques and Gianni Vattimo, 1998, *Religion: Cultural Memory in the Present*, Stanford, CA: Stanford University Press.

Emmanuel, Steven M. (ed.), 2013, *A Companion to Buddhist Philosophy*, Oxford: Wiley Blackwell.

Friedman, Maurice, 1981, *Martin Buber's Life and Work: The Early Years, 1878-1923*, New York: Dutton.

Ghosh, Jhadeswar, 2017, "Climate Change: A New Challenge to Moral Philosophy", *Ravenshaw Journal of Philosophy*, vol. III, December.

———, 2020, "Role of Buddhist Philosophy in Addressing Climate Change and Global Warming", in *Tradition Religion and Morality: An Indian Perspective*, ed. Bibhuti Bhushan Nayak, pp. 222-31, New Delhi: New Academic Publishers.

Guthrie, W.K.C., 1962 (1978), *A History of Greek Philosophy*, vol. I, Cambridge: Cambridge University Press.

Heidegger, Martin, 1959, *An Introduction to Metaphysics*, tr. R. Mannheim, New Haven: Yale University Press.

———, 1980, *Being and Time*, tr. John Macquarrie and Edward Robinson, London: Blackwell.

———, 1988, "The Question Concerning Technology", in *The Question Concerning Technology and Other Essays*, tr. William Lovitt, New York: Harper & Row.

———, 1988a, "Modern Science, Metaphysics, and Mathematics", in *Basic Writings*, ed. David Krell, New York: Harper & Row.

———, 1988b, "The Word of Nietzsche", in *The Question Concerning Technology and Other Essays*, tr. William Lovitt, New York: Harper & Row.

———, 1988c, "Age of the World Picture", in *The Question Concerning Technology and Other Essays*, tr. William Lovitt, New York: Harper & Row.

Jaspers, Karl, 1966, *The Great Philosophers: Spinoza*, ed. Hannah Arendt, tr. Ralph Manheim, New York: Harvest Books.

Jha, Arun Kumar, 2006-07, "Environmental Awareness in Buddhism", *Proceedings of the Indian History Congress*, vol. 67: 1059-60.

Kant, Immanuel, 1991, *The Metaphysics of Morals*, tr. Mary Gregor, New York: Cambridge University Press.

Leopold, Aldo, 1949, "The Land Ethic", in *A Sand County Almanac*, pp. 201-26, New York: Oxford University Press.

McKibben, B., 1989, *The End of Nature*, New York: Random House.

Mitchell, Donald W., 2002, *Buddhism*, Oxford: Oxford University Press.

Moncrief, Lewis W., 1970, "The Cultural Basis for Our Environmental Crisis", *Science*, 170: 508-12, repr. in *Western Man and Environmental Ethics*.

Müller, J. and M. Reder, 2009, "Religions and Global Justice: Reflections from an Intercultural and Interreligious Perspective", in *Absolute Poverty and Global Justice: Empirical Data - Moral Theories - Initiatives*, ed. M. Schramm, pp. 91-99, Aldershot: Ashgate.

Reder, M., 2009, "Religion als kulturelle Praxis an der Grenze zwischen Glauben und Wissen: Anregungen von F. Schleiermacher und J. Derrida", in *Moderne Religion?: Theologische und Religions Philosophische Reaktionen auf Jürgen Habermas*, ed. K. Wenzel and T.N. Schmidt, pp. 128-52, Freiburg: Herder.

———, 2012, "Religion in the Public Sphere: The Social Function of Religion in the Context of Climate and Development Policy", in *Religion in Environmental and Climate Change: Suffering, Values, Lifestyles*, ed. Dieter Gerten and Sigurd Bergmann, pp. 32-45, New York: Continuum.

Russell, Bertrand, 1967, *A History of Western Philosophy*, New York: Simon and Schuster.

Stace, W.T., 1960, *A Critical History of Greek Philosophy*, New York: Macmillan.

Weart, Spencer R., 2003, *The Discovery of Global* Warming, Harvard: Harvard University Press.

White, Lynn Townsend (Jr), 1967, "The Historical Roots of Our Ecologic Crisis", *Science* 155, cumulative no. 3767 (10 March): 1203-07.

14

The Universal Religion
Swami Vivekananda and Bhīmā Bhoi

Basant Kumar Dash

THE present world is witnessing such events which gives an impression of a human civilization without human beings. A remarkable material progress has been achieved due to the scientific and technological advancement. Development in information technology has brought the entire world to our living rooms. People in general are leading a prosperous luxurious life. But they are not happy. Truly speaking, they have become bankrupt both in the sphere of morality and spiritual life. They have no view and vision. Strife and war are the orders of the day. There is intra and interreligious conflicts throughout the globe for selfish motive. So stability and peaceful coexistence are the bygone orders. Caring of and sharing with fellow beings are outmoded values.

At such a juncture of time, certain philosophical and ethical views provide the sap of human being and becoming. The philosophical views of revolutionary thinkers do not come to the forefront of discussion. But we cannot provide to forget, bypass, suppress the enabling views of past-masters, the ideas that have nourished the human beings in society. I consider Bhīmā Bhoi of Odisha, as such a past-master.

The present-day social religious political scenario of India as well as the world is overburdened with religious fundamentalism leading to religious chauvinism and resulting in religious conflicts. Religion has been the main target of "severe" attacks from different quarters, primarily due to the desire for political advantage, narrowness of mind, racial prejudice and general ignorance. But it has stood the test of time and kept itself quite alive because it is eternal.

A critical insight into these conflicting claims clearly articulates conceptual disorder in the area of the understanding of the exact connotation of religion. So the thesis of universal religion has been proposed by the great thinkers and religious figures starting from Jesus, Mohammad, the Buddha, to the present-day thinkers like Ramakrishna Paramahamsa, Swami Vivekananda, Mahatma Gandhi and others as a possible solution to the conflicting trend which, at present, stands as a great threat to international understanding and world-peace. But adequate focus is not given to the idea of universal religion. So I feel, there is an urgent need to have a clear conception of religion, in order to realize the idea of universal religion. I therefore propose to address myself to the questions in this presentation: What is religion? What is universal religion? How this notion of universal religion is reflected in the writings of Bhīmā Bhoi?

Religion

Literally speaking, religion is a principle of unification and harmonization. It suggests that two objects of unification were originally unified and have been only temporarily separated. Religion is thus based on the faith in the ultimate unity of man and the reality, i.e. the finite and the infinite. So, the only religion worthy of its name would be a living religion or religion of Divine.

While defining religion we find philosophers differ in giving emphasis either on reasoning or on feeling or on morality, which constitutes the three important aspects of it. Emphasizing on the element of reasoning. McTaggart (1910: 9) says:

> Religion is clearly a state of mind. It seems to me that it may best be described as an emotion resting on a conviction of harmony between ourselves and the universe at large.

Gentile conceives religion as "not the exaltation of the object released from the chains of mind" (1922: 277). Emphasizing on moral aspect Bradley defines religion as "morality is led beyond itself into a higher form of goodness, it ends in what we may call religion" (1893: 388). William James (1902: 32) defines religion as

> the feelings, acts and experiences of individual men in their solitude so far as they apprehend themselves to stand in relation to whatever they may consider the divine.

According to Alexander, "Religion is faith in Deity" (1927: 608). Kant defines thus:

> Religion is a matter of the will, it being understood and identified with practical reason, that is to say certain acts ought to be done or that certain attitudes ought to be adopted.
> – Ibid.: 429

The above definitions fail to explicate the real significance of religion, since they stress on the outer aspect of it. In outer aspect, religion signifies a body of beliefs, set of rites and rituals, mode of prayer, set of prescriptions and prohibitions and a world view. But religion in its core aspect is called *dharma* or the a-cosmic principle which contains the basics of life. The Upaniṣads describe it as *sat* or *tat*. Man is necessarily spiritual. Thus spirituality is the very core of true religion. The purpose of religion is to know the unknown in the realm of known, to see the unseen in the world of seen and to realize the self in the region of not-self. It is a way which the finite trends to be tuned with the infinite. Sri Aurobindo (1950: 160) rightly observes:

> The inmost essence of religion ... is the search for God and finding of God. Its aspiration is to discover the infinite, the Absolute, the one, the Divine who is all these things and yet no abstraction but a Being. Its work is a sincere giving out of the true and ultimate relations between man and God, relations of unity, relations of difference, relations of an illuminated knowledge, an ecstatic love and delight, an absolute surrender and service, a casting of every part of our existence out of its normal status into and up rush of man towards Divine and a descent of the Divine into man.

To Swami Vivekananda (1947: 253):

> Religion is not in doctrines, in dogmas nor in intellectual argumentation; it is being and becoming, it is realization of the absolute.

For him, religion is an attempt to transcend the limit of senses and the limits of intellect. It is not only individualistic but also has social content. The entire fabrics of society will collapse without the bond of religion. Thus, religion, in true sense, is spiritual life, which is different from a vague religiosity. It is a change of consciousness, from ordinary ignorant state, to a greater consciousness in which we find our true being. Thomas Hardy rightly remarks:

> The main object of religion is not to get man into heaven but to get heaven into him.

Comparative Religion

Before going to focus on universal religion, I would like to give a brief idea of comparative religion which makes way for universal religion. Comparative religion is not a new kind or special kind of religion. It is only a way of thinking of religion.

It is a particular method of treating religion. It tries to impress upon human mind the simple truth that no particular religion, however charming and attractive it might be, is not final and absolute. It is a movement from imperfection to perfection and perfection to still more perfection. Vivekananda has rightly remarked that "man never progresses from error to truth, but from truth to truth, from lesser truth to higher truth". Comparative religion gives a new meaning to each religion and develops a new attitude or a new way of life. The essence of this new attitude is expressed by the terms "sharing" and "caring". It teaches us to show regard, respect and love for entire humanity, by developing the spirit of toleration and acceptance towards other faiths.

Universal Religion

Swami Vivekananda, the worthy disciple of Ramakrishna, proposed for universal religion, derived from his standpoint of practical Vedānta to resolve the conflicting claims of various religions. Universal religion is a synthetic approach to religion, means, nothing more than perceiving the fundamental unity that exists in all religions, maintaining an attitude of religious tolerance and benevolence, and realizing that each religion tries to achieve the same goal by different routes. The study of different religions or sects shows that they appear to be different in form or in surface level but in deeper level or in essence they are one. Ramakrishna Paramahamsa has rightly said: *jato matā tato pathā* (Gupta 1902: 124). This concept is as old as other Vedic origin. *Ṛgveda* I.164.46 says: *ekam sad viprā bahudhā vadanti* (the Ultimate Reality is one, though it is being described in many ways).

The essence of universal religion is that it is not based on a narrow sense upon universal consent. Variety, diversity and multiplicity is the very beauty of the universe as well as the beauty of all religions. It is not a separate religion. It has no geographical boundary. It has no political content, national meaning and sectarian significance. It is a peculiar frame of mind, a certain attitude, a code of conduct and a direction of thought. It stands on the basis of a universal mind, which transcends the limitation of space and time. Universal mind identifies itself with the entire universe. It recognizes the essential unity and identity of humanity. It is the willing to give up the sectarian pride and prejudices and to be one with the whole universe.

Universal religion is the fruit of the meeting of religions. All religions must meet in the same spirit if they really want to achieve something. The universal toleration, sympathy, love, acceptance, respect, self-sacrifice and unity are the prime concerns of universal religion. This way of life is not only accepted by the Vedas but also is approved by the *Gītā*, when it speaks of generosity, liberality, universality and catholicity as the distinctive marks of universal religion. Now a question may be raised that, does a religion of this kind exist? The answer is yes, such a religion is the Hinduism or the Vedāntism which is otherwise known as the Sanātana Dharma. Vivekananda goes to the extent of saying that it is Vedānta and Vedānta alone is the universal religion of man. It would be the future religion of the world.

With the above observations, on the universal religion, let me examine the contributions of Bhīmā Bhoi, the exponent of Mahimā Dharma, for the realization of the same. Now two fundamental questions may be raised. Is Mahimā Dharma be called a universal religion? And can Bhīmā Bhoi the expounder of Mahimā Dharma, be called the propagator of universal religion? To my mind the answer in affirmative. Still I keep the door open for others to differ. I therefore think, it will be proper on my part to analyse the nature of Mahimā Dharma to justify my stand.

Bhīmā Bhoi's socio-religious ideas, follow from his metaphysics of *śūnyatā* or *pūrṇatā* and is justified to be named as a universal religion, since it fulfils all the basics of a true religion. Mahimā Dharma enjoys not only the sanctions of scriptures but also the sanction of spirituality. It is based on the rock pillars of universal love, universal acceptance, tolerance, respect, self-sacrifice and unity. For Bhīmā Bhoi spirituality is both a regulative and harmonizing force in the collective body. Therefore, he admits no distinction of caste, creed and colour. True religion consists in cultivating the cardinal values like love, compassion, non-violence, and truth. It practises the vision of unity so that one can see one, in everything and everything in one.

Bhīmā Bhoi considers religion a way of life. So, for him ritualism, casteism and idol worship are the hazards of religion, which stand on the path of spiritual progress. Ritualism gives birth to sectarianism and fundamentalism which the present world witnesses. Since the reality is of the nature of *śūnya* (*pūrṇa*), having no form, *rūparekhā nāhīṅ, he śūnya dehī*, He cannot be confined to any particular form. So, all Hindu deities like Brahmā, Viṣṇu and Śiva cannot be exalted to the status of reality. These lifeless idols can never satisfy the spiritual cravings of all individuals. Out of ignorance people worship them considering them as savour, with a hope, of redemption. So, the living gods are ignored. He describes:

acetare sina jana-prāṇī mane karucanti deva pūjā ।
pade padi rakṣakara bolucanti debu khiri pūrī khajā ॥

mūrti sina sehi jīva ātmā nāhīṅ kāhuṅ jācideva bara ।
viṣṇu natakuta māyāku najani ajñanare muḍha nara ॥

jehu gadhici āpanā piṇḍa prāṇa tāku samarpaṇa nāhīṅ ।
dāru pratimā mūrtikī bolucanti prāṇaku bañcā tuhī ॥

manuṣya hoi nirjīva saṅge bhāva dekhānti keḍe ajñāna ।
śūnyaru jehu piṇḍa prāṇa gaḍhilā nāhīṅ tāku anumāna ॥
– *Stuti Cintāmaṇi* 95-98

Bhīmā Bhoi is also against ritualism. He says that *observance* of rites *and* rituals is sheer wastage of one's precious life, since it stands on the path of his spiritual realization. The so-called places of worship become the places of exploitation. It is only through deep love for the inner self, immorality can be achieved. Thus, he describes:

japa tapa sandhyā homa jajña teji dhari nirveda pātha ।
ātmā bhagatire a mṛtyu saṅsāre manili mun eka mata ॥
– Ibid.: 33

Bhīmā Bhoi is also against caste-division. He says that the caste-division is man-made which does not enjoy even the sanctions of the scriptures. For him, there is only one caste, i.e. the caste of the humanity, only one class, i.e. the class of beings. He describes thus:

chatisakula je bauna patāka je aca stirī puruṣa ।
ūcanīca boli baraṇa nākari nāmare sarana pasa ॥ – Ibid.: 92

We find a spiritualistic appeal or universal outlook in the writings of Bhīmā Bhoi. He is influenced by our Upaniṣadic ideals which considers man as the end but not a means to an end. The Veda says:

sarve bhabantu sukhinaḥ sarve santu nirāmayāḥ ।
sarve bhadrāni paśyantu mākaścit duḥkhabhāgbhavet ॥
– *Bṛhadāraṇyaka Upaniṣad* 1.4.14

This Vedic vision of unity gives rise to universal love or divine love that spreads beyond the human species which has rightly been envisaged by Bhīmā Bhoi. For him, every manifestation is the living expression of the reality. So, he prays Alekha, not only to save the human beings but also all non-human beings too, from the clutches of misery and sufferings. He thus sings:

rakṣakara svāmī naraloka
kibā juba-bṛdha stirī puruṣa bālaka
kīṭa pataṅgādi jalapoka
jāku jeuṅ rūpe kara karaṇa viveka ।
tīraṇa stabara taru bṛksa
saraṇa sambhali rakha e jantu jiveka ॥ – *Bhajanamālā* 17

For Bhīmā Bhoi, the reality called Alekha is all-pervasive and takes care of the whole creation includind all things and beings. He writes:

stabaru jaṅgama kīṭaru pataṅga canhidele anusārī ।
sakala ghatare purī samanare nuheṅ sanabada karī ॥
– Ibid.: 15

As the reality pervades equally, all including the immobile, insects and worms are all equal. This shows how Bhīmā Bhoi is against the discrimination and is in support of universalism.

As a follower observes the presence of the reality in every object and every being, he cannot be unjust to any of them. On the other hand, he adores everyone with love that breeds social harmony. Thus, Bhīmā Bhoi as an exponent of Mahimā Dharma prescribes nondiscrimination as a way for attainment of universal peace. Bhīmā Bhoi warns the followers of Mahimā against discrimination thus:

bramha bhagatire bhedābheda jebe bajra padu mo muṇḍaku ।
kahe Bhīmā Bhoi brahma sāpa dei jālī dia e piṇḍaku ॥ – Ibid.: 27

If I discriminate in realization of Brahmā, may thunder strike my head, may thou burn my body with celestial curse.

Mahimā Dharma is against casteism. Mankind can only be divided into two categories, as male and female. So, it believes in universal brotherhood. It always prays and works for the benefit of all beings. This is emphatically pronounced by Bhīmā Bhoi thus:

> *prāṇī manaṅkara ānanda maṅgala, anyare ki kārya achi?*
>
> – Ibid.: 22
>
> People's welfare and joy is the goal, what use is there in any other work?

His view of universal love makes way for self-sacrifice for the cause of fellow beings. Being a realized man, he looks after the interest of others, at the cost of his own interest. Salvation is considered as the *summum bonum* of life. But for Bhīmā Bhoi salvation is to lead a life of perfection. He never seeks his own salvation, rather, he seeks the liberation of the mass, which shows, his spiritual wisdom and universal love for the fellow beings in the society. He thus says:

> *prāṇiṅka ārata dukha apramita dekhu dekhu kebā sahu* ।
> *mo jīvana pache narke paḍithau jagata udhāra heu* ॥
>
> – *Stuti Cintāmaṇi* 27
>
> Who can bear to see the plight of people, their suffering immeasurable. Let my life be left to rot in hell, but let the world be saved.

Bhīmā Bhoi has tried to reduce the difference between man and man, and man and nature through his spiritualistic outlook and humanistic appeal for which, I consider him as a pathfinder of universal religion. Universal love and self-sacrifice lead to acceptance, toleration and respect towards other religions which is described by him as:

> *sadguru dharma ehi kāhāku manā nāhīṅ*
> *ekajanakara nuhanti ṭhākura achi saburi bhāga*
> *koṭṭha loka heba antara nohiba.*
> *jeunmāne bhajuthibeti āga* ॥ – *Bhajanamālā* 62

satyare maribi satyare tarībī ehi ajña mote heu ।
kahe Bhīmā Bhoi e martya maṇḍale jasa apajasa thau ॥
– Ibid.: 22

The core of universal religion is the realization of universal brotherhood.

The *R̥gveda* says:

saṅgachadvam sambadabam sambo manāṅsi jānatām ।
devabhāgam yathā puruve sañjanana upāsate ॥
samano mantraḥ samitiḥ samāni ।
samānam manaḥ sahacitam eṣām ॥
samānam mantra abhimantrayebaḥ ।
samānenabo habisa juhomi ॥ – X.191

Let you live together, discuss together and let your minds be united with the reality. With the divine knowledge through discussion, let your minds be one and act for the divine cause. Let your motto be universal brotherhood.

This Vedic truth is also enriched in our scriptures. The same is reflected in the writings of Bhīmā Bhoi. The same Vedic truth is also described in our literature thus:

ayam nija parobeti ganana laghu cetasām ।
udara caritānām tu vasudhaiva kuṭumbakam ॥
– *Hitopadeśa* 1.71

The whole universe is a family and we are the members of that family. This shows the catholicity and broadness of true religion.

Bhīmā Bhoi also expresses the same truth thus:

chapana koṭie jete jīvachanti mora ātmāprāe dise ।
– *Stuticintāmaṇi* 92

Conclusion

Like Swami Vivekananda, Bhīmā Bhoi accepts Hindu Dharma or Sanātana Dharma as the true religion or universal religion. He says that Mahimā Dharma is the repetition of Sanātana Dharma. Thus, it follows that Mahimā Dharma of Bhīmā Bhoi is universal in its outlook and appeal like the Sanātana Dharma. He says:

> *jeuṅ satyadharmare e piṇḍa brahmāṇḍa purbe hoithila jāta* ।
> *sehi satyadharmare e piṇḍa brahmāṇḍa sanstapane heba mukta* ॥ – *Stuti Cintāmaṇi* 44

Bhīmā Bhoi is thus optimistic like Swami Vivekananda, that the Sanātana Dharma will be the future religion of the world.

References

Alexander, S., 1927, *Space, Time and Deity*, vol. 2, London: Macmillan.

Aurobindo, Sri, 1950, *The Human Cycle*, Twin Lakes: Lotus Press.

Bhīmā Bhoi, *Bhajanamālā*.

Bhīmā Bhoi, *Stuti Cintāmaṇi*.

Bradley, F.H., 1893, *Appearance and Reality*, London: Cambridge University Press.

Gentile, G., 1922, *The Theory of Mind as Pure Act*, tr. H. Wildon Carr, London: Macmillan.

Gupta, Mahendranath, 1902, *Sri Sri Ramakrishna Kathamruta*, Calcutta: Kathamrita Bhawan.

Hardy, Thomas, 1991, *The Woodlanders*, vol. 1 (originally published in 1887 by Macmillan, London).

James, W., 1902, *Varieties of Religious Experiences*, London: Longmans, Green and Co.

McTaggart, John M.E., 1910, *Some Dogmas of Religion*, Cambridge: Cambridge University Press.

Sharma, Pandit Vishnu, 2019, *Mitralabha Pancatantra*, Delhi: Manoj Publications.

Vivekananda, Swami, 1947, *The Complete Works of Swami Vivekananda*, vol. III, Calcutta: Vedanta Press and Book Shop.

15

Sociocultural Significance of Mahimā Dharma

Harischandra Sahoo

Culture is a way of life. It is manifested in different activities of life like art, literature, religion, philosophy, music, painting, dance, beliefs and practices of rituals. Culture is an ongoing process. It grows, develops and culminates in course of time. Therefore, it is often been said that culture is a sedimentation. Odisha is the land of Lord Jagannātha. Major religious cannons have been accommodated and synthesized in the Jagannātha cult. Buddhism, Jainism, Vaiṣṇavism, Śaivism, Śakti cult, Tantra cult and the Gāṇapatya school have found their culmination in the philosophy of Lord Jagannātha. It has been aptly called that Jagannātha cult is the unity of all religious thoughts and citadel of all religious cults. But in course of time, the temple of Lord Jagannātha comes under the control of the rulers and *paṇḍā*s (worshippers) as a result of which the so-called *harijans*, tribals and people of low caste were disallowed to enter into the temple for *darśana* of Lord Jagannātha. The Lord who called as the diety for the rescue of the *patita*s no longer remains as *patitapābana*. As such a critical juncture, in the late nineteenth century a new religion flourished in Odisha. It is Mahimā Dharma, an indigenous religion of Odisha, emphasizing on the welfare of human beings at the cost of superhuman concepts of godhead and aims at the mitigation of sorrows and suffering of entire mankind. Some thinkers advocate that it is not a new religion altogether but a reformation in the fold of Hinduism. Some consider it to be a syncretism. Dhaneswar Sahoo points out that Mahimā Dharma can be called as a religion in true sense of the term because it possess all the salient features of a religion.

Mahimā Gosāiṁ is considered to be the founder of Mahimā Dharma who is often called as Mahimā Swāmī, Gupta Prabuddha Saṁnyāsī who is the wisdom incarnate. He is not an ordinary human being. He is an *avatārī*. He is not born from womb (*ajonī sambhūta*). The arrival of Mahimā Swāmī in Purī town is a turning point. He argued in favour of Ekeśvaravāda (Advaita) and expressed boldly by strong arguments before the *paṇḍitas* of *mukti maṇḍapa* in the Jagannātha Temple in favour of reality to be one and only one.

"Dhūliā Bābā" (since he was rolling on ground) then comes to Kapilas Hill to have meditation for a long period in *ātma-yoga samādhi* and attended *siddhi*. He wants to propagate a new religion called as Mahimā Dharma devoid of idol worship. It is worship to "Mahimā" who is the Saviour of the Universe, the Creator and Preserver of the world. As the incarnation, he (Mahimā Swāmī) has descended down on the earth to mitigate the sorrows and sufferings of the downtrodden human beings with the ultimate motive to establish a casteless and a classless society. He is an *abadhūta* (wandering mendicant). He is Mahimā Alekha. The meaning of "*mahimā*" is the greatest of the great and *alekha* means one who cannot be described in mere words. He is *nirguṇa* (without any quality or attributes). He is thus described *via negativa* like *ajehī*, *arūpa*, *akalpana* and *nirveda*. He is formless (*anākāra*) and *anākṣara Brahman*. He is Alekha and Śūnya Puruṣa.

The concept of visualizing the supreme reality in negation, needless to mention, jettisons the practices of idol worship which is elementary to Hindu worship.

Mahimā Dharma has been popularized by two important saint-like persons. One is the saint-poet Bhīmā Bhoi, a *gṛhī-saṁnyāsī* (a saint who has maintained family life) and the other one is Biswanāth Bābā, a saint (*bakkaladhārī saṁnyāsī*) a *brahmacārī* from the childhood. While Bhīmā Bhoi composed *bhajanas, cautīsās* and prayers dedicated to Mahimā Swāmī for mitigation of sorrows of the world, Biswanāth Bābā advocated for Bisudhādaitavāda (unalloyed Advaita theory) with strong logical arguments by the support of scriptures. Both propagated in favour of Mahimā Dharma but from two different angles.

In this connection, it can be pointed out that Mahimā cult has close affinity with the *neti* concept of Advaitic notion of reality as one and non-dual and Śūnyavāda in Buddhism. In Advaita Vedānta, the reality is one and only one devoid of any quality. Mahimā Dharma accepts the reality to be one, and only one devoid of any attribute. The reality is Śūnya Puruṣa. Here *śūnya* does not stand for emptiness or void. Rather, it is concrete and complete. The *Śūnya Brahman* is *Pūrṇa Brahman*. The Ultimate Reality is one without the second, unalloyed and non-dual. He is *Akhaṇḍita Pūrṇa Brahman*, the supreme creator of the universe who is both transcendent and immanent. As the supreme reality, he resides in *brahmaloka, mahānityapura* and *mahāmahimaṇḍala.* He is found everywhere, i.e. immanent and is all-pervasive. In this context, Bhīmā Bhoi writes:

sthābaru jaṅgama, kīṭaru pataṅga cāhīṅ dele anusārī ।
sakala ghaṭare, purī samānare nohe sana baḍa kārī ॥

– *Stuti Cintāmaṇi* 15

The tangible and intangible, the palpable and the inpalpable, and the animate and the inanimate, the tiniest worm and the

> mightiest creatures are if one looks closely, indeed of the same essence. The content and not the container is significant, the question of superior and inferior is redundant.

He is the creator of the universe but none has created Him. Thus, on one hand the Ultimate Reality (*mahimā alekha*) is found to be formless (*anākāra*), *alekha* (indescribable) but on the other hand, as an *avatārī*, he descends down in human form to mitigate the sorrows and suffering of mankind. Such a view reveals that transcendence and immanence are but two aspects of the same non-dual *Brahman*. Alekha is both *nirguṇa* and *saguṇa.*

The concept of *jīva* (individual self) is an important concept in Mahimā cult. The human body (*piṇḍa*) is a world in miniature (*brahmāṇḍa*). Such a concept of *piṇḍa brahmāṇḍa tattva* found in the *pañcaśākhās*. Human life is precious in the sense that only a human being can aspire for the Ultimate Reality. The *summum bonum* of life is to attain salvation from the earthy bondage. A man in bondage leads to a miserable life because of greed, intolerance, poverty, illiteracy and helplessness. Bhīmā Bhoi writes:

> *lobha, moha, kāma, krodha, ahaṅkāra nirantara lagi bādi* ।
> *dānaba parāye hoi e samaste dhari marucanti sādhi* ॥
>
> – *Stuti Cintāmaṇi* 15
>
> Within human individual, there rages a monstrous struggle between greed, attachment, carnal desire, wrath and pride which reduces human being to be a helpless victim at their hands.

Mahimā cult differs from Advaita Vedānta on the ground that while Advaita Vedānta considers world (*jagat*) to be a product of *māyā* (cosmic illusion), for Mahimā cult, world is not a *māyā.* The whole creation is a manifestion of the divine will. When Advaita Vedānta speaks of the liberation (*mokṣa*) of the individual self, Mahimā cult emphasizes on welfare of the humanity at large.

Mahimā cult is a reaction against the social stigmas like caste system, class system and blind beliefs like rituals and idol worship. On the one hand, there is a ruling class comprising of the *rājās–zamīndārs–gauṇṭiās* who are exploiting the peasants, farmers of lower caste (*prajās*) and, on the other, the brāhmaṇas, the so-called higher elite class try to harass the people of lower caste. In the name of caste and class, there is division among the people. There is gap between the rich and the poor, the ruler and the ruled. Mahimā cult, especially its propagator Bhīmā Bhoi, was vocal on these issues. He explained through his poems that caste system is man-made; not made by any god to make division among human beings. Thus, the revolt of Bhīma was against the prevailing social system and rulers. The main factor for the fall of society is casteism, class-division, illiteracy (lack of education) and suppression of women. It is exploitation of a man against man. Bhīma was anticipating a social change, to see a better world of tomorrow for a classless society with equal rights for men and women. Women are also eligible to accept any religion they like.

Bhīma said that Mahimā Dharma is opened to all, irrespective of caste, creed and religion. In the vernacular language he composed poems for the spreading of Mahimā Dharma. He wanted that people should have applied their conscience (*hetu-ceta*). There should be change in social as well as individual level. A man should keep himself away from *lobha* (greed) and *moha* (attachment). Bhīma writes that there is no harm if one becomes a household or follows a life of a *saṁnyāsa* (hermit/*yogī*). Bhīma's poems attracted the simple and poor villagers living in nook and corner of Odisha. The people like agricultural workers see a humanistic undercurrent in the Mahimā cult. It is *spiritual humanism*, where not only human beings but also all the creatures including the flora and fauna will be taken care by man, who is the crown of the creation.

The *śūnya upāsanā* is performed as a prayer so that the entire cosmos including ecosystem may flourish in right proportion to each other.

S. Nath (1990: 87) writes:

> It is for a blissful universe, a world order in harmony with all creations, animate and inanimate, on the land and in water and space. This is indeed an orientation of the devotees, towards *satcidānanda* for a balanced and interdependent eco-system.

Nowadays, we express our grave concern for the imbalance in ecology and for protecting our environment. But since a long, Mahimā Dharma, in tune with Vedāntic ideology of *vasudhaiva kuṭumbakam*, pleads for the peaceful coexistence between man and non-human beings including the flora and fauna and advocate for a holistic ethics. Mahimā cult is seen to be propagating the truth of unity in diversity and welfare of all beings.

References

Bhīmā Bhoi, *Stuti Cintāmaṇi*, Bhubaneswar: Utkal University.

Biswanath Baba, 1974, *Satya Mahimā Dharma Pratipādaka*, Cuttack: Dharmagrantha Store.

Nath, Satrughna, 1990, *Mahima Dharma Dhara*, Bhubaneswar: Hemalata Nath.

16

Mahimā and Mahāyāna

Decoding the Concord

Patitapaban Das

For preliminary clarification, Mahimā Dharma is said to be the last and latest movement of post-classical phase as it came to the fore during 1860s. With a significant fan-following in Odisha as well as the neighbouring states of Bengal, Chhattisgarh and Andhra, Mahimā Dharma presented a magnificent philosophical underpinning and an alternative religious movement to the mainstream religions like Hinduism. However, unlike recently, this genuine indigenous religio-philosophical system has been subjected to the political as well as philosophical subjugation of mainstream religions like Hinduism, (particularly Vaiṣṇavism and Buddhism). Scholars often banish this creed as merely an offshoot of Vedāntin tradition having sometimes as distorted views of the original. Scholars also sometimes equate it with neo-Buddhist cult slowly popularizing in rural Odisha to save the downtrodden from the religious discrimination clung by the mainstream Hindu tradition. Another school of thought smells religious syncretism in it by that branding it as philosophically empty. Numerous literatures are available, though, to show that Mahimā Dharma is not an offshoot of Vedāntic thought in modification. Similarly, though scholars smell seemingly similarity between Mahimā Dharma with Kashmir Śaivism, Vīraśaivism, Nātha Dharma and Buddhism, this paper is, however, an attempt to decode the seemingly concord between Mahimā and Mahāyāna sect prevalent in Odisha. It tries to establish that the religious experiences shared by both these sects are quite dissimilar but shaped in seemingly similar socio-political situations.

While most religions are found to be necessary, some of them are due to their extraordinary exploration of religious experience and some others are due to their social cohesive value. The history of world religions has traversed a long journey in the timeline of human civilization. Many of them bank heavily on the idea of a supernatural entity or godhead, while some others are heavily dependent on the idea of social cohesiveness as the core of religious phenomenon. In India, the division is more conspicuous but highly complex. Religions like Hinduism and Christianity believe in gods/God as the core of their religious experience while religions like Buddhism detach themselves from this idea. Sects in each section again differ from each other on the basis of their varied metaphysical, epistemological and ethical concerns. This is how group similarities and differences occur among religious sects that give rise to religious differences as well as possibilities of religious syncretism.

Religious syncretism comes forth either due to the process of assent or sometimes due to dissent too. In common parlance, we call it religious syncretism, when one sect of a particular religion adopts or assimilates similar beliefs from one or more foreign group/s. In many parts of our country, we find different sects follow important teachings from two different religions and are amalgamated into one. This is called a flat and simple kind of syncretism. Is it not possible to have a kind of syncretism, when a sect sets out of defiance from the original religious creed? Mahimā Dharma originated from Odisha could be in this group. However, before we delve deep into the nature and structure of this kind of syncretism, a preliminary introduction of the creed is essential. Moreover, it is also important to discuss one of the major sources of syncretism said to be happened in this.

Mahimā Dharma: An Introduction

While introducing the need of taking up a study on the Mahimā Dharma, Tandra Patnaik (2016: 11-12) counts two major motivations:

1. Mahimā Dharma is said to be the last and latest movement of post-classical phase as it came to the fore during 1860s.
2. During the last two decades, there has been a sudden spurt in attention to Mahimā Dharma, especially from the Western scholars.

The study could have another reason of motivation too. Mahimā Dharma is unique in its form of defiance or dissent and strong commitment to the social cohesion. This is the reason that motivates me to take up the study as a moral philosopher in the field. Mahimā Dharma originated for the uprising of the downtrodden, socially backward class. Tandra Patnaik, while deliberating the uniqueness of the creed from other contemporary movements, also points out this aspect of the creed very aptly:

> During this period, India had witnessed the rise of neo-Hinduism like Brahmo Samaj, Arya Samaj movement and many more. But they were more or less elitist movements ... but Mahimā Dharma is exclusively a movement meant for the underdog.
>
> – Ibid.: 11

And this is the precise reason for which it is more often considered to be an offshoot of another major religion prevalent in Odisha, i.e. Mahāyāna Buddhism. The present paper rejects this thesis in claiming that though Mahimā Dharma was influenced by the Mahāyāna tradition prevalent in Odisha at that moment, it retained its uniqueness as a novel religious movement for the downtrodden people. Having said so, it is not denied that the process of syncretism did happen through many of the peripheral beliefs that form the edifice of this religious section in Odisha.

The Voice of Dissent

Both Mahimā and Mahāyāna set out as voices of dissent. Mahāyāna recorded its defiance against its distant other – Brāhmanism – as all the sects of other Buddhism. It also records its defiance against its nearest other – Hīnayāna – in many significant ways. Mahāyāna as an important sect of Buddhism opposes the caste discrimination and oppression inherent in the Brāhmanic tradition. It opposed the whole gamut of Brāhmanism from many fronts – nature of the godhead, sources of religious authority, nature of *mukti*, ways to obtain *mukti*, social accountability of a creed, etc. It is difficult to discuss all these in detail here due to the paucity of space. However, one thing is very obvious that Buddhism is known for its voices of dissent in India. It originated as a rebellious movement in Indian religious milieu.

Down the line, Buddhism also got divided into two major groups: Hīnayāna and Mahāyāna. Two major differences could be recorded between the two:

1. The small vehicle (Hīnayāna) as to say emphasizes on individual liberation, while the Mahāyāna (great vehicle) reiterates on the collective liberation.
2. The Mahāyāna believes that each individual can become the Buddha, while the Hīnayāna believes that only Śākyamuni has potential to become the Buddha.

To show the difference between the two sects, Hirakawa Akira (2007: 296) writes:

> A *bodhisattva* must believe that he has the character or nature necessary to become a Buddha. In this respect, the Mahāyāna practitioner's position differs from that of Hīnayāna. ... Hīnayāna or Nikāya Buddhist doctrine was formulated with the intention of enabling the practitioner to become an *arhat*. The Hīnayānist could not conceive of himself as attaining the same degree of enlightenment as the Buddha and consequently did not recognize in himself the qualities that would enable him to become a Buddha. This difference in the ways in which the practitioner viewed himself and his potential constitutes the basic distinction between Hīnayāna and Mahāyāna Buddhism.

This is exactly the point for which Mahāyāna Buddhism became popular in India by which human beings can retain or gain their own confidence. This is humanistic so far to say that it lays utmost importance on human capability than some predetermined and predestined characteristics. This also provides a ray of hope for human accomplishments; provides reason as well as certainty for human endeavour. The underlying principle however is equality and value on the dignity of labour – human enterprise. This has the potential to destroy the dividing line between men and promises for a collective liberation. As we discussed earlier, Mahimā Dharma also recorded a tone of defiance to its nearest other – the Jagannātha culture – popular in Odisha. To delineate the nature of defiance echoed by the Mahimā Dharma, Tandra Patnaik (2016: 11-12) writes:

> Its voice of dissent came from within the heart as the society during that period had witnessed the worst forms of atrocities and ignominy meted out to the marginalized section of the society in the name of Sanātana Dharma. So when Mahimā Swāmī, the founder of the *dharma*, came out

> with the revolutionary idea of no idol, no caste distinction, no religious pomposities, but a simple life of surrendering to the one and ineffable Alekha Mahimā it ignited a new hope in the heart of the people who have been treated as pariahs.

Just like the Buddhist tradition, Mahimā Dharma questions the very nature and function of the godhead from the social point of view. It questions the very existence of the Lord Jagannātha, the Supreme Lord, worshipped by Odias unanimously. The *sādhus* and saints say that Lord Jagannātha resides in the grand temple. But had he been the real master of the universe (the eternal meaning of Jagannātha) why he should have confined himself within the precincts of the temple? Why should he have created the discrimination between man and man? He is called Jagannātha because in his eyes everybody in the world is equal (ibid.: 130).

The scepticism against the capability of the Lord himself triggered a violent attack on the sacred temple by the Mahimāpanthīs and the religion gets its first martyr. When the Lord abandons your hand, either destroy the Lord or dismantle the very idea of the lord *in toto.* The first happened by the attack on the Jagannātha Temple at Purī by some Kumbhipaṭiās hailed from Sambalpur, whereas the later was initiated by innumerable writings by Bhīmā Bhoi, the ardent champion of the religion. Both the events can be seen strategic in their goals – freedom from the religious subjugation done by the upper caste on the lower caste. The reaction of the violent Mahimāpanthīs through destroying and de-sacreding *prasāda*s in the temple and attacking it or by Bhīmā Bhoi through his writings is the result of perennial frustration accumulated over the years by constant apathy towards sufferings inflicted on a particular group due to their group identity. The reaction could be seen in the backdrop of large-scale religious atrocities inflicted on the downtrodden groups of the society. The fact remained that the period was contaminated by the unholy accord between the king and the high-caste people. The state of affairs in Odisha especially in religious matter was hijacked by this unholy bonhomie. The Jagannātha culture considered to be an excellent epitome of syncretism was in a quandary. The gloomy state of affairs can be warranted from Hunter's report in *A Statistical Account of Bengal* in 1870 as follows:

> The temple of Jagganātha in which every creed obtained an asylum and in which every class and sect can find its God now closes its doors to its low caste population. – 1876: 62

It is noteworthy that Jagganātha culture in Odisha was considered to be the epitome of religious inclusiveness as it encompasses glimpses of different religions like Brāhmanism, Buddhism, Tantra and some amount of *śabara* (aborigins) religious world view into its ambit. However, soon this stupendous syncretism turned out to be a worst instance of religious obscurantism and exclusiveness for the downtrodden. It turned out to be strict orthodoxism and caste-bound society. This created a great amount of frustration and agony in the mind and heart of those belonging to the lower strata of the society. Discussing the sorry state of affairs in Odisha, Ishita Banerjee-Dube (2001: 158) observes:

> The close association with royalty, coupled with the introduction of caste discrimination in practices of the temple at Purī, made Jagannātha appear in the nineteenth century as an exclusive and distant Lord, a monopoly of brāhmaṇas and rulers. He had moved away far from his initial devotees and had come to be identified with those who wielded power and authority.

This affair can reason the rationale behind the violent attack on the temple as well as find the germination of a new revolutionary cult at hand. The Kanapaṭiās attacked the temple while Bhīmā

Bhoi attacked the very foundation of the cult itself where he intended to destroy the very idea of a god that is a symbol of subjugation and silent apathy. In one of the verses, Bhīmā Bhoi clarifies:

> *Jagannātha is within your heart*
> *You unnecessarily worship his idol.*
> *His idol is made after all, with dry-wood*
> *Can the worship of such an idol take you to* Vaikuṇṭha?
>
> – Patnaik 2016: 10

A submissive reading can be rendered for this stanza that prescribes for the supremacy of Lord Jagannātha that should be cultivated in one's heart not through idolatry. This means to oppose the medium than the goal. From this, many scholars might think that Bhīmā Bhoi prescribing to worship Jagannātha cannot be a separate sect but the same culture. This can be seen through in other lens. In order to destroy an idea it is preliminary to destroy the symbols symbolizing that idea. Hence, the idea of keeping the Lord in the heart occurs. If the divinity does not exist in the temple what shall happen to the institution around which all kinds of atrocities happen in the name of divinity. Just like the Buddhist movement, it opposes idolatry by tooth and nail. It believes that idols are just made of five gross elements. Therefore, the idols are not the source of divinity but thought so due to ignorance. In another verse he declares:

> *Look how ignorant the people are?*
> *They fall at the feet of idols and promise to offer all delicacies*
> *For the fulfilment of their prayer,*
> *They are but statues without consciousness or soul.*
> *How can such a god grant you boons?* – Ibid.

Not that Mahimāpanthīs are against idol worship, they are also against worshipping many gods and goddesses prevalent in the Sanātana Dharma. They strongly believe that the innumerable gods and goddesses worshipped in the temple are no more sacred. The divinity has vanished (*Stuti Cintāmaṇi* 95) from all those so-called sacred places as temples had turned into the centre of institutionalized oppression of the poor and the deprived. Where these two sects differ is their underpinning metaphysical stance behind the idolatry. Mahāyāna believes in metaphysical emptiness for the ultimate, whereas Mahimāpanthīs regard Him to be full of possibilities. They believe in the epistemological emptiness in the sense that since the reality is full of *guṇas*, determination limits it and therefore ineffable.

Not only against gods and goddesses, Mahimā Dharma is against the authority of Vedas or Śāstras in the journey of self-realization. Bhīmā Bhoi discards Vedas as "moth-eaten dry leaves" and declares that most treacherous torture on the oppressed are due to the injunctions in the Śāstras. As he declares:

> *Many may talk of the reality and show the path*
> *narrated by Śāstras,*
> *Without everknowing what the* Brahman *is.*
> *That is why the experts in Veda are called "drunkard"*
> *The knowledge of Śāstras makes them more confused.*
> *As a drunkard under the spell of liquor talks without senses,*
> *Similar is the attitude of the people adept in Śāstras*
> *How can they explain the nature of* Brahman*?*
> *They can go as far as Veda can dictate them not more.*
>
> – *Brahma Nirūpaṇa Gītā* 14.127-30

God as Śūnya

This is the single point similarity by which scholars as well as commoners equate Mahimā Dharma with Mahāyāna. Mahāyāna tradition is known for its notion of *śūnyatā* in relation to the Ultimate Reality. Mahāyāna, in its many branches, advocates both metaphysical as well as epistemological Śūnyavāda. The reality is *śūnya* as well as it is devoid of any cognizing categories. The reality is beyond *catuṣkoṭi*, the fourfold logic. Nāgārjuna, the ardent advocate of the notion of *śūnyatā*, believes that the reality is *śūnya* in the sense that it lacks inherent *svabhāva*.

Vajrayāna, the Tāntric version of Mahāyāna Buddhism, provides a religious tint to the original idea of *śūnyatā*. It epitomizes *śūnyatā* in the form of the *vajrasattva*. This Tāntric sect of Mahāyāna Buddhism not only considers that *śūnyatā* as ineffable, incomprehensible highest reality, but also it is the object of devotion. Says this tradition:

> *Śūnyatā* is said to be *vajra* (*śūnyatāvajramityuktam*) and all manifestation in form is said to be *sattva*; so *vajrasattva* implies the unity and identity of the two.
>
> – Quoted in Dasgupta 1974: 78

Mahimā Dharma is also centred on the notion of God as *śūnya*. In this case, God does not stand for a symbol or idol but a formless principle. Bhīmā Bhoi through his writings elaborates the notion of *śūnya* frequently. Therefore, scholars tend to think that Mahimā Dharma is influenced by Mahāyāna in respect to this central concept. Let us quote some of the verses from Bhīmā Bhoi showing his notion of *śūnya* as well as how it is different from the other traditions.

> *He roams in the* śūnya, *his footsteps*
> *You fathom within your heart,*
> *Limitless is the ocean called Mahimā.*
>
> – *Bhajanamālā* 1.5

> *He has neither form, nor outline*
> *The* śūnya-*bodied has appeared in the* śūnya.
> *He has neither form nor a contour*
> *Whose abode is the temple of* śūnya. – Ibid. 1.53

One can see that Bhīmā Bhoi provides a wider connotation to the concept of *śūnya*. It is the all-pervading principle. One becomes amazed to find that the idea of *śūnya* was gradually being used interchangeably with the notion of *Brahman*. One feels amazed as well as frustrated to find such a combination in Mahimā literature where the *Śūnya Brahman* was coined to refer to God. The frustration deems when it is seen in the wider canvas of Odishan cultural milieu of the period. The use of the term *śūnya* in consonance with *Brahman* was so common in Odishan culture that neither the common men nor the philosophers of the land who wrote their philosophy for this segment of the populace were aware of the fact that these two words – *Brahman* and *śūnya* – are drawn from the two so-called inimical tradition, Brāhmanical and non-Brāhmanical, respectively. Does not the combination of the concepts – *śūnya* and *Brahman* – sound a little queer, since no other philosophical or religious tradition of India uses these two terms conjointly? One may ask: why did Bhīmā Bhoi, for that matter his predecessors, append the word *Brahman* to *śūnya*? One of them has its roots in the Buddhist tradition and the other one is the Vedic/Upaniṣadic tradition. It seems that there existed a distinct philosophical tradition in Odisha that did not view these two concepts as originating from rival metaphysical sources.[1] This fusion also proves that the ideas of *śūnya* and *Brahman* are not extracted directly either from Buddhism or from Advaitism. However, at certain places Eschmann claims that Mahimā Dharma takes up "the Buddhist concept of emptiness (*śūnya*) and identifies with the Hindu

---

1 *Eschmann* (1978) rightly points out about this fusion of cultures. Tandra Patnaik entirely agrees with her that Mahimā Dharma has its roots in the medieval Vaiṣṇava tradition of Odisha, a tradition that defied all the philosophical norms of Vaiṣṇavism. Vaiṣṇavism as a sect of Advaita Vedānta then borrows the concept from the original.

conception of *Parama-Brahman* and *Īśvara-Puruṣa*."[2]

Not only the notion of *Brahman* was repeatedly associated with the notion of *śūnya*, but also it is associated with another popular term *pūrṇa* (full). For the first association, he writes:

The indivisible Brahman *is One and unique*
He lacks nothing as he is self-complete (pūrṇa)
This is what is called as śūnya *and* mahāśūnya
Nothing transcends Him. – Brahma Nirūpaṇa Gītā, 3rd Canto

The use of terms like *śūnya* and *pūrṇa* defines Mahimā Dharma's ontological stand on the principle that the Ultimate Reality is not ontologically empty, rather, it is complete with all possible possibilities. Hence, it can be contrasted with Mahāyāna in this respect. On the other hand, it is said that the notion of *śūnya* as *Brahman* and *pūrṇa* is influenced by Odia culture that was quite ubiquitous at the time. For example, Acyutananda Dasa says:

It has no shape no colour
It is invisible and without a name.
This Brahman *is called* Śūnya Brahman.
– *Śabda-Brahman Saṁhitā*, 4th Canto

Similarly, it seems similar with the idea of *śūnya* developed by the Mahāyāna also, yet it differs from it in a significant way. Scholars like Patnaik and S.C. Panigrahi delineate the difference deeply. However, I take a separate root to show the difference between the two. The difference lies in the commitment of the two traditions in respect to the notion of *mukti*.

Redemption

We witnessed that Mahāyāna Buddhism is known for and differentiated from the Hīnayāna Buddhism in respect to the achievement of *mukti*. Mahāyāna Buddhist believes that

---

2 Eschmann (1978: 389). Though in the next lines she admits the role of the Odia medieval *sants* in the development of Mahimā Dharma.

everyone can become a Buddha because everyone has the potential to become the Buddha (*bodhisattva mahāsattva*). Since everyone is a potential Buddha, the practitioner has to know his inner potential and become the Buddha. However, he may seek help from others in the form of experience only. However, Bhīmā Bhoi seems to believe that in order to get *mukti*, the appeasement is necessary. This can be validated from the wide quoted verse:

> *prāṇiṅka arata dukha apramita*
> *dekhudekhu kiba sāhu* ।
> *mo jībana pāche narke paḍithau*
> *jagata udhāra heu* ॥ – *Stuti Cintāmaṇi* 27.19
>
> Why do bear the mortal pain and scream yet noticed though my life yills in bull let the world be (trnslation author's).

From this verse one can be baffled by the altruistic tinge of Mahimā Dharma as a revolutionist movement. It also shows the existing social suffering and the helplessness of the poet in eradicating it. He has to offer his life to be yelled in the hell for the upliftment of the downtrodden but he himself cannot redeem them. This is the stark difference between the two traditions. It shows the poet's magnanimity, humility as well as sense of agony and social commitment. While Mahāyāna Buddhism bestows on each individual to be a potential Buddha, having abundant power not only to become the Buddha himself but can help others being Buddha or at least to get *arhat*ship, one has to sacrifice even his own life to the godhead for the liberation of oneself or the other. This can be treated as a single point difference that keeps Mahāyāna and Mahimā apart.

Conjecture and Concord

However, many a time, scholars see seemingly a concord between Buddhism (Mahāyāna Buddhism) and Mahimā Dharma. In fact, N.N. Vasu was the first scholar credited for this conjecture. Vasu terms Mahimā Dharma as new Buddhism and Mahimāpanthīs as crypto Buddhists who due to fear of royal castration, envelop them in the cocoon of Mahimā Dharma. To prove the assumption, Vasu (1986: 150) writes:

> Following this the Utkal community of Buddhists has given the name "Mahimā Dharma" to its creed and styles itself as Mahimā Dharmin.

To strengthen the argument further, Vasu argues that Buddhists never designated their faith as Buddhism, rather they are fond of calling it *sadharma* or *sad-dharma*. Since, Mahimā Dharma uses the term *dharma* extensively to characterize the creed, it is not another new creed, but only a new name to the existing Buddhist creed of Odisha. Vasu (ibid.) concludes from this argument as the following:

> Under the benign spirit of religious toleration and the noble and fostering spirit of freedom of thought inaugurated and scrupulously adhered to by the British government, this community has began, for forty years to rouse itself up, to throw its masks and to reassert duly.

Tandra Patnaik rebuffs these twofold justifications for the seeming concord between Buddhism and Mahimā Dharma. First, Patnaik argues that only by extensive use of the word *dharma* by the Mahimāpanthīs to define their creed cannot make them a Buddhist in disguise. To record the counter, she shows that the term *dharma* was also extensively, rather profusely, used by Sanātanadharmīs in general and as "Bhāgavata Dharma or Śaiva Dharma", etc. Therefore, extensive and abundant use of the term *dharma* is not sufficient to bring the conclusion that Mahimādharmīs are crypto Buddhists.

Second, Patnaik argues that Vasu's second argument lacks enough empirical data. Vasu argues that the Birtish positive predicament towards non-Semitic religions helped rising the Buddhist into a modified creed. While Patnaik shows the empirical deficiency in the argument, it could also be argued that if the British attitude was favourable for the non-Semitic religions, what was the emergency the Buddhist creed took a modification and a brand new name. This seems quite illogical *de novo*. To show the empirical deficiency, Patnaik (2016: 159) argues that no records in the British rules show to support this claim. Hence, Vasu's claim of Mahimā Dharma as a neo-Budhism does not stand.

The Thesis

Patnaik rejects Vasu's claim only to align with Vedāntins. For her, Mahimā Dharma can be better called as an offshoot of Vedānta. However, this is also a misnomer and too simple to brand this indigenous cult as an offshoot of another. Sporadic similarities in principle as well as practice can be traced in two creeds due to mutual coexistence for a longer time. That also goes with the Buddhism. While Patnaik rejects these similarities with Buddhist practice naming them as baseless conjectures, she does not do so in the case of Vedāntin practices.

It could be argued then that the concord between Buddhist creed and Mahimā philosophy is not of genuine syncretism. Some of the practices do converge due to the migration of original Buddhist practitioners to Mahimā Dharma. However, due to some sporadic convergence of practices this new creed cannot be termed as a syncretic religion too. Reason could be manifold. The conceptual and metaphysical worlds of two religions do take diverged directions. The reflections of those conceptual worlds however do take occasional convergence due to long cultural belonging. Therefore, it can be concluded that Mahimā Dharma is a genuine indigenous creed flourished in Odisha.

References

Akira, Hirakawa, 2007, *A History of Indian Buddhism: From Sakyamuni to Early Mahayana*, New Delhi: Motilal Banarsidass.

Banarjee-Dube, Ishita, 2001, "Issues of Faith, Enactment of Contest: The Founding of Mahimā Dharma in Nineteenth Century Orissa", in *Jagannath Revisited: Studying Society, Religion and the State in Orissa*, ed. H. Kulke and B. Schnepal, New Delhi: Manohar.

Bhīmā Bhoi, *Bhajanamālā*.

Bhīmā Bhoi, *Stuti Cintāmaṇi*.

Dasa, Acyutananda, 1979, *Śabda-Brahman Saṁhitā*, 4th canto, Cuttack: Book and Books.

Dasgupta, S.B., 1974, *Introduction to Tantric Buddhism*, Calcutta: University of Calcutta.

Eschmann, A., 1978, *Mahima Dharma: An Autochthonous Hindu Reform Movement*, in *The Cult of Jagannath and the Regional Tradition of Orissa*, ed. A. Eschmann et al., New Delhi: Manohar.

Hunter, W.W., 1876, *A Statistical Account of Bengal*, vol. XIX, repr., Delhi: Concept Publishing.

Panigrahi, S.C., 1998, *Bhima Bhoi and Mahima Darsana*, Cuttack: Santosh Publication in Collaboration with the Postgraduate Department of Philosophy, Utkal University.

Patnaik, Tandra, 2016, *God as Śūnya: The Philosophy of Mahimā Dharma and Bhīmā Bhoi*, New Delhi: D.K. Printworld.

Vasu, N.N., 1986, *Modern Buddhism and Its Followers in Orissa*, New Delhi: Gian Publishing House.

Sritinisedha Gītā.

Brahma Nirupaṇ Gītā.

17

Interreligious Dialogue and Reflective Equilibrium

Gopal Sahu

Introduction

Religion has been an integral part of human civilization and continues to play a significant role in shaping individual and societal beliefs and values. However, the diversity of religious beliefs and practices has often led to conflicts and tensions among different religious communities. Moreover, religious conflicts in liberal democratic societies can arise when there is a clash between religious beliefs or practices and the values and principles that underpin liberal democracy, such as freedom of expression, equality and the rule of law. The tension often arises from the fact that liberal democratic societies prioritize individual rights and autonomy, while religious beliefs and practices may prioritize communal values and obedience to religious authority. Finding a balance between religious freedom and other fundamental values can be a complex and ongoing challenge, particularly as societies become more diverse and religiously pluralistic.

In recent times, there has been an increasing need for interreligious dialogue as a means of promoting mutual understanding and peaceful coexistence among people of different faiths and resolving value conflicts between religions and democratic societies. In order to address these conflicts, liberal democratic societies, though often, rely on a range of mechanisms, including legal protections for individual rights and freedoms, it follows dialogue and engagement with religious communities as well. This article aims to examine some of the practical and philosophical problems that arise in the context of religious conflicts and interreligious dialogue. It will explore questions such as the nature of religious belief, the role of reason and criticism in religious discourse and the limits of interreligious dialogue in addressing deep-seated religious disagreements. The paper will discuss some such practical and philosophical issues in interreligious dialogues, such as no interreligious dialogue is possible as religions are based on faith and doctrines that are to be respected and revered and not be debated through logic, reasoning, reflection and formal dialogue. Second, if dialogue is set in informal setting, it will turn to rhetoric and risk the problem of proselytizing and indoctrination. Besides, there are problems in the modality, procedure and decorum of holding the informal dialogues. Third, even if dialogue is possible, the ontological difference across the religions on the nature of God, world and the man will lead to difference in epistemology and axiology. Ultimately, the article seeks to shed light on the challenges and complexities involved in promoting religious harmony and understanding in a pluralistic and liberal democratic world. The paper suggests "Reflective Equilibrium" as a conceptual model for strengthening interreligious dialogues in resolving religious conflicts.

In what follows, the second section will discuss the nature of religious conflicts and explains the causes of such conflicts with examples. Third section will discuss interreligious dialogues as a means of resolution of religious conflicts and will discuss some practical and philosophical problems in it. Fourth section deals with the role of reflective equilibrium in strengthening interreligious dialogues in resolving religious conflicts. Fifth section concludes that though may not resolve conflicts and establish consensus in the logical sense, people of different faiths can work towards a more peaceful and harmonious world, one in which religious diversity is celebrated rather than feared. Further, it concludes that the interreligious dialogue among the believers, followers and experts of different religious traditions and world view, though may not resolve conflicts and establish consensus in the logical sense, will definitely create conducive environment for mutual understanding, communication and integration in matter pertaining to the peace, harmony and general well-being among the interreligious traditions.

Religious Conflicts

Religion is a complex and multifaceted phenomenon that encompasses a wide range of beliefs, practices and institutions. At its core, religion involves a set of beliefs and values about the nature of reality, the meaning of life and the relationship between human beings and the divine or supernatural. These beliefs and values often provide a framework for understanding the world and one's place in it and may be expressed through rituals, prayers and other forms of worship.

Religion can take many different forms and there is significant diversity within and across different religious traditions. Some religions are monotheistic, meaning they believe in one God or deity, while others are polytheistic, as they believe in multiple gods or deities. Some religions emphasize personal salvation or enlightenment, while others focus on social justice or ethical conduct. Some religions have well-defined hierarchies and institutional structures, while others are more decentralized and loosely organized.[1]

While religion can be a source of comfort, meaning and harmony for many people, it can also be a source of conflict and division as well. Religious differences have been a persistent source of conflict throughout human history and continue to pose significant challenges to global peace and security. Religious conflict refers to conflicts or tensions that arise between individuals or groups of different religious backgrounds. These conflicts can take many different forms, ranging from relatively mild disagreements to violent clashes and acts of terrorism. Religious conflict can occur at the individual, community, national, or international level and can be driven by a wide range of factors, including ideology, politics, economics and social issues.[2]

Religious conflicts arise both at social and individual levels. One example of religious conflict that arises at social level is the ongoing conflict between Israel and Palestine. This conflict has its roots in the competing claims of Israelis and Palestinians to the same land, which is considered holy by both Jews and Muslims. The conflict has been characterized by violence and bloodshed, with both sides engaging in acts of terrorism, military action and other forms of violence. Another example of religious conflict is the conflict between Hindus and Muslims in India. This conflict has a long history, dating back to the partition of India in 1947, which led to the creation of Pakistan as a separate Muslim-majority state. Since then, there have been numerous instances of violence

---

1 For a comprehensive and comparative study of the different beliefs, practices, and world views of different religions, see Ridgeon 2003.

2 For an overview of the various ways in which religion can contribute to conflicts, including through identity politics, exclusivism, and extremism, see Carlson and Burns Jr. 2013.

and tension between Hindus and Muslims in India, including riots, bombings and other acts of terrorism. It is important to note that while religious conflicts are often framed in terms of religious differences, they are often driven by deeper political, economic and social factors. For example, conflicts between Sunni and Shia Muslims in the Middle East are often driven by political and economic grievances, rather than purely religious differences. Understanding the complex dynamics of religious conflicts requires looking beyond surface-level differences and examining the underlying causes and motivations.

Religious conflicts can also occur at the individual level, such as in cases where family members or friends have different religious beliefs and values. These conflicts may be less violent than large-scale conflicts, but can still cause significant stress and tension within families and communities. Religious conflicts involving values are conflicts that arise when different religious groups hold conflicting beliefs about the nature of morality, ethics and values. These conflicts can occur at both the individual and societal level and can be driven by a wide range of factors, including religious doctrine, cultural traditions and political ideologies.

One example of a religious conflict involving values is the debate over abortion. Many religious groups, including Catholics and Evangelical Christians, believe that abortion is morally wrong and should be illegal. On the other hand, many secular and liberal religious groups, as well as some more progressive religious groups, believe that women have the right to choose whether or not to have an abortion. This conflict has led to heated debates and protests, as well as legal challenges and attempts to restrict access to abortion. Yet another example of such conflict is the tension that can arise between freedom of expression and religious sensitivities. In liberal democratic societies, freedom of expression is a fundamental right, which includes the right to criticize and even ridicule religious beliefs and practices. However, some religious groups may find such expressions offensive or blasphemous, leading to tensions and conflicts (see Mousma and Soper 2008).

There arise some religious conflicts of philosophical nature. Religious conflicts involving philosophy are conflicts that arise when different religious groups hold different beliefs about the nature of reality, the existence of God or gods and the nature of the universe. These conflicts can be particularly deeper and logical as they involve core beliefs that are often deeply ingrained and resistant to change. One example of a religious conflict involving metaphysics is the debate over the existence of God. Many religious groups, such as Christians, Muslims and Jews, believe in the existence of a single, all-powerful God who created the universe and governs it through divine providence. On the other hand, many atheists and secularists reject the idea of God as a matter of metaphysical principle, arguing that the universe can be explained solely in terms of natural laws and empirical evidence.

Another example of a religious conflict involving philosophy is the debate over the relationship between science and religion. Some religious groups, such as fundamentalist Christians, reject the findings of science on metaphysical grounds, arguing that scientific theories and evidence that conflict with their religious beliefs should be rejected. On the other hand, many scientists and secularists argue that science provides the most reliable and objective means of understanding the nature of reality and that religious beliefs should be subject to scientific scrutiny and evaluation.[3]

Interreligious Dialogue and Its Problems

In order to address these conflicts, liberal democratic societies

[3] For religious and ontological conflicts, see, Schmidt-Leukel 2013.

often rely on a range of mechanisms, including legal protections for individual rights and freedoms, as well as dialogue and engagement with religious communities. However, finding a balance between religious freedom and other fundamental values can be a complex and ongoing challenge, particularly as societies become more diverse and religiously pluralistic. In recent times, there has been an increasing need for interreligious dialogue as a means of promoting mutual understanding and peaceful coexistence among people of different faiths.

Interreligious dialogue is a process of communication and understanding between individuals or groups of different religious traditions. The goal of interreligious dialogue is to promote mutual respect, understanding and cooperation between different religious communities and to build bridges of understanding and cooperation across religious and cultural divides. Interreligious dialogue can take many different forms, ranging from formal discussions and debates to informal conversations and shared activities. Interreligious dialogue can play an important role in resolving religious conflicts by creating opportunities for individuals and groups of different religious backgrounds to engage in respectful and open-minded communication with one another. Through dialogue, individuals and groups can gain a better understanding of each other's beliefs, values and perspectives and work towards finding common ground and shared values that can help to bridge the divide (for details, see Eck 2006; Phan 2013). Interreligious dialogue is a process of conversation and engagement between individuals or groups representing different religious traditions. Its aim is to foster understanding, promote mutual respect and explore common ground while acknowledging and appreciating religious diversity. Interreligious dialogue can take various forms, such as formal discussions, conferences, seminars, or informal conversations.

One example of interreligious dialogue is interfaith prayer services, where members of different religious communities come together to share prayers and reflections. These services can help to promote understanding and respect between different religious traditions and can provide an opportunity for people of different faiths to come together in a spirit of unity and cooperation. Another example of interreligious dialogue is the work of organizations such as the *sarva dharma sama bhāva*, which aims to promote interfaith cooperation and understanding among people of all religions. The congregation works to bring together people of different religious backgrounds to engage in dialogue, service projects and other activities that promote understanding and cooperation.

Interreligious dialogue can also occur at the political level, such as through diplomatic efforts aimed at promoting peace and understanding between countries of different religious backgrounds. For example, the United Nations Alliance of Civilizations is an international organization that works to promote intercultural and interreligious dialogue as a means of promoting peace and stability around the world (Tomalin and Starkey 2018).

One way that interreligious dialogue can help to resolve religious conflicts is by promoting empathy and understanding between different religious groups. By engaging in dialogue with people of different religious backgrounds, individuals can gain a deeper appreciation for the experiences, values and perspectives of others, and develop a greater sense of empathy and connection with people from different backgrounds. This can help to break down stereotypes and prejudices and create a greater sense of mutual respect and understanding.

Another way that interreligious dialogue can help to resolve religious conflicts is by promoting the exchange of ideas and perspectives. Through dialogue, individuals and groups of different religious backgrounds can share their beliefs and perspectives on complex and sensitive issues and work towards finding common ground and shared values that can help to bridge the divide. This can help to promote greater understanding and cooperation between different religious communities and can create opportunities for creative problem-solving and collaboration.

A concrete example of how interreligious dialogue has helped to resolve religious conflicts can be seen in the peace process in Northern Ireland. The conflict in Northern Ireland was driven in part by religious differences between Protestants and Catholics, and was characterized by sectarian violence and deep-seated animosity between the two communities. However, through a sustained effort at interreligious dialogue and reconciliation, including the work of religious leaders and peace activists, significant progress has been made towards resolving the conflict and promoting peace and stability in the region.

Interreligious dialogue can play an important role in resolving religious conflicts by promoting empathy, understanding and the exchange of ideas between different religious communities. While interreligious dialogue is not a panacea for all religious conflicts, it can create opportunities for individuals and groups to work towards finding common ground and shared values that can help to bridge the divide and promote greater understanding and cooperation between different religious traditions (Cornille 2012).[4]

---

[4] See, *The Ethics of Interfaith Dialogue.* This book offers a philosophical and ethical reflection on the nature and purpose of interfaith dialogue, particularly from a Christian perspective. It includes discussions on the concept of religious pluralism, the role of reason in religious discourse, and the challenges and opportunities of engaging with people of different faiths.

While interreligious dialogue can be a valuable tool for promoting understanding and cooperation between different religious groups, it is not without its challenges and limitations. Some of the problems may be called as practical because they are contextual and historical. The follwing are some of the practical problems and challenges associated with interreligious dialogue.

First is the lack of trust. Interreligious dialogue requires a high degree of trust between different religious groups. However, in some cases, deep-seated historical, political or social divisions may make it difficult for groups to trust one another. Second, interreligious dialogue can be complicated by power imbalances, where one group may have more influence or resources than another. This can make it difficult for groups to engage in dialogue as equals and may undermine the effectiveness of the dialogue process. Third, there are cultural and linguistic barriers. Interreligious dialogue may be complicated by cultural and linguistic barriers, as individuals from different religious backgrounds may have different cultural norms and speak different languages, which can make communication difficult. Fourth, there are intra-religious differences. Interreligious dialogue may be complicated by differences within religious traditions, such as between different denominations or sects. These internal differences may make it difficult for religious groups to speak with a unified voice or may create tensions within the group that spill over into the dialogue process. Fifth, there is the problem of fundamentalism and political interference. Interreligious dialogue may be hindered by - that reject the possibility of dialogue or cooperation with other religious groups. Fundamentalist beliefs may be driven by a deep-seated sense of religious exclusivity and may view other religious groups as inherently inferior or misguided. Further, interreligious dialogue may be complicated by political interference, where political leaders or governments may seek to use dialogue as a means of advancing their own political agendas or interests. Another practical challenge is the question of how to measure the impact of interreligious dialogue. While it is clear that dialogue can promote understanding and respect, it can be difficult to quantify these outcomes or to assess their long-term impact. Moreover, there is a risk that dialogue can become merely symbolic, without leading to any real change on the ground. Besides, one of the most significant challenges is finding the right participants for the dialogue. It is important to ensure that the participants are representative of their respective communities and have the necessary knowledge and expertise to engage in meaningful dialogue.

In addition to the above practical challenges, there are also philosophical challenges to interreligious dialogue. One of the central philosophical challenges is the question of how to balance the demands of reason with the demands of faith. Religious beliefs are often deeply held and can be resistant to rational critique, which can make it difficult to find common ground across different traditions. At the same time, reason and rational argument are essential tools for resolving disputes and finding common ground, which means that they cannot be completely set aside in the context of interreligious dialogue.

Religious conflicts involving values can be particularly challenging to resolve, as they often involve deeply ethical and conceptual issues. The Euthyphro dilemma is a philosophical argument that challenges the idea that values and virtues are dependent on religion. It is named after the dialogue "Euthyphro" written by Plato, in which Socrates engages in a discussion with Euthyphro about the nature of piety. If morality is simply determined by the commands of the gods, then what is considered morally good would be arbitrary. The gods could command anything and it would be considered morally good solely because they commanded it. This implies that morality is subject to the whims of the gods and lacks a rational basis. If morality exists independently of religion and the gods simply recognize and communicate it, then religion becomes unnecessary as a foundation for morality.[5]

Another philosophical problem is the question of how to deal with the diversity of religious beliefs and practices. Different religions often have very different conceptions of the nature of God, the purpose of life and the meaning of morality, which can make it difficult to find common ground. Moreover, there are often significant differences within individual religions, as different communities interpret their scriptures and traditions in different ways. This diversity can be a source of richness and complexity, but it can also make it difficult to identify shared values and principles.

Interreligious Dialogues and Reflective Equilibrium

Despite these challenges, there are good reasons to be optimistic about the potential of interreligious dialogue to promote peace and understanding. Interreligious dialogue can be challenging, as it requires individuals and groups to engage in respectful and open-minded communication with people of different religious backgrounds. However, the benefits of interreligious dialogue are significant and include greater understanding and cooperation between different religious communities and a more peaceful and harmonious world.

Philosophers have played an important role in developing theoretical frameworks for understanding the nature of religious belief and the challenges of interreligious dialogue and their insights can help guide practical efforts to promote dialogue and understanding. Reflective equilibrium is one such philosophical

---

[5] For more in-depth information and analysis of the Euthyphro dilemma, you may refer to the original text of Plato's "Euthyphro" dialogue.

concept that can be used as a model for interreligious dialogue to resolve religious conflicts, particularly those involving philosophical aspects of religious conflicts. It is a method of moral reasoning that seeks to achieve coherence and consistency between our moral intuitions, principles and judgements. The basic idea of reflective equilibrium is that we start with our considered moral judgements and principles, and then work to achieve coherence and consistency between them. We may need to revise some of our initial judgements or principles in order to achieve this coherence, but the goal is to arrive at a set of moral beliefs that are mutually supportive and consistent. Reflective equilibrium is a method of moral reasoning that involves bringing one's beliefs and intuitions into coherence by adjusting them in light of one another. It has been discussed by many philosophers across different traditions.[6] In the context of interreligious dialogue, reflective equilibrium can be used to promote mutual understanding and cooperation between people of different faiths. It involves engaging in a process of dialogue and reflection, in which participants share their moral beliefs, values and principles, and seek to achieve coherence and consistency among them.

One way in which reflective equilibrium can be used in interreligious dialogue is by identifying areas of agreement

---

6 John Rawls: Rawls is perhaps the most well-known philosopher associated with the method of reflective equilibrium. He introduced the concept in his landmark book *A Theory of Justice* (1971) and developed it further in subsequent works. According to Rawls, the method of reflective equilibrium involves testing our moral principles against our considered judgements about particular cases, and then revising both our principles and judgements until they are in harmony with one another. Besides, Rawls, other eminent philosophers such as Nelson Goodman, Philippa Foot and Robert Nozick have used this principle in different fields of philosophy.

and disagreement between different religious traditions and working to achieve coherence and consistency between them. For example, participants may identify shared values such as compassion, justice and respect for human dignity, and work to develop a shared understanding of these values that is consistent with their respective religious traditions. Another way in which reflective equilibrium can be used in interreligious dialogue is by identifying areas of moral disagreement or conflict and working to achieve a resolution that is acceptable to all parties. This may involve revising some of our initial moral judgements or principles, or developing new principles that can accommodate different perspectives and beliefs.

Overall, reflective equilibrium offers a model for interreligious dialogue that seeks to promote mutual understanding and cooperation, while also respecting the diversity and complexity of different religious traditions. By engaging in a process of dialogue and reflection, participants can work towards a shared understanding of moral values and principles and develop strategies for resolving moral conflicts and promoting social harmony.

Reflective equilibrium is a method of moral reasoning that involves bringing one's beliefs and intuitions into coherence by adjusting them in light of one another. This method has important implications for interreligious dialogue. By testing our moral principles and intuitions against the beliefs and intuitions of others, we can arrive at a more coherent and consistent understanding of our own beliefs. At the same time, we can become more open to the perspectives of others and more willing to revise our own beliefs in light of new information and insights.

Reflective equilibrium can also help us navigate the philosophical and practical challenges of interreligious dialogue. By testing our beliefs and intuitions against the beliefs and intuitions of others, we can identify areas of agreement and disagreement, and work towards a more nuanced and sophisticated understanding of the issues at stake. Moreover, by engaging in reflective equilibrium, we can become more aware of our own biases and assumptions and more willing to consider the perspectives of others.

Conclusion

In conclusion, we can say that religious conflicts are a complex phenomenon that requires careful consideration and analysis in order to be properly addressed. Philosophers have contributed much to this effort, offering insights into the nature of religious belief, the role of reason in interreligious dialogue and the challenges of finding common ground across different traditions. While there are no easy solutions to the problem of religious conflict, it is clear that interreligious dialogue has an important role to play in promoting understanding, respect and peace. By engaging in respectful and open-minded dialogue with one another, people of different faiths can work towards a more peaceful and harmonious world, one in which religious diversity is celebrated rather than feared. In the end, it is only through mutual respect and understanding that we can hope to overcome the practical and philosophical problems that underlie religious conflicts and build a better future for all.

Interreligious dialogue is an important means of promoting understanding and peace across different religious traditions. While there are philosophical and practical challenges to this dialogue, the method of reflective equilibrium can help us navigate these challenges and arrive at a more coherent and consistent understanding of our own beliefs. By engaging in respectful and open-minded dialogue with one another, people of different faiths can work towards a more peaceful and harmonious world, one in which religious diversity is celebrated rather than feared.

Ultimately, the success of interreligious dialogue depends on a willingness to engage with one another in a spirit of openness and respect. While there will always be philosophical and practical challenges to such dialogue, the benefits of promoting understanding and peace across different religious traditions are too great to be ignored. By working together, people of different faiths can build a more harmonious and peaceful world, one in which religious diversity is seen as a source of strength rather than division.

References

Carlson, John D. and J. Patout Burns Jr. (eds), 2013, *The Oxford Handbook of Religious Conflict*, Oxford: Oxford University Press.

Cornille, Catherine, 2012, *The Ethics of Interfaith Dialogue: A Christian Perspective,* New York: Wiley-Blackwell.

Eck, Dianna L., 2006, "Religious Pluralism and Interreligious Dialogue", in *The Blackwell Companion to the Study of Religion*, ed. Robert A. Segal and Kocku von Stuckrad, New York: Wiley-Blackwell.

Mousma, Stephen and J. Christopher Soper (eds), 2008, *The Challenge of Pluralism: Church and State in Five Democracies*, Maryland; Rowman & Littlefield.

Phan, Peter C., 2013, "Religious Diversity and Interreligious Dialogue", in *The Cambridge Companion to Religious Diversity*, ed. Robert McKim, Combridge, MA: Cambridge University Press.

Rawls, John, 1971, *A Theory of Justice,* Combridge, MA: Harvand University Press.

Ridgeon Lloyrd (ed.), 2003, *Major World Religions: From Their Origin to the Present*, London: Routledge.

Schmidt-Leukel, Perry, 2013, *Religious Pluralism and Interreligious Theology: The Gifford Lectures*, New York: Orbis Books.

Tomalin, Emma and Caroline Starkey (eds), 2018, *Interreligious Dialogue: From Religion to Geopolitics*, New York: Palgrave Macmillan.

18

Revelation in Classical Indian Philosophy of Religion

A Śaṅkarite Approach

Surya Kant Maharana

Introduction

PHILOSOPHY of religion is construed as a philosophical understanding of religious concepts. It consists in validating and justifying the religious teachings on rational grounds. As John Hicks puts it, philosophy of religion is the philosophical or critical evaluation of religion. It is not a part of any religious conversation but just related to it. It is an offshoot of philosophy on which anyone, a theist or atheist, can philosophize. The function of philosophy of religion is to undertake a systematic study of the concepts and belief systems of religions. Besides, it also involves serious inquiry into the nature of religious experience, the acts of worship and meditation. It is a second-order activity since it keeps itself apart from its field of inquiry. Being a second-order activity, it addresses the issues of specific religions just like philosophy of science addresses the issues of particular sciences. Further, it intends to arrive at a logical and conceptual analysis of the religious entities, viz. God, soul, etc. Philosophy of religion, for Hicks, seeks to analyse concepts such as God, *dharma*, *Brahman*, salvation, worship, creation, sacrifice, *nirvāṇa* and eternal life and to determine the nature of religious utterances (2004: 1-2).

Indian philosophy of religion is construed in general as a critical and systematic study of some basic tenets and issues embedded in the Hindu religion by the Indian philosophers. The Indian philosophers, by and large, have been engaged with a rational approach to the essential contentions of the Hindu religion. For the philosophers of religion in India the problems of religion have arisen out of the aural tradition of Hinduism, technically and popularly known as Śruti. The aural tradition of Hinduism and its truth claims have drawn the kind attention of the sharp logical minds of the Indian philosophers of the classical period. The task of the philosopher of religion was then the philosophical analysis, critical examination or vindication of the religious dogmas on rational grounds. In the context of classical Indian philosophy it may be observed that the philosophers of the Āstika school are naturally inclined towards the religious assertions of the Śruti tradition and resolved to protect it. For instance, the Mīmāṁsakas intend to defend and justify the Vedic ritualism. Ritualism is based on the authority of the Vedas. The Vedas are eternal and self-existing. The affirmative prescriptions of the Vedas are called *dharma* or *vidhi* while the forbidden actions are called *niṣedha*. In order to justify such claims, they have developed a philosophy known as Pūrva-Mīmāṁsā. So, the approach of such philosophers may not be taken seriously from the standpoint of philosophy of religion as they are often found biased towards the Śruti. On the contrary, the philosophers of the Nāstika school have from its very inception developed a highly critical attitude and aptitude towards the Śruti tradition by questioning its very foundational beliefs on the Śruti itself. Consider, for example, the case of the Buddhism. The very inception of Buddhism is rooted in a revolt against the Śruti, the Veda and its systems of belief. To do philosophy of religion was not the intention of the Buddhists. To repudiate the Śruti tradition and establish Buddhism was rather the goal. But nevertheless it laid the foundation of erecting a philosophy of religion out of the classical Indian philosophical systems. In this regard, A. Ramamurty (2016: Intro.) observes:

> ... the Buddhist analysis and criticism of the beliefs and doctrines of the Śruti tradition of Hinduism is not just for the sake of understanding the problems of religion, but to reject or demolish them with a view to establishing Buddhist position. Though the Buddhist intention is polemical, it helped the development of philosophy of religion in India.

Thus, the distinction between the Āstika and Nāstika schools itself portrays the kind of positive and negative attitude and approach respectively the Indian philosophers have cultivated towards the Śruti tradition. In other words, the Nāstika philosophies such as Buddhism remain far more critical towards Śruti than the Āstika tradition, for instance, Mīmāṁsā, which is quite favourable and lenient to the Śruti tradition. Often, they defend the position of the Śruti guarding it against the critics such as the Nāstikas.

One significant point that needs to be noted here is that Śaṅkara, the champion of the Āstika school of Advaita Vedānta, is perhaps the only philosopher who has shown promising philosophical attitude and aptitude to religious contentions of the Śruti (ibid.). Except Śaṅkara, hardly we come across a philosopher of a critical bent of mind who has imbibed in him the quality of being honestly putting forward what truth is without any sort of favourtism to Śruti. To my mind, therefore, it is Śaṅkara, despite of being a member of the Āstika school of thought, who is endowed with the qualification of being called as a philosopher of religion simply because he possesses a critical or philosophical attitude towards both the schools of Āstika and Nāstika not because of the tradition which nurtured him but by virtue of the critical or philosophical bend of mind he maintained.

So far it is attempted to make out the nature of the Indian philosophy of religion whose sole function is to rationally analyse and criticize the religious beliefs and doctrines of Śruti tradition of Hinduism irrespective of the doctrine they wanted to establish through such activity known as philosophy of religion. In the paper, I endorse Śaṅkara to be one of the reliable philosophers of religion who impartially and rationally attempted to point out the nature and acceptability of Śruti or revelation on rational and honest grounds. What follows therefore is a critical discussion of the doctrine of revelation from the perspective of Śaṅkara's philosophy of religion.

The Nature of Revelation

Revelation in classical Indian philosophy of religion stands for the Vedic literature of the Hindus or the followers of the Sanātana Dharma. They believe that the Vedas are impersonal (*apauruṣeya*), not expressed by any human individual. It is revealed by a divine source or God-revealed. It is called the Śruti as it constitutes the record of the spiritual experiences of the seers (*ṛṣis*) and direct realizations based on extraordinary insight. The word *śruti* means "that which is heard". The Śruti comprises of the eternal principles which are ever good. It is therefore treated as revelation. Śaṅkara's philosophy is mostly based on the Upaniṣads, the concluding portion as well as the essential submissions of the Vedic literature. The word revelation logically implies that there must be a revealer. To Śaṅkara, *Brahman* is the revealer and the Śruti or the Veda constitutes *Brahman*'s revelation. It is from the Śruti that we come to know that the world has its origin in the "word". The words that come to the mind of the creator prior to the origination of the world are eternal. And, therefore, eternal words are the words of the Veda.[1] *Brahman*, the revealer, reveals Itself through the Veda. Revelation of *Brahman*, to Śaṅkara, is conceived in various ways. First, revelation is understood in the sense that the world is a revelation of *Brahman*, the Ultimate Reality. *Brahman* has revealed or manifested Itself as the world of name, form and life. *Brahman* keeps on evolving from the very lowest unconscious to the highest conscious states, such as, of the human being.[2] *Brahman*, with its essential nature as existence–consciousness–bliss (*sat–cit–ānanda*) manifests itself in a hierarchical order and culminates in man as the topmost manifestation wherein man realizes that he is non-different from *Brahman*.[3] It is the inner self of man whose nature is self-luminosity. Thus, *Brahman* expresses itself in various layers of existence giving rise to the manifold universe of beings (Murty 1974: 6). Second, to Śaṅkara, the Śruti is the only source of knowledge which imbibes in us the certain knowledge of *Brahman*. Other sources of knowledge, such as perception and inference, are not so capable. Therefore, Vedic revelation conflicts a significant form of revelation (ibid.: 7).[4] Third, revelation can be construed through the concept of incarnation (*avatāra*) in the philosophy of religion of Śaṅkara. To him, Nārāyaṇa, the *saguṇa* form *Brahman*, is the creator of the world. Having created it, He delivered the knowledge of

1 Gambhirananda, 2000b, *Brahmasūtra Śāṅkara Bhāṣya* 1.3.28.

2 Madhavananda, 1975, *Bṛhadāraṇyaka Upaniṣad Śāṅkara Bhāṣya* 2.5.2, p. 264.

3 Gambhirananda, 2000a, *Bhagavadgītā Śāṅkara Bhāṣya* 7.8, pp. 329-30.

4 Ibid., p. 7.

righteousness (*dharma*) comprising of different *yogas*, such as the *karma-yoga*, *jñāna-yoga* and *bhakti-yoga* to the initial creatures, i.e. the sages (*ṛṣis*) and the forefathers (*prajāpatis*). Later on, owing to the increasing sensual cravings and decreasing morality, such knowledge was somehow forgotten as a result of which there appeared a deterioration of righteousness. In order to revive it back and reveal the path of liberation, Nārāyaṇa was partially born as Vāsudeva Kṛṣṇa, the son of Vasudeva.[5] Thus, Śaṅkara clearly admits the doctrine of incarnation and asserts that Kṛṣṇa is none other than the *Saguṇa-Brahman* or *Īśvara*. Incarnation is conceived as revelation because incarnation is essentially aims at revealing the forgotten eternal truth, the quintessential truth of the Śruti which always remains latent in it. It reveals the crux of the Śruti in a capsulated from.[6] Lastly, to Śaṅkara, intuitive vision or immediate experience of *Brahman* (*aparokṣānubhūti*) also constitutes a form of revelation which reveals the essential nature (*svarūpa*) of *Brahman*. Such revelation is an outcome of what is called as *śravaṇa*, *manana* and *nididhyāsana* (hearing, reflecting and meditating) on the *mahāvākyas*, the great sayings of the Śruti, the Upaniṣads, such as, I am *Brahman*, the Ultimate Reality (*ahaṁ brahmāsmi*) (Murty 1974: 9-10).

Śaṅkara's Critique of Revelation as Śruti

Śaṅkara has remained a staunch follower of the Śruti. His uncompromising respect for the Śruti was so much that in its honour he could sometimes even compromise his philosophical position as a philosopher of religion. He exhibited great reverence for the Vedic wisdom. For him, *vedavākya*, the statement of the Veda is eternal by nature. But then, his support for the Veda is not dogmatic. He substantiated the support by the following argument.

---

5 *Bhagavadgītā Śāṅkara Bhāṣya*, Introduction.

6 Ibid.

> The world consisting of fixed forms or species has been produced from the sounds of the Veda; hence those sounds must be believed to be eternal. – Devaraj 1962: 44

He sometimes seems to be critical of the above *śrutivākya* which he has supported. And, this reveals the real temperament of a philosopher of religion like Śaṅkara. The following lines demonstrate it. In his commentary on *Chāndogya Upaniṣad* 7.1.3, while discussing the connection between a word and its meaning, he boldly states without any hesitation that such a connection is just an appearance only (ibid.: 144). Besides, in paying tribute to the revealed tests, such as the Vedas as well as the Itihāsas and Purāṇas, he contends that the seers whom the Śruti revealed itself are endowed with the power of seeing the unseen and therefore their reflective strength cannot be captured by mundane reason. However, he did not leave any stone unturned in criticizing his fellow Āstika philosophies, such as the Sāṁkhya, Yoga and others (ibid.: 45).[7]

Thus far, it can be observed that although Śaṅkara is a great admirer of the Śruti and its tradition, he is not a blind follower. He always applied reason as a standard instrument for interpreting the Śruti along with its authenticity and validity. His unbiased approach and independent interpretation of the Śruti call for criticizing the other Āstika systems. While criticizing them for their biasness and leniency towards their own systems, he comments that many of them do not have unbiased temperament in asserting the real contention of the Śruti (ibid.: 47-48).[8] The logical approach of Śaṅkara did not compromise with his regard for the Śruti. Besides his objective logical approach to the Śruti and other systems of philosophy, he stresses on the ordinary day-to-day experiences technically

---

7 *Bhagavadgītā Śāṅkara Bhāṣya*, p. 45.

8 Ibid., pp. 47-48.

called as *loka-vyavahāra*. He laid great importance upon the very familiar happenings and facts of our life and asserted that in those instances where the contention and meaning of the Śruti is not lucid, the day-to-day familiar experiences can be our guide in interpreting and unravelling the appropriate meaning of the Śruti.[9] For example, in the preamble to the *Brahmasūtra*, popularly known as *Adhyāsa-Bhāṣya*, he states that the decision of the day-to-day experiences must be regarded as final with reference to the cases such as appearance of nacre as silver and a single moon as double. In this regard, he follows a law which states that the unperceived has to be proved from the perceived one.[10] There are many occasions where Śaṅkara emphasizes on day-to-day experience or *loka-vyavahāra* of common man in order to establish his rational thesis. For example, in the *Brahmasūtra-Bhāṣya*, he advocates that if something is limited, it logically implies that it is not eternal as well just like a piece of cloth or anything like it.[11] Thus, it is evident from the above discussion that Śaṅkara's fascination towards *loka-vyavahāra* is in no sense less than that of his admiration to the Śruti. A pertinent question that arises here is: in case of a contradiction between *loka-vyavahāra* and Śruti, which one has to be preferred? Responding to this question, Śaṅkara holds that there cannot any opposition between the two, for their domains are well-defined and therefore both excel in their respective domains of operation. Even not a single *pramāṇa* can clash with another *pramāṇa*. If hundreds of the Śruti assert that fire is cold or bereft of luminosity, even then none will concede to it.[12] On another occasion, Śaṅkara reconfirms that hundreds of the Śruti cannot compel the objects to discard their nature (*svabhāva*) in different

9 *Brahmasūtra Śāṅkara Bhāṣya* 4.1.5.

10 Ibid. 2.2.2.

11 Ibid. 2.2.41.

12 *Bhagavadgītā Śāṅkara Bhāṣya* 18.66.

places and times.[13] However, Śaṅkara does not stick to this position in all of his writings. For instance, he sometimes seems to hold that the kind of logic we apply to the domain of day-to-day affairs cannot be *always* applied to the objects and domains belonging to the transcendent. But, then, often emphasizing the significance and force of both the Śruti and *loka-vyavahāra*, and sometimes overemphasizing the latter, he advocates that the basic intention of the Śruti is to impart knowledge of the unknown. Nevertheless, the Śruti cannot do so without referring to and relying on the relationship between the words and their meanings as it is prevalent in the domains of *loka-vyavahāra*.[14]

Despite refuting the various Āstika and Nāstika schools of philosophy on logical grounds per se without referring to the Śruti, why did Śaṅkara wish to provide a Śruti-foundation to his philosophy of non-dualism? The reason is simple. For Śaṅkara, human reason by nature is conflicting and suffers from many shortcomings unless and until it is tied up with certain experienced facts. Undoubtedly, reason being a good means of knowledge and argument, it can by no means give rise to truth of facts or reality. It is endowed with the power of evaluating, analysing, coordinating and even inferring. This power can be exercised on the basis of direct experience or certain past experiences. Reason cannot give rise to new facts and their nature since it is dependent upon the facts themselves. For example, a lamp cannot produce an object but only can show the objects that exist around it. It is the experience of things that yields knowledge, not the things themselves. In case of any erroneous perception, reason is called for to rectify the error with reference to previous perceptions or experiences. Reason is therefore is a very instrument in attaining valid knowledge

13 Gambhirananda, 1990, *Kenopaniṣad Śāṅkara Bhāṣya, Vākya Bhāṣya*, pp. 3-7.

14 Madhavananda, 1975, *Bṛhadāraṇyaka Upaniṣad Śāṅkara Bhāṣya* 2.1.20, pp. 202-20.

through analysis, coordination, etc. and put forward fresh data following inference which can further be validated by immediate experience. However, the point to be noted here is that the sources of knowledge pertaining to the two domains of knowledge, viz. the empirical and the transcendental, are entirely different. The senses act as the sources of knowledge for obtaining empirical knowledge while immediate experience (*aparoṣānubhūti*) is the source of knowledge for the transcendental reality or truth. Logic or reason has no role to play in the case of the letter as the reality of logic is also immediately experienced needing no further reason to establish its truth. Logic by itself has no solid foundation, for one person's ascertained position can very well be rejected by another's well argued ascertainment and so on, so forth. Such series of ascertainments will confine us within reasoning itself throwing us far away from the reality. The transcendental truth can never be experienced by such reasoning. And the Śruti stands for the collection of transcendental experience of truth. Reason can be used here just to submit that the truth-claim of the Śruti is valid or error-free. Śaṅkara for this reason emphasizes more on the Śruti than reason or other sources of knowledge (*pramāṇa*s). Nevertheless, the Śruti never conflicts reason. Had it conflicted with reason, any tom and jerry would have claimed its writing as the Śruti (Mukhyananda 2004: 42-43).

Conclusion

To sum up, revelation as the vision of the Ultimate Reality remains the final aim of religious endeavour. However, if we look for an objective proof of revelation, in the scientific sense, perhaps we cannot have one. It is not possible to verify if a text is based on revelation or if there is a revelation at all. Subjective effort is the only way to realize the truth of revelation which is claimed to be revealed and embodied in a religious tradition.

Such a truth, if not lived or experienced, turns out to be an untruth and non-revelation. Religious truth cannot be grasped in its entirety. This, however, does not entail that they are unfounded on reason. Reason has its own limits in capturing the ultimate, infinite truth.

References

Devaraj, N.K., 1962, *An Introduction to Śaṅkara's Theory of Knowledge*, Varanasi: Motilal Banarsidass.

Gambhirananda, Swami (tr.), 1990, *Kena Upaniṣad with the Commentary of Śaṅkarācārya*, Calcutta: Advaita Ashrama.

Gambhirananda, Swami (tr.), 2000b, *Brahmasūtra Bhāṣya of Śaṅkarācārya*, Calcutta: Advaita Ashrama.

Gambhirananda, Swami (tr.), 2000a, *Bhagavadgītā with the Commentary of Śaṅkarācārya*, Calcutta: Advaita Ashrama.

Hick, H. John, 2004, *Philosophy of Religion*, 4th edn, Delhi: Pearson Education.

Madhavananda, Swami (tr.), 1975, *The Bṛhadāraṇyaka Upaniṣad with the Commentary of Śaṅkarācārya*, Calcutta: Advaita Ashrama.

Mukhyananda, Swami, 2004, *Life and Philosophy of Śaṅkarācārya*, Kalady: Shri Ramakrishna Advaita Ashrama.

Murty, K.S., 1974, *Reason and Revelation in Advaita Vedanta*, Delhi: Motilal Banarsidass.

Ramamurty, A., 2016, *Indian Philosophy of Religion*, New Delhi: D.K. Printworld.

19

Ambedkar's Deconstruction of the Bhagavadgītā

A Philosophical Appraisal

Akoijam Thoibisana

I

THE paper is a philosophical appraisal of Ambedkar's reading of the *Bhagavadgītā* from his "Essay on the *Bhagavad Gita*: Philosophic Defence of Counter-Revolution – Kṛṣṇa and His *Gita*".[1]

---

[1] The essay is published in part III, chap. 9 of my unfinished book "Revolution and Counter-Revolution in Ancient India". The same essay is also published in *Dr. Babasaheb Ambedkar: Writings and Speeches*, 2014, vol. 3, chap. 13. All references of the "Essay on the Bhagavat Gita: Philosophic Defence of Counter-Revolution – Kṛṣṇa and His Gita" are from *Dr. Babasaheb Ambedkar: Writings and Speeches*", vol. 3, chap. 13, pp. 357-80. Hereafter the book is abbreviated as *BAWS*. The Essay is popularly referred to as Kṛṣṇa and His Gita. It was also published in his book *Revolution and Counter-Revolution in Ancient India*, part III, chap. 9.

The paper also takes into account his other works like *Riddle of Hinduism: The Annotated Critical Selection* (2017) and *Philosophy of Hinduism* (2016).

What Is Bhagavadgītā?

The *Bhagavadgītā*,[2] according to Ambedkar, is neither a book of religion nor a treatise on philosophy. Ambedkar reads the *Bhagavadgītā* as a text composed to defend certain dogmas of the Hindu religion. It illustrates ideological and moral support for the Hindu religion or Hinduism. Ambedkar writes:

> What the *Bhagavadgītā* does is to defend certain dogmas of religion on philosophic grounds. If on that account anybody wants to call it a book of religion or a book of philosophy, he may please himself. But essentially it is neither. It uses philosophy to defend religion. – *BAWS*: 361

Ambedkar quotes from many modern scholars as well as orthodox Hindus to discuss the nature of the *Bhagavadgītā*. Whereas some modern scholar point out the various contradictions, repetitions and inconsistencies in the *Bhagavadgītā*, there are orthodox *paṇḍits* who argue that the *Bhagavadgītā* is not a sectarian book but upholds equal respect to the three ways of salvation, viz. *karma-mārga*, *bhakti-mārga* and *jñāna-mārga*. This is because the Paṇḍits pointed out that the *Bhagavadgītā* devoted an equal six numbers of chapters for each *mārga*. Chapters 1 to 6 for the preaching of *jñāna-mārga*, chaps 7- 12 for the *karma-mārga* and chaps 12-18 for the preaching of *bhakti mārga* (*BAWS*: 360). Still, there are others who give a different interpretation of the *Bhagavadgītā*. For example, Śaṅkarācārya's account of the *Bhagavadgītā* differs from Tilak's view of the *Bhagavadgītā*. The

---

[2] The *Bhagavadgītā* has been read in many ways. Because, the *Bhagavadgītā*, comes in verse, it is narrative in nature. In this paper, my sincere effort is to give a philosophical appraisal of Ambedkar's reading of the *Bhagavadgītā*.

former held that the *Bhagavadgītā* preaches the *jñāna-mārga* as the only true way to salvation. The latter insisted that the *Gītā* teaches the path to liberation through *karma-yoga* and not *jñāna-yoga*.[3]

The diverse opinions in interpreting the preaching of *Bhagavadgītā*, according to Ambedkar, arise because of the false expedition and the presupposition that the *Bhagavadgītā* is a gospel like the Koran, the Bible or the *Dhammapada*. Ambedkar, however, argues that the *Bhagavadgītā* is not a gospel. He writes:

> The *Bhagavadgītā* is not a gospel, and it can therefore have no message and it is futile to search for one. – *BAWS*: 361

According to Ambedkar, the *Bhagavadgītā* states certain dogmas of Hinduism and gives philosophical insight to defend them. Ambedkar, in his reading *Essay on the Bhagavadgītā*, also popularly known as *Kr̥ṣṇa and His Gita*, listed the three dogmas that the *Bhagavadgītā* has stated and illustrated how the *Bhagavadgītā* has defended each one of them on the philosophic ground.

---

3 For Gandhi, the *Bhagavadgītā* was his spiritual dictionary. There is also the commentary of Swami Mukundananda, *Bhagavad Gita: The Song of God.* Paramahansa Yogananda in his two volumes on the *Bhagavadgītā* stresses the training of one's mind or *rāja-yoga*. And, there is Swami Dayananda Saraswati's four volumes of the *Bhagavadgītā*. Swami Vivekananda also refers to the *Bhagavadgītā* as a bouquet composed of the beautiful flowers of spiritual truths collected from the Upaniṣads. Nehru noted the *Bhagavadgītā* as the spiritual foundation of human existence. He described it as a call of action to meet the obligations and duties of life, yet keeping in view the spiritual nature and grandeur purpose of the universe. There are also academic commentaries of the *Bhagavadgītā* from Jeaneane Fowler (2011), Ithamar Theodor (2010) and R.C. Zaehner (1973). Mention may also be made of Christian commentaries on the *Bhagavadgītā* that compares and contrasts a wide range of views by theologians and religious studies.

The Three Dogmas of the Bhagavadgītā and Ambedkar's Deconstruction

First is the dogma concerning the justification of war. The *Bhagavadgītā*, reads Ambedkar, is Kṛṣṇa's account of the justification of war when Arjuna was caught in the ethical dilemma of ethics and war. Ambedkar summarized Kṛṣṇa's philosophical defence of war and killing along two lines of argument. One justification is based on the nature of the world and man. The world is perishable and man is mortal, things are bound to come to an end, and man is bound to die. And, Kṛṣṇa, in the *Bhagavadgītā*, also added that there is no difference as to how a man dies, naturally or through violence. The other line of argument in justification of war is the mistaken notion of the identity of body and soul. That is, the body is different from the soul. Whereas the body is perishable, the soul is eternal and imperishable. And, when death occurs, it is the body that dies, the soul never dies. Hence, it is wrong to say that when a man is killed, his soul is killed. The dead body only discards his old clothes and wears a new one and carries on. Hence, Ambedkar reads that Kṛṣṇa [and his *Gītā*] justifies killing on the ground that the soul is never killed. Ambedkar writes:

> War and killing need therefore give no ground to remorse or to shame, so argues the *Bhagavadgītā*. – *BAWS*: 361

According to Ambedkar, this defence of killing and justification of war is juvenile. To say that killing is no killing because what is killed is the body and not the soul is an unheard of defence of murder. It is bizarre and childish. He writes:

> If Kṛṣṇa were to appear as a lawyer acting for a client who is being tried for murder and pleaded the defence set out by him in the *Bhagavadgītā* there is not the slightest doubt that he would be sent to the lunatic asylum. – Ibid.: 364

The second dogma that the *Bhagavadgītā* put forward to offer a philosophic defence is the theory of *cāturvarṇya*. Ambedkar argues that the *Bhagavadgītā* offers a philosophic basis for the theory of *cāturvarṇya* by linking it to the theory of innate, inborn qualities in men. That is, the *Bhagavadgītā* approves the fixing of the *varṇa* in man not as an arbitrary act but according to his innate, inborn qualities. Kṛṣṇa in the *Bhagavadgītā* defended the *cāturvarṇya* on the basis of the Guṇa theory of the Sāṁkhyas. Brāhmaṇas have the nature of *sattva guṇa*, kṣatriya has the nature of *rajas guṇa* as primary and *sattva guṇa* as secondary, Vaishya nature is *rajas guṇa* with *tamas guṇa* as secondary, śūdras' nature is *tamas guṇa* and has the *rajas guṇa* as secondary. Furthermore, each of them is the manifestation of the same Divine.

Ambedkar argues that Kṛṣṇa's defence of the *cāturvarṇya* in the *Bhagavadgītā* is illogical on the ground that whereas there are four *varṇas* in the *cāturvarṇya*, the *guṇas* [of the Sāṁkhya] that determine the *varṇas* are only three in number. Ambedkar writes:

> How can a system of four *varṇas* be defended on the basis of a philosophy which does not recognize more than three *varṇas*?
>
> – *BAWS*: 364

Besides the *guṇa-karma* theory of *cāturvarṇya*, Kṛṣṇa, reads Ambedkar, also issues two positive injunctions to the theory of *cāturvarṇya*. The first injunction is not to agitate or excite people to rise in rebellion against the theory of *karma-kāṇḍa* and all that it includes. That is, it is inappropriate for a wise man to counter-propagate or create doubt in the mind of an ignorant person who is a follower of *karma-kāṇḍa* and those who observe the rules of *cāturvarṇya*. In the second injunction, Kṛṣṇa tells that everyone should do the duty prescribed for his *varṇa* and no other. He also warns that those who worship him and are his devotees will not obtain salvation by mere devotion but by devotion accompanied by observation of duty laid down for the *varṇa*. Accordingly, Ambedkar concluded that this means that a śūdra, however great he may be as a devotee, will not get salvation if he transgressed the duty of the śūdra – that is to live and die in the service of the higher classes.

The third dogma of the Hindu religion that the *Bhagavadgītā* defended is the doctrine of *karma-mārga*. According to Ambedkar, *karma-mārga* is the soul of the *Bhagavadgītā* and it refers to the performance of the observances, such as *yajña* as a way to salvation. To quote Ambedkar:

> The *Bhagavadgītā* most stands out for the *karma-mārga* throughout and is a great upholder of it. – Ibid.: 362

According to Ambedkar, the *Bhagavadgītā* tries to remove the excrescence grown upon *karma-mārga* in two ways. First is by introducing the principle of *buddhi-yoga* as the necessary condition of *karma-yoga*. Ambedkar writes:

> Become *sthitaprajña*, i.e. "befitted with *buddhi*" there is nothing wrong in the performance of *karma-kāṇḍa*. – *BAWS*: 362

The second excrescence on the *karma-kāṇḍa* according to Ambedkar was the selfish motive behind the performance of the *karmas*. Ambedkar writes:

> The *Bhagavadgītā* attempts to remove it by introducing the principle of *anāsakti*, i.e. performance of *karma* without any attachment for the fruits of the *karma*. Founded in *buddhi-yoga* and dissociated from selfish attachment to the fruits of *karma* what is wrong with the dogmas of *karma-kāṇḍa*? This is how the *Bhagavadgītā* defends the *karma-mārga*.

Ambedkar also noted that the *Bhagavadgītā* in speaking of *karma* is not speaking of activity or inactivity, quieticism or energism, in general terms, but religious acts and observances of that act. According to him, the confusion surrounding the dogmas of *karma-yoga* is due to the wrong translation of *karma-yoga* as action and *jñāna-yoga* as knowledge, and the subsequent discussion of the *Bhagavadgītā* in terms of the comparison and contrasting of *jñāna* versus *karma* (knowledge vs action) respectively. Ambedkar asserts that the *karmā-yoga* or action in the *Bhagavadgītā* means the dogmas contained in Jaimini's *karma-kāṇḍa*; and the *jñāna-yoga* or knowledge means the dogmas contained in Bādarāyaṇa's *Brahmasūtra*.

Although there are many other dogmas of Hinduism, Ambekar, in his reading of his essay, "Krishna and His Gita", listed the above three dogmas as the most important ones. These dogmas, according to Ambedkar, are also the dogmas put forth in Jaimini's Pūrva-Mīmāṁsā.

Ambedkar also noted that the *Bhagavadgītā* is one of the eighteen Smṛtis and stands very close to the *Manusmṛti* in terms of the teachings and type of philosophy it preaches. In his "Philosophy of Hinduism" (*BAWS* 2014: 3-92), Ambedkar goes to the extent to state that the *Bhagavadgītā* that everyone reads and upholds is nothing but the *Manusmṛti* in a nutshell. He remarks that the *Bhagavadgītā*'s insistence on the performance of *varṇa* duties, even when devoid of merit, echoes the *Manusmṛti*'s insistence on following one's own duty even without any good qualities is still better than someone else duties, for a man who makes a living by someone else's duty immediately falls from his caste.

Hence, Ambedkar claims that although the *Manusmṛti* is considered irrelevant and no longer has a significant place in the philosophical doctrine of Hinduism, it still continues to live on in the *Bhagavadgītā*.[4]

---

4 This is because the *Bhagavadgītā*, as Ambedkar reads, still continues to defend the philosophical insight of the dogmas of Hinduism. It also takes insight from other systems of thought. For example, the concept of *guṇa* and *karma* in the *Bhagavadgītā* is not invented by the *Bhagavadgītā* itself. Whereas the concept of *guṇa* is inherited from Sāṁkhya philosophy, the concept of *karma* was taken from Upaniṣadic philosophies.

Ambedkar, further, argues that the *Bhagavadgītā* is not an independent self-contained book. It should be read alongside the literature that has preceded it. He also places the *Bhagavadgītā* in a specific historical context. He asserts that the *Bhagavadgītā* is the aftermath of the rise of what he terms the "counter-revolution" of Brāhmanism. In other words, for Ambedkar, the *Bhagavadgītā* is a philosophical text of counter-revolution to the attack on the theory of *cāturvarṇya*, that was subject to the revolutionary and rationalist account of Buddhism. Ambedkar writes: "It was to save them from the attack of Buddhism that the *Bhagavadgītā* came into being."

What follows is an account of Ambedkar's understanding of the *Bhagavadgītā* and its simulacrum to Buddhism.

II

Ambedkar's Bhagavadgītā and Buddhism

The Buddhist age, according to Ambedkar, was the most enlightened and the most rationalistic age of India. The age of Buddhism was an age where people accepted the gospel of social equality. The Buddha's doctrine of non-violence has become not only the *guiding principle of life* but has also gone so far as to make it a *rule of life*. The teachings of Buddhism refuse to accept the theory of *cāturvarṇya* that justified killing and violence in the name of duty. The teaching of the Buddha broke down the framework of *cāturvarṇya*. Ambedkar writes:

> Buddha preached against *cāturvarṇya*. He used some of the most offensive similes in attacking the theory of *cāturvarṇya*. The framework of *cāturvarṇya* had been broken. The order of *cāturvarṇya* had been turned upside down. Śūdras and women could become *saṁnyāsīs*, a status which counter-revolution had denied them. Buddha had condemned the *karma-kāṇḍa* and the *yajñas*. He condemned them on the ground of *hiṁsā*

> or violence. He condemned them also on the ground that the motive behind them was a selfish desire to obtain bonus.
> – Ibid.: 363

The teaching of the Buddha marked a rationalistic revolution in the mindset of the people. Ambedkar writes:

> How could they [people] be expected to accept the dogma that the kṣatriya may kill without sinning because the Vedas say that it is his duty to kill? ... How could they accept the *cāturvarṇya* theory of gradation, and separation of man based on birth simply because the Vedas say so? – *BAWS*: 364

THE BHAGAVADGĪTĀ AS THE PHILOSOPHICAL TEXT OF COUNTER-REVOLUTION

Ambedkar argues that it was to defend the dogmas of the Hindu orthodox text attacked by Buddhism that the *Bhagavadgītā* came up as a philosophical text to defend the same. Ambedkar writes:

> The *Bhagavadgītā* is not against the authority of the Vedas and Śāstras. Nor is it against the sanctity of the *yajñas*. It upholds the virtue of both. – Ibid.: 365

Ambedkar's essay "Krishna and His Gita" also goes on to prove that there is no difference between Jaimini's Pūrva-Mīmāṁsā and the *Bhagavadgītā*. He argues that *Bhagavadgītā* is a more formidable supporter of the counter-revolution than Jaimini's Pūrva-Mīmāṁsā could have ever been. Ambedkar's reading of the *Bhagavadgītā* also asserts that the *Bhagavadgītā* was an addition to the *Mahābhārata* and was composed after Jaimini's Pūrva-Mīmāṁsā and even after Buddhism.

BETWEEN THE BHAGAVADGĪTĀ AND BUDDHISM

Ambedkar's "Essay on Bhagavat Gita", gave three illustrations to show the affinity between the *Bhagavadgītā* and the teaching of Buddhism. First, the *Bhagavadgītā*'s account of *brahma-nirvāṇa* (stated as *śraddhā*, *vyavasayā*, *smṛti*, *samādhi* and *prajñā*) and the Buddhist concept of *nirvāṇa*. Second the *Bhagavadgītā*'s understanding of the character and qualification of the devotee (*maitrī, karuṇā, mudita* and *upekhā*) and the Buddha's concept of *bhavanas* (mental attitude that is necessary to cherish for the training of the heart). Third, the *Bhagavadgītā*'s subject of *kṣetra-kṣetrajña* (the difference between what is knowledge and what is ignorance) is not different from the Buddha's doctrine of the same.[5]

He also gives the following account to show the affinity between the *Bhagavadgītā* and the ideology of Buddhism. He writes:

> [First] To sum up the *Bhagavadgītā* seems to be deliberately modelled on Buddhist Suttas. The Buddhist Suttas are dialogues. So is the *Bhagavadgītā*. [Second] Buddha's religion offered salvation to women and śūdras. Kṛṣṇa also comes forward to offer salvation to women and śūdras. [Third] Buddhist says, "I surrender to Buddha, to Dharma and to Sangha". So Kṛṣṇa says, "Give up all religions and surrender unto Me." No parallel can be closer than what exists between Buddhism and *Bhagavadgītā*. – *BAWS*: 371

Kṛṣṇa and the Four Patches of the Bhagavadgītā

Ambedkar's reading of the *Bhagavadgītā* also argues that the *Bhagavadgītā* is not a single book written by a single author. He concludes that there are four separate parts of the *Bhagavadgītā*, written at different times by different authors. The first is the original *Bhagavadgītā*, that consists of nothing more than a heroic tale told or a ballad recited by the bards of how Arjuna was not prepared to fight and how Kṛṣṇa forced him to engage in battle,

---

[5] Ambedkar also compares the verses of the *Bhagavadgītā* from chap. XIII.5-6, 28-29 with that of the Buddha's report in the *Majjhima Nikāya* 1.286 and *sutta* XVI, and argues that the former is a verbatim reproduction of the words of the Buddha.

how Arjuna yielded and so on.[6] Ambedkar calls it a romantic story but without any religious or philosophical account in it. This original unphilosophic *Bhagavadgītā* was part of the first edition of the *Mahābhārata* called Jaya.[7]

The second is the addition of the *first patch* on the original *Bhagavadgītā*. Here, the part of Kr̥ṣṇa is spoken of as *Īśvara*, the god of the Bhāgavạta religion. According to Ambedkar, this part of the *Gītā* is embedded in those verses of the [present] *Bhagavadgītā* which are devoted to *bhakti-yoga*. This [first] patch on the original *Bhagavadgītā*, argues Ambedkar, must be placed sometime later than the Megasthenes when Kr̥ṣṇa was only a tribal god. Ambedkar noted that the brāhmaṇas at that time were not friends of Kr̥ṣṇa, but could have become reconciled to Kr̥ṣṇa worship only at a later stage.

Third is the addition of the *second patch* on the original *Bhagavadgītā*. It is the path that introduced the Sāṁkhya and the Vedānta philosophy as a defence to the doctrines of Pūrva-Mīmāṁsā. It gives a deliberate philosophical account of Kr̥ṣṇa's defence of war (II.11-39). Here, Kr̥ṣṇa propounded that (i) grief is unjustified because things are imperishable, (ii) it is a false view that a man is killed when the *ātman* is eternal, and (iii) he (Arjuna) must fight because it is the duty of the kṣatriya to fight (*BAWS*: 377). Ambedkar notes that this path came later to the *sūtras* of Jaimini and Bādarāyaṇa somewhere between 200 and

---

6 According to Ambedkar, the original *Bhagavadgītā* is found in chapters I, II verses and chapter IX.32-33.

7 The Indian tradition divides the composition of the *Mahābhārata* into three stages: (i) Jaya, (ii) Bharata, and (3) Mahābhārata. Each of them was also assigned to a different author. According to the tradition, Vyāsa was the author of the first edition, that is the *Mahābhārata* called Jaya; Bharata was the second edition and the authorship was assigned to Vaiśampāyana and the third edition called the *Mahābhārata* was assigned to Sauti. – *BAWS*: 372

450 CE. The philosophical portion of the *Bhagavadgītā* was a later intrusion to the original dialogue and the sequence of it.[8] Kr̥ṣṇa gives a philosophical defence of war when he explains the nature of the world and man, and the distinction between the perishable body and the eternal soul. Kr̥ṣṇa also gives emphasis on action and duty to fight, as a path to salvation. This philosophical part of the *Bhagavadgītā*, reads Ambedkar, was absent from the original *Bhagavadgītā*.

Fourth and the last is the *third patch* on the original *Bhagavadgītā*. It consists of verses in which Kr̥ṣṇa is elevated from the position of *Īśvara* to that of *Parameśvara*. References to this patch notes of Ambedkar can be detected in chaps X and XV. Ambedkar places this during the reign of the Gupta king. The brāhmaṇa, to which religion has been a trade, came forward to worship the deity of the ruling race, making the family deity into a high and mighty Parameśvara. Ambedkar marked this between 400 and 464 CE.[9]

Based on his research, Ambedkar claims that the place of the *Bhagavadgītā*, especially with its doctrinal value, cannot have come prior to Buddhism. Ambedkar also refuses to accept Tilak's argument that the *Bhagavadgītā* came after Hīnayāna Buddhism, but before Mahāyāna Buddhism. Following Kimura's account of

---

[8] Ambedkar refers to *BG* I.20-47, where Arjuna mentions the difficulties, and Kr̥ṣṇa in chap. II attempts to meet the difficulties of Arjuna. This is followed by arguments and counter-arguments. Ambedkar notes that Kr̥ṣṇa's first argument is contained in verses 2 and 3. The reply of Arjuna is embodied in verses 4 to 8. In verse 11-39 Kr̥ṣṇa replies that grief is unjustified because things are imperishable; it is a false view that a man is killed when the *ātman* is eternal; that he must fight because it is the duty of kṣatriya to fight.

[9] Ambedkar, however, was not interested in searching for the precise date for the composition of the *Bhagavadgītā*. He also writes that to do so, would be a fool's errand.

the Mahāyānist as another name for the sect of Buddhists known as Mahāsāṅghikas,[10] Ambedkar concluded that the *Bhagavadgītā* does not precede Buddhism. It is not pre-Buddhistic in origin. It could also be not independent from Jaimini's Pūrva-Mīmāṁsā. Ambedkar concluded that the *Bhagavadgītā* is fundamentally a counter-revolutionary treatise of the same class as Jaimini's Pūrva-Mīmāṁsā; it is the official Bible of counter-revolution.

III

The Bhagavadgītā and the Trial of Philosophy of Hinduism

Ambedkar, in his *Philosophy of Hinduism*,[11] provides the philosophical ground for the trial of Hindu religion based on two criteria, viz. "the test of justice" and "the test of utility" (Ambedkar 2016: 41). The former is the test of individual justice and the latter is the test of social utility. According to Ambedkar, the philosophy of Hinduism failed both trials because the religious ideal of Hinduism [for the divine governance of human society] is an *ideal* that is neither central to the individual nor to society. The religious ideal of Hinduism has "class" as its centre. It is the class of what Ambedkar calls the "Superman" or *Brahman*.

Ambedkar argues that the philosophy of Hinduism is founded neither on individual justice nor on social utility but on a totally different principle. It is a principle that serves

---

[10] The sect of Mahāsāṅghikas came into being at the time of the First Buddhist Council held at Pāṭaliputra, 236 years after the death of the Buddha, i.e. 307 BCE for setting the Buddhist canon. It is also said to have led the opposition to the Theravāda sect of Buddhism which later on came to be stigmatized as Hīnayāna. There could be no trace of *Bhagavadgītā*, argues Ambedkar, when the Mahāsāṅghikas later known as Mahāyānists came into being (*BAWS* 2014: 379).

[11] All references from *Philosophy of Hinduism* are taken from B.R. Ambedkar, Philosophy of Hinduism 2016.

the interests of the *brāhmaṇa class.* It concerns sustaining and supporting the rights of that class. It is not interested in the common man. Society is denied, suppressed and sacrificed to the interests of *this class of Superman/Brahman.* Ambedkar writes:

> Hinduism is a gospel of the Superman and it teaches that what is right for the Superman is the only thing which is called morally right and morally good. – 2016: 111

Ambedkar argues that the core of the *Manusmṛti* discloses this account very clearly. Drawing from German philosopher Nietzsche, Ambedkar even drew an analogy between the *Zarathustra* and the *Manusmṛti,* and noted that *Thus Spake Zarathustra* is a new edition of the *Manusmṛti.* Ambedkar took the *Manusmṛti* as the book of the Hindu religion and argues that it is not different from other Hindu orthodox books like the Vedas and the *Bhagavadgītā.* The latter, i.e. *Bhagavadgītā,* only gives the philosophical insight to it. The teaching of the *Gītā* is nothing but *Manu in a nutshell.* Ambedkar writes:

> What difference is there between it and the *Manusmṛti*? *Gītā* is Manu in a nutshell. Those who run away from *Manusmṛti* and want to take refuge in *Gītā* either do not know *Gītā* or are prepared to omit from their consideration that soul of *Gītā* which makes it akin to *Manusmṛti.* – Ibid.: 121

Ambedkar also argues that the essence of the *Manusmṛti* is not fundamentally different from the teaching of the Vedas. The latter is called *śruti,* literally meaning "things which were heard" and *smṛti,* meaning, "things which are remembered" (ibid.: 117). There is also a difference in the status of their author. The authors of the Vedas were *ṛṣis*, whereas for Smṛtis they were the learned men. And since the *ṛṣis* were superior in status and sanctity than those of the learned, the Vedas were treated as more authoritative than the Smṛtis. However, Manu and Yājñavalkya are reckoned as *ṛṣis* and by this means, the status of the Smṛtis was equated to that of the Śrutis. The Smṛti, as the record from the memory of a Śruti, came to be regarded as akin to and indistinguishable from a Śruti. And Ambedkar (2016) stated that in Kumārila's commentary on the *Pūrva-Mīmāṁsā-Sūtra*, the Smṛtis were made as authoritative as the Śrutis (Ambedkar 2016: 117-18).

Here, the point of argument is that both the Smṛti and the Śruti advocate the doctrine of caste, the doctrine of the superiority of *brāhmaṇa*s, their rights and privileges, the doctrine of the subordination of the kṣatriyas and vaiśyas and the doctrine of the degradation of the śūdras. They are, therefore, fundamentally the same. Ambedkar writes:

> It seems to me that it matters very little whether one takes the Smṛtis, or the Vedas or the *Bhagavadgītā*. – Ibid.: 119

He asks:

> Do the Vedas teach something which is fundamentally different from what the Smṛtis do? Does the *Bhagavadgītā* run contrary to the injunctions of the Smṛtis?"

Ambedkar argued that the essence of Puruṣa Sūkta [that recognizes the division of society and inequality between them] given in the Vedas is not different from the theory of *cāturvarṇya* of the *Bhagavadgītā*. Ambedkar writes:

> Compare the teaching of the Vedas and of the *Bhagavadgītā*, with what is contained in the *Manusmṛti*. ... What difference does one find? The only difference one can find is that the Vedas and the *Bhagavadgītā* deal with General Theory while the Smṛtis are concerned in working out the particulars and details of that theory. But so far as the essence is concerned all of them – the Smṛtis, the Vedas and the *Bhagavadgītā* - are woven on the same pattern, the same thread runs through them and are really parts of the same fabric. – Ibid.: 121

Hence, Ambedkar concludes that the philosophy of Hinduism will remain the same whether one takes the *Manusmṛti*, the Vedas or the *Bhagavadgītā* as its gospel.

So, What [then] Is the Essence of the Deconstruction[12] of the Bhagavadgītā?

Ambedkar's *Bhagavadgītā* or his deconstruction of the *Bhagavadgītā* embodied his deep desire and continuous effort to reform Brāhmanic Hinduism. In his introduction to *Riddles in Hinduism* (2017), Kancha Ilaiah noted that Ambedkar's deconstruction of Hinduism explores the many "brazen contradictions that exist within the texts of Hinduism" (2017: 33). It is the deconstruction of the deepest metaphysical doctrine of the Hindu religion.

However, the controversies surrounding the relation between the deconstruction of the *Bhagavadgītā* and the trail of the philosophy of Hinduism demands a prior understanding of what Ambedkar means by Hindu, religion, philosophy, philosophy of religion and also philosophy of Hinduism.

WHO IS A HINDU?

Ambedkar in his riddles no. 1 raises the difficulties of knowing "Why One Is a Hindu?" (2017: 58-65). He argues that whereas it is not difficult to ask the same question to a Christian, Parsi or Muslim because each would reply that they are Christian, Parsi or Muslim because they believe in Jesus Christ, Zoroaster and Mohammad respectively, the same is not true for the Hindus. This

---

12 Here the term deconstruction is used in the sense of a critical study, as a style or more specifically as revolutionary methodology for examining the philosophy of Hinduism, more so in terms of its orthodox Hindu text. It concerns the destruction of the metaphysics of presence operating in the *Bhagavadgītā*. It, however, is not Derridian, because Ambedkar's deconstruction of the *Bhagavadgītā* operates in another metaphysics, that of Buddhism.

is because Hindus can believe in many gods or worship only one god. Hindus can be monotheistic, some of them are polytheists and some still are pantheists. Even the monotheist can worship different gods. The difficulties in answering this question is because of the fact that Hinduism has no definite creed as such. Ambedkar noted that the Hindus also differ among themselves as to which beliefs are of cardinal importance. However, Ambedkar noted that Hindus always belong to one caste or the other and any man who does not belong to a recognized Hindu caste cannot be a Hindu. Therefore, the caste system, according to Ambedkar, is an essential feature of Hinduism (ibid.: 64).

WHAT IS RELIGION? WHAT IS PHILOSOPHY? AND WHAT IS PHILOSOPHY OF RELIGION?

According to Ambedkar, a study of the philosophy of religion has three dimensions that also include within itself an understanding of the prior two questions. The first dimension is the definition of religion to mean theology. Whereas there are different theories of theology like mythical, civil, natural and revealed theology, by religion, Ambedkar refers to natural theology,

> which is the doctrine of God and the divine, as an integral part of the theory of nature.[13]

The second dimension for the philosophy of religion is to know *the ideal scheme* for which a religion stands. According to Ambedkar, the Hindu scheme of divine governance is enshrined in the written constitution of the *Manusmṛti*. It is a divine code

---

13 There are also two other kinds of theologies, viz. mythical theology and civil theology. The former refers to tales of gods and goddesses, the latter consists of feasts and fasts of the state calendar. Ambedkar does not use the word in either of the two senses. Another theology is the revealed theology. It concerns the spontaneous self-disclosure of divine reality. All this is different from the natural theology that Ambedkar abides to (Ambedkar 2016: 12).

which lays down the rules which govern the religion, ritualistic and social life of the Hindus in minute detail. The *Manusmṛti*, noted Ambedkar, must be regarded as the Bible of the Hindus and contains the philosophy of Hinduism (2016: 15). The third dimension in the philosophy of religion is the *criterion* to be adopted for judging the value of the ideal scheme of divine governance for which a given religion stands for. A study of the philosophy of any religion, argues Ambedkar, must put that religion on trial.

Following the last dimension, Ambedkar noted that a study of the philosophy of Hinduism is the study of the trial of the philosophy of Hinduism. Whereas Ambedkar has listed two criteria for the trial of the philosophy of Hinduism, viz. the trial of utility and the trial of justice; he has also given us a *new methodology* to do the same. It is what he calls the *revolutionary method.*

Ambedkar argues that revolution is the mother of philosophy and to know the philosophy of any movement, or any institution, one must study the revolution. The study of religion is no exception to this rule. He writes:

> To me therefore it seems quite evident that the best method to ascertain the criterion by which to judge the philosophy of religion is to study the revolutions which religion has undergone. That is the method which I propose to adopt.
>
> – 2016: 16

REVOLUTION AND THE PHILOSOPHY OF HINDUISM

Ambedkar refers to the first revolutionary shift of religion - from savage society to the religion of civilized society. Whereas there was no trace of *the idea of God* and no bonds between *religion and morality* in the savage society; God is an integral part of the civilized society. Also, morality in civilized society was sanctified by religion (ibid.: 20-21). The second revolution in religion was marked by the radical change in the split of civilized society into antique society and modern society on the basis of the relations between the concept of God, society and man.[14]

Ambedkar classifies the revolution in religion into two types: external revolution and internal revolution (2016: 22). The former concerns the field within which the authority of religion was to prevail. It was a revolt of science against the extra territorial jurisdiction assumed by religion over a field which did not belong (ibid.: 33). The latter has to do with the changes in religion as a scheme of divine governance for human society. It is the latter [internal revolution] methodology of revolution in religion that Ambedkar was interested in. This is because the internal revolution involves a constitutional change that can alter, amend and reconstitute the scheme of divine governance. Ambedkar illustrated the profound changes that the internal revolution has made in the antique scheme of divine governance (ibid.). It is the revolution that has changed the concept of God from a member of a community to God as the creator of the universe. This revolution has also changed the concept of man from a blind worshipper of God to man as a responsible person who is required to justify his belief in God's commandments by his conviction. This revolution has also replaced God as the centre of the divine order of society with *man* as the centre of this divine order.

---

14 In ancient society, religion was founded on the kinship between God and his worshippers. God, that way, has direct relations with society and was the father of his people, in a physical sense. God was exclusive and owned by one single community. In the modern society, the concept of God as father is divine and entirely dissociated from the physical basis of natural fatherhood. Modern society also eliminates God from the centre of religious composition and replaces it with men. God was dissociated from physical contact with man and conceived as capable of absolute good and absolute virtue (Ambedkar 2016: 22-26).

The purpose of the religious revolution in the ruling concept of religion [as the scheme of divine governance] for Ambedkar was to discover the norm for evaluating the philosophy of a religion. He concluded that the norms or the criterion for judging the antique society was utility, whereas, in modern society, it is justice. This is because, in the antique world, society being the end, the moral good was held to be something which has social utility. In the modern world, the individual being the end, the moral good is held to be something which does justice to the individual.

Keeping in view the above arguments, Ambedkar proves that the philosophy of Hinduism fails the trial of religion. He argues that *justice* is the only suitable standard for the moral and ethical values of a religion. Justice for Ambedkar contains within itself the idea of liberty, equality and fraternity. He applied the test of justice and the test of utility to the philosophy of Hinduism and came to the conclusion that there is nothing sacred about it. He deconstructed the sanctity of *varṇa* preached by the *Manusmṛti*. It is hierarchical and promotes inequality and discrimination. Ambedkar writes:

> In the scheme of Manu, the brāhmaṇa is placed at the first in rank. Below him is the kṣatriya. Below the kṣatriya is the vaiśya. Below the vaiśya is the śūdra and below the śūdra is the ati-śūdra (the untouchables). This system of rank and gradation is simply another way of enunciating the principle of inequality so that it may be truly said that Hinduism does not recognize equality. ... Manu has introduced and made inequality the vital force of life. – *BAWS*: 25

Hinduism, according to Ambedkar, also denies freedom of a vocation. The scheme of the *Manusmṛti* preordained each man's occupation even before his birth. It does not allow choice. It has no relation to capacity and inclination. It denies man's ultimate liberty. Hinduism also compels people to serve ends chosen by others. The *Manusmṛti* not only preaches the śūdra that he is born to serve the higher classes but also exhorts him to make that his ideal.

Hence, according to Ambedkar, the trial of the philosophy of Hinduism [from the point of view of justice] reveals that Hinduism is inimical to equality, antagonistic to liberty and also opposed to fraternity. And this is also how Ambedkar deconstructed the philosophy of Hinduism as a religion.

Conclusion

To sum up, Ambedkar concludes that Hinduism fails as a religion because the metaphysical aspects of Hinduism are one-dimensional, asymmetrical and full of contradictions. It is rooted in the binary of pure and impure, the sanity and the demon. Although the *guṇas* are inevitably given, they are not equally valued or recommended. Ambedkar also argues that the spiritual message of Kṛṣṇa in the *Bhagavadgītā* is grounded in a metaphysical that negates the fundamental equalities of all men. Ambedkar's deconstruction of the *Bhagavadgītā* is also a philosophical reflection on injustice and the social power of religious dogmas operating in the philosophy of Hinduism. His deconstruction of the *Bhagavadgītā* is the deconstruction of the core philosophy encoded in the [divine] text of Hinduism. His deconstruction of the *Bhagavadgītā* [and other Hindu orthodox texts] is the necessity of subjecting these dogmas to critical reason, that would [latterly] provide a clear lens to read the same.

References

Ambedkar, B.R., 2014, *Dr. Babasaheb Ambedkar: Writings and Speeches* (*BAWS*), vols 3-4, New Delhi: Dr Ambedkar Foundation.

———, 2016, *Philosophy of Hinduism*, New Delhi: Samyak Prakashan.

———, 2017, *Riddles in Hinduism*, New Delhi: Navayana.

20

Religious Understanding and Global Peace

Sudhakar Jally

Introduction

It is worthwhile to note that religion is not a mere necessity but a noteworthy part of human life. Every facet of human life has been influenced by religion either directly or indirectly. All world religions have preached and promoted tolerance, brotherhood and coexistence, and strive for peace. Sociologists have advocated religion as a social phenomenon. The pioneer, French sociologist, Emile Durkheim has reiterated that religion is a social affair of man. He has stated that religion is a source of stability.

In the spirit of the term religion, it is observed that a very sublime status has been accorded to man. Religion is made for man but man is not made for religion. Man cannot neglect, torture, disgrace and humiliate. Man cannot be treated as subhuman. Man is treated as a rational animal for an extended period in Greek tradition, whereas man has been treated to be identical with *Brahman* in Upaniṣadic period of India. In some religious traditions man is treated to be the child of God whereas some others consider man to be essentially selfish. Man has the special privilege of thinking for the betterment of society; reacting against exploitation and having the capacity to overcome adverse circumstances. Man has occupied the state of supreme importance in Hinduism, Buddhism, Jainism, Christianity, Islam and Sikhism. Religions take part in a seminal role in the life of man and society. It is mostly aimed at some scholars and religionists have advocated that the principal objective of religion is to enhance brotherhood, fellow feeling and harmony amongst people at large. In religions, it is observed that man's position is very significant.

The present-day world is beset with animosit, bloodthirsty, communal bigotry and man-made suffering. International terrorism is one of the nagging problems the world is facing. Today, mankind all over the world is suffering from multidimensional crises such as racial discrimination, religious intolerance, social injustice, economic inequality, exploitation, oppression and terrorism. Most of the terrorist activities are spearheaded by religious fundamentalists and vested interests. The very pertinent question which is striking our mind is that in spite of tremendous advances in science and technology why society is being dehumanized? A humanitarian crisis is a generalized urgent situation that affects an entire community or a group of people. In present-day society, we face a global crisis that is unprecedented because of the misunderstanding of religion. In this context, S. Radhakrishnan (1939: 41) proclaims:

> Life today, in spite of our material possession and intellectual acquisitions, in spite of our material codes and religious doctrines, has not given us happiness. If we knew the deepest thoughts of men today, we should find that there are millions who are dissatisfied with themselves and with the pursuits

> that absorb their energies. They have lost the radiance and gladness of life, they have no hopes to inspire, no ambitions to realize, no happiness to which they can look forward, no faith to live by.

In this context, the proper understanding of religion is very significant to solve the problem. Conversion and proselytization play a very remarkable role in the domain of religion. There is a subtle distinction between the two. Conversion means, on account of spiritual experience, change from an irreligious life to a holy/divine life. It can openly be admitted that religious conversion is a multifaceted and multi-dimensional phenomenon. It has always been a sensitive issue throughout the world. On the other hand, proselytization means one has come over from one religion to another. Mostly in the spirit of the term "religion" it is stated that if God is one, religion in its basic nature is one, there is no need to change one religion to another religion. Some religious persons have thought that it is their duty to convert the Hindus to Christianity.

Hence, S. Radhakrishnan writes:

> Our aim should be not to make converts, Christians into Buddhists or Buddhists into Christians, but enable both Buddhists and Christians to rediscover the basic principles of their own religions and live them. – Masih 1960: 368

That is why Radhakrishnan had raised his voice against missionary zeal.

In *Bhagavadgītā* III.35, it is reiterated:

श्रेयान्स्वधर्मो विगुणः परधर्मात्स्वनुष्ठितात् ।
स्वधर्मे निधनं श्रेयः परधर्मो भयावहः ॥

śreyān svadharmo viguṇaḥ para-dharmāt svanuṣṭhitāt ।
svadharme nidhanaṁ śreyaḥ para-dharmo bhayāvahaḥ ॥

> It is far better to perform one's prescribed duty, though tinged with faults, than to perform another's prescribed duty, though perfectly. In fact, it is preferable to die in the discharge of one's duty than to follow the path of another, which is fraught with danger. – Radhakrishnan 2015

The famous Vedic dictum *ekam sat viprā bahudhā vadanti.* (*Ṛgveda* 164-46) meaning the seers call in many ways, that which is one.

It is observed that intolerance is a species of violence. Religious intolerance is expressed by discrimination, religious rivalry, communal bigotry and hostility. It is a mental attitude that is characterized by a narrow approach and outlook. Contempt, mistrust and political tactics are the principal causes of religious intolerance. Intolerance destroys the growth and development of human society and causes violence between different faiths. Religious tolerance is imperative in modern society. It advocates the peaceful coexistence of all religions without any one group being discriminated against or oppressed. It is crucial that any type of religious hostility and communal bigotry may be eradicated in the true spirit of the term religion. Hence, the most significant point is to realize that every form of religion is relative, including one's own. So, the cross-fertilization of ideas and principles takes place as Radhakrishnan had emphasized. Guru Tegh Bahadur was the ninth *guru* of Sikhism, who preached tolerance and interfaith harmony.[1]

The lexical meaning of the term "sectarianism" is pertaining to a particular sect. It means strong support for one particular political or religious group, especially when this leads to hostility between different groups. Sectarianism is a cultural, political and religious variance between two groups. Sectarian religion is neither ethical nor rational nor humanistic. A religion that has an honoured position for mankind is necessarily ethical

---

1 "The Speaking Tree", *Times of India*, 21 April 2022.

and humanistic. Sectarian conflicts are often breeding grounds for acts of terrorism and the formation of terrorist groups. It is also leads to political or cultural conflicts between two groups. In this context, M.K. Gandhi reiterated:

> Religion should provide every one of our actions. Here religion does not mean sectarianism. It means a belief in the ordered moral government of the universe. It does not less real because it is unseen. This religion transcends Hinduism, Islam, Christianity, etc. It does not supersede them. It harmonizes them and gives them a reality. – *Harijan* (10-2-40), p. 445

As stated, it is very important to note that every form of religion is relative including one's own. Men differ in their types, temperament, disposition and religious bent of mind; but from the humanitarian point of view, all are equal. It is stated that in the case of religious attitude, there is divergence (not absolute difference) on the ground of sentiment and emotion without any sense of ultimacy or absolute reality.

Religion is generally implicit in every political institution and political party. That is why; our first prime minister Jawaharlal Nehru advocated not to mix up religion and politics in the affairs of the state. The reason is that the state and nature are separate in the context of aim, objective and methodology. The state is this-worldly and the religion is other-worldly.Religion is a private affair, on the other hand, the state is a public affair. It is stated that for the betterment of a society, government should remain neutral as for as religion is concerned. The political use of religion is not the basic nature of democracy. For instance, at the time of natural disasters or calamities, science and technology are used, not necessarily mass prayer. Mass prayer is not indispensable, though some have preferred to go on that on their own.

It is stated that interreligious dialogue is required to

solve social conflicts. The term "dialogue" means discourse or conversation. Most of the problems in our society arise because of ignorance and misunderstanding between two individuals or communities. Interreligious dialogue is not something new. Dialogues were held between the Hindus, Buddhists and Jaina thinkers often quite. with the advent of Islam, later Christianity, in India, the native religions could not continue the dialogue in the same spirit. Interreligious dialogue necessitates a minimum level of education and understanding on both sides. It is evident that bilateral dialogue is more academic and expedient than triangular and multi-angular dialogue. The dialogue depends upon two prominent levels, i.e. faith or belief and reason. The objective of any world religion is to bind human beings with the bond of cosmic love. To restore peace and prosperity in society, both on per sonal and social levels, interreligious dialogue or mutual debate (*saṁvāda*) is pertinent.

It has been said that all religions must be tolerent. For man, there is no coercion and compulsion in religion. For instance, as the bee collecting honey from different flowers, a religious person can accept the essence or real meaning of different scriptures. M.K. Gandhi reiterated, as Masih say:

> I believe in Bible, as I believe in *Gītā.* I regard all the great faiths of the world as equally true with my own. It hurts me to see any one of them caricatured as they are today by their own followers. – Masih 1990: 371

The lexical meaning of the term "blasphemy" is a behaviour or language that insults or shows a lack of respect for God or a religion. It means the act of veiling, ridiculing, being disrespectful by words or conduct. It is generally defined as an act or offence of speaking sacrilegious about God or the basic tenets of different religions. It is an impious utterance, irrelevant behaviour or action concerning God or sacred things.

In the spirit of the term "religion", blasphemy should not be entertained. Religion has utilitarian value for the human being in the personal as well as social platform for the sustenance of a humanitarian sense of attainment. This seems to have sustenance of value in the sphere of attainment of peace and tolerance on the basis of faith and reason to some. Though it is found that both these together are not necessarily indispensable, they can be independent.

It is worthwhile to note that religion is man-centred. Naturally man has been given a very sublime status. Religion is the most important feature which has found its significance in various activities in human life. Because of the misunderstanding of a person, any type of inhuman and sad incidents which have occurred in the human society, a man needs to be realized the core meaning of the term religion and tries to refrain from the narrow approach and outlook towards other religion.

Terrorism is regarded as an act of politically motivated violence. It is a mental attitude, characterized by narrow-minded approach and outlook. It is the unlawful use of force or violence against the government or its citizens. Terrorism does not lie in the use of weapons but has its genesis in the mind, in the unconscious. Every human being needs to understand the ignorance and the misunderstanding of religion. Despite differences at the surface, all religions share a common plank. A proper understanding of religion makes them realize that they are not competitive players in the field but co-travellers traversing a common path leading to a common goal.

Religious beliefs, customs, rituals and traditions have played a key role in man's life and, in this regard, man's freedom has found a prominent place in it. However, the concept of freedom in man is not so much autonomously taken up. Further, for such an outlook, it is quite often considered as prone to reason and justification than having any learning with belief and faith, immune from reasonable validity. Hence, it is found in many quarters as the inclusion of scientific findings which is one helpful device for analytical dissection of the concept of man and also its freedom, not ignoring the role of science. In this context, the religious sense of man, that is often presented and advocated in diverse religious sources, is also touched upon. It is shown thereby as to what extent the religious sense of freedom, in one way or another, is extraordinary and uncommon.

There are a number of religions, out of which the major religions are Christianity, Judaism, Hinduism, Buddhism, Jainism and Islam. In all such religions, there is a general acceptance of the concept of man. There are references to man, his well-being and mutual relationship among men on the basis of love, trust, reliance, fellow-feeling and goodwill. In the course of development, each religion, in this regard, has formed different classes, divisions and sects. Of course, such classification is found to be somewhat more rigid and specific in the context of Hinduism than in others. Despite the well-being of man in general, the fundamental goal, or aim of such religions, is extended beyond the earthly living sojourn of man.

The social dimension aims at the study of behaviour and custom of a group or community of men in different situations and times. It thereby analyses the change and modification of such facets in individual life as per the social or social needs, necessities and aspirations. The analysis is specific or particularized but it never aims at a common universal solution of man for all the time (past, present and future). Any such speculation at a universal level is also not entertained.

Religion, in general, has obviously been found to have a powerful role in man's life irrespective of the fact whether one is a theist or an atheist. The nature and status of religious beliefs, ideas and views of life are seen to have a considerable impact on human thinking. Both on individual and social levels, to articulate and develop a view of life or lifeworld is a necessity and, in that way, it appears to be unavoidable. From the religious and theological level, several attempts are made to justify the sense of the absolute/infinite as something proper and logical over and above the issue being treated limitedly or relatively.

One finds that there do exist a number of religious traditions. Their followers do have different modes of prayer, worship practices, rites and rituals. So long as they continue to believe in their respective religious traditions, they are bound to follow such mode of worship, etc. in a liberal form of governance for different religious traditions within the prevalent political system. It is evidently more in such a non-theocratic state than in some other form. It becomes notably dominant in a non-conservative liberal system. It may be noted that all this, possibly, leads to a meaningful review of religion, its necessity and also its contemporary relevance. It is, of course, noticed that religion, as it is meant in its traditional setting, is bound with the rigidity of stern belief (often looked down on as dogmatic/prejudices), being impractical (sometimes harmful and injurious to the individual person and also to the society), posing itself as beyond reason and sense, often being against scientific and technological developments that are beneficial to human welfare and progress. Religion needs undoubtedly change and reform.

It is more or less accepted that religion has a stronghold both among its followers and the common man traditionally. It is found that the status of religion in man's life as a whole has been affecting and, accordingly, the followers of religion have changed their stand to a great extent without, however, not dismantling but retaining the core of their religion. That means, still, even now religion is a living phenomenon to a large majority at the common platform.

Hinduism in general is prone to diverse kinds of traditions, customs and conventions, resulting in various dogmas and prejudices that are found to be amoral as well as logical. Hinduism being a complex religion has given rise to many shades of opinions and views. For example, one comes across Hinduism, theism and atheism, monotheism and polytheism, male supremacy and female supremacy, etc. As such, to suppress the differences between different cults one comes across Ardhanārīśvaravāda aiming at, integrating and harmonizing Sikhism and Śāktism. Taking this to be a significant move, some commentators and interpreters of Hinduism maintain that belief in many cults and sects is visually based on the inner unity among them in one single theistic source. Hinduism, despite their differences on some religious issues, accepts the view regarding the unique status of man.

There is a common and also lexical approval of the meaning of religion to which it more or less believes in God; but in the modern age, there is also an acknowledgement of religion without the acceptance of God. Such a wider meaning of God (as both an inclusive and an exclusive sense of God within it) is now admitted on the basis of some religions being grouped as world religions like Buddhism, Confucianism and Jainism. The positive point of the Buddhist religion is undoubtedly to emphasize avoidance or suppression of egoity, advancing the sense of *karuṇā* (mercy) and life of compassion for the fellow-beings by means of practising morality (*śīla*) and wisdom (*prajñā*); the religion as very much persuasive. As a result, it is more confined to a group of individuals in a limited locality and circle, it has attained the status of a world religion having profound human significance.

There is a dominant view in certain circles that philosophy and religion are inalienably related. Even though there are instances of reputed philosophers who never want to be associated with any type of religious belief or faith, there are some thinkers who take up the view that since religion in some form or other is found to be prominent in any civilizational set-up thought-out the globe. A philosophical study or appraisal of religious concepts, ideas and different forms of activities, championed in different religious traditions, cannot be set aside. Those definitely need some philosophical probing. Philosophy may not be fully identical to religion, but there seems to be nothing improper in advancing a philosophical study of religious concepts and ideas. In that sense, the philosophy of religion is as important as the philosophy of science, the philosophy of different social sciences and so on. Philosophy as viewed in terms of analysis of concepts, there is no harm in making a free and open analysis of religious concepts and ideas. Also, in this way, nothing is irregular in moving for a comparative study of different religions with a view to unravel and explore the philosophical significance/excellence among them if any.

It is a very pertinent point to note that religious utterance is not cognitive but emotive. But, in that sense, it cannot be nonsensical. A scientist, so far as the scientific endeavour is concerned, is neither committed to such "isms" like spiritualism or mysticism. It is generally accepted that religion is spiritual, being based on spiritual experience that is intuitive. Spiritualism essentially aims at man's inward transformation, leading to the realization of the self in the sense of transcending egoism. Both science and spirituality use the term knowledge but they use and interpret the term with completely different meanings. In this context, Albert Einstein (1940) stated:

> Science without faith is lame. Religion without science is blind.

It is a very evident point to note that spirituality is mainly concerned with the purpose of life and its spiritual movements.

Religions both in Eastern and Western traditions, we can find, deal more or less with the same basic issues. Mystery in science and mystery in religion both have different settings. Mysticism is often regarded as something anti-intellectual, obscure, confused, impractical and unconnected with normal experience. The essence of spirituality can be further clarified if we look into the contrast between spirituality and materiality. Both spirituality and materiality are two views based on philosophy with a metaphysical foundation, i.e. spirit alone is real or matter alone is real. It is a very prominent point to note that the goal of both science and spirituality is common, though adopting different names. When the scientific approach is drawn towards objectivity, the spiritual approach is dominated by some sort of subjectivity. While one gives emphasis on evidence, proofs and objectivity, the other only rests on belief/faith. Spirituality is fundamentally based on subjective experience with a view to comprehending reality as a whole. Science is not designated to frame any conjecture about reality. It only deals with the fact of phenomena. It does not raise any issue regarding the purpose of the ultimate life. It studies life only as it occurs or happens. So it is probable in character. In view of all these and related grounds, it becomes highly questionable to assert that objectivity in science and imaginative speculation in spirituality are complementary and compatible with each other. It rather seems that they stand poles apart.

In the true sense of the term religion, there is no room for ethnic conflict. It may be caused by social inequality and lack of assimilation. The source of conflict may be social, economic, political and religious. It arises if ethnic groups compete for the same goal, notably power and position. India is regarded as a multi-ethnic and highly diverse nation. Once ethnic conflict breaks out, it is difficult to stop. For example, the present in Manipur conflict is predominately an ethnic conflict.

Religion plays a fundamental role in human life. For the smooth function of human life religion is made for man but man is not meant for religion. The aim and objective of all religions is to lead man to a lofty life. That is why, social scientist Emile Durkheim remarked that religion is a social affair of man. People belonging to different faiths, cultures, races, traditions and habits, constitute the noble feeling that there is no discrimination, division or difference among human beings. Peace in human society is possible with the help of a universal outlook, dynamic attitude, open-mindedness, belongingness and peaceful coexistence.

To understand the true spirit and essence of religion, it is a prerequisite to know the basic tenets of different religions. Religions are wanted to see the establishment of brotherhood in this empirical world. They emphasize that selfless service, true friendship, compassion, fellow-feeling and respect for all living religions. These are the basic principles that are pathways for the coexistence and well-being of mankind. Religious harmony is exercised where people of different religions share mutual understanding and refrain from religious violence. To establish peace and harmony in society, there is required to develop interreligious and intercultural understanding. There is no superiority or inferiority in the basic tenets of religion. It means no religion is superior to the service of human society. The feeling of equality and unity is the sustaining life force of any religion. That is why it is really admitted that oneness is the essence of all religions.

Religion provides human understanding, awareness and responsiveness. It is considered a way of life, just an understanding. It holds the key to the contentment of human society. It is ideally serving several functions. It has innumerable effects. The intrinsic nature of religion is influencing, assimilating, fusing, interpenetrating and assuming one another. The humanistic approach is found in almost all religions of the world. From the socio-religious point of view, man is considered a free, rational and conscious being who has the purpose of human solidarity. A man should live in this society with socio-empirical principles. Human society is called an ideal society if there is no opportunity for ill-will feelings, bloodthirst, communal bigotry and man-made suffering. Proper understanding and appreciation of religion reinforces social solidarity, stability, peace and unity.

Religion, in general, has obviously been found to have a powerful role in man's life. The nature are status of religious belief, their ideas and views of life are seen to have a considerable impact on human thinking. At the same time, it needs to be emphasized that religion needs change and reformation (not rejection) in personal as well as social spheres for the sustenance of peace and stability. Hence, change and reformation are necessary at all levels for the cause of the sustenance of global peace, along with personal, social, regional and national interests and obligations.

References

Radhakrishnan, S., 1939, *Eastern Religions and Western Thought,* Oxford.: Oxford University Press.

———, (ed.), 2015, *The Bhagavad-Gita,* new edn, Harper Collins.

Masih, Y., 1990, *A Comparative Study of Religions*, New Delhi: Motilal Banarsidass.

21

Jainism

Meeting of the Sacred and Secular

Alakananda Parida

In common parlance, the term "sacred" is associated with religious beliefs, practices, notion of "holy", whereas the term "secular" is associated with things that are non-religious, religious neutrality, beliefs and practices pertaining to the empirical and pragmatic concerns of life. Secular came into currency in the post-Renaissance period when there was radical change in the collective psyche on account of discoveries, inventions and rapid march in science and technology. Human mind, by and large, became more objective, rational. Renaissance witnessed a revolt against religious authoritarianism and intervention of the holy authorities in affairs of the state. In the medieval age, it was faith which was ruling the collective psyche. People were, by and large, driven by the articles of faith rather than by the demands of reason. Secular stood for the characteristic mindset of the people which is more inclined to believe things on the strength of experience and reason rather than the dictates of the religious authorities which demanded unconditional obedience. People began to raise questions about the received views which were considered to be sacrosanct. There was also the rejection of the articles of faith which did not have the sanction of reason because there is nothing in principle which is beyond the grasp of reason and experience. Thus, secularism came to vouchsafe principles and norms which were distinct from religious views. Thus, sacred which were associated with religious and secular are conceived as an incompatible system of beliefs and practices. Sacred was opposed to religious hegemony. The belief patterns and institutions with the backing of religious institutions were considered to be irrelevant and sometimes harmful for the real growth of human personality. Knowledge through reason was preferred to knowledge through faith. The whole body of knowledge stood for the whole corpus of scientific and there is nothing in the principle which cannot be comprehended by human reason and experience.

As a result of the rise of secularism, there were efforts to liberate social and political institutions, and practices from the control of the religious authorities. On the contrary, anything which was not in consonance with the fundamentals of religion or scriptural injunction was considered to be heretical. Thus, the secular revolt was directed at rescuing human reason and experience from the grip of the irrational or the non-rational. Everything that was transcendental or non-empirical was rejected as unacceptable. Instead of God, man came to the centre stage. Society became more and more human-centric than God-centric. This eventually led to rise of individualism and affirmation of reason against the dictates of faith. Things came such a pass that though initially secular signified for beliefs and practices that were non-religious, eventually came to be equated with things that are irreligious. Thus, secular and sacred came to be considered to be mutually incompatible and dichotomous. Though secularism stood for the pragmatic values in the beginning, later on it stood for anything that was not keeping with the spirit of faith. There are attempts by scholars to reconcile the claims of sacred versus the secular by pointing out that there are fundamental values that are responsible for the holistic growth of human society which is the commonality between the proponents of sacred and secular.

> Secularism signifies a kind of life that is lived in complete indifference to God. – Hackma et al. 1957: 283

> Secularism as an ethical system, founded on the principles of natural morality, independent of revealed religion and supernaturalism. – Lieber 1960: 259

Every religion is defined in terms of the world views, body of beliefs, rituals, dos and don'ts, mode of prayer, concept of "holy" and observances. Religious pluralism is a social reality which cannot be explained away. It is because religious urge is innate in every individual irrespective of time, place and community. The religious urge is nothing but the spontaneous desire of every individual to move from imperfection to perfection. The invocation; "Oh God! take me from untruth to truth, darkness to light, mortality to immortality"[1] is the song of every soul. Religions prescribe ways which are to be lived in order to attain the highest state. The concept of highest state is explained differently in different religions. The views and practices enjoined by founders of different religious faiths appear to be contradictory. But a closer reflection on them would reveal that the founders or proponents of different religions address their contemporary people in a language which they can understand. The beliefs and practices are dependent upon the relativities of context or community. But a closer look into the original texts which are considered to be holy in different

---

1 *asato mā sadgamaya,*
tamaso mā jyotirgamaya
mṛtyormāmṛtam gamaya । – *BṛUp* 1.3.28

religions would convince one that though they differ in respect of legends, narratives, language they have a common message for the followers to be good and do good, helping people to live an ethical life is the goal of every religion. Thus, plurality of religions is inevitability. The fact remains that though different religions came into existence to bring peace and harmony in the collective body but in the name of religion, there has been a great deal of bloodshed. This is the irony in the history of religions. Many religious wars have been fought. Religious intolerance in the form of fanaticism, bigotry has taken away the peace of the humanity. This is because the followers fail to understand the common message behind the differences pertaining to the nature of practices and religious teachings. There are two distinguishable aspects of religion, viz. the message of peace, harmony, tolerance, mutuality and the practices which are prescribed to enable people to live a value-centric life. It is worth noting that the religious beliefs and practices owe their justification to the world views.

Faith is considered as central to religious pursuits. It is claimed that it is only the faithful who can comprehend the nature of the Ultimate Reality. The Ultimate Truth remains veiled from those who insist on logicality or empirical verification. In other words, religious truths are construed as articles of faith. Faith is considered as subjective. If religion is bound up with the notion of faith, then religious claims may turn out to be subjective. But the proponents of religion hold that the articles of faith are not opposed to reason but are beyond the purview of reason; religious truths are not illogical but a-logical. It is claimed that given the nature of the Ultimate Reality, it is only the faithful who can have the vision of truth and faith is the only mode to know reality in its true nature. As sense-experience is the objective means to have valid cognition in respect of the reality in space and time, faith is the objective mode of knowing that which transcends the world of spatiotemporal. Thus, faith and reason appear to be antithetical. There have been ongoing controversies to safeguard the articles of faith against the touchstone of reason.

It is often thought that concept of God or transcendental being is central to every religion but it is not so because there are non-theistic religions like Buddhism and Jainism which do not moot the existence of God. Rather, the notion of highest state, highest good is central to every religion. Religious consciousness presupposes the inherent limitations of human mind to comprehend the highest truth. Realization of God, attainment of godhood or the highest state is considered to be the be all and end all of human existence across lives. Religious path helps one move expeditiously on the God-ward path. What is essential to every religion is the consciousness of one's limitation in the form of bondage and suffering and the firm belief that one can move from state of limitation to state of perfection through self-effort by following the path prescribed by the respective religions. The set of prescriptions and prohibitions contains guidelines by following which one can move from ignorance to knowledge. No religion leaves room for any privileged access. Rather, everyone is considered to be holy at the core and everyone does possess the ability to undertake the journey to perfection. The proponents of religion hold that the notion of highest reality or world view provides foundation for building an ethical system. As is the world view so is the ethical paradigm. Therefore, belief in a trans-empirical is necessary to understand the nature of the empirical. Dogmas in the form of fundamental beliefs and practices provide justification for the ethical norms or prescriptions. Dogma is used in two different senses. Dogmas refer to the fundamental beliefs which remain unquestioned in a religious framework. In social domain, dogmas stand for those irrational beliefs which are injected in the minds of people by the vested interests. Though morality constitutes the core of every religion often people tend to take the myths, beliefs and practices to be essentiality as a result of which there are religious conflicts, making way for religious fanaticism. People take to different religions depending on the social context in which one is born or exposed to. In course of ti-[me, superstitions and dogmas creep into religions. As a result, religions degenerate into a set of mechanical rituals and abstentious observances.

What is paramount is the fundamental values that constitute the commonality between the sacred and the secular. The proponent of secularism would argue that it is possible to embrace an ethical life without subscribing to a religious belief or dogma but the advocates of religion would argue that it is the ontology which lends rationale to an ethical system. In the event of resolution of conflicts among metaphysical world views the more comprehensive world views constitute the foundation for building a holistic value system. Respect for values does not discount the role of reason. Rather, the religious ontology is a step forward in arguing in favour of the ethics of "live and let live" by taking the non-humans as part of the moral community. Since everything is an expression of the fundamental consciousness, everything is holy and sacrosanct and it points to the interconnectedness of things and beings. This world view prepares the ground for building a holistic ethics which would help human beings to live in harmony with the non-humans.

Unlike religion, philosophy undertakes rational comprehension of reality. The moot question is, are religious pursuits incompatible with the critical thinking of a philosopher? It is evidently not so. Philosophy as second-order discipline analyses the concepts and issues in the first-order disciplines such as natural sciences and social sciences. Unlike empirical sciences which aim at explanation and prediction of facts and events, philosophical investigations aim at gaining clarity about concepts, methods employed in first-order disciplines. A scientist undertakes to explain facts by means of causal dynamics, whereas a philosopher takes analysis as its method. Philosophy does not compete with sciences insofar as it does not add to the body of already known facts but enhances our clarity about the logic of different foundational concepts. In this sense, philosophy is empirically uninformative, whereas growth of science witnesses our increasing knowledge about facts or reality. Conceptual questions or foundational questions in sciences are philosophical in nature. Therefore, there is a passage to philosophy from every empirical discipline. Concepts are used as tools of investigation by first-order enquirer, whereas understanding the nature of the concepts is the sole objective of philosophical analysis. Philosophical explanations are given in terms of reason, whereas the scientific explanations are given in terms of causality. Religion can be likened to the first-order discipline insofar as one through out in quest of the knowledge of the Ultimate Truth undertakes the journey with certain discipline. Philosophy of religion tries to help religious followers to have adequate clarity so that one does not fall into dogmas or superstitions or ways that are contrary to the spirit of the spiritual quest and which otherwise would defeat knowledge of truth.

Philosophy of religion seeks to analyse the seminal concepts in religion like faith, self, God, liberation, devotion and intuition. Religious claims need to be subjected to philosophical scrutiny so that the articles of faith do not degenerate into dogmatic beliefs. Truths accepted on faith need not be taken as dogmatic because there are certain areas of human experience that defy the canons of logic. Philosophers have their bounden role to analyse the nature of faith and limit of faith vis-à-vis the limit of reason. In this sense, faith does not negate the claims of reason but points to a domain where reason being inadequate, faith remains as the only mode of knowing the trans-empirical or non-empirical.

Jainism is one of the oldest religions of the world. It is a religion and philosophy in one. As a religion, Jainism stands unique as it is based on a metaphysics which sets the ground for reconciliation of the divergence of religious views and practices and also explains why there are alternative metaphysical systems when all of them seek to comprehend a singular truth. Truth, by definition, is objective and impersonal. If truth is one, why do people view it in different ways, making room for conflict of views and eventually leading to conflicts in the society? The metaphysical view of the Jaina thinkers takes the form of metaphysical pluralism. It is assumed that reality is infinite and multifaceted and human mind is finite. Therefore, any attempt on the part of a finite mind comprehend the infinite is bound to fall short of the infinite. Every object in the state of nature possesses infinite properties, both positive and negative (*ananta dharmakam vastu*). It is observed that no finite mind can comprehend all the properties of an object.

> One who knows all the qualities of one thing, knows all the qualities of all things and he who knows all the qualities of all things knows all the qualities of one thing.[2]

Such knowledge is attributed to *kevalīs* who have attained the highest state in the scale of evolution. The great philosophical and religious legacy is handed down the centuries through the life and teachings of the *tīrthaṅkaras* (*kevalīs*). Their way of life testifies to the truths and explanations in the Jaina scriptures. Relativity of empirical knowledge is lucidly illustrated by the analogy of five blind men, each trying to comprehend the nature of an

---

2 *ekobhāvaḥ sarvathā yena dr̥ṣṭaḥ sarve bhāvaḥ sarvathā tena dr̥ṣṭaḥ* ।
– *Tattvārthasūtra* 37

elephant. Because of their inherent incompetence, they know a part of reality but unfortunately they mistake the knowledge of the part to be the knowledge of the whole. That is how the conflicts among different blind men set in but one who can see the elephant in its completeness, understands the reason behind the conflict which in nutshell arises due to the native ignorance or limitations on account of which the relative is mistaken as absolute. This view of reality constitutes the foundation of the theory of relativity of knowledge termed as epistemic relativism. Whenever a judgement is pronounced about reality as such, it has to be qualified by "relatively" (*syād*). It means that every judgement about reality suffers from relativity as it is true insofar as the perspective or framework of the knower. Every knowledge claim is significant only in relation to a framework or perspective. Framework is understood in terms of concepts, values, mode of interpretation such that given the same sensory field it can be interpreted differently by different individuals. Since human mind has access only to finite aspects of the reality which is infinite no knowledge should be claimed as absolute. The epistemic relativism of Jainas is expressed in Syādvāda. To look upon the partial knowledge of reality as the absolute amounts to fallacy of exclusive predication (Ekāntavāda). From this perspective, one can understand why there are conflicts of world views. The proponents of different metaphysical views should not construe themselves as mutually conflicting viewpoints but views that are mutually complementary insofar as they illuminate different aspects of the same reality. A substance is that which is subject to production, destruction and permanence. The same reality which is viewed as eternal from the standpoint of substance is looked upon as transitory from the standpoint of the modes. This sets the base for resolution of metaphysical conflicts. Such a metaphysical and epistemic relativism constitutes the basis of the ethical paradigm which Jainism advocates.

Sacred is associated with religion or religious pursuits. The word "secular" came into currency in the sense of religious neutrality, in view of the divisive fallouts of different sectarian practices in the name of religion. It is worth underlining that though the religions differ in respect of the beliefs and practices the universal values constitute the foundation or rock bottom of every religion. The cardinal values like love, mutuality, tolerance, sacrifice, forgiveness cut across different religions. Verily, they constitute the secular core of the sacred. In other words, values form secular core of the sacred. In Jainism one notices unique confluence of the sacred and the secular. The ongoing debate between the claims of faith and reason have been sought to be resolved by scholars who argue that given the limitation of human reason, it is wrong to presume that the limit of the reason is the limit of the reality. Therefore, reason has to draw its own boundary and make room for the realm of faith. Jaina ontology prepares the ground for respect for alternative views about the reality thereby paves the way for coexistence and ethics of non-violence as tolerance of dissenting opinions and beliefs.

So, given the fact that reality is multifaceted and human knowledge is relative, it paves the way for tolerance or accommodativeness. In Jaina metaphysics, there are two distinct metaphysical entities, viz. *jīva* and *pudgala*. *Pudgala* is nothing but matter which is the habitat of the unitary consciousness, i.e. *jīva*. Every atom is inhabited by *jīva*. The difference between one *jīva* and another depends on the degree of expression of the consciousness. In case of the emancipated souls (*kevalīs*), consciousness finds its optimal expression. Every *jīva* contains infinite faith (*ananta darśana*), infinite knowledge (*ananta jñāna*), infinite bliss (*ananta sukha*) and infinite power (*ananta vīrya*) as its essential nature. The more and more one evolves, the more and more the qualities become pronounced. From this perspective, the difference between one and the other is one of degree and one stands related to one another by the bond of kinship. Hence, it remains the ethical imperative of every individual to evolve into perfection by taking others along in creating an enabling environment for others to evolve. As every being is sacred in being the habitat of the consciousness, "non-violence" constitutes the highest ethical paradigm. Non-violence in its subtlest form, takes the form of *mānasa ahiṁsā*. Even hurting the other in the psychic plain amounts to violation of the principle of non-violence (*ahiṁsā*).

Interestingly, Jainism is a religion without God. Jaina metaphysics does not leave room for a personal God or a transcendental entity but Jaina literature enunciates the nature of the highest state (*kaivalya*) which can be attained here and now through self-effort. Since every being (*jīva*) is potentially infinite, everyone is worthy to attain the highest state. Like other classical systems of Indian philosophy, the Jainas hold that action performed with ignorance is the cause of bondage. Bondage means that one remains subject to the cycle of birth and death. On account of the accumulation of the kārmic-dross an individual who is essentially infinite and blissful, comes under bondage. Hence, the only way to overcome bondage is to cultivate right knowledge. Real knowledge can be attained only when we have the right faith. So, the journey towards perfection has to begin with right faith. Faith, here, is not opposed to reason but signifies the transformation in one's mind or attitude to believe in the lives and teachings of the *tīrthaṅkaras*. The lives of the *tīrthaṅkaras* exemplify their teachings enshrined in scriptures and sermons. Faith stands for deep convictions about the truths, advocated by the *tīrthaṅkaras* who have attained the state of omniscience. Faith is the basic prerequisite for knowledge. Faith makes one accept the path shown by the liberated souls. Knowledge is necessary but not enough to move on the path leading to liberation. True knowledge must have its manifestation in one's conduct. So, the right conduct is said to be the immediate cause of liberation. In this respect, there is an affinity between the Jaina epistemology and Vedāntic epistemology. In Vedānta, it is said that knowing is being. The knower of *Brahman* becomes *Brahman* (*brahmavid bramhaiva bhavati*). Similarly, we find that in Jaina system, the knowledge together with the conduct is the cause of liberation. On the contrary, knowledge without its manifestation in real life-situations remains a mere body of information. A body of information neither benefits the knower nor the society but when knowledge gets manifested in real conduct it not only benefits the knower but also the society at large. So, right faith (*samyak darśana*), right knowledge (*samyak jñāna*) and right conduct (*samyak cāritra*) constitute the three jewels (*triratna*) in the Jaina system. In other words, it lays down the objective ways by which the life and teachings of *tīrthaṅkaras* can be relived so that one can progressively move towards the state of perfection. In this respect, the lives of the *tīrthaṅkaras* remains as the milestones for an aspirant who seeks to attain the highest state. Highest state is not only conceived as impersonal in the sense that anybody can achieve it and the ways laid down by the Jaina thinkers hold out the hope and assurance that anyone and everyone can attain the highest state. Thus, the philosophy and the practice enjoined in Jaina philosophy and religion are secular in letter and spirit. Jainism not only indicates a perspective from which the religious and ideological conflicts can be resolved but also shows the way by which any individual can attain the highest state by following the ways spelt out in the Jaina literature.

The ethical paradigm advocated in Jainism is a necessary corollary of the metaphysical relativism on the one hand and epistemic relativism on the other. In other words, the ethics of the Jainas is built on the bedrock of metaphysics and ethical practices mark the meeting of the "sacred" and the "secular" providing a shared platform for peaceful coexistence.

References

Hackma, Gerge G., Charles W. Kegley and Viljo K. Nikander, 1957, *Religion in Modern Life,* New York: Macmillan.

Lieber, Francis, 1960, *Encyclopedia Americana,* vol. XXIV, New York: Americana Corporation.

22

J.N. Mohanty on the Structure of Religious World and Religious Experience

Manoj Kumar Panda
Pragyanparamita Mohapatra

Introduction

In the history of mankind, nothing is as controversial as the subject matter of being religious has been. What is it to be religious? The answer to this question radically varies if we look at different world religions, and some barbaric and inhuman ways of being religious sometimes come to our notice which are beyond our comprehension for rational and logical minds. Can we make any consensus against this background to reach at a common framework so that we can understand the structure of religious experience independently of any particular religion?

In this paper, we are going to discuss and critically engage with J.N. Mohanty's thought-provoking and very engaging take on being religious (2000: 40-52). The questions that we reflect on are: What is a religious point of view? What is the essence of a religious point of view? How the world presents or appears for a religious point of view? What is the nature and structure of religious world? Answering these questions will lead to an understanding of the structure of religious world and also the structure of religious experience. Mohanty's primary engagement in his writing is the structure of religious world. But the discussion that follows has important relevance and repercussions for the structure of religious experience. Both complement and supplement each other and one can also say that the understanding of one will not be complete without understanding the other under a broader phenomenological framework. As part of the phenomenological investigation, phenomenologists have tried to understand the structure of reality by means of understanding the structure of experience. This has been the way of understanding reality by various phenomenologists. In this context also, Mohanty tries to understand the structure of religious world by means of understanding religious experience. Another complementing way to understand the reality by phenomenologists is through describing the way in which the phenomena are given in experience. This first personal givenness of the phenomena is the key to understand our situatedness and the phenomena surrounding us including our lived experience. Mohanty while trying to understand the structure of religious world has given emphasis on our lived religious experience. The religious experience, according to Mohanty, is part of our lived experience and does not transcend the world where we live. Our ordinary daily experiences can also be the key to understand the religious world.

The Meaning of a Religious Point of View

The truth and falsity of a religious point of view or how religious point of view is about the world or how is it related to the world depends on the very meaning of a religious point of view and in this sense the question of meaning, according to Mohanty, is logically prior to the question of truth involving religious points of view (2000: 40). If we do not sufficiently determine, what is it to be religious or what makes a religious point of view religious or what it means to be religious, we will not be able to understand the semantics or truthfulness of a religious point of view which is determined in relation to the world. The meaning of a religious experience or religious point of view will take us to decipher the structure of religious world. The question of religiosity or the question of what makes a religious point of view religious can be asked and answered independently of any particular religion or any particular religious point of view. If a point of view or perspective is religious, it can be religious without depending on any particular religion or particular God. Dependency of "religiosity" on a particular religion would not leave scope open for other ways of being religious which are not dependent on that particular religion.

Since being religious in general would not depend specifically on any particular religion, there is a need of common framework to be developed in order to understand what does it involve to be religious. Many would object to this point by saying that a point of view cannot become a religious point of view without becoming part of a specific religion be it Hinduism or Islam or any other religion. It is the religion or religions and more importantly being part of a religion, which gives necessary meaning to a religious point of view. The sense of sacred we have in this world depends primarily on being religious. Mohanty by going against this point would say that the notion of sacred is independent of being religious in the sense that we do not have to be part of an objective religion. We will discuss what Mohanty meant by objective religion in the later part of this paper. The notion of sacred that we have is not something we derive from being religious, i.e. depending or being part of a religion. If being religious does not depend on believing in God, then being sacred is not dependent on believing in being religious in the sense of believing in God. Mohanty categorically states: "He is not asking what makes a point of view of Hindu? Rather he is concerned with the very question of religiosity (2000: 40)." This statement implies that he is trying to pursue the question of religiosity independent of any particular religion. Mohanty's distinction between pre-objective religion and objective religion is significant in this context which we will discuss in the later part of this paper. Perhaps Mohanty wanted to rise above various objective religions of the world in his inquiry of the notion of "sacred". It seems from his writing that Mohanty emphasizes on being sacred over and above being religious. One can ask, in this context, what is it that is involved in being truly becoming religious or having a religious point of view if not it is by being part of a specific religion? Mohanty points out three negative criteria for the same:

1. For being religious, it is not necessary to believe in God.
2. A person can be irreligious even if she believes in God. Therefore, believing in God will not lead to being religious.
3. A believer can be irreligious (ibid.: 40-41).

These above criteria do not tell us what is involved as a positive criterion in being religious. It tells us what is not involved in being religious. Mohanty goes on to discuss what the true religiosity consists in which is independent of all the above criteria. In his opinion,

> [the true religiosity] consists in some inner attitude towards things, i.e. some way of looking at oneself and the world.
>
> – Ibid.: 41

Believing in God, if not the necessary criterion, then what is its status in relation to a religious person. Believing in God may be a part of a religious point of view, but it does not constitute the very religiosity we are talking about. Even for a believer one can say that her true religiosity goes beyond her belief in God. But the inner attitude that Mohanty talks about is not something one would believe stems from believing in God or infinite power. Being religious is a way of experiencing the world. What is it actually? Being scientific and appreciating beauty are also different ways of experiencing the world. Then, what is distinct about being religious which is a way of experiencing the world? Mohanty applies the noema-noesis framework of phenomenological method to understand further what is involved in having an inner attitude towards things. In every experience, the object presents itself in a certain way. Or, in following the framework of phenomenological investigation, one can say that for every experience, there is meaning associated to the object that is being experienced. For example, in aesthetic experience, the object is experienced as beautiful, for a loving person, the object is presented as lovable and for the attitude of a scientist, the object is presented as decomposable into various elements and properties (Mohanty 2000: 41). The question that can be asked here is: how the world and its object are presented to a religious point of view? The very meaning of a religious point of view consists in answering the above question. Mohanty's answer to this question is: the true religiosity which is having an inner attitude towards things, the world is presented to it as *sacred* and religious world is a *sacred* world. Being sacred is at the heart of being religious instead of believing in God. One of the implications that we derive from the above point is that "sacred" or "being sacred" is taken in much broader sense than the notion of "being religious".

There are two questions that can be asked in this context, the first one is: what is the very constitution or the source of this inner attitude? The second one is: how are the things presented as sacred and to whom? In answer to the first question, one can say that those have this inner attitude who are truly religious. And if we ask, who are truly religious? The answer is those who have this inner attitude towards things. This explanation becomes circular as it does not say anything at all about either being religious or about having some kind of inner attitude. It is true that being religious is a kind of experiencing the world. But what is involved in this experience? This inner attitude towards things or a kind of experiencing the world may involve other things which are not sacred as such.

Being Religious and Being Sacred

For Mohanty, the religious world is a sacred world. For a religious person, the world is presented as sacred. It is not clear in Mohanty's writing what this being sacred consists in. What kind of experience is this for which the world is not a brute fact as Mohanty stresses on? Everything has a value of its own without being valuable for some other purpose. For a religious person, the world itself has value not for some purpose outside of it (Mohanty 2000: 42), but for itself and in itself. For a religious person, things in the world do not have values for serving some purpose outside of it like other things in our life such as wealth, health and power. The world for an authentic religious person is intrinsically sacred. There is some kind of conflict or may be seemingly so between two points, i.e. being religious is having inner attitude towards the world and the world presents itself as sacred. How the world presents itself as sacred if true religiosity consists in some inner attitude? Is the world represented as sacred depending on inner attitude of a religious person? If yes, then world being religious or experiencing the world as sacred is purely a subjective attitude. The implication of this point would be that the world as such then is not sacred. Moreover, is the sacredness or being sacred a property of things or an attitude of a subject? If the world is a sacred world objectively, then why are we not all experiencing it as sacred? Mohanty, it seems, would say that this distinction between subjective and objective is superficial in the context of our lived experience of sacred. One may add to this that the world as sacred is not something which figures in scientific naturalism or pure materialism. The world itself, for scientific naturalism, is brute in the sense that it is governed by causal or nomological laws of nature. If that is the case, then experience of sacred seem to be something imposed by human beings, not that the world itself is sacred. It leads to supernaturalism in the sense that the experience of sacred is not something natural for human beings. Experience of sacred takes place due to some kind of intervention of something supernatural. But as Mohanty points out that being religious is independent of God, then the experience of sacred as part of being religious must be independent of God. Being sacred may serve some extrinsic purpose, not that it is the mark of it. For example, a person who is an authentic religious person may contribute in a significant way towards society and for its people. But surely, he is religious not by depending on this.

Mohanty is of the opinion that our religious attitudes may differ among themselves depending on the following aspects:

1. For some, religious attitudes may differ relating to the kind of experience they are having presently, more specifically depending on the kind of objects that one is experiencing as sacred. For some, everything in this world present itself as sacred starting from high mountain to a blade of grass. Some people may see only a few things as sacred, for example, the temple, church or mountain tops, but not all things. They may not see the fearful animals in the jungle as something sacred. Here one point that can be made is that for authentic religiosity, everything (every object) may seem to be sacred. Why only mountains or temples? The reason for which one may not see everything as sacred

is that everything in the world is not good, for example, heinous crimes against humanity or killings of animals at large scale that is going on all around the world.

2. Another point of difference among religious attitudes is that the intensity of experience. One may have the believe that the world is sacred but not the experience of it. The intensity of experience of sacred would of course differ from mere belief that the world is sacred. Whether one has experience of sacred or one has mere belief that the world is sacred depends to some extent on the kind of attitude that one has.
3. A very significant point of difference, according to Mohanty, is the kind of experience one has of sacred. One's experience of sacred may be poetic–aesthetic in nature. Some other's experience may be mystic in nature. Mohanty's one of the interesting points is that the religious experience can be aesthetic–poetic. He tries to develop this point further.

Mohanty explores further the moral, aesthetic and poetic dimensions of our religious experiences. It is important to note that he tried to understand the nature of religious experience in terms of the above and independent of theistic (belief in God) aspect of religion. The moral dimension tells us that one of the ways to see the world as sacred is to treat others not as a means but as an end in itself. Kant's categorical imperative, i.e. respect for all humanity is the moral basis of religious experience. But what one may note here is that the moral basis of religious experience as a whole does not encompass or based on respect for humanity only. Respect for nature as a whole must be the basis of our religious experience. Otherwise, how could one see sacred in every creature. Moral basis of religion must be nature-centric not anthropocentric. Mohanty cites a famous line of Tagore's poem *amār māthā nato kore dao he tomār caraṇa dhulār tale* for explaining the poetic–aesthetic aspect of religious experience. It is interesting to understand the *tumī* or *tumār* of Tagore's poem. Who is this *tumī* before whom my head bows down? Can it be personified? For an atheist believer, *tumī* cannot be any particular God from any particular religion. For Mohanty, it is the universe as a whole to whom the poem refers. How can one understand the universe as a whole? Mohanty rightly points out that universe as a whole or nature as a whole cannot be from a physicalistic point of view. One of the implications of the above point is that the universe as a whole cannot be exhausted by a physicalistic or scientific perspective. Rather, here the universe as a whole is the experience of sacred. Scientific naturalism is not the only explanation of nature as a whole or universe as a whole. It has room for moral, aesthetic and other dimension. Can we say that the experience of sacred has to be situated beyond this nature so that it does not come in conflict with the scientific explanation of nature? Mohanty would not take experience of sacred beyond the realm of nature or beyond the realm of our lived experience. He would rather stress on the point that religious experience or the experience of universe as sacred is part of our lived experience.

Mohanty makes an important distinction between the experience of sacred and other experiences. In the experience, for example, "*X* is red" there is a distinction between "*X* appears to be red" and "*X* is really red" (Mohanty 2000: 44). Experience of red may be due to the fact that an object appears to be red, not because it is actually red. But this is not true so far as the religious experience is concerned. The experience of *X* as sacred is not due to *X* merely appears as sacred and not really sacred. If the experience of *X* as sacred depends on merely on *X* appears to be sacred, then the experience turns into a subjective one. But Mohanty argues that the experience of sacred is not a subjective experience, but an objective one. That means if *X* is not sacred it cannot appear to be sacred. There is no gap that exists between "*X* is sacred" and "*X* appears to be sacred". It is the sacred itself which appears to be sacred or one can say that what appears to be sacred is sacred. The appearance of sacred is itself sacred. If something appears as sacred then it cannot but be sacred. Something cannot appear to be sacred if it is not sacred. But why *X* may not appear to be red, if it is really red? It could also be case that *X* appears to be red because it is really red. What is it in the religious experience we cannot be wrong about? One of the implications of the above point is that we cannot be wrong about our experience of sacred. If something is sacred, it will appear as sacred independently of any subject.

Mohanty makes a revealing point about religious experience when he says that the experience of sacred or sacredness does not belong to things. It is not the being which, following Heidegger's formulation, one can say that belongs to the things or present at hand. Rather, according to Mohanty, it is the manner in which the things act upon us. It is the power of the things which is experienced as sacred (ibid.: 45). The sacred is not a thing and not due to any physical property of a thing. Rather, the impression of sacred is due to the way something acts on us (ibid.: 46).

Sacred Space, Sacred Time and Sacred Causality

While discussing the nature of sacred world, Mohanty identifies three fundamental categories known as sacred space, sacred time and sacred causality (2000: 46). These categories are not categories that are available to the world of physics or one can say that these categories are not explainable by the account that we have from the physical science. The notion of space, time and causality is applicable to the empirical world or to the world of physics. But this is not the way in which the notion of sacred space, sacred time and sacred causality work in our lives. Space, time and causality usually are the notions described as belonging to the physical world, and the physical or the empirical world is described with the help of these notions. But how is anything sacred described with the help of these notions? How is sacred world itself is described as determined by space, time and causality? It is in this context Mohanty points out that the space, time and causality pertaining to the religious world are not described by physical laws. He rather tries to give a different interpretation of these notions away from the realm of natural science or physical science. One of the implications of his view is that then the notions of space, causality and time are not exhausted by natural science as it is commonly believed. The sacred world, not the physical or empirical world, is characterized by sacred space, sacred time and sacred causality. These three are not the only exhaustive categories to characterize the sacred world. Sacred space, for Mohanty, is not homogeneous and symmetrical. Rather, it is qualitatively differentiated. The homogeneity and uniformity of the empirical world or physical world is breached or interrupted by the sacred space. A temple or a mosque, for example, is not just a physical structure occupying some space. Rather, a temple and a mosque are a sacred space. Our physicalistic understanding of this structure is interrupted by the sacred space. But one might ask here that is it a temple, mosque or church that is sacred. If being religious is independent of God, then the whole space is a sacred space. Sacred time, according to Mohanty, is not the time which is "uniform, symmetrical, quantitative, one-dimensional flow (2000: 47). There are multifarious modalities in our experience of time, for example, the experience of a specific religious event or being part of such an event leads to qualitative experience of time and this experience of time is not uniform for everyone. The sacred time is meaningful for different people differently. Sacred time or auspicious time is repetitive and circular as it does not have one-dimensional flow. Sacred time always comes back and one can re-experience sacred time or occasion or event repetitively in one's lifetime. Sacred causality, according to Mohanty, is not the law of causality in physical science where there is "predictable lawful regularity" (ibid.: 48). Sacred causality is not the physical property of something which leads to a particular effect. Rather, it is, according to Mohanty, a practical causality. Mohanty is of the opinion that science by means of the principle of causality can explain why is there cancer, by identifying the particular cause–effect relationship in the form of "if *A*, then *B*". But it does not explain why a particular person is having that disease, not others.

Mohanty argues that the predicate "is sacred" like aesthetic impression such as "is beautiful" is a modifying predicate and not a determining predicate (1994: 55-59). It is important to understand the distinction between modifying predicate and determining predicate in order to understand what is the true nature of the predicate "is sacred" or how this predicate figures in our religious experience. Mohanty is of the opinion that modifying predicates and determining predicates are not just different predicates such as there is a distinction between the predicates "is red" or "is blue". These are rather a different kind of predicates, i.e. they "are qua predicates different" (ibid.: 55). Modifying predicates are the predicates of religious and aesthetic experiences such as "is sacred" and "is beautiful". These predicates, according to Mohanty, "express the how of a certain kind of working on the subject who is the bearer of this experience (ibid.). These predicates work on the subjects in an appropriate manner. For example, a beautiful thing creates the impressions-of-beauty on the subject. A sacred thing creates the impression of sacred in a subject. But the impression-of-beauty or the impression-of-sacred unlike the impression of red is immanent to the objects which are sacred or beautiful. The impression-of-sacred is the constituent object. One of the implications of the above point is that the religious experience, according to Mohanty, is objective in the sense that it does not depend merely on the subjective appearance of the something as sacred. It is not just a mental construction by a few who have the experience of the sacred. The impression-of-beauty or the impression-of-sacred is not merely a beautiful impression or a sacred impression which is purely subjective depending purely on the subject. The object in its being sacred or being beautiful itself creates the impression of sacred or beautiful in the subject. A certain object is sacred and its work as sacred on the subject are not different. Rather, they are one and the same thing. But in this context, Mohanty argues that sacred is not a thing but an activity. Something or some space is sacred due to the way it affects the subject. Something is sacred because its sacredness consists in acting-as-sacred. On the one hand, Mohanty tries to argue that the sacred is an original being in the sense that it does not just depend on its mere appearance for a subject. Its being sacred belongs to the reality itself. It is not just a conceptual or subjective reconstruction. On the other hand, Mohanty tries to put forward the point that sacred is not a thing, but a power of being sacred. There is a difference one can identify here between the expression "a thing is sacred" and "sacred is not a thing". It seems from Mohanty's account that we can say that "a thing is sacred", whereas he rejects the view that "sacred is not a thing". How can we accept the former and reject the later? Things, for example, a religious symbol, a statue, a text, are sacred. Since sacred is not a subjective reconstruction, it must belong to the things themselves. If that is the case, then how can we not say that sacred is a thing? We cannot accept this, because for Mohanty, sacred is not due to merely being a thing, but due to the way it acts or affects.

He states:

> The description of an art work is like the description of a thing. But an aesthetic impression is not. It speaks, as it were, for itself, bears its own testimony. "X is beautiful" describes the impression-of-beauty. Aesthetic sensing and aesthetic describing are inseparable moments of one experience of beauty. This is what "is beautiful" means, and it should not be construed to mean that "X only appear to be beautiful". We are not permitted to make that distinction between being-beautiful and appearing-to-be- beautiful. The aesthetic judgement is objective. – 1994: 56

Science, Religion and the Sacred

The relationship between science and religion has been one of the controversial topics of discussion in the history of mankind. The aim behind bringing in to the discussion the notion of sacred space, sacred causality and sacred time is that the religious world is not a scientific world. Mohanty argues that religion is science. The experience of sacred is not a scientific experience as is the case in natural science. The description of religious world and corresponding religious experience is not a scientific experience. Interpreting religion through science, which leads to the interpretation of science through religion, actually has two negative implications. Either it leads to the creation of pseudo-science or it leads to pseudo-religion. Religion is not pseudo-science. Rather, it is more fundamental as a way of experiencing the world in comparison to scientific investigation. Science, on the other hand, is not a competitor to religion. The discourse of science is different from that of the discourse of religion. Mohanty is not only arguing that religion is not to be determined by and studied by science, he is also stating that, as we witness these days, science is not to be studied or investigated or appropriated by religion. The question of whether science will discover sacred or not, according to Mohanty, is a mistaken question. Mohanty points out that science will not be able to discover the sacred. One might be impressed by the holistic implications of science and work towards it. But Mohanty argues that the holism of the science is not the holism of the holy. The sacred, according to Mohanty, is experienced in a different way independently of the mechanism that is provided to us by science.

One of the important points of Mohanty's discussion of the notion of religiosity is that religion does not necessarily have to transcend the world where we live. According to Mohanty, it transcends the profane world, but not the world as such. Rather, the experience of sacred is a lived experience and it is grounded in our lifeworld. One way of understanding this point is that if religious experience is very much related to our lived experience and it is not something which can be a subject matter of science, then this implies that the world is not exhausted by science or our lived experience is not exhausted by scientific experience. It has other dimensions, i.e. moral, aesthetic and religious. The question that arises here is that, if religious experience or point of view gives a new meaning to the world we live in, then can we not have any room for transcendence? Mohanty would argue that his conception of religious experience has the scope of transcendence, but not for transcendence to another world, i.e. heaven or God, etc. It is the transcendence we realize while living in this very world. Hence, the experience of transcendence as part of religious experience is not a supernatural experience. It is an experience like other experiences of our lifeworld.

Mohanty argues that our understanding of religious point of view or the experience of sacred is neither be discovered by science nor by a philosopher. Philosophical arguments like scientific reasoning cannot help us understand or describe religious point of view or the experience of sacred. Religious experience cannot be originated by philosophical arguments. Philosophical arguments, Mohanty states, cannot have a transformative effect like the poem of Rabindranath Tagore or participation in the *kīrtana* of Vaiṣṇavite tradition. Mohanty, in this context, made a distinction between pre-objective religion and objective religion. The pre-objective religious texts are the source of religious experience which is poetic in nature. He says, "the original religious world is a poetic world" (2000: 59). Vedic hymns, Upaniṣads, the poems of Tagore, Tukārām and Kabīr, and the *kīrtana* of Vaiṣṇavas are some of the instances which are the source of pre-objective religious experience. It is the pre-objective religion which comes as a mode of experience where the world gets a new meaning for the experiencer. It is not the objective religion where, according to Mohanty, these primitive experiences are solidified, freezed and dogmatized.

Conclusion

We have discussed in this paper J.N. Mohanty's account of the structure of religious experience and the structure of religious world. Mohanty's interpretation of the notion of religious and sacred is different from its usual interpretation and it gives us a common framework to understand the very nature of religiosity. Various attempts have been made, we think, by Mohanty, in his analysis of religious experience, to make the religious world and religious experience as part of our lifeworld. We have also discussed following Mohanty the moral, aesthetic and poetic dimensions of the religious world.

References

Mohanty, J.N., 1994, "Religion and the Sacred", in *From the Sacred to the Divine: A New Phenomenological Approach*, ed. Anna-Teresa Tymieniecka, *Analytica Husserliana*, XLIII, Berlin: Springer.

———, 2000, "The Structure of the Religious World", *The Self and Its Other Philosophical Essays*, New Delhi: Oxford University Press.

23

Universal Religion

The Indian Perspective

K. Om Narayana Rao

Hinduism is Vedic religion. The Vedas that constitute the basis of Hinduism are *apauruṣeya* and this implies their divine origin. But the scriptures in different other religions owe their origin to some divine inspiration or to some sacred message delivered through angels or to some special messengers of God; and this implies some author(s) of the respective scriptures. The latter scriptures being shaped out in different points of time in history, the religious currents in each of these scriptures have their own grounds for the conceptions, principles, ideals, etc. that they advocate and grow up as independent and self-evident systems. This being so, the revelatory events that have led to the birth of these religions, their principles and practices, and their modes of religious experience differ from one another. With this background in mind, an attempt is made here to *define* and see how far the idea of "universal religion" is relevant and appropriate in the Indian context.

Universal religion is neither a separate (or new) religion nor a particular religion, but is any religion that exhibits the element(s) of universality. The universal elements of love, friendship, brotherhood, cooperation, understanding, etc. can be seen in religions and these elements bring different religions on to a common platform, despite of the differences at the superficial level. These differences without understanding the true spirit of religion bring in problems of a much conflicting nature and, hence, there is a need to go deep into each of the religions to search for universal aspects in them that support and supplement each other's religion. The universal aspects or elements have a great force to build a platform where different religions are expected to agree on issues confronting them without any compulsion or force. The religions may have different mythologies, rituals, practices, beliefs, etc. but they all have one important aim, i.e. unfurling Ultimate Reality. The Ultimate Reality is one and the same though it looks different to the advocates and followers of various religions. A true realization of this point paves the way for universal religion.

Universal religion has its basis in the philosophy of humanism wherein everybody is respected and the principle of equality is recognized, irrespective of caste, creed, colour, sex, nationality, etc. Any establishment of such a universal religion requires the fulfilment of three basic conditions: first, it should respect, honour and give value to each and every religion; second, it should keep its doors open to one and all without any distinction and provide them satisfaction; and finally, it should allow individuals to practise any religion of their choice without in any way disrupting the basic structure of oneness, unity and integrity on the one hand and love, charity, compassion and sympathy on the other hand that constitute the universal facets of a true religion.

In the Indian context, a look into Hinduism reveals that it is more a flexible than a rigid religion. This is because it accommodates all the beliefs and practices of all those who call themselves Hindus. A monist or a monotheist or a polytheist or even an atheist can be called a Hindu. A God believer and a disbeliever can be equally called a Hindu. Even within the same Hindu family, there may be differences in the belief patterns among the members. The elderly people may be orthodox, the middle-aged liberal and new generation theistic or atheistic or with no proper belief-patterns. But still they live together harmoniously as a unit in the family. Because of the diversity in the features that underlie Hinduism, it is a bit difficult to draw a clear-cut sketch of Hinduism. A new belief all of a sudden may come into being and get incorporated into the belief-system of the Hindufold without much opposition or no opposition. Sometimes, an opposition to a particular belief is sidelined if a greater community intends to go on with the belief. Though a number of new beliefs come in and the old beliefs vanish or lose strength, there is no impact on Hinduism as a religion. This is because, as said earlier, Hinduism is not a staunch and rigid religion. There is always a scope for change without hitting at the interest of the community. This feature keeps Hinduism dynamic and also keeps its doors open to welcome new ideas, conceptions, beliefs, etc. into its fore and here lies an accommodative element in Hinduism that gives more or less a universal character to the practice of Hinduism.

A glance into Buddhism brings to fore that though Buddhism came into being as a reaction against traditional Hinduism, the influence of the Vedas and Upaniṣads on it cannot be completely denied. Buddhism was much influenced by the spiritual ethics of Hinduism. There are certain features in Buddhism that greatly contribute to the idea of universal religion and some of them are:

a. The simplicity in the personality of the Buddha; and his deep sense of love, charity and compassion for others that had a huge impact on the minds of the people, attracted them in large numbers to the Buddhistfold.

b. The teachings of the Buddha were simple and could be practised by anyone without discrimination, and also they were against unnecessary *yajñas* and sacrifices and this greatly inspired the people.

c. By totally discarding the metaphysical speculations, the Buddha laid emphasis on getting rid of human sorrows, pains and miseries that every human being undergoes.

d. The Buddha made no discrimination on the grounds of caste, creed, colour and sex, and preached the gospel of equality and brotherhood.

e. Buddhism emerged as a liberal religion – liberal not only to human beings, but also to animals. It totally discarded/discards animal sacrifices. Violence and bloodshed has no place in Buddhism.

f. Buddhism shaped out as a practical religion. It took/takes into account the problems confronting man and tried/tries to show the way out of them. It is humanistic in its outlook and approach.

g. The Eightfold path that Buddhism prescribes has elements acceptable to all.

h. Apart from teaching the ideals of self-reliance and self-help, it also teaches the ideal of mutual interdependence, friendship and coexistence.

These features can be taken to serve as the basis to think of Buddhism as a universal religion.

Now moving through the contribution of Jainism as a religion, we find that it has produced a tremendous impact on the social, religious, political and cultural life of the people of India. In the social sphere, we find that Jainism denounces caste system, practises *ahiṁsā* (non-violence), preaches the principles of brotherhood and undertakes activities for the benefit of the society. In the religious sphere, it denounces unnecessary rituals and sacrifices. In the political sphere, it sees the practice of *ahiṁsā* as instrumental for maintaining peace and harmony in the society. And in the cultural sphere, the Jaina literature among other things contains fairy tales and stories that reflect the importance of the philosophy of *ahiṁsā.* As a religion contributing to world peace, there is no better religion than Jainism. With *ahiṁsā* at the core, Jainism also speaks of *satya* (truth), *asteya* (non-stealing), *aparigraha* (non-possession) and *brahmacarya* (celibacy). It advocates the practice of ten kinds of *dharma*, viz. forgiveness, humility (or softness), simplicity, truthfulness, cleanliness, self-control, austerity (or penance), sacrifice, non-attachment and celibacy. These fundamental principles are for *all men*, irrespective of the cross cultures and traditions, since they are meant for ensuring a pure and simple living that religion can offer.

A reference can be made here to the Mauryan period of ancient India that witnessed a number of religions and their sub-sects, which often expressed the sentiments of intolerance and mutual disrespect. Emperor Aśoka got rid of such a conflicting situation by formulating the policy of *dhamma. Dhamma* is the law of piety that contained the fundamental principles of *saṁyama* (mastery over the senses), *bhāvaśuddhi* (purity of thought), *kr̥tajñatā* (gratitude), *dr̥ḍha-bhakti* (devotion), *satya* (truthfulness), *dayā* (kindness), *dāna* (charity), *suśruṣā* (service), *apiciti* (reverence), *śauca* (purity) and *saṁpratipatti* (support). These principles created an atmosphere of mutual trust, respect and toleration for each other's religion. *Dhamma* may be seen in the light of universal religion that could bring together the people belonging to different belief-patterns on to a platform of mutual harmony and coexistence.

It is also relevant here to state the Bhakti movement in medieval India where the mystic saints expressed views that were non-sectarian and humanistic, and tried to realize the unity of God through different names as Rāma, Kṛṣṇa and Allāh. *Bhakti* implies a single-minded, uninterrupted and extreme devotion to God who is the source of all joy and eternal bliss; and that which can be practised by any person through the purification of body and mind, and personal love of God. Though this movement can be traced back to Ādi Śaṅkarācārya, his monistic system was too philosophical for the masses to follow. Rāmānuja restricted the study of the Vedas to the higher classes, but he advised *all* to completely surrender themselves to *Īśvara* by having an absolute faith in Him. Kabīr, who spoke of himself as belonging to a lower caste and probably brought up in the family of a Muslim weaver, was the greatest of the *bhakti* saints who through his association with the saints of different religions acquired a balanced world view and made the movement very meaningful by focusing on the needs of the people. Macauliffe (quoted in Mahajan 1991: 391) writes:

> Kabīr has written works which all religious denominations can accept, and which, if pursued without bigotry, are advantageous for the salvation of all persons.

Kabīr's poems, especially his *dohās*, had an impact on the people, but most importantly on the common people. His *dohās* can also be found in the *Ādi Granth*. For him, Rāma and Rahīm, Kṛṣṇa and Karīm, Kāśī and Mecca express the same Divine Force. His teachings are still relevant today. Another *bhakti* saint, Caitanya upheld Kṛṣṇa-*bhakti* and advised all to respect others and surrender to God in love and devotion. He advised the different religious teachers not to abuse gods, belief-patterns and scriptures of other religions and also advised them not to pose up as a teacher continuously criticizing and elucidating religious views. Caitanya's message of love for a personal god consoled the suffering humanity, created freshness in human relations and provided a base for morality and goodness in the

Indian character. Further, Guru Nanak's Oneness or unity of God; Mīrābāī's love for Kṛṣṇa; Tulsīdās's Humanism; Dādū Dayāl's emphasis on love, brotherhood and toleration among people; Raidās's doctrine of "Hari in all and all in Hari"; Śaṅkaradeva's *niṣkāma bhakti*; and the contributions of Jñāneśvara, Nāmdev, Tukārām, Rāmdas, Eknāth and others may greatly be taken as unifying forces for human well-being in the divine path.

Sufism also had an impact on the Indian religious set-up. It sprang from the doctrine of *wahdat-ul-wujud*, meaning that God is the unity behind all phenomenal appearances. It was a religion belief pattern without any creed or dogma wherein the Sufi saints aimed at spreading the message of love of God among the fellow human beings. They advocated that for attaining *vasl* (liberation), poverty, tolerance, fear, repentance, non-possession, kindness, obligation, hope of spiritual glory, contentment and complete self-surrender to the Divinity are necessary. Though there were fourteen orders of Sufis in India with certain individual differences, they all had a humanitarian approach for the general welfare of all. The Sufis were more or less clear that there is one and only one God, the God of all, irrespective of whether one practises Hinduism or Islam or Sufism or any religion whatsoever. This may rightly be taken as a comprehensive feature or ground supporting the idea of universal religion.

The Sufis, viz. Sheikh Mubarak, Abul Fazl and Faizi, encouraged Akbar to follow a liberal policy in the matters of religion. Akbar too wanted to know the truth concerning world, life and existence; and he realized that the cultivation of a broad religious outlook is needed to know the truth. He constructed *ibādat khānā* at Fatehpur Sikri to carry on religious discussions with the saints, seers and prophets of different religions. Dīn-ī-Ilāhī was the product of these discussions. He promulgated Dīn-ī-Ilāhī with an objective of establishing a *national religion* that is acceptable to both Hindus and Muslims. Though Dīn-ī-Ilāhī could not sustain and met an end with the death of Akbar, a sincere attempt can be seen here to bring the various ideas in different religions on to a platform of common understanding to establish amity and peace.

In the first half of the nineteenth century, the land of Odisha witnessed the shaping of Mahimā Dharma, founded by Mahimā Goswāmī and propagated by Bhīmā Bhoi, that lays emphasis on the oneness of God who is formless, pure and indescribable. God is seen as Alekha Śūnya Puruṣa. Irrespective of one's caste, creed, colour and social status, all are eligible to receive the divine grace if they go on in the spiritual path. The humanistic overtones and the spiritual undercurrents in Mahimā Dharma are seen to help the human beings to liberate themselves from the problems and miseries of the worldly life. Since the concern here is man and his divine elevation without any sort of discrimination, it opens up its universal character to reach all.

In the modern times, we find the religious ideas of Mahatma Gandhi and Swami Vivekananda very convincing. For Gandhiji, Truth is God and the devotion to Truth is religion. He writes:

> Let me explain what I mean by religion. It is not the Hindu religion ... but the religion which transcends Hinduism, which changes one's very nature, which binds one indissolubly to the truth within and whichever purifies. It is the permanent element in human nature which counts no cost too great in order to find full expression and which leaves the soul utterly restless until it has found itself known its maker and appreciated the true correspondence between the maker and itself.
>
> – *Young India*, 12-5-1920

This definition gives primacy to the commitment to Truth, both external and internal; and there is no religion superior to the devotion to Truth.

Gandhiji had a wide understanding of different important religions and believed that every religion contains noble teachings of much value to mankind. But some misinterpretations, fanatic tendencies, irrational practices, etc. have degraded and distorted religions to some extent. However, Gandhiji believed that all religions are true, but they have certain defects or errors. The point that Gandhiji emphasized is that each of the religion must have a sense of respect for other religions, so that the people of different religious orientations find themselves in harmony with one another. He writes:

> Pray merely that your friends may become better men, whatever be their form of religion.

For him, God is the essential unity of everything which is to be realized by a truly religious man; and for this realization one has to transcend his own selfish considerations to love and serve others. If this becomes the essence of religion whatsoever, then there is a much hope of a universal consideration of religious doctrines taken with a spirit of human well-being. The rational position then is:

1. The claims of a given religion are true (from a standpoint).
2. The claims of other religions, though seem contradictory, are also true (from a different standpoint).
3. There should emerge a sense of respect for each other's claims.
4. The claims should be taken coherently in relation to one another with a clear view in mind that different claims and tendencies ultimately lead to one and the same Reality.
5. The purpose of religion is to spread love, not hatred, and for this, there should emerge a broad outlook in the matters of religion.

A very consistent position can be seen in the thought and conception of Swami Vivekananda who puts forth that the Ultimate Reality is one and the same, though it looks different to the advocates and followers of different religions. He exemplifies this as follows: The photographs of an object when taken from different angles look different. This does not make the object different for the photographers at different angles. The object is one and the same, it only looks different from different angles. Similar is the case with religions. They may appear different, but they assert the same thing. If this is so, then there is no point in mutual conflicts between religions. In the minds of the spiritual men, there is no conflict – they see everything similar in each other's conceptions and claims. It is only for the ignorant men and the men with partial knowledge who assume themselves to be absolute and true and take religion as a tool to meet their own selfish interests, there is conflict when there is actually no conflict at all. Such men close their eyes with their own hands and complain of darkness. There is a need to come to light to realize the true nature of reality which is one and only one, but with different forms and shades that are again a part and parcel of the same reality.

Thus, for Swami Vivekananda, Reality is one and a true religion is that which seeks unity and integrity, and sees the oneness of reality. A true religion must have a head to think, heart to feel and hands to work, which in other words means that the religious men must have a vision of unity despite all complex diversities and inculcate the values of love, compassion and tolerance. Such a true religion, for him, is universal religion. The aim of universal religion is to sort out the apparent conflicts and contradictions that religions have and establish peace and harmony for the good and well-being of one and all. Swami Vivekananda sees the positive side in religious conflicts as he writes:

> It is the clash of thoughts, the differentiation of thought, that awakes thought ... whirls and eddies occur only in a rushing living stream. There are no whirlpools in stagnant, dead water.
>
> – 2014: 379

Thus, variations or differences between religions may be there since men adhering to different religions differ in the way they think, but they need to be constructive and open-minded in order to have a forward thrust to shape out some novel ways of living admissible to all.

Now, on the question as to whether universal religion is ever possible, Swami Vivekananda answers that it is already there, though some of us are not aware of it. He asserts that we are at large so much involved in the external facets of religions that we fail to look and comprehend their inner facets. An insight into the inner facets of different religions shows that they are not contradictory, but are supplementary to one another. Further, in religion there are various aspects and religions do not put on their efforts on all these aspects. Each religion selects specific aspects and discusses them at length and tries to deduce other aspects from these specific aspects. That is, in each religion there are certain primary aspects and also certain secondary or tertiary aspects. An aspect that is primary in one religion may be secondary or tertiary in other religion. Thus, each religion, focusing on a specific aspect, gives to the world a total account of the aspect that could be better understood by other religions too. For instance, spirituality in Hinduism, universal brotherhood in Islam, self-purification in Christianity, *ahiṁsā* in Jainism, middle-path in Buddhism, are not just confined to the respective religions, but they do serve as the path-showers to all, beyond religious distinctions. There is an open choice to give and take without any conflict. This widens the scope of interreligious communication and paves a path for mutual cooperation and understanding, and more importantly helps to make a transit from a lesser to a higher truth. If this really happens in reality, then universal religion is already there. In a line it can be said that religions at the surface are diverse, but at the core they are all one. The realization of this point is important to understand or know the very nature of universal religion. Further, the differences vis-à-vis religions at the surface level, though look contradictory, in reality, are supplementary to one another if seen in a broader perspective. In the words of Swami Vivekananda (2001: 19):

> ... if there is ever to be a universal religion, it must be one which will have no location in place or time; which will be infinite like the God it will preach, and whose sun will shine upon the followers of Kṛṣṇa and of Christ, on saints and sinners alike; which will not be Brāhmanic or Buddhistic, Christian or Mohammedan, but the sum total of all these, and still have infinite space for development; which in its catholicity will embrace in its infinite arms, and find a place for every human being, from the lowest groveling savage not far removed from the brute, to the highest man towering by the virtues of his head and heart almost above humanity, making society stand in awe for him and doubt his human nature. It will be a religion which will have no place for persecution or intolerance in its polity, which will recognize divinity in every man and woman, and whose whole scope, whose whole force, will be created in aiding humanity to realize its own true divine nature.

Further, Swami Vivekananda makes it clear that by universal religion, one should not mean that it would have universal philosophy or mythology or rituals or doctrines; and again, one also should not mean that it advocates the common characteristics or features of different religions. A person may said to be within the fold of universal religion even though he practises the customs and rituals of a particular religion, provided that he respects all other religions and their doctrines the way he respects his own religion and its doctrines. It goes with an admission that though one is born in a family having a belief in a particular religion, he has his inner choice to expand his self to the practices of some other religion. Or again, he practises his own religion and also some other religion(s) without any discrimination and offers prayers in a temple or a church or a mosque or in an open field and finds utmost satisfaction and peace in all of them. Here lies the practice of a universal religion. Universal religion is not any specific religion, but any religion, in whose practice one does not get limited or bounded by its doctrines, principles, rituals, philosophy, etc., but keeps his heart open for all other religions with an equal sense of reverence and respect. B.K. Lal (1995: 45) writes:

> The one watch-word for universal religion, according to Vivekananda, is acceptance. Acceptance is not just tolerance. Tolerance is negative in its import, it implies, at least at times, that something is being allowed in spite of its being wrong. Vivekananda recommends positive acceptance. That is why he says that he can worship in any form with any individual or sect. He says that he can enter and offer his prayers anywhere, in a temple, or a church, or a mosque, or any other place. The believer in the universal religion has to be broad-minded and open-hearted, he would be prepared to learn from the scriptures of all religions, and keep his heart open for what may come in the future.

This feeling and emphasis on keeping the heart open for all religions makes Vivekananda to find out the essence of religions, which for him, is the conscious or unconscious struggle for the realization that we are all one in God. This realization reflects the ideal of universal religion. In the words of Vivekananda (1963: 432):

> Religion is realization; not talk, nor doctrines, nor theories, however beautiful they may be. It is being and becoming,

> not hearing or acknowledging; it is the whole soul becoming changed into what it believes.

This reflects the universal character acceptable to all races of mankind.

In the final analysis, it may be said that the Vedas which are *apauruṣeya* contain teachings for the whole of mankind beyond religious distinctions. But somehow the entire Vedic literature is thought to be the sole treasure and guide of Hinduism. There is a need to come out of this attitude to keep the doors of Vedic learning open to all. But how far the people belonging to different historic religions accommodate the Vedic spirituality into their fold much depends on their outlook and attitude. At the same time, there is also a much need in Hinduism to discover the facets of different historical religions in its own fold. This is because if God is seen as the author of the Vedas, then nothing outside the Vedas can ever be conceived of. Thus, the very ideal of universal religion is already there in the Vedas itself.

In the light of the rich cultural tradition of India, which while passing through various phases right from the Vedic age to the ancient and medieval periods to the modern period, though saw the spiritual light of the Vedas and Upaniṣads, the attachment to the excess of unnecessary rituals, sacrifices and *yajña*s, and also caste discriminations, largely overlooking the social problems and human sufferings somehow shook the minds of the lower sections of the society who turned to newly shaped religions, viz. Buddhism and Jainism, and especially Buddhism, and also to the Bhakti and Sufi movements because of the simplicity in their teachings. But the transition to Buddhism or Jainism or the involvement in Bhakti movement or Sufism or Mahimā Dharma was without bloodshed and this is the remarkable feature of this land that opens up the fact that the right of the people to profess, practise and propagate the religion of one's choice or to adhere to a set of belief-patterns is not something new, but has its roots that can be traced back down the history. This remarkable feature and the incorporation of the Buddha as the ninth *avatāra* of Hinduism speak of the universal character of Hinduism. Further, Aśoka's Dhamma, Bhakti and Sufi movements, Akbar's Dīn-ī-Ilāhī, Mahimā Dharma, Gandhiji's religion of Truth and Swami Vivekananda's practical Vedānta speak of the possibility of universal religion that has at its core the ideal of realization of oneness with the fellow beings and the concern is humane; and this can very much be seen to fit to the dynamics of Hinduism. Again in the Indian tradition, the religions and the religious movements have the messages of universal love, compassion, friendship, peace and law that reflect unity, integrity and oneness. This constitutes the very basis and foundation of *universal religion.*

References

Datta, D.M., 1953, *The Philosophy of Mahatma Gandhi*, Madison, WI: University of Winconsin Press.

Lal, Basant Kumar, 1995, *Contemporary Indian Philosophy,* Delhi: Motilal Banarsidass.

Mahajan, V.D., 1991, *History of Medieval India*, New Delhi: S. Chand & Co.

Vivekananda, Swami, 1963, *The Complete Works of Swami Vivekananda*, vol. III, Calutta: Advaita Ashram.

———, 2001, *The Complete Works of Swami Vivekananda*, Mayavati Memorial Edition, vol. I, Kolkata: Advaita Ashram.

———, 2014, *Jnana Yoga*, 34th repr., Kolkata: Advaita Ashram.

24

Tribal Religious Beliefs and Practices

A Philosophical Study on Koraput Region

Lakshman Patra

Introduction

The beliefs and practices of each and every society of the world have manifested through celebration of ritual and ceremonies, while going by Tylor (1871) (Chatterjee and Ghosh 1998: 120-22), "animism" is the common phenomenon among the tribes. Therefore, the religious beliefs and its performances among the tribals consist with their life-cycle rites, communal rites and worship practices along with their ancestral worship practices followed by their different totems and taboos. Religion, as a social singularity, is challenging to explain. Tribal people believe in gods and goddesses, witchcraft and magic, and disaster is attributed to the displeasure or malicious acts of the supernatural forces, malevolent spirits. Tribal rituals associated with birth, death and marriage, performed by priests, who own certain magical power, connect with the gods and spirits for their interference and blessing. However, religious beliefs and practices play an important role in the tribal myth. Their religious beliefs arranged on nature and the creativity unless the gods are first placated and the signs.

However, India has different ethnic communities, and tribal ethnic community is one of them. However, the Koraput tribe is also known as the Bonda tribe in the western parts of Odisha; apart from this, the Kora-Mudi is a minute tribe scattered in eastern India. In Odisha the Bondas are approximately 3 per cent out of the total tribal population. However, the Bonda tribal community maintains their existence and religious practices in the threshold of Hinduism. Therefore, in the year 1891, H.H. Risley (Deogaonkar 1994: 151-52), specifically pointed out that the Bonda tribe has been fully influenced by the Hindu religion; thus, Risley said, the Bonda religion stay under the "Hindu orthodox" and the practices of collective mobility which outstanding to extensive assimilation with the Hindu religion are static to the Bonda. Therefore, Risley in his *Castes and Tribes of Bengal* states:

> Moreover, the present study has been made an effort to understanding the religious belief and practices of the Bonda tribe who lives in Sangabadi village under Gadapadar Gram Panchayat of Koraput district, Odisha. Thus, the author attempts to identify the beliefs in religious and worship and rituals practices to regulate the spirit and soul which maintain the harmonious relationship among themselves. The study may be simplified to recognize their religious views and beliefs and how they practise their religious worships.
>
> Why do sociologists study religion? For centuries, humankind has sought to understand and explain the "meaning of life". Many philosophers believe this contemplation and the desire to understand our place in the universe are what differentiate humankind from other species. Religion, in one form or another, has been found in all human societies since human societies first appeared. Archaeological digs have revealed ancient ritual objects, ceremonial burial sites, and other

> religious artefacts. Much social conflict and even wars have resulted from religious disputes. To understand a culture, sociologists must study its religion.
>
> – District Welfare Office, Rayagada 2005: 111-12

What is religion? Pioneer sociologist Émile Durkheim described it with the ethereal statement that it consists of "things that surpass the limits of our knowledge" (Mandal et al. 2002: 195-96). He went on to elaborate:

> [Religion is] a unified system of beliefs and practices relative to sacred things, that is to say set apart and forbidden, beliefs and practices which unite into one single moral community, called a church, all those who adhere to them.

Some people associate religion with places of worship (a synagogue or a church), others with a practice (confession or meditation) and still others with a concept that guides their daily lives (like *dharma* or sin). All of these people can agree that religion is a system of beliefs, values and practices concerning what a person holds sacred or considers to be spiritually significant (Mankadi and Gangopadhyay 1983: 17-18).

Religion can also serve as a filter for examining other issues in society and other components of a culture. For example, after the 11 September 2001 terrorist attacks in the United States, it became important in North America for teachers, church leaders and the media to educate citizens about Islam to prevent stereotyping and to promote religious tolerance. Sociological tools and methods, such as surveys, polls, interviews and analysis of historical data, can be applied to the study of a religion in a culture to help us better understand the role religion plays in people's lives and the way it influences the society (Mishra 1989: 120-22).

Every religious system consists of a set of three essential elements:

a. belief in the existence of a superhuman world;
b. human's relationship to it; and
c. practice of ritual as an instrument of establishing relationship.

Here (a) refers to the belief system, (b) to the value system, and (c) to the action system. The form and meaning of these elements, i.e. religious belief, religious value and religious action, may differ from one order to another. Religion of a tribe is simple insofar as it is expressed in everyday language and experienced in everyday life. It is descriptive, demonstrative and readily discernible. Among the tribe's religious myth, belief, religious value and religious action are not treated as something apart from other kinds of belief and behaviour, as followed in social, economic and political contexts. Yet, the meaning of beliefs and behaviour of the tribal's appears mysterious to the outsiders. This is precisely because theirs is a religion without explanation. However, tribal religion is no less complete than the highly developed form of complex religion to the extent that its implicit philosophy recognizes the same universal truth (Mohanty 1994: 128-29).

Let us now explain all these features of tribal religion, its implicit philosophy and the world view. This we will do by discussing tribal lifestyle, tribal ritual complex and tribal world view.

Important Features of Tribal Sociocultural and Religious Life

1. They live in relative isolation usually in hills and forests in interior area.
2. Their social identity is defined and redefined from time to time.

3. They constitute simple societies which are socioculturally homogeneous.
4. They have their written and oral language or dialect for communication.
5. They have their rich cultural tradition and heritage although their social organization is simple.
6. They possess their own sociocultural history which may be shallow and unwritten.
7. They have low access to education and health care services.
8. A particular tribal community is endogamous and is divided into a number of exogamous divisions.

Other Cultural Features

1. *Traditional Village Council* – The village council is considered to be the cultural centre of a tribal village. The head of the village council is the head of the village. He is normally selected as per seniority and talent. Almost all the tribes call the head as *naiko*. Assistant is chosen to help the head, who is called as *challan*. The duty of convening a meeting is rested on the shoulder of *barika*. The priest of the village is regarded as *dehuri*. The head of the Koya village is *warde*, the Paraja's the *muduli*, the Sauras the *gomaṅgo* and so on. The religious head of the Kondh community is the *jani* who is assisted by *bis-mājhī* during the time of meeting (Patnaik 2006: 220-22).

2. *Worship of Nature* – All tribes are the worshippers of nature as they feel the presence of divinity in nature. Indeed, this is important from the religious ground. They give more emphasis on three elements of nature. They worship the soil as mother earth, the sun as religious god and water as the life giver. The aim and objectives of religious objects are as follows

a. Prayer for blessing
b. System of improved bread earning

c. Worshipping and remembering of forefathers
d. Welfare of the world
e. Recreation
f. Environment protection
g. Integration among communities.

The religious practices go on in tribal culture throughout the year.

Chief Characteristic of Tribal Societies: Simple Form of Religion

Every religious system consists of a set of three essential elements:

a. belief in the existence of a superhuman world;
b. human's relationship to it; and
c. practice of ritual as an instrument of establishing relationship.

Tribal Lifestyle

Religion pervades all aspects of tribal life that is why for understanding the tribal lifestyle we need to first understand the tribe's religious notions. To explain this, we will take an example of the Bonda of the Koraput in south Odisha. By their own account, the Bonda and their long horned buffaloes were created on the high massif of the hills by the great Goddess. Their settlement is marked by the unique barrel-vaulted houses and dairy buildings. The dairy buildings are temples. The Bonda people alone can own the most sacred dairy temples with their associated herds; the religion in tribal societies' *pujārī* men, called "the servants of the gods" fulfil the highest priestly tasks associated with them. Their economic and social lives are centred on the buffaloes. The greater part of their religious observance is also focused on this animal. The buffaloes are ritually guarded.

Every task of the dairyman, every object and place associated with the herds has received the impress of ritual. The Bonda observe a number of special ceremonies related to the dairies, the buffaloes and the pastures. There are rites by which they honour the dairy, purify it when it has been defiled and make offerings to it. There are rites associated with rebuilding and ret hatching. Next are the rites for naming a buffalo, milking a temple buffalo for the first time, giving salt to the herds and moving them to the new pastures. There is also the rite of lighting the gods' fire to ensure the fertility of the pastures. Life's major events are highly ritualized among the Bonda.

Tribal Ritual Complex

For a religious human, the superhuman world is the real world, which is ritually replicated in space and time. The believer communicates with this world through a symbolic code which calls the ritual language, consisting of

a. esoteric word (*mantra*),
b. gesture (*mudrā*),
c. sound (*dhvani*), and
d. everyday language of interaction (*vyāvahārikī*).

The tribal ritual complex may be described along this line. Here we will first speak of ritual space and then of ritual time. Next, we will discuss ritual language in terms of *mantra*, *mudrā*, *dhvani* and *vyāvahārikī*.

Ritual Space

In the tribal perception the space is filled with spiritual beings. There are two classes of space: cosmic space and physical or object space. The Bonda believe that the creator Ṭhākur Jiu dwells up in the sky; the sun-God also occupies the cosmic space. There is also the land of the dead. The spirits occupy concrete objects in and around their settlement. Such spaces are named after the spirits associated with them. For instance, the spirit of the region, the spirit of the village boundary, the house spirit, the spring spirit, the mountain spirit, the forest spirit, the spirit of the rice field, the spirit of the threshing floor, spirit of the cremation ground, etc. The ritual space is different from the ordinary space inasmuch as it is sacredly effective. But any ordinary space can become a ritual space, depending on its association with the spirit. Generally, it is allowed to retain its natural form.

Ritual Time

The tribes order their ritual time on the nature's signal, i.e. on the blossoming plants and trees, on the position of stars and moon, the biological time, and, if the circumstances so demand, by direct divination. The principal festival is the Caitī Parab. Another festival, known as Pūṣa Parab, is celebrated when rice grains have formed in the rice plants. The Bonda perform their rituals according to the position of stars and new moon. Most rituals are performed on or about the new moon. The moon-time is followed rather strictly. The first funeral rite is also held on the day of the new moon. Most tribes consider biological time as an occasion to perform ritual, such as the first menstruation, childbirth and death.

Ritual Language

Forms of ritual may vary from one tribe to another, but the basic ritual code of *mantra*, *mudrā*, *dhvani* and *vyāvahārikī* is applicable to all cultures.

a. *Mantra*: In the complex form of religion, such as in the Vedic and Tāntric traditions, the conception of *mantra* is fully developed. The Vedic *mantra* is not considered as the primordial word of which neither human nor God is the author. It is not even the message of God; it is God itself. Briefly, a *mantra* is that letter, or combination of letters, which evokes the deity. The *mantras* used by the tribes in the performance of a ritual are simple words of everyday language. For instance, the Bonda tribal priest recites the following *mantra* to the village spirits:

> Oh ye Khunt and Baghia spirits! Today I am offering sacrifices. Today in your name I am offering to you *mahuā*, *bera*, fig – all these fruits, I am worshipping you. Do ye protect (our) bullocks, buffaloes, goats, men, etc. in jungle and brushwood, from tigers and bears.

This *mantra* may appear as prayer. For, the Bonda priest offers a sacrifice to the spirit, which in return is asked to reciprocate. But, on a closer inspection, one will find that in this, there is both a command for boons and the hope of reciprocity. Some scholars (for instance, Woodroffe 1955) are of the opinion that *mantra* is not the same thing as prayer. A *mantra* intoned in the proper way becomes effective by the very structure of its sound body; a prayer, on the other hand, is a mere individual thinking expressed without determined sounds.

b. *Mudrā*: There are various kinds of hand gestures and bodily positions representing specific feelings and esoteric actions. In tribal dance, the movement of steps, interlocking of hands and other hand gestures have both aesthetic and ritualistic significance. The most common forms of the tribal dance *mudrā* are interlocked arms at the waist level in front and back; swinging of one leg while holding all the weight on the other foot; open movements of arms above shoulder level; outstretched hands held diagonally – one above the level of the head and the other at the level of the knee; taking such tiny steps that the lifting of the feet from the ground is hardly perceptible, the arms held down to the sides and the eyes downcast; fast movement of foot back and forth; swinging; rolling; rotating; hanging head down; and so on and so forth. There are also gestures of ceremonial greetings, such as Johar of the Bonda.

c. *Dhvani*: Sound is the third component of the ritual language. The sound of musical instrument guides the dance *mudrā*. Certain forms of sound have special significance. The Bonda produce peculiar sound at the annual hunt. They shout *der der, deper deper* during the Dhemasa dance. The Bonda shout *oh haw haw* during the thatching of their sacred dairy temples. The tribes of north-east India also produce a wide variety of sounds, sometime giving expressions to their virility. The sound of flute, the sound of drum, whistle and cries are associated with a number of ritual performances. Certain forms of sound are considered inauspicious. According to the Bonda tribal, if a jackal of the Fekar kind (which emits a peculiarly hoarse sound) is heard calling near the settlement, it is apprehended that someone in the community will fall sick or die. The croaking of a raven near the hut is believed to indicate that the news of the death of some near relative is about to come. Ceremonial weeping at the time of death may also be included in the category of ritualistic sound.

d. *Vyāvahārikī*: In course of the performance of a ritual what follows in the form of prescriptions or instructions, thoughts, methods and behaviour is the *vyāvahārikī* code. The following description (Walker 1986) of making offerings to a Bonda dairy will be a good illustration: All Bonda dairies must be kept in a state of high ritual purity. Dairies are participants in the divinity of the gods of the sacred places believed to be able to grant boons and punish wrongdoers. The manner in which the Toda go about requesting a boon from a dairy is strictly prescribed. It involves presenting to the dairy certain gifts: a buffalo or a dairyman's black loincloth, silver coins or a silver ring. If religion in tribal societies, the presentation is to be a buffalo, the ceremony lasts two months; if it involves no more than a silver, the whole affair can be completed in a couple of days. But in any case, it involves all the male adults of the patrician and the ritual interaction of the two clan divisions known as horns.

On the day before the new moon following the announcement of the act of offering a buffalo, all female members of the chief settlement must leave the hamlet, as must all males of the buffalo-givers. On the Sunday following the new moon, the buffalo will be presented to the dairy. The man who wishes to propitiate the dairy must provide a female calf, between one and two years old, unblemished, with clear eyes and no parts of its ears or tails cut. On the morning of the ceremony, members of the gift-giving must bathe from head to foot and abstain from food. When they are ready, they assemble at the outskirts of the chief hamlet from where they approach the settlement in a group with the calf; each man bares his right arm (a ritual sign of respect) and carries a green stick. When the members of the resident see these people approaching, they shout, "Give the buffalo! Come here". The gift-giving enters the hamlet and the two divisions face each other. The dairyman addresses a ritual three times with the question "Shall I give the buffalo!", to which the reply each time is "Give the buffalo!". Then all the men drive the calf past the buffalo-giving stone, by which act it becomes the property of the resident. The whole assembly now bows towards the dairy entrance as they recite a short prayer, which differs from clan to clan. After the prayer, all approach the dairy and bow, one by one, at the threshold, after which everyone partakes of a feast prepared by the receiving. The food on this occasion is a Bonda delicacy, large balls of puffed millet and jaggery, served with generous helpings of honey and *ghee*. After eating, the gift-giving must again leave the chief settlement and stay away for another lunar month. Members of the gift-receiving may come and go as they please, except the resident dairyman. Two or three days after the new moon, everybody (including the womenfolk) may return and the whole community is invited to participate in a celebratory feast. Dancing is an integral part of the festivities. Life in the chief hamlet now returns to normal, having been disrupted for two months. The underlying structure of the tribal ritual complex, as you must have realized, is not a mere reflection of and association with the superhuman world, but a strong reinforcement of the human world itself. Both social and aesthetic aspects of life are enriched. The social implications of primitive religion have been highlighted by Durkheim and Weber and many other sociologists of religion. The integrative function of religion in tribal society is demonstrated in their common goal (superhuman world) and common means (ritual). Unlike the salvation-seeking complex religions, tribal religion is concerned with the maintenance of social and cosmic harmony and with attaining this worldly goods – rain, harvest, children, health, victory and so on.

Method of Treatment

Among the most primitive tribe of Odisha, there is the belief that disease is caused by hostile spirits, the ghosts of the dead or due to the violation of some taboo. They have their own doctors. In the realm of netting the tribal's are still living in the age of magic with its practitioner. By their magical performances they also cure various kinds of disease like stomach trouble and fever. Before proper treatment, the tribal doctor (*disan*) called upon to attend a patient for diagnosis. For the diagnosis, what is known as *chaula khojā* any male relative of the patient brings a handful of rice which the patient is made to touch. Indigenous methods of treatment of the diseases among the tribal can be divided into two categories, viz. magical cure and medicinal cure. In case of epidemics like small pox, cholera or cattle disease they believe that it is caused by the evil influence of the *duma* (ghost). The family has to celebrate a worship to village Goddess (Ṭhakurānī) (Roy 2003: 70-72).

Hinduism and Tribal Religions

Ethnographic studies of different tribal groups show that the contact of the tribals with their neighbours varied from part-isolation to complete assimilation. The Tharu and the Khasa (William 1981: 114-15), the two central Himalayan tribes in north India, are a good example of completely assimed or Hinduized tribes. By adopting Hindu caste names, wearing the sacred thread, establishing social links with the local Rājpūt and brāhmaṇa groups, these tribals have incorporated their identity with high-caste Hindus. Similarly, the kṣatriya model (Alez 1994: 180-82) of Hinduism has been adopted in central India by the Chero, Kharwar, Pahariya of Bihar and the Bhumij of Madhya Pradesh. The Bhumij Kshatriya Association, founded in 1935, showed wider implications of Hinduization of the tribals. The concept of tribal Rājpūt continuum was evolved in the course of historical studies of the Bhumij Raj of Birbhum. In eastern India, the Bauri of West Bengal (Verrier 1943: 160-62) accepted to observe the prescribed number of days of pollution for mourning, wear the sacred thread go to pilgrimage and follow Vaiṣṇavism. They now claim to belong to the brāhmaṇa caste (Mohapatra et al. 2006: 17-18).

Christianity and Tribal Religions

Christianity has brought about many changes in the cultural life of the tribals in India. The missionaries attempted to convert numerically major tribes. As a result, minor tribes remained untouched by the new religion while mass conversion of major tribes gave the impression of the hold of Christianity on tribal India. We can also mention the element of fusion with Christianity introduced among the tribal groups. Under the rubric of one denomination of Christianity some of the previously separated tribal groups came together and even accepted marital relations across tribal boundaries. Under the church organizational network, many tribal groups, scattered over a wider area, came together and built contacts not only with the provincial and national but also international church bodies. Sahay (Samal 2000: 65-66) has studied the process of Christianization of the Bonda tribals and identified a set of five processes, signifying different forms of interaction between the tribal Christian norms and values. Under the patronage of British rule, conversion to Christianity had found a favourable environment while in independent India, many revivalist movements among the tribal groups have led the tribals to go back to their traditional religious beliefs and practices.

Art and Crafts

The artistic skill of the tribal people is not only manifested in their dance and music, but also in their dress and ornaments, wall paintings, wood carving and toy making. But through art and craft, their self image and aesthetic sensibility are visualized. The Sauras, the Koyas, the Kondhas decorate their houses with motifs of flowers, birds and geometrical designs. The Bonda paintings are intimately related to religious beliefs and drawn in order to appease demigods and spirits. The wood carving of Kondhas, metal work by Bathudis are really things of attraction to outsiders. The Bonda and Gadaba have their own looms by which they weave cloth for their own use. The Bonda women, though are considered to be very primitive, look majestic when they wear head bands of grass, necklace of coloured beads and girdles made of brass on their bodies. All these are expressions of their artistic quality and aesthetic sense.

Conclusion

The tribal culture is so much liberal and simple. A deep observation, study and analysis regarding tribal culture will clarify our understanding. On account of the above reasons, the tribals of these parts are considered as simple, truthful and freedom-oriented. Although modernization and the process of globalization have already entered into the hills of Koraput region changing their lifestyle, their costumes, tradition associated with cultural history will remain evergreen in the world. Now it is the need of the hour to study and highlight the rich culture of these south Odishan tribals of Koraput region, though they are unaware of their contribution for widening and enriching the scope of global culture. In the words of Verrier Elwin (2000: 162), the notable scholar of tribal studies in India:

> Let us teach them that their (tribals) own culture, their own arts are the precious things that we respect and need. When they feel that they can make a contribution to their country, they will feel part of it. It is, therefore, an important aspect of their integration.

References

Alez, K.P., 1994, *The Gospel of Indian Culture*, Calcutta: Punthi Pustak.

Chatterjee, A.K. and B.N. Ghosh, 1998, "The Impact on Culture on Development: A Critical Response", in *Tribal Development Option*, ed. P.K. Samal, Nainital: Gyanodaya Prakashan.

Deogaonkar, S.G., 1994, *Tribal Administration and Development*, New Delhi: Concept Publishing.

DWO, Rayagada, 2005, *A Note for Information on the visit of Commissioner-cum-Secretary to the ST & SC Development Department,. Government. of Orissa, Bhubaneswar*, Rayagada: District Welfare Office.

Elwin, Verrier, 1943, *The Aboriginal*, London: Oxford University Press.

Mandal, H., S. Mukherjee and A. Datta, 2002, *India: An Illustrated Atlas of Tribal World*, Anthropological Survey of India, Kolkata: Goverment of India, Ministry of Tourism and Culture.

Mankadi, K. and T. Gangopadhyay, 1983, *Rehabilitation: The Ecological and Economic Costs*, Surat: Centre for Social Studies.

Mishra, S.N., 1989, *Party Politices and Electoral Choice in an Indian State*, New Delhi: Ajanta Publication.

Mohanty, M., 1994, *Politics of Under-Development: Orissa,* New Delhi: University of Delhi.

Mohapatra, P.C., K.K. Mohanty and J. Samal, 2006, *Tribes of Koraput*, Koraput: Council of Analytical Tribes Studies.

Patnaik, N., 2006, *Primitive Tribes of Orissa and Their Development Strategies,* New Delhi: D.K. Printworld.

Roy, A.K., 2003, "Jharkhand: Internal Colonialism", in *Jharkhand Movement: Indigenous Peoples' Struggle for Autonomy in India,* ed. Ram Dayal Munda and S. Bosu Mullick, Copenhagen/Jharkhand: IWGIA and BIRSA.

Samal, J., 2000, *Values in Tribal Culture, Parab*, Koraput: District Council of Culture.

Walter, R.B.J., 1986, *Culture, Discourses, Insecurity, Alternatives, Global, Local, Political*, 11(4).

William, R., 1981, "The Analysis of Culture", in *Culture, Ideology and Social Process*, ed. Tony Bennetl, London: Batsford Academic and Educational in association with Open University London.

Woodroffe, J., 1955, *The Garland of Letters*; Varnamala: Studies in the Mantraśāstra, Madras: Ganesh and Co.

25

The Concept of Premādvaita[1] through the Lens of Swami Vivekananda

Dibyendu Mondal

Introduction

THE *truth* can be discovered in a variety of ways, which explains why it takes many forms. But the validity of the truth is always remained constant at the level of feeling. Reviewing the entirety of human history reveals that people have been actively looking for this truth, whether consciously or unconsciously. Truth is one and infinite; so, the way to get close or see this truth in a

1 [1] The term *premādvaita* refers to the understanding the nature of the non-dual state of reality through the path of love or devotion. In Sanskrit the word *prema* is refers to love. Here love has not been understood in ordinary relational aspect; rather it is defined as the relation between an individual and the higher reality. The nature of the highest state (expression) of this relation, the duality between the *sādhaka* and the loving being would not persist. This notion of love if it is attached with the term *advaita* (non-dual) then it's called *premādvaita*. In *bhakti-yoga* to describe the state of *parā-bhakti* Swami Vivekananda has indicated this non-dual nature of love, which I have tried to explore in this paper.

new way also be infinite. In this context, it can be stated that – an infinite way to an infinite path. In the rich land of spirituality in India, since ancient times, various saints or sages have been searching for this single truth in different ways. Various kinds of wise sages have been looking for the truth in accordance with their personal tastes. In this article, we will try to find out only one way out of this infinite paths and that is the path of devotion.

The word "devotion" simply means a passionate search for higher being. *Bhakti-yoga* refers to the practice of meditation, adoration or lovingly seeking God. *Brahmasūtra* 1.1.2 states: *janmadasya yataḥ* (Vyāsadeva 2014: 96). It translates as follows:

> *Brahman* is the source from which the entire cosmos was formed, sustained and ultimately destroyed.

Note, that this is the definition of the qualified nature of the reality (*Saguṇa-Brahman*). Now the question naturally arises: Is there more than one God? In another language, the concept of highest reality comes with duality or it is exclusively non-dual in nature. Are those attempting to distinguish reality through the procedure of elimination (*neti-neti*) and the devoted person's *loving being* distinct from one another? More specifically, is there any difference in the state of liberation where a student or a meditator (*sādhaka*) is following the path of knowledge and another learner (*sādhaka*) who is following the path of devotion? For a devotee, can it be possible to experience the absolute nature of reality (*Nirguṇa-Brahman*) and be considered as her favourite? Following Swami Vivekananda, the nature of reality is qualified and non-qualified at the same time. In this context, he gives an example:

> *Brahman* is as the clay or substance out of which an infinite variety of articles are fashioned. As clay, they are all one; but form or manifestation differentiates them. Before everyone of them was made, they all existed potentially in the clay, and,

> of course, they are identical substantially; when formed, and so long as the form remains, they are separate and different; the clay-mouse can never become a clay-elephant, because as manifestations, form alone makes them what they are, though as unformed clay, they are all one. *Īśvara* is the highest manifestation of the Absolute Reality, or in other words, the highest possible reading of the Absolute by the human mind. Creation is eternal, and so also is *Īśvara*. – 1958: 37

From a shared perspective, it seems that there is a significant distinction between knowledge and devotion, both conceptually and methodically. However, it may be demonstrated via philosophical study that, despite their outwardly appearing distinctions, knowledge and devotion ultimately converge in the same place. Although there is a theoretical and practical difference between the different teachers (*ācāryas*) of the path of knowledge and the path of devotion, both are believed in the effect of devotion. The contrast between the two, from an ideological or theoretical standpoint, is that whereas devotees see devotion as both a means and an end, teachers of the path of knowledge see devotion as a route to liberation. Explaining the concept of *bhakti*, Rāmānujācārya, while explaining the *athāto brahmajiñāsā sūtra* (Vyāsadeva 2014: 65), said:

> *dhyānaṁ tailadhārā-badavicchinna-smr̥ti-santānarūpā dhuravā smr̥tiḥ.* – Ibid.: 145

In *Brahmasūtra-Bhāṣya* 3.2.25, Sri Nimbārkācārya said:

> *prakāśyādibaccābaiśeṣyaṁ prakāśaśca karmaṇyabhyāsāta* ।
> – Ibid.: 452

This means, that just as the sun and fire. are manifested using such specific conditions, so also *Brahman* is manifested by means of devotional worship. Vallabhācārya was also a believer in the path of devotion. According to him, even if both knowledge and devotion are accepted as the means of liberation, liberation is not possible only through knowledge. In this context, Vallabhācārya says:

> *kr̥tisādhyaṁ sādhanaṁ jñānabhaktirūpaṁ śāstreṇa bodhyate* ।
> *tābhyāṁ bihitābhyāṁ mukti maryādā* । *tadrahitānāmapi svarūpavalena svaprāpaṇaṁ puṣṭirucyate.* ।
>
> – Chaudhari 2016: 302

Says Swami Vivekananda (1958: 33):

> Three things are necessary for a bird to fly – the two wings and the tail as a rudder for steering, *jñāna* (knowledge) is the one wing, *bhakti* (love) is the another and *yoga* is the tail that keeps up the balance.

Now, to establish the idea of devotion in the house of non-duality is important to demonstrate that knowledge and devotion are "one" (*advaita*) at the highest level of experience. Because, from the perspective of the path of knowledge, although the highest form of *Brahman* is absolutely non-qualified (*nirguṇa*) by its nature, *Brahman* becomes qualified (*saguṇa*) by the interpretation of the universe. But if we observe the whole structure of the path of devotion, then devotion is clearly dual in all cases. In other words, the devotee can experience the most desired liberation by performing her spiritual practice (*sādhanā*) in the context of *sālokya, sārūpya, sāmīpya* or *sārṣṭirūpa mukti.* In the path of devotion, there is never a state of harmony (*sāyujya*) between the chosen ideal (*iṣṭa*) and student (*sādhaka*); because of this reason, they are not one (*advaita*). In this context, any scriptural interpretation establishes the duality of the path of devotion. Following Swami Vivekananda, we can say that even though the path of devotion begins its journey with duality, the highest feeling of devotion is always non-dual. His view in this regard is at the lower level of *bhakti* (*gauṇī bhakti*), the devotee starts her spiritual practices (*sādhanā*) in a number of methods, such as symbols (*pratīka*), idols (*pratimā*), worship (*pūjā*) and words (*mantra*) and can purify the body and mind. Through this process, the student constantly aspires to reach herself to the next level of devotion, and the gap or the distance between the student and the Supreme Being disappears in the highest state of devotion. The student continually aspires to reach higher levels of devotion through this process, and in the highest state of devotion, the gap or separation between the devotee and the Supreme Being disappears.

Renunciation is the Primary and Natural Key to Understand the Premādvaita (Non-Dual State of Love)

Swami Vivekananda explicitly stressed the significance of renunciation or sacrifice as the first step in the pursuit of the student (*sādhaka*) at the higher level of devotion (*parā-bhakti*). This "sacrifice" is thought to be necessary for spiritual advancement. At this level of *parā-bhakti* (renunciation) is specifically mentioned as the first preparation for the student's pursuit. So it is practically impossible to advance spiritually without this kind of renunciation. Now, this essential characteristic of "renunciation" is not applicable to *parā-bhakti* or *bhakti-yoga* only. Renunciation has been regarded as a crucial and necessary requirement for all paths, regardless of the path (*mārga*) that the emancipated person chooses to follow. A student who is a follower of the path of service (*karma-yoga*) must constantly keep in mind that she has no control over the outcomes of *karma* when practising *sādhanā*. In this context, it is said in the *Gītā* (V.10):

> *brahmaṇyādhāya kramāṇi saṅgaṁ tyaktvā karoti yaḥ* ।
> *lipyate na sa pāpena padmapatramivāmbhasā* ॥

In other words, a person who conducts deeds without attachment and surrenders complete control to the Supreme Soul does not engage in sin like a lotus leaf submerged in water. As a result, *karma-yoga* does not tell us to stop doing our *karma*; doing our *karma* is the most socially acceptable means of achieving *nirvāṇa*. But it is important to keep in mind that every route has its own benefits and drawbacks. For example, while *karma-yoga* has the benefit of non-renunciation, it also has the drawback of working independently. Every action is motivated by the modest "ego" of everyday beings like us, and from this sense of self-interest, selfishness is created. We do all our daily actions from the profit and loss calculation. Therefore, the main obstacle to practising *karma-yoga* for the common student (*sādhaka*) who has gained freedom is their inability to practise it without attachment or emptiness. In *rāja-yoga*, the student is always required to think of herself as *Puruṣa* (Pure Consciousness) through meditation and, in this sense, one must reach the level of feeling which is distinct from *Prakr̥ti* (Insentient Nature). The Sāṁkhya school says about *Prakr̥ti*:

> *mūlaprakr̥tiravikr̥tirmahadādyāḥ prakr̥tivikr̥tiyaḥ* ।
> *saptaṣoḍaśakastu vikāro na prakr̥tirna vikr̥tiḥ puruṣa* ॥
>
> – Mishra 2016: 35

In other words, the form of non-deformity (*avikr̥ti*) is the fundamental nature. The seven substances (*tattvas*), starting from the sublime (*mahat*), are both nature and deformity (*vikr̥ti*) and eleventh senses and *pañca-mahābhūtas* – these sixteen categories are only deformity (*vikr̥ti*). And beyond that *Puruṣa* (Pure Consciousness) is neither nature nor deformity (*vikr̥ti*). The practice of renunciation of the path of knowledge is the most rigorous; on this path, the student has to reject the world in front of her as a lie, an illusion. Through the varied events of the world, we have expanded our range of experience; also through our various external and internal senses, we relish the various forms, juices, tastes, smells, etc. of nature; it is almost impossible for an ordinary living being to give up or imagine a lie in an instant. Besides, it is said in the *Gītā* (II.19) regarding *jñāna-yoga*:

ya enaṁ vetti hantāraṁ yaścainaṁ manyate hatam ।
ubhau tauna vijānīto nāyaṁ hanti na hanyate ॥

That is, one who considers this soul to be a killer or one who considers it to be slain both do not know the true nature of the soul. Because this soul does not actually kill anyone and is not killed by anyone.

It is mentionable that all other paths also consider that renunciation is a necessary condition to progress in the spiritual journey. But significantly, in the path of devotion this "renunciation" is very normal. It means, like the other paths, here in the *bhakti*-path there is no need to give up the effect of action (*karma-phala*) or not necessary to separate herself from nature (*rāja-yoga*) or not at all to separate herself from the whole living world (*jñāna-yoga*). Flowing Swami Vivekananda, we can say naturally the way we look at the world and life without forcing ourselves to leave it, we need to surrender all our small narrow loves and attachments to the higher reality. In this context, he (1958: 73) says:

> So in this renunciation auxiliary to devotion, there is no harshness, no dryness, no struggle, nor repression, nor suppression, the *bhakta* has not to suppress any single one of his emotions, he only strives to intensify them and direct them to God.

The Natural Manifestation of Love and Its Secrets

If renunciation is a necessary component of the path, it is evident from the explanation above that renunciation is quite natural in this kind of *bhakti-yoga* and does not call for the forceful suppression of any emotion; rather, only those sentiments need to be directed towards higher reality. Now, the question is why is this "sacrifice" treated as normal in the path of devotion? Why is there no dryness in renunciation in the *bhakti* path compared to other paths? In other words, how can devotional sacrifice be so lively? Now, if we examine the issue carefully, it will become clear that any good or terrible deed done in this world is accomplished via the power of love. People are prepared to commit any good or wicked deed when they are inspired by this love, which is quite inherent in human nature. According to the philosophy of *bhakti-yoga*, the evolution of the numerous and varied forms of love that can be seen in nature is really just the evolution of the single "one" love. The various ugly and demonic things that we do in our daily life and all the great things that are happening in the world are all motivated by the same love. For instance, one person may want to or actually do her best to help the less fortunate, while another murders her closest relative and makes off with everything. Both of these acts are carried out by people who are driven by the same love force. The love of the two people in this situation is equal, but the second person's love is mistaken since the second person performing the act loves herself while the first person performing the act loves the other. It is noteworthy that love here is indifferent or love has no faults or qualities of its own. Similarly, pure love is unconditionally manifested through all the entities; but the reason for the discrepancy is in the way how we use it. So, in such a situation *bhakti-yoga* can be considered as a scientific path as a means of attaining pure love. The path by which we control our petty selfish love, channel it and use love for a new purpose can ultimately lead to spiritual peace and joy. So, our attraction to and love for lovely things and people should be channelled towards the way of devotion to the higher reality. There is simply turning love towards a higher entity; there is no forced surrender. The student must now let go of all small attachments in order to participate in this kind of natural renunciation. She must also stand on the high ground of devotion and observe the world and its events from a distance with perfect detachment. Only then will it be understood that the same love energy is playing everywhere. As common people, we are constantly fighting for the petty interests of the world with the various forces of society and, while doing this struggle, people forget about themselves, i.e. their true nature. However, it should be noted that from the perspective of *bhakti-yoga*, this conflict with life's existence does not have a completely pointless outcome. According to the path of love, every living thing is advancing towards the Supreme Being through this effort. The meaning of the words can be said, when a person embarks on a life struggle and continues to fight for her own and her family's self-interest throughout her life, then she only experiences conflict or struggles. But, the idea of *bhakti-yoga* is that if a woman comes out of the conflict as a seer or witness and observes all worldly happenings cautiously but dispassionately, she will gradually feel, through all worldly activities, the same *loving being* is manifesting itself. At the root of all, our attraction is the presence of this one supremely loving being. Because it is necessary to think that our attraction to material objects, i.e. the attachment we are constantly expressing to various objects, is it only because of the attraction to the material, or is there any invisible conscious being working behind it? Only the presence of a conscious entity within an inanimate object can trigger excitation in matter because no inanimate object has the ability to do so. Swami Vivekananda (1958: 75) says in this context:

> Who can attract a soul really? Only He! Do you think the dead matter can truly attract the soul? It never did, and never will. When you see a man going after a beautiful face, do you think that it is the handful of arranged material molecules that really attract the man? Not at all. Behind those material particles there must be and is the play of divine influence and divine love.

In this context it is said in *Bṛhadāraṇyaka Upaniṣad* 2.4.5:

> *na vā are patyuḥ kāmāya patiḥ priyo bhavatyātmanastu kāmāya patiḥ priyo bhavati na vā are jāyāyai kāmāya jāyā priyā bhavatyātmanastu kāmāya jāyā priyā bhavati* ।
>
> – Sankhya-Vedantatirth 1331 BS: 111

From the foregoing discussion, it is evident that modest or large worldly concerns can never be the single or primary aim of the enormous job that is being done in this world, through which different people keep the work of the world going. According to *bhakti-yoga*, the ignorant person is not aware of her actions; the real and highest goal of person's hard life struggle is to reach the Supreme Being and finally merge with it. Because only a sincere student is able to sense from this world what is the fundamental objective and purpose of human life's struggle, only devotion can lead to this ultimate realization. Intense attraction to higher reality is the source of a student's renunciation; by this attraction, the learner rejects all trivial attachments and is perpetually overcome by her love for the Supreme Being. This natural dispassion of a student towards loving being is different and everything is actually the key to enter into *parā-bhakti*. And the person who has attained the heights of *parā-bhakti* via *sādhanā* alone has the right to assert that idols, worship and worship techniques are not necessary for *dharma* or God-feeling because she got into *parā-bhakti* with such a deep love for loving reality in her heart. In the language of Swami Vivekananda (1958: 76):

> He sees no discriminations; the mighty ocean of love has entered into him, and he sees not man in man, but beholds his Beloved everywhere. Through every face shines to him his Hari. The light in the sun or the moon is all His manifestation.

The Conditions of Premādvaita (Non-Dual Love)

The discussion above makes an indication that there is no distinction between knowledge and devotion when one is on the plateau of meditation (*sādhanā*); while the student who is flowing the path of knowledge (*jñāna-mārgī sādhaka*) can experience herself as one, identical with the absolute reality (*Nirguṇa-Brahman*), the devotional ascetic is fortunate to taste the love of the one single loving being through all things. Although the higher state of knowledge (*parā-jñāna*) and the higher level of devotion (*parā-bhakti*) are one on the level of feeling, the two paths are certainly different in terms of external character. It will be possible to achieve the state of oneness or non-duality if the student can detach herself from the world, body, mind, intellect, etc. while experiencing the knowledge of *Brahman*. In the same vein, *parā-bhakti* possesses some distinctive character traits that set the higher field of devotion apart from other routes and allow her to properly enjoy the loving Being's presence and its affection. Now on the stage of *bhakti* path only when these certain conditions are fulfilled can a student be properly claimed to have set foot on the land of *parā-bhakti*. *Bhakti* path advises against harbouring any thoughts of physical or mental gain, no matter how small or overt, in order to reach the highest level of love. Second, in a relationship between the student and the higher reality that is based on genuine love, there should be no fear. And the last condition is the time of interaction with any limited person or entity you should impose your highest ideal; it means that true one, non-dual love manifests through everything.

First, the true learner is distinguished from others in spiritual life by this sign of love. People, who are in those interested in transcendence reality or *loving being*, the whole community roughly can be divided into two types: The majority of individuals adore or use the Supreme Being as a tool to satisfy their materialistic ambitions. In other words, they are committed to the higher reality in the hopes of obtaining something. People worship that Supreme Being in hopes of health, wealth, status, prosperity, etc.; higher reality is only the medium of seeking here. A small group of people also like discussing, hearing about or thinking about this higher reality because they genuinely adore it and cannot imagine living without doing so. We can compare this condition of the higher realm of devotion (*parā-bhakti*) with *ahetukī bhakti.* The word *ahetukī* means the complete sense of desireless. It means, in the true sense of devotion one does not want anything other than God. Even at this stage of devotion, the devotee does not pray for the most desired liberation. In this context the *Bhāgavata* (2014: 241) says:

> *na pārameṣṭhyaṁ na mahendradhiñcyaṁ na sārvabhaumaṁ na rosādhipatyaṁ* ।
> *na yogasiddhīrapunarbhavaṁ vā maypitātmecchati madvināhanyāt* ॥

When the devotee does not desire anything other than *a loving being* (God), it is called *ahetukī bhakti.* Another great example of *ahetukī bhakti* is:

> *yadi bhavati mukundena bhaktirānandasāndrā* ।
> *viluṭhati caraṇāje mokṣamrayajyalakṣmīḥ* ॥
>
> – Dutta 1920: 8

As this advanced stage of *bhakti* devotee does not beg for *mokṣa*, but liberation itself repeatedly prays for shelter at the feet of the devotee. Here for a devotee, liberation itself is very significant as a highest post in spiritual journey. At such a stage of devotion we can recall the prayers of the devotee to Mother who says:

> *māṭḥ kiṁ baramaparaṁ yāce* ।
> *sarvvaṁ sampāditomiti satyam* ॥
> *yattvaccaraṇāmbujamiti guhyaṁ* ।
> *dṛṣṭaṁ vidhiharamuraharajuṣṭam* ॥" – Ibid.: 13

The above verse is a reflection of a sincere prayer to the highest being as a mother of the Universe and the *sādhaka* is expressing her internal disposition like. Hey mother! what want a groom? Brahmā, Viṣṇu, Lord Śiva worship your feet, the rare lotus feet, when I saw what else? All my quests are fulfilled; I no longer desire anything. She who is a true devotee can have no desire for anything other than Her loving being who is the Lord. There is a story in this regard, while walking through the jungle, a king came across a sage and asked him to visit his kingdom so he might receive some alms. In response, the sage said he would not travel since he was content with his natural wealth and had no possibility of acquiring more. But after numerous demands, the sage subsequently consented to go to the king's palace with him. Prior to offering the sage alms, the monarch prayed to God for greater health, money and prosperity, among other things. Upon witnessing this prayer, the sage decided to depart from there. When the monarch questioned the sage about why he had left the palace before taking the gift, the sage replied – I am not interested in accepting alms from a beggar; one who asks for more health and wealth like a beggar himself has not qualified to give alms. The moral of the narrative is that true love cannot be developed if there is a sense of reciprocation or demand; instead, it merely results in "shoplifting". The idea behind *bhakti-yoga* is that one should love the higher reality without asking for anything in particular, not even liberation. I should love Her, my Lover, without expecting anything in return. Just as when we see a natural scenery and are enthralled by it, we do not want anything from that scenery, nor does the scene demand anything from us. In the *bhakti* path, true love has the same characteristics; she only loves the Supreme Lover only for love's sake. In this context, it is said in the *Bhaktisūtra*:

> *tribhuvana vibhavahetavehapyakuṇṭhasmṛtirajtātmasaṁ ārādibhivimṛgāt* ।
> *na calati bhagavatpadārvindālpava nimiṣārddhamapi yaḥ saḥ* ॥
>
> – Jīva Gosvāmī 1955: 33

This means, if you remove your mind from the feet of the Lord just for a moment, you can possess all the riches of the universe. The great devotee is the one who, when confronted with such a temptation, remembers that the Lord's lotus feet are unique and that nothing else in the universe is a substance, refusing to take her attention away for even a moment from those precious lotus feet of those passionate gods. In this context, Swami Vivekananda (1958: 88) says:

> Love knows no reward. Love always for the love's sake. The *bhakta* loves because he cannot help loving. When you see beautiful scenery and fall in love with it, you do not demand anything in the way of favour from the scenery, nor does the scenery demand anything from you. The real nature of love is the first of our triangle. Ask not anything in return for your love; let your position be always that of the giver; give your love unto God, but do not ask anything in return even from Him

Fearlessness emerges as the second requirement of love. The requirement for love or devotion depends to some extent on the first condition. Because, if there is a desire in love, that love is inevitably low-level and accompanied by fear. Being selfish creatures, we become more scared the more limited our thinking becomes; it is this limited selfishness that isolates us from the rest of the world. True love can never be born in such a narrow-mindedness of *bhakti-yoga*; it is necessary to think of higher being not as a punisher or as a rewarder but only as a *loving being*. For instance, the judge is accepted by her husband as a lover or wife rather than as a partner; similarly, on the spiritual path, the student will accept her will as the supremely loving man. Simply expressed, fear is an impediment to true love. A significant indication where true love resides without fear when a devotee is so attached to the higher being that anger or price is born in the devotee's heart at the one sight of her *loving being*. Swami Vivekananda (1958: 89) says:

> Love conquers naturally all fear. Think of a young mother in the street and a dog barking at her; she is frightened and flies into the nearest house. But suppose the next day she is in the street with her child and a lion springs upon the child. Where will be her position now? Of course, in the very mouth of the lion, protecting her child. Love conquers all fears. Fear comes from the selfish idea of cutting one's self off from the universe. So long as there is the least spark of fear in you there can be no love there.

The third and most important condition of love is that the lover imposes her own highest ideal on the beloved. Because on this condition lies the highest expression of love. This third condition of love is obviously the most philosophically significant from the perspective of devotion; in other words, we can think of this circumstance as the strongest indication that love or devotion has non-dual foundations. This circumstance lends itself to an easy demonstration that there is no significant distinction between knowledge and devotion in the stage of *sādhanā*. However, it is important to highlight that while the non-dual feeling of love and knowledge is identical, their modes of expression are not. Three kinds of limitation are recognized in Indian philosophy, primarily in Advaita Vedānta: first, special limitation; second, temporal limitation; and third, object limitation. First, special limitation entails that all living and non-living phenomena in this universe are constrained to a certain location at a specific time. It implies that anything will always be restricted to a certain location in this complete globe at any given time; that is, at that specific moment, that thing is only capable of existing at that specific location and nowhere else in the entire cosmos. For instance, if someone is seated in a specific chair in her own room, it indicates that she is not at that moment anywhere else in the world. The second limitation that we observe is temporal limitation. This perspective holds that everything in the universe, whether it be an item or a living thing, is subject to a law; the law is that everything that exists in the universe must eventually disappear in accordance with the unavoidable rules of nature. There is nothing in this world that does not eventually perish. Therefore, all of the objects in this world are not immortal; otherwise known as matter with no origin – destruction. All things in the world are located within a certain period of infinite time; the existence of that object before its creation or after destruction, cannot be grasped in time. The third type of constraint is object-related constraint; any object in this world is related to that object only in identical and the difference or contrast of that particular object with all other objects exists. For example, an individual human being is related to herself only in non-differentiation and is different from all other human beings and all other things in the world. Now, according to *jñāna-yoga*, the idea of *Nirguṇa-Brahman* is an object that is above all of these categorizations; if *Nirguṇa-Brahman* does not contain these three types of differences, then *Brahman* is an entity that permeates all locations, all periods of time and all objects in this universe. Now if we want to know the form of *Nirguṇa-Brahman* in one word, then we have to say–*sat-cit-ānanda*. In other words, infinity means that there are no such three types of limitations within the *being*. Now, one can properly comprehend the form of *Nirguṇa-Brahman* if the first two terms of *sat-cit-ānanda* are rightly related to infinity. Perfectly *Being* refers to the complete existence of a being. This means that everything in this universe, sentient or insentient, is entirely dependent upon this absolute existence or infinite existence. All things in our world have various names, shapes and purposes, and in terms of these attributes, all things are exclusive from one another and constrained by these three restrictions. But the most significant thing is that the characteristic that is present in all the objects of this world is that all the objects of the world "exist" in one way or another. For example, objects such as tables, chairs, trees, people and rivers are existent entities, even though they differ in name, form and functions. On the other hand, the word *cit* refers to infinite or pure consciousness. Consciousness is the one thing that is consistently present as a shared characteristic in all the various things we learn about. When we claim to have knowledge of something or I claim to know the subject or the object, we are always claiming to be through consciousness behind this knowing or knowledge. While there may be differences in the names, forms and functions of the subjects about which we learn, as well as in the space–time–object limitations between them, within all such limited knowledge there is the same Consciousness, and it is through this Consciousness that all knowledge is made possible. In other words, this limitless Consciousness is experienceable through the lens of finite knowledge. So, from this discussion, we can say that the complete and infinite existence and consciousness is revealed through the various small objects of the world; apparently, therefore, the existence of everything seems to be limited, but there is only one thing in this world, objective or subjective, without name–form–use. *Nirguṇa-Brahman* is therefore unlimited in nature, i.e. abiding in all places, all times and all things, according to the *jñāna-yoga* perspective. So, who completes existence (*pūrṇa astitva*) means the existence of everything is dependent on *Brahman* and who completes consciousness (*pūrṇa caitanya*) means it is possible to know all knowable objects with the help of this one, infinite or pure consciousness. So, *Brahman* is infinite existence and infinite consciousness; we are not accustomed to thinking in this way, which is one of the reasons why we do not realize that this limitless consciousness and existence is constantly present around us.

Now, if the issue is thoroughly examined, it will become clear that even though *jñāna-yoga* holds the pure existence and pure consciousness to be very high theories, the average person does not search for this infinite, all-pervading and eternal being and does not feel the need to do so. If the matter is judged from a practical point of view, rather a philosophical point of view, it is natural to ask that, if such a *Nirguṇa-Brahman* exists as the real entity of this world, what does it matter to the common man? In simple language, ordinary people do not realize the necessity of such *Nirguṇa-Brahman* in their daily activities. The concept of non-dualism, however, is quite different when it comes to *bhakti-yoga*; in the final and most extreme degree of *parā-bhakti*, the form of *bhakti* or love likewise assumes the shape of this non-duality. According to *bhakti-yoga*, the internal disposition (*bhāva*) of an average man has the trait of constantly seeking love, and it is obvious that practically all the loves in this world are constrained by space, time and objects. When a person applies her extreme ideal as love to the smallest person or thing in the world, love also becomes narrow or limited. But what is significant is that we also see within our ordinary experience a tendency to attain that extreme non-dual aspect of love; i.e. as a small common man, the tendency to go beyond the bounds of time and space is manifested only through love and devotion. Now, this sensation of transcending or overcoming everything via love is not exclusive to the conscious being. Following the *bhakti* paths, we can state that the holistic orientation of love transcending special, temporal and material borders is essentially separated into two parts: First, love is capable of bridging even the smallest gaps between individuals and across different states of awareness. As an example, we can use the friendship between two people. This relationship is not based on blood; but despite that, within a very short period of time, we unite an unknown person from a distant country with us only and only through the power of love. A person can connect with many other individuals across time and geographic boundaries solely via love, and what is crucial is that this occurs spontaneously or frequently; no further effort is needed to overcome any constraints. Another instance, if a woman works hard her entire life and invests all of her savings into building a home, her love or attachment to it is unlike any other since she has connected her very essence to each and every brick. Therefore, every minor harm to that residence damages not only her house but also her emotions. In this instance, love extends beyond its own conscious self to encompass the unconscious as well. The examples discussed here undoubtedly prove that love is limited, i.e. limited by space, time and object. However, an effort has been made to demonstrate how we as common people are attached to the transcendent being beyond the limitations of space and time. This condition is primarily relevant to understanding the non-dual foundation upon which love (*bhakti*) stands. In such non-dual love, competition has no place. By loving what a person usually loves, she actually loves her highest ideal. Significantly, when human love begins to function on the heights of devotion, then the narrow love of a person is transformed and radiates out into all things in the world. In other words, at this level of human-hearted devotion, it does not force its ideal on any inferior being or thing, but rather, because it imposes it on the highest being, it starts to manifest through all the things of the world. In this context, Lord Kṛṣṇa tells Arjuna:

> *adveṣṭā sarvabhūtānāṁ maitraḥ karuṇa eva ca* ।
> *nirmamo nirahaṅkāraḥ samaduḥkhasukhaḥ kṣamī* ॥
>
> *santuṣṭaḥ satataṁ yogī yatātmā dṛḍhaniścayaḥ* ।
> *mayyarpitamanobuddhiryo madbhaktaḥ sa me priyaḥ* ॥
>
> – *Gītā* XII.13-14

This means, such a devotee of mine, my love, is the one who is pure in all beings; who does not harbour grudges against anyone; whose every being is filled with friendship and mercy; she who has no knowledge of "mine", "mine" who is modest, to whom joy and sorrow are equal; who is forgiving; whose heart is ever content; who is a *yogī*;[2] a balanced soul; who is steadfast; and who has given her mind and intellect to me. Besides, it is said in the *Gītā* (XII.17) in this context:

yo na hr̥ṣyati na dveṣṭi na śocati na kāñkṣati ।
śubhāśubhaparityāgī bhaktimānyaḥ sa me priyaḥ ॥

That is, she who is not enamoured of anything, yet has no hatred for anything, who does not grieve for not getting anything or desires for anything, who does not wait for anything good or bad, such a devotee is my favourite. The love of human being may be misdirected in some cases, but consciously or unconsciously she loves her highest ideal. True love is not possible until we judge our beloved as the highest ideal. In this context, Swami Vivekananda (1958: 89) says:

> The highest ideal of every man is called God. Ignorant or wise, saint or sinner, man or woman, educated or uneducated, cultivated or uncultivated, to every human being the highest ideal is God. The synthesis of all the highest ideals of beauty, of sublimity, and of power gives us the completest conception of the loving and lovable God.

The Highest Manifestation of Premādvaita (Non-Dual Love)

In the state of *parā-bhakti*, the universality of love is manifested in the higher state of the various levels of feeling (*sādhanā*) or in other words the non-dual form of love is manifested in the higher state of *parā-bhakti*. The *sādhaka* will eventually be able to transcend the unique structure of love and experience love as a uniform small thing if she advances properly in the realm of *parā-bhakti*. We get limited to specific objects or people when we get caught up in the self-centredness and narrowness of the average person. According to *bhakti-yoga*, such narrow love is not always

2 The term *yogī* is referred in Gītā (XII.14) as a *sādhaka* (spiritual seeker, without any gender bias) who has same specific qualities.

bad; it is simply misdirected. And people strengthen through this special character of love in their life. In fact, when a person is attracted to something, she imposes her ideal on it, and that ideal is the object of the highest love for her; in this way, although the object of love changes, everywhere she loves, imposing her ideals. As the student works to understand or experience the ideal, she eventually comes to the realization that external items are irrelevant to her. A person gradually transcends specialized particularity in this way to experience unconditional love.

In this universal form of love, the sincere student never wants to know whether Supreme Being is omnipotent or whether Supreme Being is ruling the world. The learner (*sādhaka*) is not even interested in learning about or tasting the one, exclusive non-dual nature of the Supreme Being in this elevated condition of *parā-bhakti*. A *sādhaka* is not even curious about how or what method of knowledge can be used to know the *loving being*. When a *sādhaka* reaches the level of sovereign love, she is able to feel the one universal love within her soul through all of the fractious objects and come to the realization that if we can love the *whole* (*samaṣṭi*), then we can love the *individual* (*vyaṣṭi*). The student no longer needs temples, mosques, churches or any other place of worship in this elevated level of love because *bhakti* is able to sense that love is present both within and outside the mosque or temple. She beholds that eternally *loving being* within the saint as well; even the sinner feels the presence of that loving one within. According to Swami Vivekananda (1958: 91):

> What is the ideal of the lover who has quite passed beyond the idea of selfishness, bartering and bargaining, and who knows no fear? Even to the great God such a man will say, "I will give You my all and I do not want anything from You; indeed, there is nothing that I can call my own." When a person has acquired this conviction, her ideal becomes one of perfect love, one of perfect fearlessness of love. The highest

> ideal of such a person has no narrowness of particularity about it; it is love universal, loves without limits and bonds, love itself absolute love. This grand ideal of the religion of love is worshipped and loved absolutely as such without the aid of any symbols or suggestions. This the highest form of *parā-bhakti* – the worship of such an all-comprehending ideal as the ideal; all the other forms of *bhakti* are only stages on the way to reach it.

Conclusion

So, based on the foregoing discussion, we can conclude that the path of love is likewise a means and an end of attaining the *nirguṇa* form of nature or the taste of *Nirguṇa-Brahman*. Reaching non-dual state through knowledge is called *jñānādvaita*, while the term *Premādvaita* refers to attaining non-duality via love. Now the question is whether these words *jñānādvaita* and *premādvaita* refer to the same non-dual state? Or is the taste of achieving a non-dual state also varied since the paths are diverse? Here, we can say, when the student is able to reach this subtlest state of non-dual love, then she also gives up the desire for liberation. In such a situation, the internal disposition (*bhāva*) of a student is that she enjoys eating sugar but never wants to be sugar. At this extreme peak of love is "love for love's sake" – this is the supreme happiness of the spiritual learner. But we must keep in mind that the pursuit of love or devotion always begins with duality, where the learner believes that she and the Supreme Being are entirely different, and that love eventually brings about the union of the student and *loving being*. The gap between the *sādhaka* and her lover gets smaller as she pursues her goal and transitions from genuine devotion to *parā-bhakti*; as we continue to ascribe our petty mundane love to *the highest being* and it comes closer to us and manifests itself fully. Therefore, *premādvaita* is possible through the path of love but it is very exclusive in nature compared to the path of knowledge; but this difference does not imply that non-duality is different in nature. The living worlds that are experienced in the state of *premādvaita* do not turn out to be false because of the distinctive nature of *Premādvaita*; rather, the One, Unique *loving being* demonstrates itself via each of the many living worlds that are encountered. Second, although knowing that her nature is non-dual, the *sādhaka* wishes to experience love in duality with her *loving being* at this ultimate level of love. Here the most significant point is that the highest form of non-dual *love*, *sadhka* constantly seeks to experience with duality; because of the special character of love that it always demands duality. As a result, even though *love* is ultimately one and non-dual; but dualism allows for the highest expression and development of love.

References

Chaudhari, Rama, 2016, *Vedanta Darshan*, tr. M. Matiur Rahaman, 1st edn, Dhaka: Abasar Publication House.

Dutta, Aswini Kumar, 1920, *Bhakti-yoga*, 7th edn, Kolkata: Banerjee Dutta & Co.

Jīva Gosvāmī, 1955, *Sribhaktisandarbha*, Pandit Radha Raman Goswami Vedantabusana, Sri Krishna Gopal Goswami, Calcutta: Calcutta University Press.

Mishra, Vachaspati, 2016, *Sāṁkhyatattvakaumudī*, ed. Sri Narayana Chandra Goswami, 5th edn, Calcutta: Sanskrit Book Depository.

Sankhya-Vedantatirtha, Pandit Durga Charan, 1331 BS, *Bṛhadāraṇyaka Upaniṣad*, 2nd edn, Calcutta: BP-MS Press.

Sri Nimbārkācārya, *Vedāntapārijātasaurav*, Swami Santadasbābājī Brajabidehī, Introduction, 4th edn, Kolkata: Parbati Publisher.

Śrīmadbhagavadgītā, 1st edn, Gorakhpur: Gita Press, 2014.

Śrīmadbhāgavata, 1st edn, Gorakhpur: Gita Press, 2014.

Vivekananda, Swami, 1958, *The Complete Works of Swami Vivekananda*, vol. III, Mayabati Memorial Edition, Calcutta: Advaita Ashrama.

Vyāsadeva, 2014, *Brahmasūtra*, Swami Chidghananda, 1st chapter, 2nd edn, Kolkata: Udbodhan Karyalaya.

List of Contributors

Prafulla Kumar Mohapatra was a formerly Professor and Head of the P.G. Department of Philosophy, Utkal University. He was a Commonwealth Scholar in England from 1974-77 and also Fulbright Visiting Professor in the United States in 1989. He was a General Editor in Utkal Studies in Philosophy Series of Publications from 1992 to 2002 and also editor in *Indian Journal of Analytic Philosophy* from 1997–2002 which was published from P.G. Department of Philosophy, Utkal Universiy. He has published many articles in both national and international level and also has authored many books. One of his recent books titled *An Applied Perspective on Indian Ethics* has been published by Springer in the year of 2019, <e-mail id: mohapatra97@gmail.com>.

Ramesh Chandra Pradhan was a formerly Professor and Head of the P.G. Department of Philosophy, University of Hyderabad. He was awarded the Commonwealth Academic Fellowship at the University of Oxford during 1990-91. He was Member-Secretary of the Indian Council of Philosophical Research, New Delhi during 2000-2003. He was a National Fellow at the Indian Institute of Advanced Study, Simla during 2018-20. His field of specialization includes, philosophy of language, philosophy of mind, metaphysics, and the philosophy of Wittgenstein. His recent publications are *Mind, Meaning and World: A Transcendental Perspective* (Springer 2019), *Metaphysics of Consciousness: The Indian Vedantic Perspective* (Springer and IIAS 2020) and *The*

Early Philosophy of Daya Krishna (Springer 2021), <e-mail id: pradhanrameshchandra@yahoo.com>.

Bijayananda Kar was a former Professor and Head of the P.G. Department of Philosophy, Utkal University. He was a Governing Body Member of Indian Council of Philosophical Research (ICPR), New Delhi. His field of specialization includes, Indian philosophy, Vedānta philosophy, Odishan philosophy and ethics. His publications include *Indian Theories of Error, Major Trends in Odishan Philosophy, The Philosophy of Lokayata, Indian Philosophy: An Analytical Study and Ethics in Indian Materialist Philosophy*. He has travelled extensively in India and abroad; has visited sixteen countries of five different continents, except Antarctica, where minimum daily temperature in normal period is usually -035 Celsius. He was awarded the Commonwealth Staff fellowship in 1941 and visited different universities including Oxford, London, Cambridge, and Edinburgh, etc.

Ganesh Prasad Das was a formerly Professor and Head of the P.G. Department of Philosophy, Utkal University. He was a Governing Body Member of Indian Council of Philosophical Research, New Delhi. He was the Director of the P.G. Department of Philosophy and Critical Thinking, U.N. (Autonomous) College of Science and Technology, Adaspur, Odisha. His works are in the field of analytic philosophy, Advaita Vedānta and applied philosophy. His publications include *Vedantaparibhasa: An Analytical Study*, (Co-ed. Darsanika Ganeswar Misra [Odia]), *Bidyutara Kahani*, [Odia], *Basics of Logic* (Pts I & II, Pancashila, Bhubaneswar). He has edited books on Logic in Odia for +2 course of CHSE of distant mode and Samāja, *Sāhitya o Darśana* (collection of essays in Odia), <e-mail id: gpdas45@gmail.com>.

S. Panneerselvam was formerly a Chairperson, School of Philosophy & Religious Thought, and Professor and Head of the Department of Philosophy, University of Madras. He has authored and edited fifteen books and also published more than eighty-five research papers in the leading philosophical journals and anthologies at national and international levels. His book, *The Problem of Meaning with Reference to Wittgenstein and Sankara*, published by the University of Madras and the two volumes of *The Life-World of the Tamils: Past and Present* (as associate editor) were published by the Project of History, Indian Science, Philosophy and Culture, New Delhi (PHISPC), by the MHRD, Government of India. His book, *Understanding Hermeneutics and Postmodernism from Indian Perspective*, was published by the University of Jaffna, Sri Lanka. He has recently co-edited a book, *Conflict Resolution: Perspectives from Indian Philosophy and Traditions*, published by the Universiti Kebangsaan, Malaysia, <e-mail id: sivanandampanneer@gmail.com.

Godabarisha Mishra is a Professor and Dean, School of Buddhist Studies, Philosophy and Comparative Religion at the Nalanda International University, India. Earlier, he served as a visiting professor in the School of HSS at the IIT, Bhubaneswar. Formerly, he also worked as the Chairman of the School of Philosophy and Religious Thought as well as the Professor and Head, Department of Philosophy, University of Madras. He was the Director of the Centre of Buddhist Studies, Director of the Publication Division and the Coordinator of the University Newsletter at the University of Madras. He was the Editor at the Kuppuswami Sastri Research Institute, Chennai during 1985-88 and also was the Member Secretary of the Indian Council of Philosophical Research, New Delhi during 2007-11. During 2008-10, he was the editor of the *Journal of Indian Council of Philosophical Research*, New Delhi. He was awarded Charles Wallace Visiting Fellowship to study at Oxford University UK. He was also a visiting professor at the Oxford Centre for Hindu Studies, Oxford, UK and at Mahatma Gandhi Institute, Mauritius. His areas of specializations are Indian Philosophical Schools, Vedānta and Buddhism, especially classical and textual traditions. At present, he is busy completing a project of two volumes of "Encyclopaedia of Indian Philosophy (Advaita Vedānta)" assigned by (late) Karl H. Potter, <e-mail id: mishra.godabarisha@gmail.com>.

Laxmikanta Padhi is a Professor and former Head of the Department of Philosophy, University of North Bengal, Siliguri. He has received his BA and MA from Utkal University, Bhubaneswar, Odisha, and MPhil and PhD from Jadavpur University, Kolkata. He teaches environmental philosophy, philosophy of religion, Western epistemology and virtue ethics. Presently, he is working on Itihāsa and Dharmaśāstra, <e-mail id: laxmikantnbu@gmail.com>.

Sarat Chandra Panigrahi was a formerly Professor and Head of the P.G. Department of Philosophy, Utkal University. He has a brilliant academic career, received gold medal in MA. He was recipient of Eschmann Memorial Medal for his outstanding research contribution in Buddhism and Jainism. He has authored a number of books in English and Odia on Indian philosophy, analytic philosophy, ethics and logic. He was a member of the Governing Body of Indian Council of Philosophical Research, New Delhi. At present he is working as Professor Emeritus in KISS Deemed to be University, <e-mail id: saratpanigrahi5@gmail.com>.

Vikram Singh Sirola is a Professor of Philosophy at the Department of Humanities and Social Sciences, Indian Institute of Technology, Bombay. He received his PhD from Jawaharlal Nehru University, New Delhi and is a recipient of the Fulbright-Nehru Senior Research Fellowship at Columbia University. His research is in the areas of philosophy of language, epistemology, and philosophy of science. He has published in various journals and anthologies, <e-mail id: v.s.sirola@iitb.ac.in.

Ranjan Kumar Panda is a Professor of Philosophy in the Department of Humanities and Social Sciences, IIT Bombay, Mumbai. He specializes in the area of philosophy of mind and language and published a book *Mind, Language and Intentionality* (2008), and a few reseach papers in this area, <e-mail id: ranjan.panda@iitb.ac.in>.

Jhadeswar Ghosh is at present Professor of Philosophy at the Vidyasagar University. He has authored the books like *Naturalized Semantics: A Critical Analysis of Quine's Philosophy*, *From Meaning Atomism to Meaning Holism: A Study of Bhartṛhari, Wittgenstein and Quine*, editor of *The Engaged Intellect: Essays on the Philosophical Perspectives of Raghunath Ghosh*, co-editor of *Media Ethics in the Information Age* and the Editor-in-Chief of *Reflection: UGB Journal of Philosophy*. He has published a number of research papers in reputed philosophical journals and anthologies. His areas of interest include philosophy of language (Indian and Western), analytic philosophy, philosophy of Wittgenstein and W.V.O. Quine, contemporary Western philosophy and applied ethics.

Saroj Kanta Kar is currently serving as Associate Professor and Head in the Department of Philosophy at Utkal University. His research was concentrated on consciousness in Buddhism and Vedānta, Nāgārjuna's philosophy, and Advaita Vedānta. He has specialized in Buddhism, Vedānta, and moral philosophy. His recent interest is in critical, creative, and applied research in philosophy and allied areas of study. He has some publications to his credit including two books and several research papers published in recognized journals, <e-mail id: sarojkkar@gmail.com>.

Basant Kumar Dash at present is a visiting faculty in the Department of Philosophy at Ramadevi Women's University, Bhubaneswar. He was an formerly Associate Professor and Head of the Department of Philosophy, Ramadevi Women's

University, Bhubaneswar. He has contributed four books in philosophy such as *Essays in Philosophy: Indian and Western*, *The Philosophy of Ishopanisad and the Gita*, *Manual of Indian Ethics* and *Swami Vivekananda on Universal Religion*. His areas of interest in philosophy include Indian philosophy, philosophy of religion, philosophy of Vedānta and Western philosophy, <e-mail id: basantdash.dash73@gmail.com>.

Harischandra Sahoo is by profession a teacher of philosophy serving for thirty-seven years in different government colleges of the State of Odisha including Ravenshaw, G.M. and B.J.B. (Auto) College. At present, he is the Professor of Bhima Bhoi Research Chair in Kalinga Institute of Social Science (KISS), Deemed to be University, Bhubaneswar, <e-mail id: harissahoo9@gmail.com>.

Patitpaban Das is a professor in the Department of Philosophy, Ravenshaw University, Odisha. He is an alumnus of JNU, New Delhi. He is the associate editor of *Ravenshaw Journal of Philosophy* and *Journal of All Orissa Philosophy Association*. He has six books, more than twenty book chapters and thirty-five journal articles to his credit. His research interest includes ethics, applied ethics, socio-political philosophy, and continental philosophy. He has special interest in postmodern thought, <e-mail id: pdas@ ravenshawuniversity.ac.in>.

Gopal Sahu, working as a Professor and Head, Department of Philosophy, University of Allahabad, Prayagraj. He has received PhD in Philosophy from IIT Bombay. His areas of specializations are contemporary epistemology, scepticism, philosophy of mind and philosophy of science. His current research areas are in consciousness and applied ethics. He has published one book and fifty research papers in several philosophy journals of India. He has edited the prestigious philosophy journal, *The Philosophical Quarterly*, published from North Maharashtra University, Jalgaon from 1997 to 2002. He was awarded the prestigious Jawaharlal

Nehru Doctoral Scholarship for History and Philosophy of Science instituted by Jawaharlal Memorial Fund, New Delhi, <e-mail id: drgopalsahu@gmail.com>.

Surya Kant Maharana is Associate professor in the Department of Philosophy, University of Allahabad, Prayagraj. He has published an edited book co-authored by him titled *Perspectives on Indian Ethics*. He has accomplished a UGC sponsored research project titled "Philosophy of Mind in Advaita Vedanta" in the recent past. In April 2021, he has been awarded a research project titled: "A Study on the Minor Schools of Vedanta" sponsored by the Indian Council of Philosophical Research, Ministry of Education, New Delhi. His areas of research include continental philosophy, especially phenomenology and existentialism; Vedānta, especially Advaita Vedānta of Śaṅkara. His areas of interest in teaching include classical Indian philosophy, nineteenth- and twentieth-century continental philosophy, modern Western philosophy, logic, symbolic logic, Western epistemology, comparative religion, ethics and professional ethics, <e-mail id: maharana.suryakant@gmail.com>.

Akoijam Thoibisana is an Associate Professor and Head of the Department of Philosophy, Gauhati University, Guwahati. Her area of interest is contemporary philosophy. She has contributed papers on themes related to deconstruction, postmodernism, psychoanalysis, and phenomenology. She has in her credit two books and several research papers published in journals like *JICPR, IPQ, Sandhan*, etc., <e-mail id: akoijamthoibisana@gauhati.ac.in>

Sudhakar Jally is Assistant Professor in the Department of Philosophy at Utkal University, Vani Vihar, Bhubaneswar. He has an active professional career in philosophy by way of publishing a number of books and articles. The areas of his interest are indian philosophy, comparative religion, philosophy of social science and the study of "value" in different facets, <e-mail id: sjphilmaa@gmail.com>.

Alakananda Parida currently Associate Professor of Philosophy, Ravenshaw University, had her Post-graduation from P.G. Department of Philosophy, Utkal University and MPhil and PhD from Utkal University. She specializes in philosophy of religion, Indian philosophy and ethics. She has two books to her credit namely – *Understanding Religion* and *Mysticism in Prabhat Sangit* and translated six books from Bengali to Odia, viz. *Tamasara Arapare*, *Satyara Sandhan*, *Yogic Chikitsa*, *Ananda Vacanamrutam* (Parts 1, 2, 3), *Bhakti Rasa Kirtan Mahima* (under print). Besides her academic assignments, she was Former Coordinator, P.G. Department of Philosophy, Utkal University and Students' Welfare Officer, New Campus, Utkal University, Chandikhole. Presently, she is serving as the Director, Students' Welfare at Ravenshaw University, <e-mail id: alakanandaparida@gmail.com>.

Manoj Kumar Panda is an Assistant Professor of Philosophy at Presidency University, Kolkata. His research interests span philosophy of mind, epistemology, philosophy of perception and consciousness. His research works in the above fields draw insights from both analytic and phenomenological tradition. He has been teaching many advanced level courses on philosophy of mind, Western epistemology and consciousness. Before Joining Presidency University, he taught in Jawaharlal Nehru University and Kirori Mal College of University of Delhi. He has published several research papers in some reputed journals and edited anthologies, <e-mail id: manoj.phil@presiuniv.ac.in>.

Pragyanparamita Mohapatra is an Assistant Professor in the Department of Philosophy, Utkal University, Vani Vihar, Bhubaneswar. She has received her MPhil and PhD degree from Jawaharlal Nehru University, New Delhi. Her areas of interest are in analytic philosophy, philosophy of language, philosophy of mind and symbolic logic. She has published several research papers in recognized journals and anthologies. Prior to Utkal University she was working as a junior lecturer (Odisha Education Service), at Sashi Bhusan Rath Women's (Auto.) College, Berhampur, <e-mail id: pragyanparamita@ utkaluniversity.ac.in>.

K. Om Narayana Rao is working as an Assistant Professor in Logic & Philosophy in Niranjan Government Women's College, Aska, Odisha. He is an author of the book *Logic: Deductive and Inductive* (vols I & II) meant for the Higher Secondary Students of Odisha. His books for the Degree Students include *Philosophy of Religion*, *Systems of Indian Philosophy*, *Introduction to Gandhian Studies*, *Introduction to Applied Ethics*, *Objective Philosophy*, *Critical Thinking and Applied Reasoning*, *Introduction to Ethics* (co-author), *Symbolic Logic & Scientific Method* (co-author) and *Quantitative and Logical Thinking* (co-author), <e-mail id: omnarayana_rao@ rediffmail.com>.

Lakshman Patra is working as an Assistant Professor (Odisha Education Service) and Associate NCC Officer in the P.G. Department of Philosophy, Vikram Dev University, Jeypore. Many of his research papers have been published in anthologies and journal of national repute. He has received DG COMMENDATION National award for the year 2021 for his social activities in NCC, <e-mail id: patra_lakshman@rediffmail.com>.

Dibyendu Mondal is working as an assistant professor at Presidency University, West Bengal since 2018. His Doctoral thesis focused on the theory of Bhakti philosophy from contemporary philosopher of Swami Vivekananda. The author also interested in Bhakti philosophy of Caitanya Mahāprabhu related to Gauḍīya Vaiṣṇavism Vedānta School Acintyabhedābhedavāda; Śaktitattva, the relation between *Brahman* and its power (*śakti*).

His areas of expertise are Nyāya and Vedānta metaphysics & epistemology and contemporary issues in Advaita Vedānta, <e-mail id: dibyendu.phil@presiuniv.ac.in>.

Additional Entry

Prafulla Kumar Mohapatra, Former Professor and Head, P.G. Department of Philosophy, Utkal University, Vani Vihar, Bhubaneswar, <e-mail id: mohapatra97@gmail.com>, Mobile: 9437101511

Ramesh Chandra Pradhan, Former Professor and Head, the Department of Philosophy, University of Hyderabad, Hyderbad, <e-mail id: pradhanrameshchandra@yahoo.com>, Mobile: 9440052901

Bijayananda Kar, Former Professor and Head, P.G. Department of Philosophy, Utkal University. At Home: No. AM-16, V.S.S. Nagar, Bhubaneswar-V.S.S. Nagar, Sub-P.O. Bhubaneswar, Vani Vihar Station - 751004, Mobile: 7047133866

Ganesh Prasad Das, Former Professor and Head, P.G. Department of Philosophy, Utkal University. RUTAYANI, 396, Paika Nagar, Bhubaneswar - 751003, <e-mail id: gpdas45@gmail.com>, Mobile: 8249579548

S. Panneerselvam, Former Chairperson, School of Philosophy & Religious Thought, and Professor & Head, Department of Philosophy, University of Madras, <e-mail id: sivanandampanneer@gmail.com, Mobile: 9841059170

Godabarisha Mishra, Professor and Dean, School of Buddhist Studies, Philosophy and Comparative Religion, Nalanda International University, Flat 3, "Sunayana Apts" 49, First Main Road, RA Puram, Chennai – 600028, (Tamil Nadu) India, <e-mail id: mishra.godabarisha@gmail.com>, Mobile: 9445873557

Laxmikanta Padhi, Professor of Philosophy, University of North Bengal, Siliguri, <e-mail id: laxmikantnbu@gmail.com>, Mobile: 9832383948

Sarat Chandra Panigrahi, Former Professor and Head, Post-Graduate Department of Philosophy, Utkal University, Vani Vihar, Bhubaneswar, <e-mail id: saratpanigrahi5@gmail.com>, Mobile: 9338702401

Vikram Singh Sirola, Professor of Philosophy, Department of Humanities and Social Sciences, IIT Bombay, Mumbai, <e-mail id: v.s.sirola@iitb.ac.in, Mobile: 9869080255

Ranjan Kumar Panda, Professor of Philosophy, Department of Humanities and Social Sciences, IIT Bombay, Mumbai, <e-mail id: ranjan.panda@iitb.ac.in>, Mobile: 9869843951

Saroj Kanta Kar, Associate Professor & Head, Department of Philosophy, Utkal University, Vani Vihar, Bhubaneswar, <e-mail id: sarojkkar@gmail.com>, Mobile: 7007514251

Jhadeswar Ghosh, Professor of Philosophy, Vidyasagar University, Midnapore, West Bengal, <e-mail id: jhadeswarghosh@gmail.com>, Mobile: 6294195297

Basant Kumar Dash, Former Associate Professor, Department of Philosophy, Ramadevi Women's University, Bhubaneswar, <e-mail id: basantdash.dash73@gmail.com>, Mobile: 6372214416

Harischandra Sahoo, Professor, Bhima Bhoi Research Chair, KISS (D.U.) Bhubaneswar, <e-mail id: harissahoo9@gmail.com>, Mobile: 9438408465

Patitapaban Das, Professor of Philosophy, Department of Philosophy, Ravenshaw University, Cuttack, <e-mail id: pdas@ravenshawuniversity.ac.in>, Mobile: 7377074334

Gopal Sahu, Department of Philosophy, University of Allahabad, Prayagraj, Uttar Pradesh, <e-mail id: drgopalsahu@gmail.com>, Mobile: 8840142544

Surya Kant Maharana, Department of Philosophy, University of Allahabad, Prayagraj, Uttar Pradesh, <e-mail id: maharana.suryakant@gmail.com>, Mobile: 9120756055

Akoijam Thoibisana, Associate Professor and Head, Department of Philosophy, Gauhati University, <e-mail id: akoijamthoibisana@gauhati.ac.in>, Mobile: 6001794848

Sudhakar Jally, Assistant Professor, P.G. Department of Philosophy, Utkal University, Vani Vihar, Bhubaneswar - 751004, <e-mail id: sjphilmaa@gmail.com>, Mobile: 9777756769

Alakananda Parida, Associate Professor, Department of Philosophy, Ravenshaw University, Cuttack, <e-mail id: alakanandaparida@gmail.com>, Mobile: 7978780591

Manoj Kumar Panda, Assistant Professor, Presidency University, West Bengal, <e-mail id: manoj.phil@presiuniv.ac.in>, Mobile: 9903853702

Pragyanparamita Mohapatra, P.G. Department of Philosophy, Utkal University, Vani Vihar, Bhubaneswar - 751004, <e-mail id: pragyanparamita@utkaluniversity.ac.in>, Mobile: 7377527398

K. Om Narayana Rao, Assistant Professor in Logic & Philosophy, Niranjan Government Women's College, Aska, Odisha, <e-mail id: omnarayana_rao@rediffmail.com>, Mobile: 9937188631

Lakshman Patra, P.G. Department of Philosophy, Vikram Dev University, Jeypore, Koraput, Odisha, <e-mail id: patra_lakshman@rediffmail.com>, Mobile: 9238999875

Dibyendu Mondal, Assistant Professor, Presidency University, Kolkata, West Bengal, <e-mail id: dibyendu.phil@presiuniv.ac.in>, Mobile: 8240444048

Subject Index

Name and Title Index